D1116823

Operation
Babylon

SHLOMO HILLEL

Operation Babylon

CARNEGIE LIBRARY
LIVINGSTONE COLLEGE
SALISBURY, NC 28144

Translated
by Ina Friedman

Doubleday

NEW YORK

1987

124071

Library of Congress Cataloging-in-Publication Data

Hillel, Shlomo, 1923–
  Operation Babylon.

  Translation of: Ruaḥ ḳadim.
    1. Israel—Emigration and immigration.   2. Iraq—
Emigration and immigration.   3. Jews—Iraq—Migrations.
4. Immigrants—Israel.   5. Jews, Iraqi—Israel.
6. Hillel, Shlomo, 1923–   .   I. Friedman, Ina.
II. Title.
JV8749.I8H5513   1987   325'.2567'095694   87-9038
ISBN 0-385-23597-6

Original Hebrew edition copyright © 1985 by Shlomo Hillel and
Edanim Publishers, Israel
Translation copyright © 1987 by Bantam, Doubleday, Dell Publishing Group Inc.
All rights reserved
Printed in the United States of America
First Edition in the United States of America

TO THE MEMORY OF MY PARENTS,
AHARON HILLEL AND
HANINI (NÉE SHEMTOB) HILLEL

CONTENTS

Operation
Babylon

Prologue

PHANTOM FLIGHT #1 was airborne—right on time, almost without a hitch, safe as could be expected under the circumstances. Once the glow of Baghdad was well behind us, I asked the captain to switch on the cabin lights and walked back to greet our passengers. The fifty teenagers were still lying flat on the floor of the bare cargo plane, clutching each other rather more desperately than we had instructed them, a frightened, confused pile of humanity.

"You can sit up now and make yourselves more comfortable," I shouted over the drone of the plane's engines. "There's no need to be frightened any more."

That was not precisely the truth. We still had to reach Palestine, land there secretly, and avoid being arrested by the British. But now that we were off the ground, the worst was over. Smiles began to replace the look of sheer terror on the faces around me, and as soon as the youngsters had rearranged themselves, I began outlining the landing procedures.

When the plane began its descent, I explained, they were to lie down, hold on to each other as before, and stay that way until the aircraft came to a complete halt. Then two of the stronger boys would jump off first and two others were to station themselves inside the door to help the rest climb out. If for any reason we could not land at our secret airstrip in Yavneel and were forced to set down in one of the country's airports, they were to answer every question addressed to them by the British in Hebrew with the words "I am a Jew from Palestine"—not a syllable more. That was standard procedure in the Mossad's operations.

I returned to the cockpit as dawn began to break—a process that lingers when you're flying westward—and sat peering silently at the arid, monotonous desert landscape. When we crossed the Iraqi-Syrian border, about halfway through the three-hour flight, Mike pointed out our position on the map. But there was no change in the scenery, just as there was no difference in the hostility or danger we faced on the two sides of the frontier.

The closer we came to Palestine the more the sunrise caught up with us. And then suddenly the dull brown Golan Plateau gave way to the blue Sea of Galilee below us, and we were home. As the sun's first rays glinted off its waters, I was gripped by such a pang of emotion that I pressed my forehead against the window to hide the moisture glinting in my eyes. West of the lake, I could see the squads of Palmachniks deployed to defend the landing strip. Parallel pillars of smoke marked the edges of the make-shift runway, and whatever else I might say about Leo Wessenberg, he certainly knew how to make a perfect landing, setting us down on the first run. As we bumped across the field to a halt, I saw familiar faces in the crowd. It seemed as if the whole Mossad had come out to greet us, and off to the side someone was operating a small moving-picture camera to capture the event for posterity.

Within minutes, the last of the immigrants was on the ground and the plane was airborne again. Two trucks carried the youngsters off to be scattered among the nearby settlements. The fires were doused, the troops dispersed, and Yavneel returned to its pastoral ways, as if the whole drama had been an illusion, fata morgana. Standing in the deserted field, I gave my last order of the operation: code and send the following message to our people in Baghdad over the clandestine wireless network:

TO: Yerach
FROM: Shammai
August 23, 1947
1. Arrived safe and sound to an enthusiastic welcome.
2. Check and report whether there are any repercussions on your end.
   Take care that all the participants in the operation are kept quiet.

Then I, too, went home, back to the kibbutz, and made straight for Temima's tent. Finding it deserted, I lay down for a few minutes—just to unwind, gather my wits—and instantly lapsed into a sleep of utter exhaustion. Suddenly I woke with a start. The light was on and I heard Temima's voice chiding me about sleeping in my clothes.

"Quiet! I told you not to make a sound!" I hissed at her in complete disorientation, then heard her soft laughter in reply. The last thing I can remember from that historic day was my fury and confusion over why she was making such an infernal racket at a time like that. "My God," I remember thinking in panic, "she'll give us all away!"

When I next opened my eyes, the sun was high in the sky and I was alone in the tent. It was years before I discussed the matter with Temima again. She didn't ask and I didn't volunteer anything. In those days people like us didn't talk about such things. It just wasn't done. But now I think the whole story can be told.

ONE

From Underground to
Under Cover

ON A GRAY, CHILL MORNING in December 1945, Christmas Day to be
exact, a black Hillman plied its way northward over the narrow asphalt
road that was the main highway between Haifa and Tel Aviv, taking the
puddles at full speed and splattering the windshield at uneven intervals as
it penetrated deeper and deeper into citrus country. About half an hour
outside of Tel Aviv, the car slowed down, turned off the highway onto a
dirt path, and wound its way through the orchards until it rolled up to the
gate of one of the fenced-off groves. Placing the car in neutral, the driver
gave three short blasts of the horn in a broken rhythm, then waited until a
man dressed in wrinkled, greasy overalls lumbered out to unlock the iron
chain holding the gate closed. The car drove through and continued to
bump its way slowly down the path to a rundown wooden shack that
looked much like all the other packinghouses dotting the citrus orchards of
the Sharon Plain.

The driver of that car was Moshe Baron, of Ta'as, the clandestine arms
industry of the Haganah, or Jewish underground in Palestine. Next to him
on that journey sat yours truly, then the economic administrator of a
young kibbutz that didn't even have a name yet but certainly had a mission

and was deeply involved in that industry. And the packinghouse was not a packinghouse at all, but a secret factory for manufacturing small arms and ammunition. It was staffed by some fifteen of my fellow kibbutzniks who on that particular morning were embroiled in a rather prosaic labor dispute with the Haganah. Not over wages, of course; the problem, as I understood it, was a personality clash with their foreman. In any case, as the man in charge of our labor force, I was the natural choice to step into the breach.

Baron, as I was now to learn, took an idiosyncratic but highly effective approach to labor negotiations. Bypassing the subject of their grievances, he sat the group of rebellious workers down in a circle and broke the news about the *Hannah Senesh,* a rickety little boat that had slipped past the British naval blockade to safely deposit its 250 passengers ashore. The British, I should explain, had a mandate over Palestine and were determined to keep Jews out. Equally determined to get in were the survivors of the Nazis' "Final Solution to the Jewish Problem," bare shadows of human beings who jammed onto the decks of the creaking, leaky boats scared up by another arm of the Haganah, the Mossad for Illegal Immigration.*

The *Hannah Senesh* was one of those boats, and Baron held my workers spellbound as he told the story of its arrival. Two days before, when it was still outside Palestine's territorial waters, a British plane had flown past the boat, and all aboard were sure it had been spotted. But no patrol came out to intercept it, and after nightfall on December 24 the *Hannah Senesh* changed course and moved in toward the coast near the town of Nahariya. Then, as it was approaching the shore, a storm broke, driving the boat onto a shoal. It tilted on its side, threatening to capsize, and the waves were so high that they swamped the lifeboats. But the Haganah people showed great resourcefulness: they strung a heavy rope from the ship to the shore so that, clinging to this single thread, literally for dear life, the passengers could pull themselves to safety through the crashing waves. At the same time, a Haganah unit and young people from the town of Nahariya swam out to the stranded ship to rescue those unable to make it on their own. When it was all over, one man was missing and was presumed to have drowned.

"Since they couldn't move the ship anyway," Baron concluded his narrative in a crescendo, "our people decked it out with a sign reading: 'Hannah Senesh—Haganah Immigrant Ship: Memorial to Six Million of Our Brethren; Badge of Infamy on the British Government.' The British police found the boat this morning, and they're piping mad. Right now

* Not to be confused with the arm of Israeli Intelligence now widely referred to as the Mossad.

they're scouring every inch of the surrounding area, and they have road-blocks up all over the place."

"But how come they didn't discover the boat as it was coming in?" someone asked.

Baron chuckled, as if he had saved the best part for last. "Tucked away here in the orchards, you probably didn't notice. Last night was Christmas Eve. But I assure you it wasn't goodwill toward men that had prompted the soldiers and police to let the boat slip through. They were simply busy celebrating. Many of them were probably dead drunk."

There was celebration in the air that morning too. Having steeled them-selves for a scolding, my comrades were doubly delighted by Baron's tidings. And with spirits so high, no one had the heart to ruin it all by haggling over labor conditions. So the meeting promptly adjourned and everyone went back to work with redoubled energy.

"What you did in there was pure demagoguery," I grumbled at Baron as we drove back to Tel Aviv. "What does the *Hannah Senesh* have to do with the way their foreman is treating them?"

"You're wrong, my young friend," he chided me gently. "The story of the *Hannah Senesh* enabled them to put things in their proper perspective. Suddenly they realized that great things are going on here and it's a pity to waste time squabbling over trifles."

I wasn't entirely convinced by that, but the truth is that I, too, had fallen under the spell of the tale. On the way from Tel Aviv, I had been thinking about my decision to pass on the job of economic administrator, a post I had held for far longer than I liked. We were still in temporary quarters, and the whole kibbutz—barn, chicken coops, kindergarten and all—was scheduled to pick up and move to a hill outside the town of Rehovot (not far from the Weizmann Institute), where it would serve as the cover for a subterranean arms factory to produce most of the ammunition for the Haganah. I was in charge of the move, and it was one of those tasks that seemed to require endless arguments with every last member of the kib-butz. Somewhere in the course of those "negotiations," I decided that, once the move was over, someone else could have the pleasure of finessing my comrades. I had had it. All I wanted was to settle into some quiet job—in the fields, the fishery, or even in the projected arms factory.

Then Baron's story stirred a new feeling in me and conjured up memo-ries of other boats that had tried to make their way to Palestine. Illegal immigration had been going on since May 1939, when the British pub-lished a White Paper that marked a drastic reversal in their policy. Con-trary to the promise, embodied in the Balfour Declaration, to create a "national home for the Jewish people" in Palestine, the 1939 White Paper contended that His Majesty's Government had fulfilled its obligation in that respect and could now proceed to create an independent Arab state in Palestine within ten years. The change of heart was clearly prompted by self-interest. Since the Arabs were so strongly opposed to a Jewish national entity in the region, and since they had the potential to cause quite a headache to the British throughout the Middle East, London was loath to lock horns with them—especially with a war looming on the horizon in Europe. If they wanted the Jews kept out of Palestine, that's what they would get. Thus the British decided first to limit Jewish immigration to the country, fixing a very small quota for the coming five years, after which they would bar Jews from entering altogether.

The most shocking part of this announcement was its timing. By May 1939 there could be no question about what awaited the Jews of Germany and the other countries already in the Nazis' grip. It was more than a year after the *Anschluss,* Germany's annexation of Austria, and a few months after the dismantlement of Czechoslovakia. It was six months after the shattering *Kristallnacht* pogrom, the start of a campaign of murder, plunder, and deportation that would ultimately spiral into the extermination of the Jews of Germany and the rest of Europe. It was close to a year after the Évian Conference to solve the European refugee problem had come to naught. And it was well after everyone realized that if the broader refugee problem defied solution, the fate of the Jewish refugees was doubly grim, for the only place they could turn to was Palestine. Now the White Paper had sealed off that haven as well.

The Jews of Palestine were not prepared to accept Britain's edict while the threat of destruction loomed over their brethren in Europe. Their answer to the White Paper was to organize Aliyah Bet (Illegal Immigration)—if action in defiance of a monstrous policy can be called illegal. Throughout the war, the Mossad for Illegal Immigration worked tirelessly to get people out of Europe by any means possible. But the names of three boats in particular were etched in my memory and probably in the memory of every Jew who lived in Palestine during that period. The first of them was particularly symbolic because it arrived here on September 1, 1939, the day on which the war broke out.

The *Tiger Hill* had left the Romanian port of Constantsa almost a month earlier carrying fourteen hundred Jews from Poland, Romania, and Bulgaria. It tried to evade detection as it approached the coast but was met by a volley of machine-gun fire, from British patrol boats, killing two refugees and wounding fourteen others. Though the boat turned around and headed back out to sea, essentially it had nowhere to go. Its stocks of food and fuel had run out, and it lacked provisions for treating the wounded. So, the next morning, the *Tiger Hill* set its bow back toward Tel Aviv and its engines at full speed till it ran aground, not far from the house in which

I was living. My friends and I ran out to gaze at the surrealistic sight of a large boat stuck just off the beach we considered our playground. The immigrants began jumping into the shallow water, and a few hundred managed to reach the shore and mingle with the crowd there. But then the police arrived, rounded up twelve hundred of them, and carted them off to a detention camp. It may not have been a spectacular operation, but the *Tiger Hill* went down in history if only because—as one irate eulogist observed at the graveside of its victims—the first British shots fired in World War II were not at Hitler's advancing divisions but at pitiful Jewish refugees fleeing from the Nazi terror.

The second ship, the *Struma,* a battered cattle boat, left Constantsa in December 1941 carrying 769 Jewish refugees who had already witnessed the abuse and slaughter of Jews by the Nazis and the equally sadistic Romanian Iron Guard. The boat reached Istanbul and tied up at the dock, but though its passengers were not allowed to disembark, neither were they permitted to continue on their journey. It seems that the British had caught wind of the affair and prevailed upon the Turks to keep the boat from passing through the Dardanelles—in violation of an international convention assuring free passage to civilian ships at all times.

For over two months, through the worst of the Turkish winter, the *Struma* remained tied to that dock, its passengers deprived of the most elementary sanitary conditions. Then, toward the end of February 1942, it was towed back through the Bosporus into the Black Sea, and the captain was warned not to return to Istanbul. The *Struma*'s wheezing engine was barely effective, and essentially the barge was carried along by the current. But not for long. When it was less than ten kilometers from Istanbul, a loud explosion was heard and the *Struma* sank within minutes, leaving only one survivor. The cause of that explosion was never determined, but the odds are that it was a torpedo launched by a Russian submarine.

The image of a sinking ship naturally led to thoughts of the *Patria,* an incident that touched closest to home, not least because it was played out right in Haifa Harbor. The story involved 3,642 Jews who had escaped from Germany and the countries under its control at the end of 1940: Austria, Czechoslovakia, and Poland. Strange as it sounds today, they left for Palestine with the knowledge and even the aid of the Nazi authorities, who were prepared to let Jews go in return for a hefty "ransom." To reach the Black Sea, they sailed down the Danube on riverboats—though theirs was no pleasure trip. Yet as soon as they reached the port of Tulcea and boarded the three steamers that were to carry them to Palestine, they were filled with new hope. Not even the terrible crowding and shortage of food and water could dampen their spirits. When they ran out of fuel midway, they readily—almost eagerly—burned the boats' meager furnishings, including the narrow wooden bunks on which they slept.

The war seemed to follow hot on their heels. Soon after they left Tulcea, the anti-Semitic Iron Guard effected a coup, turning Romania into a cog in the German war machine. As they sailed past Crete, they learned that the Italians had attacked Greece. In the race between life and death, again and again they had been awarded life. "It must be the finger of God," they murmured, and as they neared the coast of Palestine they dared to hope that, despite official policy, the British would let them in. Indeed, when the first two boats arrived, on November 1 and 3 (the third was delayed in Cyprus), the British authorities allowed them to enter Haifa Harbor. They tied up at the dock but were not allowed to release their passengers until "the matter" had been "clarified." The refugees accepted this delay with resignation, never dreaming what lay in store.

For in the meanwhile, the British authorities had cooked up yet a new policy: to deport the refugees to Mauritius, a remote island colony in the Indian Ocean. The notion seemed absolutely mad. In the midst of a world war, when ships were at a premium and enemy predators lurked in the seas, the British Government was prepared to allocate boats for the purpose of carrying off to exile, thousands of miles away, hapless Jews whose only crime was escaping the claws of the Nazis and who were willing to give their all to the war effort against Germany! Mad, indeed—but true.

Docked in Haifa Harbor, waiting to carry them off, was the *Patria*, a large, old ship. When all efforts failed to dissuade the British from executing their plan, the commanders of the Haganah came up with a plan of their own: to cripple the *Patria* and gain time for additional protests and appeals against this truly cruel scheme. When the refugees from the first two steamers were already on the *Patria* and the immigrants from the third ship were being transferred aboard, explosives were smuggled on with the aim of creating a serious leak—though nothing so grave as to endanger the passengers. But someone must have miscalculated the ship's age and decrepit condition, for when the blast went off it made a gaping hole. The *Patria* listed sharply, and its panicked passengers began jumping into the water, which was soon streaked with the blood of the injured. The air vibrated with the screams of parents seeing their children drown before their eyes and others desperately searching for their partners or offspring. As the ship listed farther, the cargo on deck broke loose and slid into the water, crushing anyone in its path and many of those who had already jumped to safety. The *Patria* went down in a quarter of an hour, taking 260 people to their deaths as scores of others looked on helplessly in horror from the shore.

Fished out of the bay, the survivors of the *Patria* were held in detention for an entire year. Yet, due either to a sudden humanitarian impulse or the pressure of public opinion, they were not deported in the end.

One of the *Patria*'s survivors was a charming, chestnut-haired twelve-year-old named Temima Rosner, who on that Christmas morning five years later was my girlfriend and would later become my wife. Perhaps that, too, had something to do with the fact that suddenly I knew I was not cut out for a quiet job in the fields or the arms factory. All at once, almost like an epiphany, I was struck with the perfect certainty that I wanted to be part of this cause, that I wanted to work with Jews abroad and bring them to Palestine. Before we reached our destination, I found myself sharing these thoughts with Moshe Baron, who raised one of his dark brows to flash a message of skepticism but finally said, "If you really mean that, Lord knows there's plenty to do."

"I don't want to force myself on anyone," I hedged, embarrassed by my impetuosity—to say nothing of my frankness with a man who, not twenty minutes before, I had tagged as a demagogue. But Baron was reassuring.

"I'm sure your suggestion will be welcomed," he said. "The headlines are all about the immigration from Europe, but you know that we're bringing in Jews from the Arab countries too. In fact, the Mossad has decided to make a special effort in that direction. You could probably fit right in there."

I replied with a dubious shrug, not out of modesty but because I knew that my Arabic was a bit rusty. True, I had been born in Iraq. But I had come to Palestine as a child and was far from sure that I could pass for a native. Still, I certainly had an advantage over others on that score, as I discovered a few days later when I met with Yonatan Rabinowitz.

A kibbutznik who went by the nickname of Yunis, Rabinowitz invited me to lunch at a class of restaurant that we proletarians did not usually frequent. Over the appetizer, he told me he would be leaving for Baghdad in a few days to direct the illegal immigration from Iraq. Since he had heard of my willingness to work abroad, he wanted to propose that I join him in Baghdad and take over the job of directing the Zionist underground there. To help me consider the offer, he began to fill me in on all he knew about the Zionist movement, its clandestine operations, and the illegal immigration coming from Iraq.

Prompted by the age-old religious injunction to live—or at least to die—in the Holy Land, Iraqi Jews had been making their way to Palestine for generations. But the modern Zionist movement—meaning the resolve to build a vibrant Jewish society in the ancient Jewish homeland—did not strike roots in Iraq until after World War I, when the British occupation led to a greater openness toward the West in general. By the end of the 1920s, Zionist activities were flourishing in Iraq, particularly in the form of the Ahiever movement to foster Jewish culture (of which my brother Eliyahu was a founder) and the work of Hebrew teachers who had come from Palestine.

Yet this golden age was short-lived. Iraq received its full independence in 1932, and in the following year—after the death of the liberal King Feisal I—the country embarked upon a fervently Arab-nationalist course under his successor, Ghazi. By sheer coincidence, these developments coincided with the Nazis' rise to power. Yet perhaps it was more than coincidence that the Germans' viciously anti-Semitic policy intrigued the Arab nationalists in Iraq. In any event, the Jews could not ignore the fact that the climate in Iraq had turned radically against the cultivation of a Jewish-nationalist outlook. The Hebrew teachers from Palestine were expelled; the members of Ahiever either emigrated to Palestine or dropped out of the movement; and slowly but surely, Jewish cultural programs were officially prohibited. Here and there Jews even found themselves under physical attack—an extension, so to speak, of the anti-Jewish ferment in Palestine. A demonstration might get out of hand, and before you knew it Jewish shops were the target of wanton destruction and plunder. The best defense in these circumstances was to hole up at home and wait for the storm to pass. A day or two later, life would resume as usual, though a hint of menace lingered beneath the surface.

Despite (or perhaps because of) this change in atmosphere, the younger generation of Jews began to immerse itself in Arab literature and culture. Until then, most of the Jews in Iraq had spoken their own dialect of Arabic and wrote it in Hebrew letters (much as Yiddish was a derivative of German written in Hebrew letters) but were illiterate in Arabic proper. The generation growing up in the 1930s was schooled in Arab culture, however, and for the first time in the community's long history, Jewish writers and poets composed their works in Arabic and were regarded as *Arab* writers. Rather than be identified as Jews, they were Iraqis of the Jewish faith.

Had this process continued, things might have turned out very differently. But it came to an abrupt halt on June 1, 1941, when, sparked by the incitement of Iraq's pro-Nazi regime, a pogrom broke out in Baghdad. It raged for two whole days, during which 180 Jews were massacred and countless homes, shops, and synagogues were destroyed. Jews were literally snatched off the streets or dragged out of buses and cars and summarily beaten or knifed to death. Hysterical mobs burst into homes and savagely slaughtered their inhabitants. Not even infants were spared, and in the most ghoulish act of all, pregnant women were slit open and left to die in agony. When the frenzy had spent itself, the Jewish community was left dazed and traumatized.

Still, the Jews of Iraq were divided over the lessons to be drawn from this *farhoud*. The traditional approach was that, ghastly as it had been, the pogrom was essentially a freak tantrum that was over now, and life should return to normal. Many of the intellectuals blamed it, along with Iraq's other ills, on the reactionary government and channeled their energies into the Communist movement in Iraq. It was the Jewish youth who tended toward a more immediate and pragmatic solution. First they organized self-defense units, and soon they were thinking of leaving Iraq for Palestine. It was out of this dual impulse that a Zionist underground began to take shape.

When the British reoccupied Iraq, in the summer of 1941, to protect the flow of oil to the Allies, along with His Majesty's forces came many Palestinian Jews serving either in combat units or in the auxiliary corps as bus and truck drivers, foremen in the units building roads and airfields, and the like. The constant traffic between the two British strongholds in the Middle East made it relatively easy to smuggle Jews from Iraq to Palestine. And once Palestinian Jews had made contact with the young Jewish activists in Iraq, it was possible to send emissaries in the opposite direction to help cultivate the budding movement there. But when the war ended and the British withdrew their forces from Iraq, this overland channel was blocked, and the Zionist movement was forced to go deep underground. Our emissaries had to enter Iraq under cover, and Jews had to be smuggled at both ends of their journey westward: first out of Iraq, then into Palestine. Nevertheless, during the war years the Zionist enterprise had established itself as a going concern in Iraq, and there was no reversing that now.

As I took this in and listened to Yunis speak of the dangers involved in the clandestine life, I stared at him—a flaming redhead with eyes as blue as the sea—and wondered how he would ever survive there. But when I asked him precisely that, he just smiled broadly and assured me, "Don't worry. We'll con them." Seeing that I was far from convinced, he added with a wicked look, "Don't you know about the Australian soldiers who were stationed in Iraq during the last world war and were separated from their wives for years? Let the Iraqis think what they like about my venerable forebears." As matters turned out, the details of his cover differed, but the outcome was as he had promised. After entering Iraq as a stowaway on a truck, Yunis Rabinowitz spent an entire year there as one Dr. Salman, a veterinarian of "Armenian extraction." And to his great fortune—and that of the animals of Iraq—he was never called upon to extend his professional services.

The dangers notwithstanding, I confess that the prospect of going to Iraq was very appealing to me. According to family lore, our roots there went back to the days of King Nebuchadnezzar of Babylonia and our name traced to the great Jewish sage Hillel the Elder, making us an illustrious line. While none of my immediate family was living there now, I did have a few more distant relatives in Baghdad and still felt a tie with them and with the community as a whole. Besides, I felt it almost a moral obligation to take up Yunis's offer. So I made my decision then and there and promised Yunis that we would meet again soon—in Baghdad.

The process of becoming a secret agent took far longer than I had expected, however. It began with the first of many visits to the headquarters of the Mossad for Illegal Immigration, in Tel Aviv. I remember being surprised, even disappointed, to discover that the entire Mossad—the spearhead of the struggle against all the resources of the mighty British Empire and the nerve center of illegal immigration from all over the world—was housed in a total of three cramped and rather dingy rooms. It was hard to believe that such a complex and ramified international underground engaged in such dramatic and heroic actions could be run from such modest, to say nothing of shabby, quarters. A secretary in the front room directed me to one of the men in an adjoining office, who dispensed with formalities (no swearing-in ceremony or anything like that) and brusquely informed me that the Mossad had decided I should try to obtain an Iraqi passport.

"How do I do that?" I asked, truly surprised by the directness of this approach.

He explained that I should apply to the Iraqi consul in Jerusalem, saying that I had been a minor when my family came to Palestine and therefore had had no say in the matter. But now that I was of age, I wanted to take out a passport and return to Baghdad.

So, a day or two later, dressed in my kibbutz-issue finery and armed with my father's long-expired passport, I strode into the Iraqi consulate and explained my request in Arabic, in the best Iraqi brogue I could muster, to a distinctly unimpressed reception clerk.

"Out of the question!" he snapped. Not easily daunted, I demanded to see the consul, who heard me out with pronounced impatience and finally asked in near disgust, "How old are you?"

"Twenty-three," I said.

"And when did you come to Palestine?"

"In about 1934," I said. "The exact date is here in the passport."

"That was twelve years ago," he observed sourly but quite accurately.

"About," I mumbled in growing discomfort.

"How many brothers and sisters do you have?"

"We're eleven children. Seven brothers and four sisters. I am the youngest."

"Are any of your brothers or sisters living in Iraq?" he pressed. I lowered my eyes and did not answer.

"All of them in Palestine?"

"No," I perked up again, hoping for a lead out of this spot. "One brother is in India, one in Japan, one in America, and one in England."

"Mashallah," he sneered, using an Iraqi idiom, particularly popular among the Jews, meaning "how fortunate for you." I think I may have turned red, but I held my tongue.

"And you're not ashamed to turn up here now? You've been living in Palestine since childhood. You've studied here—and I don't dare ask what else you've been doing here since high school. And now you have the nerve to walk in here and tell me that suddenly you remembered you're an Iraqi and want to go 'home'?"

"It's no sudden decision, sir. Life is hard for me here. I have no job. I can't support myself. And I've always wanted to return to Iraq!"

The consul's response to that profession of longing was to resume reading the paper spread out on his desk, and I understood that the audience was over. But even then I didn't give up. Returning to the waiting room, I sat myself down again, determined to keep trying my luck until they threw me out. Finally the reception clerk came to life.

"Have you at least got a cigarette to pass the time? A Players or State Express?" he asked, referring to the most expensive brands of the day.

"Be right back," I responded and dashed out, bought a large pack of Players (fifty cigarettes), and stuffed a five-pound note inside it. Back at the consulate, after the clerk had helped himself to a cigarette and gotten a glance at the note, I asked half casually, "When do you think my passport will be ready?"

He stood up, brought over the necessary forms, asked for four photographs, told me to return the next day, and advised me not to forget the cigarettes.

Having followed his instructions to the letter, I became the proud bearer of a bona fide Iraqi passport, with which I returned to my kibbutz to tie up loose ends as economic administrator. The Mossad apparently saw no need to train me in any special way or even brief me in detail on my mission. The one course I was invited to attend—either because someone was pulling my leg or because he had a wild imagination—was in hand-to-hand combat, which in those days meant mastering the use of a stick and a knife. I was taught how to jump with knife drawn, roll out of range, and throw my weapon so that it would stick in a wooden board like a dart—along with sundry other capers that reminded me of the adventure films I had seen in my childhood, like *Ali Baba and the Forty Thieves* and *Sindbad the Sailor.* Soon I began to wonder whether my days would be

spent organizing immigration or leaping off rooftops, with turbaned enemies in hot pursuit through the dark, winding alleys of Baghdad.

If my professional preparation was less than thorough, when it came to
motivation I was getting a fresh dose almost daily. After the successful
conclusion to the *Hannah Senesh* episode, the Mossad seemed unable to
duplicate the feat. From Christmas 1945 until I finally left for Iraq, in July
1946, eight immigrant boats tried unsuccessfully to reach the coast. All
were stopped on the high seas, and their passengers—the survivors of
death camps—were promptly arrested and again placed behind barbed
wire. The pictures of British soldiers dragging pale, emaciated women,
children, and old people off those ships as they resisted with the last of
their strength made our blood boil and left us with a crushing sense of
frustration. Ordinary people took to the streets in mass demonstrations
and went on hunger strikes for lack of any other way to get the British to
relent. And I, who knew what I should be doing and was prepared to take
on a perilous mission far from home—I sat with bags packed, burning with
travel fever, and waited.

Finally, on July 22, 1946, with twenty-five pounds in my wallet and the
new *nom de guerre* of Shammai (the ancient Hillel's archrival), I sat in the
departure lounge of Lydda Airport, near Tel Aviv, my eyes darting around
to see if any British policemen or agents were eavesdropping as I talked
with my brother Eliyahu in Hebrew—barely above a mumble—about how
to deal with Father's curiosity while I was in Baghdad. Eliyahu was the
only member of my family who knew where I was going and why. At that
point, no one could really say for how long. So we had concocted an
elaborate ruse whereby Eliyahu would mail Father predated postcards
from inside Palestine for the duration of my absence. It had seemed a
clever enough idea when I sat preparing that stack of vaguely worded
missives, but now I was having misgivings. Eliyahu assured me that everything would work out fine; it was just that I had never flown before and
was having a perfectly natural case of preflight nerves.

If that was so, it was mercifully brief. For in the midst of my fretting, the
flight was called, and as soon as I entered the small BOAC plane, along
with eight other passengers, I became fully immersed in the rituals and
wonders of commercial flight: the briefing, the seat belt, the leisurely taxi
to the runway, the incredible din when the engines were pushed to full
throttle for takeoff, and then the odd sensation of being airborne and
feeling that my vital organs had shifted a centimeter or two from their
usual moorings as the plane banked and headed eastward. Through the
window, I could now see the mighty Jordan—actually a narrow, winding
ribbon of rather turbid water and very disappointing. Nonetheless,
touched by the excitement of it all, I tapped the window with my finger

and proudly informed the man seated next to me, "That's the Jordan." My neighbor, very British in visage and dress, merely glared at me for this gross invasion of his privacy, thereby giving me my first practical lesson in underground etiquette: speak as little as possible. I was still digesting that point when the small, two-engine plane dipped into an air pocket over the Jordanian Desert, and the whole experience quickly lost its charm. I soon had to resort to my air-sickness bag, rousing the contempt of not only my immediate neighbor but all the other passengers as well. Bathed in a cold sweat, I closed my eyes, slouched down in my seat, and abandoned myself to a wave of self-pity.

To cheer myself up, I decided to think ahead to the end of the ordeal and concentrate on the landing in Baghdad. But suddenly I wasn't so sure that traveling on an Iraqi passport was really such a good idea. After all, there was ample reason to fear that the consulate in Jerusalem had sent a report on me to the relevant authorities in Baghdad and perhaps even suggested sending out a "welcoming committee" for me in the form of a squad of police. Even more likely, it now occurred to me, were the chances that I would be drafted upon arrival. It was touching, the MP's would tell me, that I had pined for the homeland—so touching, in fact, that now I would have the pleasure of fulfilling my national duty.

When I entered the terminal in Baghdad, however, I was awaited by neither an arrest warrant nor a draft notice but by Selim Sweri, my sister's brother-in-law, who had lived in Palestine for a number of years and had returned to Iraq for family reasons. At Selim's home I was welcomed by Yunis, who took me to the quarters we were to share and promptly outfitted me with the Iraqi identity card of one Fuad Salah, who had been smuggled into Palestine a short time earlier. With that I became a "fully legal" resident of Baghdad, and Yunis put me to work.

TWO

The Lords
of the Desert

MY FIRST MISSION to Iraq lasted one full year, and when I arrived in Baghdad what I found there was a tightly knit, passionately motivated, clandestine movement of about two thousand people, most of them young men and women. Outside of the capital—whose Jewish population numbered about a hundred thousand—were another twenty or so branches in almost every city and town where Jews were to be found. The underground operated through three arms: an educational youth movement, a self-defense organization known as the Shurah ("The Rank and File"), and the network for illegal immigration. This division had been established in 1942, when the first emissaries came from Palestine, and the wisdom of it became apparent when all the foreign forces left Iraq at the end of World War II and the Zionist movement went underground—literally as well as figuratively. We even referred to our enterprise as the "Zionism of cellars," because most of the movement's activities, from the study of Hebrew to training in the use of arms, were carried out below ground—in the basements that were a vital feature of almost every home as a refuge from the brutal heat of the Iraqi summers.

Cells of ten to fifteen members met in these windowless rooms, each completely isolated from the next. As an extra precaution, everyone was known only by an underground name, to limit the danger to our members and their families and prevent the whole network from unraveling if anyone were arrested. The emissaries from Palestine worked only with the leadership level, so that their exposure was limited. Five people alone knew where they lived, and no Iraqi Jew was even privy to their real identities. In line with this policy, we decided not to reveal that I was in fact a native of Baghdad. Within the movement I was known simply as Amo Yusuf, meaning "Uncle Joseph," and I was looked upon as an uncle —more of a big brother, really—by all the movement's leaders.

One of the bolder and therefore high-risk operations of this "Zionism of cellars" actually took place in an attic housing the precious wireless set that enabled us to communicate with the Mossad in Tel Aviv. These communications had been initiated in 1943 by Malka Rofeh, a woman who had been smuggled into Iraq disguised as a British soldier. Soon afterward, however, one of the local people was trained to operate the rather primitive set that had been brought in with Malka. The choice fell on Avraham Mordad, and a very fortunate one it was, for he proved to be diligent, resourceful, and above all persevering. In fact, he continued at this task until the underground was dissolved, in the middle of 1951. He also displayed a flair for tinkering that enabled him to repair the instrument— an invaluable talent in underground conditions. Avraham trained Eliyahu Shina as a backup operator, and I first met the two of them in the midst of their labors in July 1946, a few days after arriving in Baghdad.

When Yunis and I entered the tiny room in Avraham's attic, I was struck most of all by the stifling heat. The room's only window had been sealed, and I found myself all but gasping for air as I watched the two men at work. The sweat was literally dripping off them both, but still they sat almost motionless, the heavy earphones hugging their heads. The wireless looked much like an ordinary radio set, and Avraham was working it that day, tapping the key carefully to produce its dots and dashes. After he finished transmitting, his body stiffened and he pressed his eyes closed in concentration as he began jotting down a jumble of letters that grew into meaningless words, while opposite him Eliyahu sat briskly waving a paper fan a few inches from Avraham's sweat-soaked face. I felt as though I were standing in a holy of holies and didn't dare move or make the slightest sound. Once the transmission was over, however, and they began to decipher the coded message, I allowed myself to break the silence and greet them. Curious about the fan ritual, I pointed at the paper in Eliyahu's hand

and asked in what was meant to be friendly jest, "Haven't you heard of the invention called the electric fan?"

"As a matter of fact, we have," Avraham snapped in irritation; but then his voice softened as he explained, "The reception is poor enough as it is, and if we turn on another electrical appliance, we won't be able to hear anything."

Having opened with a *faux pas,* I decided to hold my peace about the other detail that had intrigued me as we were standing there. But as we descended the steps, I commented to Yunis about the small revolver I had noticed on the table.

"Is it really necessary?" I asked, more out of concern than criticism.

"Avraham has decided that if anything goes wrong, he won't be taken alive," he explained with a particularly grim expression, "and he's probably got a point."

It was a sobering thought that certainly impressed upon me the need for caution. Still, I had a job to do, and it required me to get around. According to the division of labor that we had agreed upon in Tel Aviv, I was to direct the movement's educational activities. That meant working with the leadership level, face to face, throughout the country—which was no mean task, because of the great distances that had to be covered (at least by Palestinian standards). Compared to Yunis and our predecessors, however, I enjoyed relative freedom of movement and exploited it to visit every one of the cities and towns in which the movement existed. I even spent extended periods in Basra, in the south, and Kirkuk, in the north, doing my best to raise a new generation of dedicated activists.

But, for all that, my pet interest continued to be illegal immigration. Considering that we had to overcome a double barrier—smuggling people first out of Iraq and then into Palestine—our work in this area called for a double measure of ingenuity. Gone were the days when British Army vehicles could be used to get people across the vast expanse of desert that separated Palestine from Iraq. On occasion, Arab drivers of the giant trucks that transported goods from various Iraqi cities to the Mediterranean port of Haifa were willing to conceal some human cargo—for a handsome fee. We were also able to get a limited number of people out on forged passports, usually in small seaplanes that took off from Lake Habbaniyah, not far from Baghdad, or the Shatt-al-Arab, in southern Iraq, and landed on the Dead Sea. But altogether this added up to a mere handful of immigrants, so the search for new channels went on without respite.

One rather audacious attempt to create an avenue of immigration began halfway through my first year in Iraq, on February 16, 1947, when, guided by a Bedouin smuggler named Sabah, six strong young men left Baghdad to make their way to Palestine on foot, or at best on donkeys—through more than six hundred miles of barren desert. In retrospect, perhaps the scheme smacked of desperation. But we genuinely believed that, with sufficient thought and guidance, a trek of that sort through the wilderness was not as outlandish as it sounds today. In fact, we thought it might even pan out into a regular route for immigration. What's more, the fact that six young men who were not reckless adventurers or desperadoes running from the law were willing to test out the route seemed a sign that it had its merits. So we sent them off with high hopes—and then had no word of them for weeks, during which our sanguine expectations degenerated to the point of outright despair. It wasn't until March 16 that we were informed of the arrival of "all six laborers"—our code word for immigrants —at a kibbutz on the Dead Sea.

But if any of us believed that this was the breakthrough we had been waiting for, the next day's transmission disabused us of such notions. Our six boys had staggered into the kibbutz in a state of utter exhaustion after having walked all the way to the Iraqi-Jordanian border, repeatedly running out of food and water, and then being shot at in the desert, arrested in Jordan, and finally left to make the last leg of their journey completely on their own. "The smuggler treated them very badly," the wire informed us with restraint, "and deserted them in Amman." But before doing so, he forced them to sign a letter confirming their safe arrival, so that he could collect the balance of his fee. At least they outwitted him on that, however: The group's leader signed his family name as Sheker, which is the Hebrew word for "lie."

"This is no breakthrough," headquarters admonished, forbidding us ever to use the smuggler again. (Evidently Sabah knew his ruse wouldn't work, for he never turned up to collect the remainder of his money.)

Though we were relieved to hear that the boys were safe, the failure of the experiment left us particularly despondent, because it followed an equally nerve-racking wait for word of a breakthrough on another route that had ended in news of tragedy. The story had begun a few months earlier, late in October 1946, with the receipt of the following wire from Tel Aviv:

TO: Berman*
FROM: Artzi†
Negotiations are going on here with very serious people who will take laborers from Berman from the vicinity of Rutba. One of them will be

* Our code word for Iraq.
† "My Country," our code word for Palestine.

arriving in Berman in another ten days. Details on him will follow after his departure. The price agreed upon is 50 Palestine pounds from Rutba to Artzi. You will have to determine the exact place where you will deposit the laborers. The first attempt will be made with 15 laborers. Further details follow.

Our initial reaction to this message was elation, for it came after a torrent of angry letters and wires to Tel Aviv demanding some serious action on the immigration front. I had been in Iraq for almost three months, Yunis for closer to a year, and during that time emigration had all but come to a standstill. Our frustration had reached the point where, a few days earlier, I had sent out a wire asking peevishly, "Is the whole purpose of our mission here just to salve someone's conscience?" So we hoped that this wire was a genuine sign that Tel Aviv was finally responding to our entreaties. At any rate, the words "Negotiations are going on here with very serious people" were heartening—until doubt began to creep into our wary minds. "Why all the mystery?" we asked each other. Why hold back details about the man on his way to us until after his departure? Perhaps the whole thing was just a cock-and-bull story served up to mollify us for a while.

The letter that arrived a few days later filled in a few more details. It seems that "three people," identified only as "Lords of the Desert," were prepared to pick up immigrants near Rutba and transport them to Palestine "with full guarantees." The unnamed man with whom negotiations had been conducted in Palestine "has returned to Ruthie to arrange his papers for Berman." "Ruthie" was, of course, Beirut, but the reference to the "Lords of the Desert" suggested that he came not from Lebanon but from Syria, whose entire border with Iraq was one vast, barren wilderness.

All in all, these "details" were not very illuminating. More to the point, the arrangements outlined in the wire may have seemed promising to people negotiating on the shores of the Mediterranean, but to us the notion of a rendezvous in Rutba seemed almost ominous. A small desert town some 250 miles west of Baghdad, Rutba lay on the road from Iraq to Palestine near the Iraqi-Jordanian border. Naturally it was an important stop for the huge trucks that traveled this route and a place where travelers in buses and taxis could get out and stretch their legs. It was also crawling with policemen, border guards, and customs agents. But, other than that, Rutba was a dumpy little town devoid of so much as a single Jew for variety. What, then, was the point of choosing it as the "staging area" for Jewish immigrants?

Quite by chance, the answer to that came from Sammi Moriah, one of

our activists who had recently begun to work on the immigration problem
—and probably the most astute and level-headed man I would ever have
the privilege to know. A short while earlier, Sammi had met a Jew by the
name of Eliyahu Inni, from the town of Ramadi, on the Baghdad–Rutba
road, and happened to hear about an acquaintance of his, Sheikh Abdullah
Sa'id of Rutba. Abdullah had enjoyed a long if not particularly illustrious
career as a police sergeant. But now, with his service about to end, he was
prepared to cross over to the farther side of the law and take on various
kinds of smuggling operations—without prejudice as to his clients or their
needs. His good standing with the police and long experience in security
operations boded well for this new career, and he certainly knew the
desert inside out. But, above all, Abdullah Sa'id was known far and wide
as a fair and honest man whose word could be trusted.

That was as much as Inni could say, but Sammi kept poking around until
he had pieced together other details. For example, that Abdullah was a tall,
swarthy man who was meticulous about dressing in a sparkling white shirt
and broad, elegant *abaiya* (the long outer gown worn by the men of the
desert), and that whenever he came to Baghdad he indulged himself by
frequenting one or another of the modern cafés on the city's main thoroughfare, Al-Rashid Street. Upon discovering that lead, Sammi began to
stake out these cafés, drinking strong, sweet tea and sometimes allowing
himself a dish of *dundorma,* ice cream as sweet as honey and as sticky and
elastic as bubble gum. Each time he caught sight of someone who approxi-
mated Abdullah's description, Sammi would approach him as casually as
possible and ask—after begging a thousand pardons—if the gentleman
were not in fact the famed Abdullah Sa'id. After a string of disappointments, one day this ritual ended on a different note. The words were
hardly past his lips when, instead of the usual negative reply, Sammi heard
the emphatic retort, "And what would you be wanting with Abdullah
Sa'id?"

"I have regards for him from a mutual friend, Eliyahu Inni," he replied
with a quiet matter-of-factness that Abdullah must have found appealing,
for he immediately changed his tone.

"Well then, any friend of a friend is a friend of mine," the sheikh fairly
cooed, gesturing toward an empty chair. "Won't you join me? What will
you drink?" Before Sammi could even reply, he had clapped his hands and
called to the waiter, "Two teas!"

Quickly sizing up his host, Sammi decided to get straight to the point.
"My friend Eliyahu tells me that you can help me. My sister has recently
married, and her husband needs medical treatment, in Palestine. But they
can't get a passport. You know, the government's policy and all—"

"It makes no difference to me who they are and why they want to go," Abdullah broke in to spare himself further details. "I am prepared to help with anything. Unfortunately, however, I cannot take them all the way to Palestine. I know the roads and paths from Baghdad to Rutba. I might be prepared to go as far as the H-4 pumping station over the border, in Transjordan. There's not a man alive who will tangle with me in those parts. But beyond H-4, that's not my territory. And I'm not one to promise what I can't deliver."

So they didn't do any business that day, and Sammi paid for the teas and left, feeling glum. Still, the contact had been made, and both sides were interested in maintaining it. "Something may yet come of it," Sammi said with a shrug when he reported on the meeting. He had been very impressed with the sheikh: his experience, his self-confidence, and especially his straight talk about what he could do and what he could not.

Now that the mysterious "Lords of the Desert" had entered the picture, it looked as if two gears were about to mesh. Was it mere coincidence that Abdullah Sa'id could take people only as far as Rutba—H-4 at the most— and that the "Lords" had agreed to take our "laborers" only from the vicinity of Rutba westward? We wondered for a while, but then the point became academic, because after that first wire and the subsequent letter about these "very serious people," nothing further happened. Yunis, who had been planning a visit home, decided not to delay it any longer, and I was left in charge of things in Baghdad. Then, after I, too, had practically despaired of the matter, on November 15 I received an urgent wire instructing me to contact one Mohammed al-Kuzbari, the agent of the "Lords of the Desert," at the Regent Palace Hotel, and "finalize arrangements with him."

That, as it turned out, was the starting signal for a wicked (and typical) game of cat and mouse. Almost daily I would receive a cable imploring me to find the man, while day after day I went out scouring the hotels and travel agencies in Baghdad, only to return empty-handed. The situation was not only frustrating and embarrassing, it was downright dangerous. For Sammi had contacted Sheikh Abdullah again, and we couldn't keep him dangling forever without ruining our relationship with him. It wasn't until December 1 that I was finally able to inform Tel Aviv of my success in tracking down Kuzbari's brother, Adnan, and arranging for him to meet with Abdullah to work out a preliminary plan (for which I had to fork over thirty pounds as a down payment).

Adnan al-Kuzbari, Mohammed's twin, was quite different from what I had expected. I went to his hotel prepared to meet a venerable, aging sheikh and found instead a man in his late twenties nattily dressed in a custom-made suit set off by a colorful tie, matching handkerchief peeking smartly out of his breast pocket, and the chain of a gold pocket watch draped out of his vest. Clean-shaven, his hair slick with brilliantine, Adnan was a paragon of good breeding and spoke with a pronounced air of self-importance. It was hard to imagine what connection he could possibly have with the desert. But when we retired to the bar of his luxurious hotel (notwithstanding the fact that Muslims are forbidden to imbibe liquor), he explained that he and his brother worked in close collaboration with Emir Fauaz Sha'alan, the head of the Ruala tribe, which effectively controlled all the territory from Damascus to the Iraqi border. In short, the emir was the unchallenged ruler of the desert (hence the Mossad's code name for Sha'alan and company). Adnan and Mohammed Kuzbari had been in the emir's service for years, acting as his foreign ministers, so to speak. The Kuzbari family, Adnan went on to inform me, was a large, wealthy, and well-connected clan whose members commanded positions of influence in all walks of life in Syria, from politics and law to the military and industry.

In fact, Adnan seemed prepared to go on about his credentials all night. But when I tried to steer our conversation toward the nitty-gritty, asking how he intended to get our people from Rutba to Palestine and where in Palestine he would deposit them, he became suspiciously evasive.

"I don't know exactly what my brother has worked out with the emir," he waffled. "Either they'll go through Damascus or we'll work out an arrangement with the Arab Legion and your people will travel in army cars, straight through Transjordan. That, of course, is the shorter and more convenient route."

Seeing the look of astonishment on my face, he explained that they had connections with a number of Jordanian army officers who were only too happy to generate additional income from their official cars and were prepared to sell even their mothers for the right fee.

"If they travel in army cars, will they have to dress in uniforms?" I asked.

"No. Either way, it's best that they go in Bedouin dress."

But I had my doubts about that, because I knew that it wasn't enough to wear an *abaiya* for a man to pass as a Bedouin. I also wondered whether the "full guarantee" Tel Aviv had promised was contingent upon our immigrants' knowing how to behave like Bedouin. Adnan promised to check whether the Bedouin outfit was mandatory, and I reported to Tel Aviv on December 4 that "the brother is not well versed in the [operational] details, which has proved to be an obstacle in the negotiations." On the other hand, the man was a stickler in another department: cold cash.

That was true of his principals, as well, and applied throughout our relationship. Money, money, and money yet again was their constant refrain.

However, despite my sense of disquiet about his vagueness, the long postponement of our meeting, and his aggressiveness about payment, there was no reason to doubt that the man sitting opposite me was indeed the representative of the legendary "Lords," who could probably solve our problem. His stories about the emir—a genuine prince who ruled a vast desert empire—could spark the imagination of the most sober. And being somewhat less than that, I found myself lapsing into a dream of caravans of immigrants overcoming all obstacles as they made their way through the wilderness to the borders of Palestine while the immigrant boats continued to do the same over the sea.

After that meeting with Kuzbari, I introduced him to Sheikh Abdullah, and we agreed that the two sides would meet near Rutba on December 8 to coordinate the action in the field. But like so many of the meetings that had been agreed upon, that one never took place—and the blame was shifted every which way. The "Lords of the Desert" and our man in Beirut, Givoli, who was our liaison with them, complained about Tel Aviv; Tel Aviv passed the buck to Baghdad; and Baghdad (need I add?) fumed about everyone. The fact that we were not in direct contact with the emir complicated matters considerably, for everything we wanted to convey to him had to be wired to Tel Aviv and then relayed via Beirut to Sha'alan's men in Damascus. All of this not only contributed to the general disarray, it also helped people escape responsibility by explaining away their negligence as innocent "misunderstandings."

Then, just when it looked as if the whole affair were little more than a hoax, Emir Sha'alan turned up in Baghdad in person. According to the latest word from Tel Aviv, we expected Kuzbari and Givoli to be accompanying him. But the emir informed us that the two had remained behind in the desert, though for the life of us we couldn't get out of him the reason why. Looking back, it's clear that money was the answer to everything. Tel Aviv had wired us that the sum of fifty Palestine pounds per person, to be paid at the end of the journey, had been settled upon with Kuzbari, and we were ordered to "give him 200–300 for expenses when the laborers are picked up." But the emir claimed that Givoli and Kuzbari—who were conveniently out of reach—had arrived at a completely different sum and demanded an advance of one thousand Palestine pounds—or no deal. We complied with this demand only because of the bait he dangled before us: he was actually prepared to take the first "shipment" of forty people (men only), and at the beginning of 1947 that was a *real* breakthrough!

The entire underground went into high gear, concentrating the candidates for immigration—healthy young men from all over Iraq—in the homes of a few movement members in Baghdad. They had been told to bring provisions for the journey, but we nevertheless prepared a container of water and modest rations for each of them: dried dates, salty goat cheese, loaves of Iraqi bread *(samoun),* and the dried Iraqi pita known as *jaradok.* Yoel Shochat, one of the movement's most talented leaders, was appointed head of the group—not least for his thoughtful expression and quiet, soothing manner that belied his twenty years.

The plan worked out among Yunis, Abdullah, and Sha'alan called for Abdullah to bring the boys as far as the H-4 pumping station, where they would be transferred onto an army truck that would continue along the main road though Transjordan to Beit Yosef, a *moshav,* or smallholders' collective, south of the Sea of Galilee. To avoid having to take the main road between Baghdad and Rutba, Abdullah placed our "laborers" in the hands of two of his best drivers, Mahmoud and Jumah, seasoned desert foxes who knew every path and rise in those wastes and didn't need anything as vulgar as a road. They would drive southward from Baghdad to Karbala and then take desert paths known "only to policemen and smugglers," as Abdullah put it, to the vicinity of Rutba. Abdullah would be waiting there to lead them around the town to their rendezvous with the emir.

At 10 P.M. on March 7, Yunis sent off the wire that we had been dreaming of:

TO: Artzi
FROM: Berman
Forty left safely tonight. Wish them well.

Those seven words made up for all the tension and irritation of the previous months. I wish I could say that they also brought them to an end, but quite the opposite was true. Three days passed without any word from Tel Aviv of their safe arrival. By the fourth day we were anxious, and on the fifth, when we received an urgent transmission from Tel Aviv, our two operators copied and decoded it with trembling hands, but it wasn't the message we had been waiting for. All it said was that Kuzbari would be arriving on Saturday to take "120 laborers." Yunis, who was a genuine trouper but whose patience failed him at that point, quickly wired back:

TO: Artzi
FROM: Berman
Has the shipment of forty arrived? Is that why you're so eager to turn 120 others over to Kuzbari?

And in case that point was lost in the airwaves between Baghdad and Tel Aviv, at the end of the transmission he added for good measure:

The abundance of unclear points in your transmission last night indicates either disorder in your method of working or a lack of talent in wording transmissions. And don't think I'm merely in a mood. You're getting on my nerves, and I have enough to cope with as it is.

Miffed by his style, Tel Aviv struck back:

7. As to disorder and a lack of talent, we'll discuss that some other time. You must be prepared to send off the shipment, even if it gets on your nerves.

The classic arguments, misapprehensions, and sheer bickering between headquarters, in the rear, and the people in the field applied to our covert war as well. But, for all this venting of frustration, the enigma remained unsolved: what had happened to the forty boys? On March 14, Tel Aviv wired that "according to Kuzbari the workers have not yet arrived because a storm has forced him to turn them back." We could confirm that a fierce storm had indeed raged over the desert, a veritable blizzard of sand and minute particles of brown-red dust that clogged the nostrils, burned the eyes, stuck to the lashes, and clouded vision more than the thickest fog. A vehicle caught in the open desert during a storm of that sort—especially a smuggler's vehicle that has been avoiding the main roads—was in far greater danger than a ship caught in a squall. Without a compass, navigational equipment, or a communications set, its driver would be blinded by the pall that settles over the desert. And the prayers and cries of its terrified passengers would be muffled to silence by the thick suspension of sand and dust.

Our forty "laborers" had driven into just such a storm on the third day after their departure. If everything had gone as planned, they would have reached their destination before the storm broke. But, as we later learned, they had suffered delays almost from the start.

The first and most nerve-racking was in Karbala. As they drove out of Baghdad, and Yoel outlined the route they would be taking, his briefing roused general consternation. And with good reason. For Karbala is a city held holy by Shiite Muslims, and Jews—whom the Shiites regard as impure —are forbidden to enter it. Karbala's sanctity dates back to the year 680, when Hussein, a grandson of the Prophet Mohammed, was murdered there together with seventy-two of his disciples. In the wake of this slaughter, Hussein's followers split away from mainstream Islam, established the Shi'a cult, and declared Karbala to be inhabited by holy spirits. When our boys heard the name Karbala, their instinctive association was with the annual Ashura processions that caused the Jews of Iraq to close themselves up behind barred doors. They recalled how as children they had peeked through the shutters in terror at the seemingly endless torch-lit parade of men dressed in mourners' black, beating their bared chests, flagellating themselves with chains, pounding their heads with the handle end of swords and daggers till they brought forth blood, and all the while bewailing the death of the martyred Hussein to the monotonous beat of a drum:

> Hussein died in Karbala
> A waterskin lay where he tread,
> And even the birds in the heavens
> Weep for the blood that he shed.

As the truck entered the deserted streets of Karbala, close to midnight, the boys seemed to huddle together and all but hold their breath until they would be clear of the town. But, to their astonishment, the vehicle came to a halt in the market square, at the very heart of the city. When Yoel jumped out to ask why, the drivers explained that from there on the route went through the trackless desert, with no signposts to guide the way, so that it was senseless to continue at night.

"You stay in the truck," Mahmoud ordered. "The most important thing is that no one leave it. And don't make any noise. We'll get going again at daybreak."

The request for silence was superfluous; no one dreamed of making a sound, for they all knew what would happen if a group of Jewish boys were caught in the precincts of Karbala. How would they explain their presence? By pleading that they meant no harm and were actually only passing through on their way to Palestine? It goes without saying that not a sound issued from the truck other than the beating of forty hearts.

When the truck set out again at daybreak, the boys heaved a muted sigh of relief. But their trials were far from over, and their second delay was far longer. The engine of the old truck—which was at any rate loaded well over its capacity—puffed and wheezed its way across the sand, and from time to time the radiator boiled over, forcing them to stop until it had cooled. During one of these stops, the radiator began to leak. Its water, dark red with rust, was instantly soaked up by the sand, leaving only a stain the color of blood.

Mahmoud and Jumah tried to repair the damaged radiator with a hammer and some rusty wire they found under the seat. When they failed to make headway, they began to dismantle it altogether. And just then, as if by appointment, a Bedouin came by on his horse, curious about the intruders who had shattered the desert quiet. Mahmoud began to haggle with him, settled on a price, hoisted the radiator onto the animal, and set off with the Bedouin toward the road, where he would hitch a ride back to Karbala to repair the defiant radiator.

Stranded, the boys amused themselves by singing songs and telling stories around a campfire till Mahmoud returned, toward noon the next day, with the repaired radiator perched proudly on the horse's back—together with a few waterskins and a basket of dates and *samoun*. By evening the radiator was back in its berth, filled with water, and successfully tested. "It's better than new!" Mahmoud exclaimed, and he decided to renew the journey at dawn.

But before daybreak, they awoke to the sound of a high-pitched whistle coming from afar that grew almost into a wail. Soon they could feel a coating of dust on their lips and lining their nostrils and the choking sensation that followed it. The drivers ordered the boys back into the truck and hastily drove off, with Mahmoud at the wheel. He tried to work up as much speed as he could in the aging truck, as it became increasingly difficult to distinguish between day and night. But from what he could see in the faint light that penetrated the dust, Mahmoud knew that he had lost his way. Afraid to stop and wait out the storm, he began to drive in steadily larger circles in a desperate attempt to find the path he had missed earlier, as the wind buffeted the truck and billowed its canvas like a sail in a typhoon.

The search went on, the circles grew wider and wider, and still there was no sign of the way. As the drivers became increasingly nervous, prayers replaced the curses on their lips until Mahmoud's red and irritated eyes caught sight of the coveted landmark: a bent, twisted date palm that had once flourished in splendid isolation in the heart of the desert, though all that remained of it now was its scarred trunk. Beside it he made out the beginning of the path he knew so well, and when he had satisfied himself that his imagination was not playing tricks, he jerked the steering wheel to the right to place the truck on the road to salvation.

Had the vehicle been loaded with the kind of cargo that Mahmoud was used to hauling, the maneuver probably would have succeeded—as it undoubtedly had in similar instances in the past. Unfortunately, Mahmoud forgot (or never knew) that a live cargo behaves like fluid and the sharp turn would induce the effect of a centrifugal force and knock the truck off balance. The result was that Mahmoud lost control of the wheel, and the truck, which was already careening from the sharp turn, flipped over twice before finally coming to a halt, hulking on the ground like the corpse of some huge animal.

The cries of the wounded finally penetrated the dazed shock of those who had emerged unhurt or only slightly injured. When they pulled themselves together, the picture before them was shattering. Two boys had been crushed to death under the truck. A third was caught under one of its wheels and lay in agony from fractures in his pelvis and legs. Three other boys had suffered less serious fractures. While tending to the injured and organizing an effort to free the boy under the wheel, Yoel suddenly noticed that their Bedouin drivers, Mahmoud and Jumah, had vanished, and he realized they were stranded. Later in the day a few Bedouin who happened by on camels set the boys in the direction of a water hole that had remained after the winter rains. One of them even milked his camels to provide a little sustenance for the injured boys.

By the time the storm had exhausted itself, the boys realized that they had no idea what day it was. But whatever the date, their chances of surviving decreased with every passing hour. This terrible realization did not show in their behavior, though. They continued to maintain self-discipline and saved the remaining drops of water in their skins for the injured.

Three days passed before their ears picked up something that differed from the usual desert sounds. Squinting in its direction, they could see a tiny cloud of dust that appeared to be moving toward them. At first they dismissed it as a mirage—which was only befitting parched people who were slowly losing their senses. But slowly the shape of a truck could be seen, and when the vehicle reached them, Mahmoud and Jumah jumped out and unloaded a veritable haul of waterskins, fried dates, and savory *samoun.* They were offended when Yoel confessed that he thought he would never see them again. "You don't know the Bedouin," one of them growled. "Otherwise you would never have let such words pass your lips." They loaded the injured on the new truck and drove back to the scene of the accident, setting the overturned truck on its wheels and extricating the corpses. Now the boys could dig graves for their comrades and allow themselves the luxury of tears.

The desert swallowed up the sound of their mourning and returned to its eternal silence, as the shifting sands soon covered all trace of the two mounds. At twilight the next day, Friday, March 14, the boys were returned by truck to Baghdad. They were deposited at the Baghdad West railway station and were met by the people who had sent them on their way a week earlier with hearts full of hope. From there they were dispersed among the homes of movement activists, and Jewish doctors were enlisted to tend to the injured. Two of them had to be admitted to the local Jewish hospital, despite the risk that their story would get out.

I was in Basra then and received an urgent summons to return to Baghdad. When my train pulled into the station on Saturday morning, I found Sammi waiting for me at the end of the platform wearing his gold-rimmed glasses (which he didn't need), a *sidara* (the boat-shaped hat that was the symbol of Iraqi nationalism and independence), and carrying worry beads in his hand. As I drew near, he turned his back to me and began walking. I followed in silence. It was only after we had reached the car, driven out of the station area, and satisfied ourselves that we were not being followed that Sammi told me what had happened.

It was a time of trial for the movement, and we feared a total collapse of morale. Far graver was the prospect that the hospitalization of the injured boys would give us away, that one of the many people who had been privy to the affair would suffer a slip of the tongue or even deliberately inform on us. We were also deeply troubled by the problem of the bereaved families. Until then we had walked a thin line in our relationship with the parents whose sons and daughters had left for Palestine—always without their knowledge and often against their will. But there's no comparison between receiving word that a son or daughter has reached Palestine safely, or even that he or she has been arrested and needs help, and learning that a son has been killed in the desert and is not even buried in consecrated ground. So we couldn't predict how the families would react. Neither could we imagine how the incident would affect our relationship with the Jewish community's official bodies—which took a rather dim view of our activities as it was.

When I met with Yoel and his comrades, heard their story firsthand, and asked if there was anything I could do for them, one of the boys said almost meekly, "Amo Yusuf, we want you to promise us that we will be at the head of the list for emigration to Palestine. It's not our fault that we didn't make it, and we don't want to stay here." I of course promised that they would be the first to go and even that they would be able to do so soon—perhaps very soon. But when I made that promise, I had no inkling of the troubles that still lay ahead.

On March 17, Emir Sha'alan again turned up in Baghdad, presumably in connection with the message we had received about the proposed shipment of 120 "laborers." This time he came at the head of a small army of advisers, bodyguards, and rifle-toting escorts who were further armed with curved daggers that peeked out of silver-plated scabbards—to say nothing of a host of servants and cooks. They arrived in a convoy of dust-covered jeeps and desert cars that pulled straight up to the door of the luxurious Semiramis Hotel, where the emir and his closest associates got out and booked their rooms, leaving the rest to settle for more modest accommodations nearby. Inside the Semiramis, Sha'alan and his entourage ensconced themselves in the lobby and the rooms as if they were the open desert, spreading mats on the tiled floors, placing a charcoal stove in the middle of the emir's suite, and setting a polished copper coffeepot over it. Just like home. The rumor that preceded them—and was evidently spread with their encouragement—was that the police had tried to bar them from entering Baghdad with their weapons. But the emir, incensed by such impudence, informed them that if he were not allowed to enter the city peaceably but armed, he would mount a raid and break in by force. Shortly thereafter the police relented and opened the way before him.

When Yunis, Sammi, and I went to call on the emir in his hotel, I couldn't help but be impressed by the man. He looked exactly as I had imagined a prince of the desert to be: tall and lean with prominent cheekbones, slightly thick lips set under a mustache, and the rest of his dark face plowed with lines from the desert wind. He wore a white *kaffiyeh* (traditional head cloth) and golden *agal* (circular band holding the cloth in place) and was wrapped in a broad camel's-hair *abaiya* embroidered in gold down the sides. When we entered, the emir was seated on a mat with his legs crossed oriental style and his elbow propped on a pile of pillows at his side. Before him stood a narghile, its small embers glowing on a bed of tobacco, with water bubbling in its elongated jar each time he inhaled through the narrow pipe in his hand.

When we entered the room, the mandatory ceremony began. We opened by offering him the traditional greeting ("May Allah bless you with a good evening"), and he replied in kind, adding that he was honored by our visit. Hardly were we seated when he clapped his hands and a servant appeared with a tray of small cups in one hand and a copper coffeepot in the other, signaling that we were about to embark upon the coffee ceremony. First he approached each of us in turn and poured a small amount of the liquid into each cup. We tasted the bitter brew—a single drop of which suffices to bring any man to his senses—and then the servant returned and filled our cups. This time we slurped it in noisily, to demonstrate our enjoyment, and when we indicated with a wave of the hand that we had had our fill, he proceeded to serve the others. In the meantime we conducted polite conversation with the emir about his health, the annual rainfall, and other innocuous subjects until Sha'alan clapped his hands again and, without another word, his entire entourage stood up and left. Other than the emir and Adnan Kuzbari, only the three of us remained.

Having dispensed with the courtesies, the emir got right down to business, telling us that this time our people would be picked up directly from Baghdad, on the western bank of the river. He even agreed to take women and children, assuring us that they would be as safe in his hands as they were in their own homes. And having offered us such improved terms, he then demanded half the money in advance.

At that point, Yunis interjected that, according to the information we had from Tel Aviv, the agreement was that the entire sum would be paid at the end of the journey.

"Moosh moomkin! Out of the question!" the emir pronounced, putting an end to the matter. "When will you be ready?"

Yunis paused for a moment, considering whether to insist on the payment at the end. But evidently he thought better of it, for when he spoke it was only to answer the question about timing.

"The day after tomorrow," he said.

Sha'alan looked pleased. "May Allah give you strength," he concluded the meeting with a blessing.

"And may Allah give you health," Yunis replied, whereupon the three of us rose and left.

Our operations, so recently stifled by the pall that had descended over us all, now proceeded at a mad pace. We had to collect 120 people in Baghdad, find homes for them to stay in, transport them from the railway station to their lodgings throughout the city (at various times, because they came from different places), tend to their daily needs, and—particularly in light of the previous experience—prepare enough food and water for the journey ahead. All this activity was like a tonic for the movement. We certainly stopped brooding about the tragedy of the last attempt; we simply didn't have time. The wireless worked overtime as transmissions flew back and forth, first to coordinate the time and place for "unloading the cargo," then to inform headquarters that the "shipment" was being postponed by a day, at the emir's request. But after all the frenetic preparations, on the twentieth Yunis had to send the following wire:

To: Artzi

From: Berman

1. The "Lords" left Berman at midnight last night without saying a word. We were in contact with them up until yesterday evening and made a date for this morning. We have no idea where they've gone or why.

2. It's hard to believe that the purpose of their visit was to deceive us.
   Perhaps they quarreled among themselves or someone informed on
   them and they were forced to flee.
3. During this visit we paid them about 4,000 pounds in addition to the
   1,000 paid out earlier.

Now we were really in a jam, and our first priority was to get the scores
of young people who had been concentrated in Baghdad out of the country to Palestine. That became a full-time job, and we exploited every possible channel. Some people were sent out on forged passports; others were
lucky enough to obtain the genuine article (for a fat bribe); and yet others
were smuggled out in the massive trucks that made their way across the
desert or were trusted to new smugglers who happened to come to our
attention. But even after we had eased the pressure, we still had a whopping account to settle with the "Lords of the Desert."

Considering the gravity of the problems we faced, it's no wonder that
we were constantly demanding reinforcements from Palestine. But even
before these requests were filled, our own little group of emissaries began
to fall apart. Yunis, who had been in Iraq for well over a year, wound up
his tour and returned home. After a year underground, I, too, began to
think about doing the same. Both of us felt bitterly disappointed about the
meager results we had to show in the sphere of illegal immigration. We
had failed to overcome the double obstacle of distance and desert that
separated Iraq and Palestine. The most we could claim was getting a handful of immigrants out. And from our vantage point far from home, it
seemed that we weren't getting our message across in Palestine—and certainly weren't getting enough help.

Added to this was the aggregate frustration of daily life in the underground. Over and above the relentless tension and fear of discovery, we
imposed a life of isolation and celibacy upon ourselves—not just for security reasons, but also to protect our already patchy relations with the Jewish community and to keep loose tongues from wagging within the movement itself. Yet there was little compensation in the sparse contact we had
with home. Obviously we couldn't use the standard postal channels, and
when longings for my family, kibbutz, and girlfriend, Temima, weighed
me down, I couldn't even let my feelings out in letters. Our use of special
secret means for transferring mail made it necessary to keep communications short and to the point, while the fact that these notes passed through
many hands precluded the least hint of intimacy and thus rendered them
almost pointless.

In short, by the end of a year I was utterly drained and ready to return home at the first opportunity. It arose when a wire arrived from the Mossad summoning me to fly back to Palestine as soon as possible. I didn't even stop to clarify what the purpose of the trip was. As soon as I had put my affairs in order, I paid a bribe to have my Iraqi passport stamped with a genuine, yet not fully legal, exit visa, and once I had that, the British consulate was good enough to accord me an entry visa to Palestine. Thus outfitted with all the trappings of propriety—for the first time in a year—I boarded a plane for Lydda and, presumably, a normal life.

But that was not quite what the Mossad had in mind. Instead, as Yunis was determined to return to his kibbutz, I was asked to fly back to Baghdad immediately and take his place. Clearly I felt a deep sense of responsibility to the members of the movement. Yet I couldn't suppress all the frustration, anger, and dismay that I had known in Iraq. And the memory of my exasperation in Baghdad exhausted my patience in Tel Aviv, so that somewhere in the course of endless hours of discussions and clarifications and reports on plans for the future, as tempers flared over a matter that escapes me now (and was probably of little consequence), I popped out of my chair and simply quit.

"Goo-ood-bye," I crooned in a fit of petulance. "I am going back to my kibbutz. If you ever decide that you would like to work seriously, you know where to find me."

And with that I stalked out of the room—stopping in the outer office only long enough to pen a testy little letter of resignation—and went off to spend a few days with my family in Tel Aviv before returning to the kibbutz, never doubting that my days as an emissary were over.

THREE

Operation Michaelberg

BACK ON THE KIBBUTZ a few days later, I gloried in the opportunity to work outside again, basking in the bright Mediterranean sun after more than a year of looking over my shoulder and feeling cooped up in cellars and attics. And I was especially glad to be able to prove to my more skeptical comrades that my stint as a "bourgeois"—who as part of his cover was fastidious about having his tie knotted just so over a starched white shirt, crisply ironed pants, and shoes shined to a gleam—had not spoiled me as a laborer or changed my convictions about the kibbutz way of life. Actually, my first assignment was little more than busywork: I was building a cage for two monkeys that one of our members, a ship's captain, had brought back from his last trip to Africa. There was no deadline on the project, and I could afford to take my time getting back into the routine. But I worked at it almost feverishly for fear of what others might think if they caught me taking a break and interpreted my idleness as "loafing on the job."

"Hey, Shlomo," one of my fellow kibbutzniks called out as he happened by, "have you been given leave?"

"No," I told him without looking up, "I've quit. All they ever do there is talk. Here at least I can put in an honest day's work."

That last sentence was punctuated by the rhythmic honking of a car's horn coming from the main gate. I was familiar with that particular "tune." It signaled that the driver was a member of the Mossad for Illegal Immigration, and when I glanced furtively in the direction of the gate, I saw a large black American car with Moshe Carmil seated behind the wheel. A short man in his late thirties, with thinning hair, a round face, and wise, alert eyes, Moshe was one of the top figures in the Mossad. Though he was not particularly dashing in appearance, beneath his easygoing exterior lay a veritable bulldozer of a man who was unsparing of his time and energies. His job in the Mossad was never clearly defined (just as none of the others were), but roughly speaking he was the agency's director. Yet Moshe's special standing derived not from any title but from the force of his personality, which inspired love, respect, and affection in everyone who knew him. Soothing ruffled feathers seemed to be his specialty, and he always succeeded at it—usually by a sincere show of friendship, human warmth, and a sense of humor that would bring a smile to the lips of even the most resolutely angry soul.

I therefore assumed that, after allowing me a decent cooling-off period, he had come to deal with my own little crisis. But I was in no rush to succumb to his charms, and rather than hurry out to greet him, I decided to behave as if I had seen and heard nothing, continuing to work with redoubled energy until I heard the hum of a motor right behind me followed by the click and gentle slam of a car door. Only then, when I could no longer feign ignorance of his presence, did I turn around.

"Hello, Moshe," I called out in what I hoped sounded like surprise. "What brings you here?"

"I came to check on whether you're really working," he teased. "Can I help?"

"Sure," I said, careful to maintain the appearance of taking him strictly at his word. I actually kept him busy for a full five minutes, as if he had come expressly for the purpose of building a monkey cage, before I felt that I had demonstrated a sufficient lack of curiosity about the real reason for his visit. Only then did I gather up my tools and invite him to join me in taking a break on a nearby patch of grass. The sun was already in the west by then, and the heat was beginning to yield to a light breeze, so that sitting outside was preferable to being in one of the huts or tents that made up the kibbutz in those days.

Having invested those five minutes of his valuable time softening me up, Moshe decided to dispense with further preliminaries and explained the reason for his appearance by telling me that our friends in America had sent us two very special characters. "They claim that the whole world is making money off illegal immigration—shipowners, captains, deckhands," he related in a way that left me unsure whether he was entirely facetious, "and they want to get in on it too."

"And what are they prepared to do—other than relieve us of our money?"

"They were combat pilots during the war," Moshe explained, "and they've got a lot of experience. From what we've been told, they evidently have guts, too. But what really counts is that they have a C-46, a fairly large cargo plane that they say is particularly suitable for our needs. It can take off and land on relatively short runways, and they can pack in fifty people on each flight."

"And?" I prodded.

"Well, you're the one who's been shouting that we're not doing enough in Iraq. I seem to recall an angry little speech and letter of resignation over that very issue, so that, unlike others, you happen to be free right now. How would you like to carry out an experiment?"

I raised an eyebrow as a begrudging sign of interest, and he rightly took it as a victory.

"Do you think there's a flat area near Baghdad where a plane can land and take off again?"

"Of course there is," I pronounced, as if it were axiomatic. "Most of Iraq is a desert, much of it as flat as a board. There's no problem landing and taking off anywhere. Why, I can personally guarantee you twenty places like that around Baghdad."

That, as matters turned out, was far from true. But it never occurred to me that such confidence and expertise might be exaggerated. As a twenty-four-year-old in Palestine in 1947, I was incapable of imagining that something might have escaped my attention or required investigation. After all, my experience with matters aeronautical extended to two whole flights: my journey to Baghdad and my return a year later. It must be said, however, that such experience was evidently impressive to Moshe Carmil, for neither he nor anyone after him questioned my judgment on the matter.

"I'm glad you're willing to sign on," he said, shaking my hand warmly and leaving me little choice. "Come into the office tomorrow and we'll continue working on it."

As we walked back to the car, I could feel my imagination go into high gear. I pictured the great steel bird taking flight in the desert as Bedouin, perched on camels in the distance, were seized with wonder at the sight.

But then, as the plane reached the heavens and began to gobble up the miles, I suddenly hit upon a major snag.

"Where will the plane land once it gets here?" I asked. The British mandate was still in full force, making it highly illegal to bring Jews into the country, by whatever means of transport. So where was this "underground flight" supposed to end?

"Our people are still working on that," Moshe conceded. "They're trying to locate an appropriate field, and the Palmach* will take care of keeping the British at bay."

The one question that remained was half frightening, half exhilarating.

"Tell me," I said, "have we ever had any experience with illegal immigration by air?"

"No, never," Moshe replied definitively. "If something actually comes out of this, we will have had a historic conversation here today. A few years ago, people had a talk much like this about bringing in immigrants by boat. Now we're talking about the first plane. Who says we're not making progress?"

Even I was smiling by then, and as I parted with Moshe, I promised to come into the office bright and early the next morning. But the next day began badly, as successive buses, packed to capacity, passed me by on their way to Tel Aviv. When I finally arrived at the Mossad's headquarters, Zafrira, the winsome red-headed secretary who always greeted us with a smile, crisply informed me that Moshe couldn't wait any longer and had gone on to Haifa alone.

"Alone?" I echoed, wondering whether the implied "missing person" could possibly be me. Moshe hadn't said anything about accompanying him on a trip today.

"Yes, and you'd better hop to it," she barked. "Everyone's waiting for you!"

Unfortunately, those emphatic orders did not carry much weight with the taxi, which broke down halfway to Haifa. By the time I reached my destination, I found Moshe and two other people from the Mossad waiting for me with unconcealed rage. They bundled me into a nearby car, and we made off on a near-madcap ride through the hilly streets of Haifa.

"You're late, Shammai," one of my colleagues snapped.

"Late!" I protested. "I had no idea that I was supposed to get as far as Haifa. And besides, the buses were full and the taxi broke down—"

"There's no time for that now," Moshe cut in roughly, and I could hear the urgency in his voice. "Listen to me carefully. We want you to go to

* Permanently mobilized "shock troops" of the Haganah underground.

Baghdad. Tonight. Everything's been arranged. We're on our way to the Carmel Court Hotel, where the two Americans are staying. And before we get there, we have to brief you on the situation."

I was flabbergasted. I never suspected that I was going as far as Haifa that day, to say nothing of Baghdad. I hadn't been granted leave from the kibbutz. I hadn't said good-bye to anyone, not even Temima. And besides, I might have complained about procrastination, but this pace was ridiculous. We had barely mooted the idea for the first time the day before, and now I was expected to fly off to Baghdad without any of the usual preliminaries—meetings, skepticism, criticism, arguments? I could barely contain my astonishment.

"How can I be going now?" I blurted out. "The idea didn't even exist until yesterday."

"But remember what we said," Moshe tried to soothe me, "about progress and all."

I studied his face for a long moment and realized that he was quite serious. This was probably one of those opportunities that had to be grasped or lost forever. And in his own quiet way, Moshe was challenging me to rise above the usual things that sway our actions, like logic and fears and qualms, and just decide to do it, to prove my mettle. I closed my eyes for a few seconds, took a deep breath, and abandoned myself to destiny.

"All right," I said softly, considerably sobered by the weight of that commitment. "What's the plan?"

The briefing had to do mostly with the price agreed upon with the pilots: one hundred pounds per passenger, for a total of five thousand pounds to be paid in gold coins upon landing in Palestine.

"And where will we land?" I again inquired.

"Ever heard of Yavneel?" Moshe asked.

"Of course I have," said I, conjuring up a picture of that quaint, pastoral village west of the Sea of Galilee—though I couldn't imagine what its shabby collection of goat pens and chicken coops had to do with the business at hand. "Is *that* your secret airfield?" I sniggered.

"No," Moshe continued dryly, "but the surrounding valley has a spot that's flat and pretty well hidden, and our people believe it's suitable for an improvised airstrip." In fact, the area was already being cleared of rocks and stones to ensure a smooth landing. "When the plane comes in, we'll light fires along both edges of the 'runway' to guide you in and indicate the wind direction."

One of the others added that a Palmach unit would take up strategic positions on the access routes to prevent any kind of British interference until all the passengers had disembarked and been scattered among our settlements in the area. After unloading its passengers, the plane would immediately take off for Rome.

There was still the risk of being detected by British planes, and I was instructed to diminish it by ensuring that our aircraft arrived either before dawn, so that the passengers would have time to disembark and leave the area under cover of darkness, or at twilight, so that the pilots could find the airstrip in the last of daylight, but everything else could be done after nightfall. Finally, I was informed that the pilots had been told "in no uncertain terms" that I was the commander of the operation and was thus solely responsible for determining every detail—other than technical matters related to the safety of the plane and its passengers. These conditions likewise applied to the captains of the immigrant boats—who were subordinate to commanders from the Mossad—and experience proved that they were vital to the success of the operations, so I was glad that they had been made clear from the outset.

The pilots were waiting for us in their hotel room, which looked as if a pogrom had passed through it, scattering clothes and shoes in all directions. In the midst of the mess, the two gum-chewing Americans were down on all fours, engrossed in a huge map of the Middle East spread out on the floor. My companions introduced me, and while we were still shaking hands, the pilot, Captain Leo Wessenberg (who, despite his name, was not Jewish), drew me down on my knees beside him, picked up a compass, and inscribed a circle on the map with Baghdad at its center.

"That's it," he announced. "Any suitable landing place within this 15-mile radius will be fine."

All eyes turned to me, but despite my earlier boast to Moshe, I now drew an absolute blank. Suppressing panic, I assumed a thoughtful expression and suggested that we postpone a decision until we had reached Iraq and could benefit from the advice of our people there. Meanwhile, we had a more pressing problem to deal with: how to get me out on this empty "cargo plane" and into Baghdad. The solution was ostensibly in Moshe's pocket, and although I wasn't very enthused about it, there really wasn't much choice if I wanted to leave the country immediately. Moshe had brought along the Iraqi passport that had served me on my last trip to Iraq and my return voyage a few weeks back. From the standpoint of the mandatory authorities in Palestine, it was a perfectly legal passport. But the situation was considerably stickier on the Iraqi end, because the exit visa that enabled me to leave Iraq openly had not been obtained legally. There was no way of knowing whether anyone in Baghdad had noticed the discrepancy in the records and had issued orders to keep an eye out for the bearer of that particular exit visa, in case he ever returned to Iraq. For lack of an alternative, I pocketed the passport and we agreed that I would be listed on the plane's manifest as a member of the crew—on the premise that the check of the crew's papers would be purely perfunctory.

To complete my new cover, on the way to the airport we stopped at a clothing store and bought a khaki shirt and pants that appeared to resemble the pilots' uniforms. Thus, to all appearances, I had been transformed into a member of the crew in almost every way. "Almost" because one detail was beyond revision: my height remained a total of five feet four inches, and when I stood between those two American bruisers—who were at least a head taller than I was—I feared that the sight was not very convincing.

But the time for entertaining misgivings was past. In contrast to that morning's delays, we were now moving at a dizzying pace. While still in the Carmel Court, I scribbled out two short letters. The first, addressed to my brother Eliyahu, explained that I was leaving the country and hoped to return shortly, but if I was delayed he was to cover for me with Father and the rest of the family, as he had done before. The second letter was addressed to Temima and obliquely outlined the reason for my absence. When I had left the kibbutz that morning, I assumed that I would be back by evening. Now I had no idea when we would be likely to see each other again. As for notifying the kibbutz secretariat, I left that to Moshe and trusted that he would smooth things over in his own inimitable way.

At the small airport near Haifa, where the C-46 was parked, we decided that Captain Wessenberg would deal with the paperwork and the rest of the formalities while I accompanied the copilot, known to me only as Mike, directly to the plane. It was during our walk that Mike proposed a way of keeping me out of sight during the rigorous check of the aircraft that could be expected in those tense days. Under the cockpit of the C-46 is a compartment filled with switches, one of which starts the propellers. As soon as the British officers came to check over the plane, Mike would order me to turn on the engines. "That will make the proper impression and save you from having to answer any embarrassing questions," he explained, and I had to assume that he knew his business.

Soon Wessenberg returned in the company of two British sergeants whose rifles were chained to their bodies to prevent them from being snatched (as happened quite often back then). As they climbed into the plane and came into earshot, Mike ordered me to start the engines to save time. I promptly vanished into the lower compartment and, to my amazement and relief, pulled the right switch among the dozens of levers that looked frightfully similar to my novice eye. The propellers began to whir with a deafening noise and white smoke plumed out of the rear of the plane (all perfectly normal, I had been told in advance). After the sergeants left the plane, I climbed back into the cockpit feeling exceptionally pleased. "Who knows?" I thought, "I might have the makings of a real pilot."

His Majesty's agents sent us off with a thumbs-up sign and a traditional "Good luck!" My American colleagues replied with a hearty "OK!" and the plane began to sweep down the runway at full power and speed. In a matter of seconds, we were airborne over Haifa Bay and my career as an air cadet came to an abrupt end. For suddenly I was suffocating and felt as if my innards were draining out of my ears. The blue sea was above my head, and Mount Carmel was listing dangerously over on an angle. I grasped the arms of the seat in panic, and just as I was on the brink of blacking out, the world resumed its proper order: sky above, sea below, and the plane on a slight but steady incline heading eastward. Clearly it was not out of control, and we were not going to crash. Our flight plan called for a 180-degree turn, and the two seasoned pilots—and amateur acrobats—simply decided to take the shortest route between west and east.

Even after I got my breath back, I continued to sit in silence, swallowing hard and breathing deeply just to regain my composure. Flying, I now recalled, really brought out the worst in me. And the addition of that loop had played havoc not only with my equilibrium but with much of the confidence I had displayed the day before, when Moshe had visited me on the kibbutz. Here I was, flying off to Iraq with two men I had met for the first time only hours before. "They've been referred to us by our friends in America," Moshe had said by way of vouching for their credentials, but we really didn't know the first thing about them. At best they were adventurers—and of the daredevil variety at that. Worse yet, the very idea of secretly landing and taking off again in the middle of the desert now seemed outlandish. What if the pilots failed to locate the spot where we had assembled the immigrants? What if the plane landed and then couldn't take off again because of some sort of breakdown? The whole plan seemed like something straight out of Hollywood. How could the Mossad ever have fallen for it?

One anxiety led to another, and soon I was ruminating on my passport again. That I was listed on the manifest as a member of the crew was not very reassuring now. On the contrary, the fact that the bearer of an Iraqi passport was flying on an American aircraft was irregular enough to arouse suspicions. If they arrested me, these two would probably leave me to rot for years in some dank prison, half-starved and tormented by the guards and prisoners—

"Do you know a place called Baquba about twenty to thirty miles north-

east of Baghdad?" asked Wessenberg, who was obviously made of sterner
stuff and seemed oblivious to all the disasters that might lie ahead. "From
the looks of this map, there's an abandoned airfield there."

The question pulled me out of my funk and forced me to grapple with
the matter at hand. I had never actually been in Baquba, but I assumed
that, since it was a small town, the sudden appearance of fifty strangers, en
masse, would surely arouse attention. In fact, the landing of a plane would
probably cause a sensation and immediately become known to every official for miles around. On the other hand, I wasn't terribly concerned about
being pursued by the pitiful Iraqi air force, and I felt confident that once
we were in the air again, the Iraqis could do little to stop us. So we
decided that before landing in Baghdad, we would fly over Baquba to get
a sense of the place. Circling low over the field, we could see that other
than being cluttered with junk and barrels that would have to be removed,
the runway was in satisfactory condition. But we could also see people
rushing out of their houses at the sound of our plane, and I realized that
my earlier assumptions had been right: if we left from there, we would
attract quite a crowd. So we flew on to Baghdad, leaving Baquba as a last
resort.

The view of Baghdad from the air was depressing in those days. Its
squat, earth-colored, mud-brick houses lacked all charm or splendor, and
the asphalt roads seemed more like alleyways. Now, at the height of summer, the Tigris River, cutting through the center of the city, was notably
shallow, and a series of islands covered with thick vegetation rose out of its
dull brown, sluggish waters—altogether an uninviting sight. Coming in for
a landing, we decided to follow much the same procedure as in Haifa:
Wessenberg would deal with the formalities while Mike and I would remain in the plane, occupying ourselves with various tasks, to keep my
visibility as low as possible.

The longer Wessenberg was gone, the more nervous I became. When I
noticed some uniformed men exiting the terminal, I fully expected them to
march toward us in formation and haul me in. But they simply stood there
aimlessly, and about ten minutes later Wessenberg returned—alone—
wearing a smug expression.

"Come on," he said in a condescending singsong as he waved my passport at me and added with a look of contempt, "No one showed the least
interest in you or your passport. They didn't even bother to stamp it. As
far as the Iraqi authorities are concerned, you're not even here.

"Well, don't stand there with your mouth hanging open," he chided.
"Let's get out of here before someone changes his mind!"

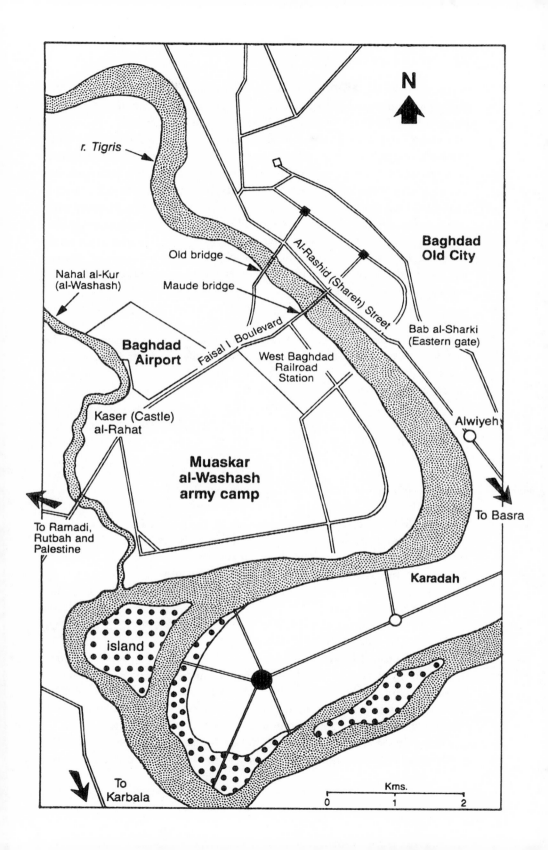

N

r. Tigris

Baghdad
Old City

Old bridge

Al-Rashid (Shareh) Street

Nahal al-Kur
(al-Washash)

Maude bridge

Bab al-Sharki
(Eastern gate)

Baghdad
Airport

Faisal I Boulevard

West Baghdad
Railroad
Station

Alwiyeh

Kaser (Castle)
al-Rahat

Muaskar
al-Washash
army camp

To Basra

To Ramadi,
Rutbah and
Palestine

Karadah

island

To
Karbala

Kms.

0   1   2

As we walked toward the terminal across the deserted field, I decided that with my passport in such a dubious legal state, rather than register in a hotel with the pilots I would go directly to the "safe house" where our emissaries lived. So we shared a cab to the posh Regent Palace Hotel, on the bank of the Tigris, and agreed to meet again for breakfast at nine the next morning. Then I made off on my own and quickly fell back into the underground ways I had practiced reflexively until just a few weeks before. First I sauntered down Baghdad's main street until I was sure that no one was following me. Then I hailed a horse-drawn carriage and told the driver to take me to Al-Alwiye, one of the city's attractive new residential quarters. The sun had already set, and with the heat having lifted somewhat, the ride through the lamplit streets in the open carriage was pleasant and soothing—almost enjoyable.

The address I had given the driver, in an area of charming villas, was the home of Menashe Shasha, a local Jew who lodged the emissaries from Palestine. The members of the Shasha family placed their lives in jeopardy by giving us a roof over our heads, but that didn't stop them from showering us with love—which was generously requited. As I climbed out of the carriage, I could see them silhouetted on the open veranda, sitting in near darkness, so as not to attract moths, and enjoying the first cool breeze of evening. I pictured them eating juicy slices of chilled watermelon, as was their custom on summer nights, and decided to surprise them by casually walking in and greeting them with a lilting "Shalom"—as if dropping in on them from Palestine were an everyday event! Luckily, however, as I walked briskly toward the veranda, I was seized by a mischievous urge to surprise them in a different way: by adopting the dialect and inflection of a local Muslim and asking after the master of the house, I would not only fool them about my identity until they actually recognized me by sight, I could also put a little scare into them for starters. But the joke, as it turned out, was on me. For when I asked in a deep voice and the proper style, "Is Mr. Shasha at home?" to my astonishment an unfamiliar male voice answered in the same dialect, "No sir. That family left the house a month ago, and we've been living here since then. But please, come in and do us the honor of joining us in a cup of coffee."

The invitation, I knew, stemmed from the dictates of oriental hospitality, and in my startled state it took all my wits just to beg off with the same good manners as my would-be host. At first he wouldn't take no for an answer. In my uniform, he apparently mistook me for an army officer and absolutely insisted on extending his family's graciousness to so distinguished a guest. It took a second, firmer refusal to get me free of the garden and back into the street, so that I could continue my getaway by some means of transport, and even then I had to suppress an instinct to run, rather than keep to the steady, measured step befitting an "Iraqi officer." Approaching the corner I saw a local bus—resembling a station wagon—pass by. Although we made a habit not to use them, because they were usually crowded and a "gentleman" did not avail himself of such facilities, I decided to take the next one that came along, just to get out of there as quickly as possible.

The story behind the Shashas' disappearance, I later learned, was a simple one. The family (and our emissaries with it) had simply moved to a larger house and neglected to inform Tel Aviv. The lapse was understandable, for in the entire history of our underground activities in Iraq, no one had ever arrived from Palestine without prior notice. As I stood stranded on that street corner, however, I imagined the worst and forced myself to concentrate on choosing my next move carefully. I decided to contact Nachman Shina, one of the movement's leading activists, whose house was like a second home to me and whose family was deeply committed to our cause. Nachman's brother and sister were both youth-group leaders, and his aging parents were fully accepting of their children's activities, despite the heavy risks to them all. It was the senior Shinas who now greeted me on their doorstep—with affection and surprise, but without a single question. They were familiar enough with underground etiquette to know not to ask. Seated safely in their drawing room, I was finally able to smile over my close call at the Shasha house. Still, the problem of locating the Shashas' new abode remained unsolved. As a result of our strict precautions, only three people in the movement knew where the emissaries lived: the two wireless operators and the coordinator of immigration. I was depending on Nachman to summon one of the three, but Nachman wasn't at home. His parents believed he would return shortly, but they couldn't be sure. And when I asked whether one of the emissaries or my old friend Sammi was expected that evening, they could only shrug in ignorance. So there I sat in the Shina parlor, having flown hundreds of miles on a daring mission, with time of the essence and the clock ticking at my back, and I couldn't even make contact with the leaders of the underground I had left just weeks before!

Nachman finally turned up at about ten, breaking into a broad smile upon seeing me and, like his parents, controlling his curiosity. To my great relief, he knew where Sammi could be found and dashed out to call him. Sammi, in turn, sped over in his car, and minutes later we were on our way "home" to the Shashas' new address, where we were awaited by my replacement, Yerachmiel (Yerach) Assa. There we made ourselves comfortable on the roof, which was the custom of the Baghdadis on summer nights. Their houses, having baked all day in the merciless sun, were still sweltering at night. But on the roof one could luxuriate in the cool breeze blowing in from the desert, and that was where the members of the household bedded down.

Despite the late hour, the mistress of the house rose to prepare a spread in my honor. Before I could protest (though I knew it would be pointless), out she came bearing a large silver tray with a pot of strong, sweet tea and an assortment of home-baked delicacies: crescent-shaped *sambousag*, the light pastry filled with salty goat cheese or chopped, sugared almonds, and round *ba'aba*, filled with luscious chopped dates. Considering that I had had nothing to eat since breakfast, the taste of these delicacies—coupled with the late hour and sudden release of tension—sent me floating into a reverie of the many mouth-watering meals that I had consumed at the Shasha table. I could almost smell the inviting aroma of warm, fresh whole-wheat pita as my mind filled with visions of the dishes that inevitably followed: platters of steaming white rice, cuts of lamb served in a delicate zucchini sauce, and the flowered porcelain bowl piled high with peeled cucumbers (considered a fruit in Iraq) and slices of sweet, pink watermelon.

"Amo Yusuf, are you all right?" I heard Sammi ask, more with reproval than concern, and suddenly I felt foolish as I imagined the bemused expression on my face. Marcelle Shasha had retired again, leaving us alone around the table. I shook my head sharply to clear it and, speaking just above a whisper both for privacy and out of courtesy to the rest of the household, explained to my colleagues why I had suddenly reappeared and what I intended to do. The darkness did not conceal the apprehensive looks on their faces. Neither did I spare them my own qualms about the plan to land the plane in the desert, pick up passengers, and head for Palestine—all with perfect timing, coordination, and secrecy.

"Sounds like you've concluded that the safest thing is to do nothing at all," Sammi remarked with his accustomed sarcasm.

In defense, I decided to broach the idea that had begun to take shape in my mind as I had walked across the airfield with the two pilots.

"Of course the simplest solution is to take off from the airport," I observed, noting as I did so that my colleagues' expressions became increasingly perturbed, as though they feared that something on the journey to Baghdad had come between me and my right mind. "Don't forget," I recited the rule so familiar to anyone engaged in clandestine operations, "that the bold, direct action mounted right under the enemy's nose is often a better risk than painstaking efforts to evade his notice."

Having sparked their curiosity, I prefaced my plan by describing our solitary stroll across the airport, mentioning that guards were stationed only by the main buildings and the planes themselves. Then, like a seasoned air traveler, I ticked off for them the stages of a takeoff: how the plane taxis to the end of the runway, turns around, and spends a few minutes warming up its engines before driving down the runway at full speed to lift off. There were usually no structures near the end of a runway —a precaution, I assumed, in case a plane failed to get off the ground or to stop in time when landing. Neither were there any guards or sentries, since there was nothing to guard. A policeman or official of some sort might climb aboard and check a plane before it had taxied out to the runway, but once it had cleared the hangar area no one was likely to recheck it. In other words, if we could get our people into the plane while it was warming up its engines at the end of the runway—and when the noise was deafening and the plane's headlights would be blinding anyone facing it—the problem was solved. Of course our timing would have to be absolutely perfect, our people would have to be lying motionless on the ground as they awaited the plane, and we'd have to find a way to get them to the end of the runway without being sighted. In short, our first priority was to check the airport out thoroughly.

"Let's go out there right now," was Sammi's instinctive reaction. "The flight will have to be at night anyway, so we might as well see how things look in the dark."

A cup of coffee later we were off in Sammi's car. It was past midnight by then, and the usually teeming streets of Baghdad were eerily deserted as we drove through the center of town, crossed over the Tigris, and proceeded on the main road westward to the airport. When we reached it, however, we made no attempt to enter through the gate. Instead, we continued up to the northern edge of the field and then drove along it to the northwest corner, which was the farthest from the gate. If you ever have to steal your way into Baghdad airport, there's no deeper flanking movement than the one leading northwestward. But as we were soon to discover, penetration from that side presented problems of its own.

Sammi remained in the car, with the motor going, while Yerach and I proceeded toward the fence. The moon had already set, leaving us to maneuver as best we could in almost total darkness. We found ourselves walking through a fallow field with a few Bedouin tents scattered in the distance. As we moved toward them to get closer to the airport, we caught our first whiff of a sharp, sour odor that is the hallmark of a Bedouin encampment. It came from the custom of burning dried grasses in their tents to keep them warm in winter. The heat value of this particular fuel is enormous, but so is the amount of smoke. Their tents and clothing remain redolent of its odor all year round, so that even at the height of summer you can smell a Bedouin encampment from quite a way off.

Now, as this classic "fragrance" filled our nostrils, the dogs in the encampment had picked up our scent in return. The Bedouins' dogs were notorious as flea-ridden, emaciated, cowardly mongrels that were without peer as barkers. Just let them hear or smell the least hint of an intruder from afar and they would break into a chorus of high-pitched yowls that suggested nothing short of the apocalypse. All it took was one alarmist to start, and immediately all the rest of the dogs in the camp joined in, whether to stiffen the courage of the lead howler or because they, too, had been infected by his fear of the night.

One way or another, within seconds we seemed to be surrounded by barking and baying, and we knew what we had come to find out: obviously there was no way to get fifty people through on this side. We would have to find another way in. Back in the car, however, Sammi surprised us with an upbeat assessment.

"All in all, I feel encouraged," he said. "True, there are dogs in this corner, but the important thing is that access to the airport is not difficult at night."

He was right, of course. We hadn't come across any policemen or civilians on the way, and we had been poking around there for over an hour without anyone paying us the least attention, despite the canine uproar.

"What we must do is come back during the day and study the area well," Sammi continued. "Then we can check it out again tomorrow night."

It was almost dawn by the time we returned to the Shasha house, climbed back to the roof, and stretched out on the beds that had been made up for us. But sleep was beyond me by then. Thoughts, plans, and tension defied my need for rest, and soon the voice of the muezzin broke through the predawn silence to announce the birth of a new day and call the faithful to prayer by reminding them that *Allah akbar* ("God is great"). But still no one stirred on the Shasha roof, and my head continued to buzz with plans and calculations.

Suddenly there was a sharp knock at the door, creating a flurry of panic. Our first instinct was to look for places to hide—none of which presented themselves on the open roof. The knocking continued, increasingly insistent, until the master of the house finally bit the bullet and called out, "Who's there?"

"Me," a male voice answered, immediately calming us all, for in Baghdad the intonation of that single word was enough to establish whether the speaker was an Arab or a Jew, and the man who had uttered it this time was unquestionably a Jew. Menashe Shasha went down to open the door, and a few seconds later Eliyahu Shina, our wireless operator, came bounding up the stairs, flushed with excitement. Upon seeing me, he stopped in his tracks and gawked.

"You're already *here?*" he cried in a tone of confusion. "I've brought an urgent wire saying that you're on your way. Look!" he waved the piece of paper in the air, as if we doubted his word on the matter, and then actually read it out loud:

To: Berman
From: Artzi
Shammai coming to you by plane today to take fifty laborers. He will arrive toward evening and explain everything.

"Better late than never," I consoled him and went on to explain that the wire had been written as soon as I had left Haifa; indeed, it bore the previous day's date. But since our communications took place only once a day, during the morning hours, there was no way of sending it any earlier. (Evidently Tel Aviv was also on to this problem, for in a wire that arrived a short while later we were ordered to man the wireless twenty-four hours a day till the end of the operation.) In its own way, though, the wire served a good purpose: the bolt of adrenaline that shot through us at the sound of the knocking left us all wide awake and on our feet. A cold shower and quick shave finished the job of readying us for the day ahead, and as we sat down for an early breakfast, Sammi reviewed the problems that required immediate decision.

The first problem had to do with timing. Since we were going to send off a large group of immigrants, it was vital—for the sake of movement morale—that they be assembled from all over the country, and the process would take a day or two. I also realized that we wouldn't be able to hold the plane at the airport for too long without inviting questions, so that the sooner we left the better. Thursday had just dawned, and according to Sammi's calculations the last of the immigrants would be able to reach Baghdad by late Friday morning—providing we summoned them immediately. I therefore decided to set the tentative departure time for Friday night and to start bringing our people in from all over the country.

The other critical decision that had to be made now would affect the fate not only of this present "shipment" but of all future airborne immigration. Until now the immigration from Iraq had been accomplished with the cooperation of local Arabs, be they truck drivers, police officers, or officials at such strategic points as border posts, the passport department, and the airport. Their motive for helping us was financial, and we made it worth their while. But this time, we felt, the secret was too big to trust to anyone from outside the movement, and no sum would be large enough to protect us against informers. We would have to bring the operation off entirely on our own.

Having established the ground rules, Sammi and I made off for the hotel and reached it at 9 A.M., the hour I had set with the pilots. When I entered the lobby, however, they were nowhere to be seen. Neither was there any trace of them in the dining room. Eventually I found them in their room, still submerged in sleep. They had evidently spent the previous night in more pleasurable pursuits than I had, and no muezzin's call had penetrated their dreams. I managed to wake them, with some difficulty, and sent them staggering off to wash, while I remained in the room, again amazed by the degree of disorder they had managed to create in so short a time. As compensation for having to wait, I "entertained" myself by going through their personal effects—passports, wallets, checkbooks, and anything else I could find on or under the beds, in pants pockets or open suitcases—and I picked up a few pointers that came in handy later. These Americans may have been crack pilots, but they certainly had a lot to learn when it came to security.

Breakfast turned into a small feast consumed with relish—by Wessenberg and Mike, that is. I was a bundle of nerves, fearful that Sammi, who was waiting for us outside in his car, would draw attention to himself and that someone might ask what he was doing there, who he was waiting for, or any number of other embarrassing questions. But since my companions were intent on gorging themselves, I used the time to present my idea of leaving from the airport and told them about our nocturnal expedition. Wessenberg responded with mild interest, remarking between bites that it would be necessary to fill in certain technical details—such as which runway was used for takeoffs. He also pointed out that the place where the plane would turn around and secretly take on its passengers would depend on the wind direction. Although he agreed to clarify which way the wind usually blew at midnight or toward morning, he was reluctant to abandon the idea of leaving from a patch of flat ground outside the city.

I finally pried them loose from the table and escorted them out to Sammi's car for the drive to the airport. It seemed considerably less redoubtable now in daylight than it had the night before. With our two Americans ensconced in the back seat, we entered it openly, through the main gate, and Sammi retained his position in the car while the rest of us walked into the terminal and strode casually past the policemen, cleaning workers, and other employees. Then each of us attended to his own tasks. Wessenberg called on the airport manager to clear up administrative and technical details related to the takeoff as Mike and I walked over to the plane, parked near the end of the runway, ostensibly to tend to some standard mechanical matters. While Mike was going through his paces in the plane, I tried to sketch an accurate picture of the airport. Perched high in the cockpit, I could see that the entire periphery was enclosed by a barbed-wire fence, which in itself did not pose a very serious problem.

The shocker was that across the main road, along the entire south side of the field, lay a huge army camp. From my vantage point I could see that it was filled with buildings and tents and was bustling with soldiers. On the western side of the airport ran an earthen embankment topped by a row of military tents, and I realized that soldiers were probably stationed there to guard the palace of Abdul Illah, Iraq's regent, which was situated nearby. All the airport's buildings—the terminal, police station, customs station, airlines offices, hangars, workshops, and the like—were on the eastern side of the field, near the main gate. Finally, to the north ran the narrow road on which we had driven the night before, with the Bedouin tents and the yapping dogs. My sketch also made note of the fact that the main runway extended from the terminal in a southwesterly direction, reaching almost as far as the army camp.

Wessenberg returned from the control tower with more information to round out our picture. The main runway could be used for takeoffs at any hour of night or day, and he had already informed the airport authorities that he would probably be departing after midnight on Saturday. I showed him my sketch of the field and suggested that we could mass our people at the far end of the runway.

"Sounds good to me," said Mike, who usually left the talking to Wessenberg. "Let's walk down there and see how it looks from that end."

So we locked the plane and began walking along the tarmac. A march like that right down the airport's main runway in broad daylight might not have been the most intelligent approach. But walking between the two Americans, I felt a pleasant—if not exactly rational—sense of security.

"Do you see what I see?" Wessenberg asked as we neared the end of the runway. How could I not see it? Just ahead of us stood a cement guard post of the pillbox variety, and as we continued toward it we noticed two men stretched out in the shade of the low structure, enjoying their midday snooze. *"That's that,"* I thought, as the whole plan began to crumble before my eyes. But then I noticed something odd: the two men I had presumed to be delinquent guards were dressed in civilian clothes. Could it be that they were merely passersby who had found a patch of shade from the burning sun? I felt driven to find out immediately, and without consultation I strode up to the closer one, woke him with a kick in the rear, and shouted at him in my most authoritative Arabic, "Sleeping here instead of standing guard, eh? These foreign pilots are going to have you court-martialed for not protecting their plane!"

"Effendi, don't be angry with *me!* I'm not a guard here," he replied indignantly, though careful not to offend me further.

"Then what are you doing here?" I continued to bark.

"We're working on the road nearby, and we've come to rest a bit."

"And where are the guards?"

"There are no guards here, effendi," he explained.

"Don't give me that. What's this position for if there are no guards?"

"It's from the time of the war. But there are no guards here now."

"Not even at night?" I asked, careful to keep my tone aggressive rather than questioning.

"Not even at night. Really, effendi, you mustn't be angry."

After I had translated the gist of this exchange to the pilots, we continued our stroll to the end of the runway. Now we could see that the embankment separating the airport from the tents of the palace guard blocked the end of the runway from their view, so we could keep walking along the fence unnoticed in the direction of the main road. Negligently built, the fence sagged not far from the end of the runway, and all we had to do was bend the barbed wire a bit and pass over it without difficulty. We lingered there awhile trying to memorize all these details before sauntering back to the vicinity of the terminal—and still no one had taken the slightest interest in our doings.

As we entered the car, which felt like an oven, I suggested a drive around the field to fill in details on my sketch. But the pilots were wilting and beginning to turn cranky, so I relented and told Sammi to drive back to their hotel. About halfway there, Wessenberg complained of a dry throat, and when I failed to take the hint he came right out and asked if we could stop for a cold drink, preferably alcoholic. I explained that Muslim Baghdad was scrupulous about keeping alcohol confined to the tourist hotels and nightclubs. But we did find a stand that sold beer, and Sammi duly jumped out to buy some—only to find that it wasn't cold. Then he recalled a tidbit that Americans were great consumers of ice. So, ever ingenious, he decided to solve the problem in the quickest and most direct way by slowly pouring the beer into two glasses over some small chunks of ice. When he came out proudly bearing the results, Wessenberg took one look at the concoction, turned a deep red (bordering on purple), and erupted in a stream of abuse about primitive idiots, a desert hellhole, and the like—not all of which I could follow or would choose to repeat. Fortunately, Sammi was even less accomplished in English, or he, too, might have blown a fuse; the tension, fatigue, and savage heat were getting to us all. As it was, he stood transfixed in bewilderment at the spectacle of this raving American, while Mike and I tried to calm the pilot down.

Softly I told Sammi to dump the beer and we continued on toward town, with Wessenberg maintaining a sullen silence. We did not make plans to investigate alternative landing sites, but even though nothing definite was said, I knew we would be leaving from the airport. It now remained for us to deal with hundreds of details before midnight on Friday.

We began operating on a number of fronts simultaneously, moving to collect the fifty candidates for immigration, finding homes in which to board the out-of-towners, and informing Tel Aviv of our intentions. Back at the Shasha house, in the midst of all the bustle, I suddenly began to wonder whether we could really trust the testimony of the startled laborer and assume that there was no guard on duty at night. That doubt led to the specter of a chance appearance by a soldier, a policeman, or even a pair of lovers, and all these perfectly possible contingencies seemed to lead me to a single, unavoidable conclusion. Until then we had made it a hard-and-fast rule not to mix emigration with arms. Stealing out of the country was enough of a crime without compounding it by being stopped with weapons. This time, however, if we were caught trying to board the plane, the consequences would at any rate be fatal: hangings in the streets of Baghdad, to be blunt. But if we were armed, we could overcome whoever happened by and caught us in the act. At the very least, we could prevent him from summoning the police before we were airborne, and if necessary we could even force a hapless witness onto the plane and let our people in Palestine decide how to deal with him.

I shared these thoughts with Yerach and Sammi, who digested them in silence, reluctant to commit themselves on so grave an issue.

"At any rate we've summoned the commanders of the Shurah to meet this evening," Yerach said. "Let's talk it over with them."

I saw the wisdom of his suggestion, but having delayed making the decision, I had an uncomfortable, if unjustified, feeling of backsliding. Almost instinctively, I again laid out the sketch made in the airport and pored over it with them, trying to cover every detail. Soon we realized that we would have to know for sure whether there was access to the end of the runway from the main road, and there was only one way to find out.

So back we were in Sammi's car, making for the airport. When the field came into view, we continued driving slowly along the main road until we had reached the western end of the army camp. Then Sammi made a U-turn and drove slowly back along the camp's northern edge, coming to a halt close to the spot where it bordered on the airport, so that the entire field was now spread out below us. At that point Yerach and I got out, crossed the road, slid down to the foot of the embankment, and began walking along beside it.

"If we see anyone along the way, we'll just stop and piss," I said, as if that pose would cover all evils. Yerach nodded silently, so perhaps there was something to it. When we reached a spot that overlooked the main runway, we stopped to check the barbed-wire fence. Then we continued walking until the end of the runway and the sag in the fence were clearly visible. That much accomplished, we turned on our heels and climbed back up to the car. The whole process took just minutes, and no one in the army camp noticed our presence.

"Well?" Sammi asked as he floored the gas pedal and we sped off in the direction of the city.

"At least there are no dogs," I quipped, though it was clear from my expression that I was delighted with our walk, for it proved that we could penetrate the airport from the direction of the palace. "We have a clear plan of action now."

By the time we drove up to Nachman Shina's house, twelve young men, all leading figures in the underground or commanders of its armed self-defense organization, were awaiting us. None of them knew why this urgent and extraordinary meeting had been called, and my entry was greeted with cries of astonishment, for obviously they had no idea that I was back in Baghdad. It took a while for even these highly disciplined young men to settle down, and considering the air of excitement, I decided not to reveal the details of the plan just yet. Instead, I explained only that we were embarking upon a bold emigration operation and that they would have to mobilize ten cars, to be driven by our most capable people, and a few more members trained in the use of revolvers. All of these people would have to drop whatever they were doing and devote themselves exclusively to the movement from the next afternoon until they were released.

Their initial reaction alarmed me. I was expecting them to nod silently and carry out my orders, but what I got was a cry of protest as they unanimously insisted that they be allowed to carry out the operation themselves. At first I wouldn't hear of it. If anything went wrong and these leaders were arrested, that would be the end of the Zionist movement in Iraq—and I, for one, was not prepared to take that kind of risk. We argued the point for quite a while, with the boys insisting that there was no other choice. "You've always taught us that the commanders should lead every action personally," they cried, "and now you're saying that we mustn't endanger ourselves!" For a fleeting moment I even considered scrapping the plan. Ultimately I yielded, ordering them to round up ten cars in good condition, fill their tanks, and be prepared to meet again at 3 P.M. the next day. But the encounter left me more anxious than ever, for now the stakes had risen considerably.

I was feeling the effects of a sleepless night and a day spent scurrying around in the desert heat by the time Sammi drove me from that highly charged session to the cabaret where I was to meet our pilots. Walking through its gate, I passed from one world into another. The cabaret was set in a rose garden with colored lights strung between the surrounding trees. The effect of the delicate scent of flowers and freshly watered grass, designed to allay the heat and dryness of a Baghdad August, was to make me feel conspicuously grubby. I spotted the pilots relaxing with what looked, to my untrained eye, like scotch, but I confined myself to a beer as I sat down and tried to get into the proper mood—if only for appearance' sake. Competing with raucous atonal music and a plump belly dancer who looked as if she were about to writhe her way right out of her diaphanous costume, I practically shouted at the pilots that I had penetrated the airfield from the direction of the main road, that we would have ten cars at our disposal, and that Tel Aviv was eager to know our exact departure time.

"Terrific!" Wessenberg said sincerely, if somewhat under the influence. "Now, what about the money?"

"No problem," I assured him brightly. "Tel Aviv has confirmed that the full sum, in gold coins, will be awaiting you on arrival."

The dancer concluded her act at that point, and the music fell silent. I was half pleased, half concerned by the quiet—at least the music had provided us with a measure of privacy—and for the first time I looked around the garden to see who our fellow celebrants were. When my glance returned to Wessenberg, I could see that he had instantly sobered.

"You must be kidding," he blurted out testily. "Now, see here: we had an agreement that the money would be paid to us in Baghdad, before takeoff. If you thought for a minute that we'd move your people without payment in advance, you can forget it, buddy!"

"There must be some misunderstanding," I protested, though it was beyond me how either side could have mistaken such clear-cut terms. "Our people understood you would receive cash on delivery. They've already got the gold coins prepared, just as you asked. Did you think I would be able to get my hands on gold coins *here?*"

"Oh, no," he countered, as if he had caught me trying to outmaneuver him with some sleight of hand. "No money, no flight!" He even offered a logical reason for his obstinacy. "We agreed that if we couldn't land at the place where your people would be waiting for us, we'd let the passengers off in one of the country's airfields and get the hell out of there as fast as possible. What about the money then?"

I assured him that he could trust us to transfer the money to wherever he asked, but he just kept shaking his head in exasperation at my appeal to his better instincts.

"Listen," he said in an unmistakable tone of finality, "we're leaving tomorrow night—with or without your passengers. We can't extend our stay here. At most we'll agree to take the money here and postpone the transfer into gold coins until we reach Palestine."

I sat there stunned. Was the whole plan going to collapse right then and there? And were these two soldiers of fortune just going to fly off and leave me stranded, so that in addition to the fiasco for Jewish immigration and the blow to the local underground, I would be stuck in Iraq indefinitely? My earlier astonishment over the pace of the operation was turning into rage over the haste with which it had been slapped together. It even occurred to me that my comrades in the Mossad might be weak in idiomatic English. Heaven knows what they thought they had, and what they *really* had, agreed on.

The hour was approaching eleven when I asked Wessenberg to sit tight while I worked out a way to arrange for the payment. Then I rushed out to Sammi's car, told him of the latest development, and made it clear that I was prepared to pay them—on my own responsibility—regardless of what arrangement had been reached in Haifa. The question was whether he could get me the necessary five thousand pounds by the next day.

Sammi's response was a skeptical frown. "Perhaps part of it," he ventured, "but not the whole sum."

"Then go to the bank and withdraw the money," I growled at yet another source of disappointment, "even if it means dipping into the personal funds of our members."

"The problem is that tomorrow's Friday," Sammi reminded me, his voice betraying his own impatience, "and most of the banks and businesses are closed." Iraq was, after all, a Muslim country. Had I forgotten?

I winced at my own stupidity and was ready to concede defeat when Sammi suggested that I return to the cabaret and keep the pilots entertained while he checked how much cash he could muster within twenty-four hours. "I'll do my best," he promised—but his tone was not very reassuring.

I returned to the cabaret to find two garishly attired hostesses drinking, giggling, and cooing with our pilots in very limited, broken English. I joined the jolly foursome, but gaiety was not my strong suit that night. Fortunately, by the time the ladies moved on and Wessenberg asked me what progress I had made, Sammi had returned with tidings of partial salvation: he could get half the sum, 2,500 Iraqi dinars (then worth the same in pounds sterling). But Wessenberg would not be moved; as far as he was concerned, it was all or nothing. Which forced me to try another tack.

"All right," I sighed, feigning capitulation in the hope of softening his obstinacy. "If you're afraid they won't come through in Palestine, I'm prepared to provide my personal guarantee. I usually don't mix my personal business with the organization's affairs," I bluffed with an assurance born of desperation, "but because I am so sure that this is just a simple misunderstanding, I'll make an exception in this case."

"What kind of guarantee can you give?" Wessenberg asked, skeptical but clearly hooked by this sudden reversal.

"I'll give you a check for the missing half of the money, and if you don't get your fee, in full, within two weeks, you can cash it."

"That sounds better," he pronounced with a satisfied grin that promptly melted into a second thought. "What bank are we talking about, and where can we cash the check?"

"I have an account in the Chemical Bank of New York," I lied brazenly.

"Hey, that's great!" Wessenberg exclaimed. "I have an account in the same bank!"

The quick rummage through their effects had paid off. The Chemical Bank was the name that I, a twenty-four-year-old kibbutznik without a penny to his name, had come across for the first time that morning in their hotel room. Yet, having uttered it, I saw it worked like magic: an instant rapport arose between us as clients of the same bank. Now I had to produce a check, however, and my expression turned to one of strain as I began to slap my pockets.

"Very bad," I groaned in helpless regret. "I don't think I brought my checkbook along."

"That's no problem!" Wessenberg assured me with new-found camaraderie. "I'll give you one of my checks and you can write your account number on it."

The result was almost predictable: I broke into a grin and offered him my hand with a sense of genuine relief. He raised his glass in a toast, and I grabbed a vacant one to reciprocate. When I suggested that I would write the check in the car to avoid curious eyes, he readily agreed.

Outside in the car, Sammi was intrigued by the strange rite. By the light of Wessenberg's Ronson, after correcting the account number, I made out a check for ten thousand dollars. Three pairs of eyes were following me as I wrote it, but my hand was steady as a rock even when I appended my signature to this felonious document. Captain Wessenberg read the check carefully, folded it, and placed it in his pocket, the picture of satisfaction.

"Well, what are you boys waiting for?" he exclaimed as Sammi turned on the ignition to drive them back to their hotel. "Let's get this show on the road!"

Friday began with a feeling that the plan had developed a momentum of its own and there was no turning back. I felt a void where my stomach should have been and couldn't even contemplate the thought of food, so while the others ate breakfast I found a quiet corner and tried to concentrate on all the things that remained to be arranged, jotting down random details that I knew could make the difference between life and death. For instance, I ordered Sammi to tell the immigrants that they would not be allowed to take any suitcases or packages.

"Why are you being so stingy about their personal belongings?" he asked, protective of the youngsters. "They won't even add weight to the plane."

"The point is that everyone's hands must be free for climbing into the plane quickly," I explained. "And they'll have to hold hands on the way to the runway so they won't go astray in the dark. They can wear as many layers of clothing as they like, but they mustn't carry anything!"

Briefing the drivers and escorts on details of that sort filled much of the day. I scheduled takeoff for 3:30 A.M. Baghdad time and told the drivers to arrive at intervals of five minutes. Each car would let its six or seven passengers off on the main road near the "seam" between the airport and the army camp. Then it was to continue driving westward for another few miles, turn around, return to the "seam," and wait until the takeoff—in case we had to evacuate the people quickly. I also held the drivers responsible for knocking it into everyone's head that the last one out must *not* slam the car door! In the dead of night, a noise like that would probably bring every soldier in the camp down on us. Also, by the calendar, we knew that there would be no moon out at the time of departure. When the cars doused their lights as they approached the area, they would be left in total blackness. So I ordered the drivers to go over the intended route a few times in daylight and familiarize themselves with every twist and dip in the road.

Finally, in contrast to our usual practice of not telling immigrants in advance about their means of transport to Palestine—to avoid leaks—this time I decided that we would not only have to explain things in detail but even try to simulate the maneuver. Otherwise we could expect problems in leading the youngsters silently from the main road to the runway—to say nothing of panic when they saw a plane coming straight at them. Among other things, they were to be drilled in walking at a half crouch and approaching the plane from the tail end, well out of the way of the propellers.

I was rattling off these instructions when the escorts filed in silently and I felt a twinge of nostalgia as I sighted Shneur, an activist from the northern city of Kirkuk, who had come to Baghdad accompanying the group of nine youngsters from the North, including his seventeen-year-old sister.

"Did you bring Grandma along too?" I called across the room, drawing a broad grin from him and curious looks from the others about the private joke between us. About half a year before, I had spent a month in Kirkuk and took up lodgings in Shneur's house. Admittedly, the accommodations were rather offbeat: because we had to take special precautions—Kirkuk being a fairly small city—I spent most of my waking hours in the cellar, which was out of bounds even to the family. Or at least that's what I thought, until one afternoon the door opened with a creak and down came a frail, elderly woman, taking the stairs one by one. My first instinct was to hide, but our eyes met before I could duck out of sight. Besides, it proved to be unnecessary. She knew I was stashed away down there, and her greeting to me—the Hebrew word *shalom*—told me that she also knew exactly who I was.

"I hear you're going to take my granddaughter to Jerusalem," she said more gruffly than I would have expected, judging by the looks of her, "and I want to tell you that it's not fair. She's still young, just sixteen, and if she doesn't go now, she'll have other chances later on. But I haven't much time left, and if you don't take me now, I'll depart this world without having seen Jerusalem. Please," she implored me, her voice softened almost to a conspiratorial whisper, "let me go in her stead."

I did my best to explain gently why I could not comply with her request, stressing the rigors, rather than the dangers, of the journey, so as not to alarm her. But she seemed quite intent on reaching the Holy City. It wasn't until after more pleading and more patient explanation that she finally settled for having me write out a blessing in bold Hebrew letters (though I protested that I was not a rabbi). She folded it carefully and tucked it deep into her head scarf, where it joined a stock of similar notes that she carried as amulets. Then she rose silently and climbed slowly back to the cellar door. But at the top of the staircase she could not resist the last word.

"Young man, I am going to keep an eye on my granddaughter," she warned me, "and when you call for her, I'm coming along too!"

Shneur's grandmother did not turn up that day, but the memory of that encounter took the edge off my anxiety—for a few moments at least. I immediately invited Shneur to join us as one of the escorts. Then I gathered the boys around me and showed them the sketch of the area, explaining that after they had directed each successive group to the break in the fence, they were to spread out and serve as guards. Two of them would help hoist the youngsters into the plane.

"What if we encounter troops?" one of them asked hesitantly.

It was a good question—unpleasant to contemplate but imperative to face.

"We're tired of backing down from a fight," Shneur said adamantly. "This time we must act, come what may."

I saw the others nodding vigorously, and I agreed that if we came upon one or two men, we would overpower them and continue as planned. But if we encountered a full troop of soldiers at the start, I made it clear that we would scatter our people and abort the operation. Only if the youngsters had begun boarding the plane would we complete the operation at all costs. In that case the guards were to do whatever necessary to block intervention. Then they, too, would climb aboard the plane and join the flight to Palestine.

The rest of the day was filled with tension as we rehearsed details again and again, stressing the need for caution and discipline. One incident might have provided a little comic relief, but I was too keyed up to appreciate the humor of it then. At one point, Eliyahu Shina came in with a wire from Tel Aviv in response to the report I had sent out earlier. He handed it to me without comment, and as I read it I could feel myself flush with anger. The message read:

TO: Shammai

FROM: Artzi

Tell [the pilots] again that they needn't worry about the money. The gold will be awaiting them upon landing. The area has been cleared of stones and marked as we agreed. If they are forced to land elsewhere, we will get the money to any address they stipulate. . . . Explain to them that they're doing business with honest people. Try to persuade them. Do not give them anything in advance. If they refuse to take off under these conditions, show them half the money but do not, under any circumstances, turn it over to them until you land here. Remember, you're fifty people and they're only two. . . .

I didn't know whether to laugh or shriek. Even if I could understand the superfluous advice about convincing the pilots that we were honest people, what was I supposed to infer from the line about being fifty against two? That all fifty of us should rush the two of them in the cockpit and leave the plane to fly itself? Or perhaps the Mossad expected *me* to pilot the aircraft to safety! Aware that my feelings were showing, suddenly I had a vision of Wessenberg railing away at Sammi and decided that I had better control myself in deference to the company. Anyway, this was no time to squabble over the airwaves. So I literally bit my lip, wrote out a curt reply—"Departure time 3:30"—and saved the rest for after my return.

Our final round of briefings began before midnight, this time on the spot. First Sammi and I picked up Shneur, and each of us pocketed a revolver in case of the worst. Then the three of us drove to the Regent Palace to collect the pilots. As we continued on to the airport, I produced a wad of bills that represented twenty-five hundred dinars—the sum obtained by Sammi—and extended it toward Wessenberg.

"You hold it for us," he said with a nod.

"Don't you even want to count it?" I asked, puzzled at his cavalier attitude over an issue that had been crucial to him the night before.

"Not necessary," he said with a sardonic smile. "After all, I've got your check in my pocket."

That actually brought a smile to my lips too—perhaps for the first time all day.

Sammi dropped us on the main road and continued driving westward, keeping to the instructions the drivers would follow later that night. The young moon, soon to set, lay low in the sky to light our way, and the silence around us was so complete that a sudden gust of wind rustling through the trees sent our pilot friends diving for cover. We hauled them back to their feet and pressed on to the end of the runway, showing them the spot where our people would be lying flat on their bellies.

"Don't run them over," I implored in a whisper and heard Wessenberg reply with a grunt. Then we turned back toward the road, and I pointed out the guard post that continued to trouble me, telling Shneur to check whether it was manned by a soldier when we returned later on.

"And if it is?" he asked.

"Kill him," I hissed, startled that those words were coming out of me. "No, knock him out and drag him to the end of the runway. Maybe we'll take him along."

Driving back to town, there were no more wisecracks or digs. We were all growing genuinely nervous and preferred to ride in silence. Upon depositing the pilots at their hotel, we parted with a laconic reminder that a car would come for them at two. Then we returned to the airport and went over the route again—twice—with the escorts. Finally, one of them remained by the break in the fence while I huddled with the others at the foot of the embankment, waiting for the cars. Once again the silence was total, almost oppressive, as the moon set and the blackness closed in on us.

After waiting for what seemed like a decade, at the sound of a muted hum I glanced up at the horizon and could see a black shape move toward us and come to a stop. The first car had arrived, lights off. As the youngsters scrambled out, my body cringed against the anticipated slam of a door. But there was only silence until the motor could be heard whining from gear to gear as the car drove off again. Catching hold of a hand, I brought up the rear of the first group on its wobbly march to the runway. The others arrived one after the next, at the planned intervals, just like clockwork. All but the last group. It simply didn't show, and there was nothing to be done about it. Meanwhile, at the far end of the runway, exactly on schedule, our C-46 turned on its headlights and began to taxi slowly toward us. As it loomed closer and larger in our eyes, I could feel my whole body vibrate with the thumping of my heart until the plane reached us and slowly turned around, almost crushing some of the youngsters lying perilously close to the runway. Fortunately they knew what to expect or they surely would have scattered in panic.

Now the plane stood with its tail toward us, lights facing the control tower and propellers turning at full power, making a deafening racket. Having overlooked that detail, I had arranged for each group to approach the plane upon hearing me call out its number, but the noise made that impossible. So I began running back and forth to summon each group with a wave of the hand, directing them to the small ladder that had been dropped and making sure that the youngsters approached the door from behind, staying clear of the propellers. The last group still hadn't arrived, but I knew we couldn't wait. That the car bringing it was being driven by Sammi made me twice as anxious, for if Sammi was late, something drastic must have happened. Yet that was all the more reason to get off the ground as fast as possible.

When the last of the youngsters had clambered into the aircraft, I bent over for a last glance at the top of the embankment outlined against the horizon. Now I could see Sammi's group approaching us, bent over in a ragged line. From inside the plane, one of the other group leaders was signaling me frantically to climb aboard, and I understood that the pilots were probably pressing him to close the door. Perhaps they, in turn, were being questioned by the control tower about why they were dawdling on the runway. Looking back, I can see that there probably wasn't much pressure on anyone at that hour in the morning. But I was in no position to analyze the situation logically just then. Instead, I pointed wildly at the group shuffling slowly toward us, but the young man in the plane couldn't see that far and just kept waving for me to come up. This charade continued for a few more seconds, which felt like hours, until the lead member of the group reached the ladder and began to climb. I practically pushed the remaining kids into the plane and started up the ladder myself, seeing the grin on my face reflected in the expression of the group leader who was holding his arms stretched down toward me.

And then I remembered the gun in my pocket. Swinging my head around to see if Shneur was still close by, I jumped back off the rung, dashed over to him, and pressed the revolver into his hand. As I moved to turn back to the ladder, he clasped my body in a strong embrace and shouted in my ear, "Amo Yusuf, come back to us!" Breaking free, I took a hard look at that strapping young man, and maybe it was just the effect of the sand and gravel being swept up by the propellers, but I could swear he had tears in his eyes.

The next thing I remember, we were airborne. For a while I sat in silence, eyes closed, head resting against the bulkhead, trying to let the drone of the motors lull me into a sense of calm before we launched into the stress of the next phase, the landing. Then I was back on duty, entering the cabin, soothing the youngsters, and finally asking what had delayed the arrival of the last group, the one in Sammi's car. Shulamit, who was later to become Sammi's wife, explained that a caravan of camels had blocked the road and there was no way around it, so that Sammi just had to wait until they were good enough to yield the right of way. I pictured poor Sammi trapped behind those camels, absolutely aching with nerves, and hoped that at least he was enjoying the knowledge that everything had worked out.

Our dawn landing at Yavneel, after a four-hour flight, was mercifully swift and undramatic: no British troops, no gunfire, no commotion. When the plane drew to a halt, I jumped out first, followed by the two pilots. We were met by a bevy of people from the Mossad, one of them prominently displaying a satchel that held the gold coins. He extended it directly to Wessenberg, but I stepped in between them and pointedly demanded my check back.

"A check with such heavy cover," I told him, "should be treated with respect."

"Right you are," the pilot conceded with a look of genuine contrition as he produced the crisply folded check. "Sorry about our little spat."

I shook his hand warmly, and while the others drifted toward their cars I waited until Wessenberg and Mike were back in the cockpit, then gave them the thumbs-up sign as they started the propellers and positioned the plane for takeoff.

"Shammai, we have to clear out of here!" one of my colleagues called from behind me.

As I turned toward the car, wondering if I would ever see those two Americans again, something told me that, either way, for me this was just the beginning.

FOUR

A Lebanese Interlude

THE NEXT MORNING, after making up for much lost sleep, I hauled myself out of bed and went to Tel Aviv to file my report and celebrate our success. Quite arbitrarily I decided to reverse the order of priorities and began on a festive note by treating myself to breakfast at a café near our headquarters. Settling into a quiet patch of shade, as I savored the first meal in days that wasn't gulped down in haste or picked at in a state of nerves, I leafed through the papers to see what I had missed since the previous Wednesday.

Admittedly, these were days in which signs of a political solution to the Palestine imbroglio were beginning to emerge, and one newspaper reported that the majority in the United Nations Special Committee on Palestine (UNSCOP) was leaning toward the partition of the country into a Jewish state and an Arab state. Other than that, however, little had changed during my brief absence. Skirmishes between the Haganah and the British authorities were fierce and increasingly frequent, but they weren't the only war going on. Far more punishing to the population at large were the bloody clashes between Jews and Arabs in Palestine. In fact, the violence had reached the level of an incipient civil war, and on some days the headlines counted the dead and injured in the dozens. Each Arab attack prompted a counterattack; each assault, retaliation; and hardly a day passed without casualties.

But despite the relentless bloodletting on the streets of Palestine's cities and villages, the boldest headlines those days were still devoted to illegal immigration. The immigrants on the *Exodus 1947,* whose stand against the British in the form of a hunger strike had made their plight an international *cause célèbre,* were now being shipped to Hamburg, in the British zone of occupation. Forcing Jews to return to Germany after the Holocaust was the final insult, the height of callousness, cynicism, and provocation. To the Jews of Palestine, nothing was more infuriating than Great Britain's mighty naval and air forces swooping down on defenseless immigrant boats—except perhaps the sight of British police and infantry pursuing their passengers like wild animals, shoving, dragging, beating, and finally deporting them to camps on Cyprus or even back to Germany. The very thought of it was enough to snap me out of my mood of self-satisfaction. I paid the bill, left the papers, and took the stairs two at a time to report for duty.

Upon arriving there five days earlier, I had been met by a dark scowl for being late. Now the light had returned to Zafrira's eyes, and she welcomed me with her usual mischievous smile.

"Where have you been, Shammai? We'd begun to worry about you."

I made a gesture of going limp with exhaustion but decided not to mention the detour for breakfast.

"We have a transmission from Berman saying that there were no repercussions to the operation there. Here either, I might add. Really neat work!"

After that start, as I entered Moshe Carmil's office I was fully expecting a hero's welcome: a bit of backslapping, a little encomium, perhaps even a toast. But he merely shook my hand, offered a terse "Well done"—as if sensing that it would be a pity to ruin the aftertaste of such a profound experience with clichés and superfluous verbiage. Then he got straight down to business, for our "neat work" had already given rise to a number of propositions.

First of all, the Mossad realized that such clandestine flights might well be developed into a new and promising channel for illegal immigration. Despite the success of the first run, we knew that the method was a precarious one of uncertain duration. But while it lasted, it could be used very effectively—and not just for immigration. Indeed, the people in charge of acquiring arms for the Haganah were already expressing quite an interest in our little innovation, and before long they would commandeer it for their own needs. But in the meantime we had to have some way of referring to such operations. Although they were officially known by the Hebrew acronym for "Winged Immigration," in the Mossad's letters and cables we referred to these flights as "Operation Michaelberg," a play on the names of Leo Wessenberg and his copilot, Mike, who were thus immortalized in the annals of Israel's history.

Another consequence of the first "Operation Michaelberg" was the prompt conclusion of my private feud with the Mossad. By tacit agreement, my letter of resignation was now consigned to oblivion, the monkey cage was assigned to a worthier comrade, and I began to commute to Tel Aviv daily, spending most of my time in meetings and consultations, reading reports and cables, and preparing for a rerun of "Michaelberg." Just as I was beginning to balk at my seeming transformation into a deskbound, paper-pushing apparatchik, Moshe Carmil mentioned that he had something to tell me and invited me to discuss it over a glass of tea, East European style. Having aroused my curiosity, he decided to keep me dangling for a while. When I entered the room, he reached into one of his desk drawers and pulled out a box of cookies. Then he produced an apple and began peeling it methodically with a penknife, putting the peels into his tea. Finally he cut the apple into small slices, laying them out neatly on a napkin and then stuffing a few into the glass.

"Want some?" he offered, pointing to the napkin.

"No, thanks," I replied. "I'll stick with the cookies."

When he had finished preparing the concoction that brought him so much pleasure, Moshe wiped his hands, took a satisfied sip, and asked, "How would you like to take a short vacation in Lebanon and Syria?"

Moshe had a way of doing that: lulling you into near boredom and then knocking you off balance. But this time I made a point of not showing my surprise.

"What's it about?" I asked casually.

"If you're ready to go, I'll tell you," he teased. But, seeing my expression darken, he cleared his throat and proceeded to explain. As everyone in the Mossad knew, one of our men, Akiva Feinstein, had been caught in Lebanon and had served a six-month term for attempting to smuggle Jews into Palestine. When he was arrested, Feinstein was carrying false Syrian papers, so that after serving out his sentence in Lebanon he was extradited to Syria to stand trial for forging and bearing a false identity card. Moshe wanted to make sure that his interests were handled properly, especially since our agent in the area, Givoli, was scheduled to leave and there was still no replacement for him.

"But why me?" I asked defensively, seeing the assignment as a detour away from my work on the Iraqi front. "If he's being tried, what can I do for him? Or am I to understand that you simply haven't anything more practical to offer me? You needn't rack your brain, you know. I'll be happy to return to the kibbutz."

Moshe's lips were pursed in an expression of reproach. "Sometimes I wonder about you, Shammai," he began chidingly. "Since when is aiding a colleague in distress a trifling matter? You know very well that we'd make any effort, invest any sum, take any risk to save one of our agents, and we assign only our best people to the task; people who have displayed initiative and resourcefulness."

He paused to let the effect of both the stick and the carrot sink in.

"I want you to find a way to meet with Akiva, see what we can do to help him, work out a line of defense, and brief his lawyer. That's a top priority for us, and I hope you won't turn me down.

"And as long as you're there," he continued, "you might as well look into ways of renewing immigration from Syria and Lebanon, which has dwindled to practically naught recently. I also want you to look up the 'Lords of the Desert' in Damascus and find out once and for all where we stand with them. I know *that's* important to you."

Our relations with the "Lords" had indeed been troubling me ever since the fiasco in Iraq the previous spring. After having left us in the lurch, they made no attempt to explain themselves in the intervening months. They also had an appreciable sum of our money, which Moshe was understandably anxious to recover. But if the truth be known, my decision was also swayed by the fond and surprisingly vivid memories of Damascus and Beirut, from visits there as a child, that wafted into my consciousness as I sat there in Moshe's room. I recalled how, after the long journey through the dull, dust-colored desert separating Baghdad from Damascus, the Syrian capital had seemed like a magical oasis of sweet, juicy fruits and cold, clear well water. And I remembered holding my father's big, warm hand as we walked along the bank of the Barada River or through the city's colorful bazaars fragrant with the spices of the East. Add to that the memories of vibrant Beirut—where we stopped later on our route from Baghdad to Palestine and made into a base for visits to the resort areas in the nearby mountains—and I had reason enough to agree to the proposed mission, especially because this was to be a short-term operation, not a year underground in distant Iraq.

"Well, what do you say?" Moshe pressed.

"When do I leave?" I smiled obligingly in reply.

"First I want you to go back to Baghdad with the plane," he said, "just as we agreed with your two boys when they landed in Yavneel. And this time let's hope we don't have a repeat of the mishap in Italy. If there's another leak, we can kiss the idea good-bye."

The mishap, the leak, and the agreement with "my boys" all had to do with the decision to turn "Michaelberg" into a standard routine. After the success of our original flight from Baghdad, the Mossad decided to attempt a similar one from Italy, with the refugees who had gathered there. Unfortunately, although the plane left from a small, remote airfield, word of its departure got out, and the next thing we knew, the popular newspaper *Corriere della Sera* had published an item under the headline:

Fascists or Illegal Jews
Flown in Mysterious Plane

Yesterday two large trucks were seen in Sesto, near Naples, with about fifteen people getting out of each. Curious townsfolk who gathered around them were told by the drivers that the guests were American citizens on a tour. Later on, a foreign plane appeared, circled several times . . . and landed in an abandoned military airfield. The mysterious group boarded the plane and took off in an undetermined direction. . . .

Ironically, the relatively lax conditions in Italy proved to be to our detriment, for our emissaries were less sensitive about the need for caution and secrecy, and as a result "Michaelberg" shot into the headlines—and almost gave up the ghost. "Almost," because the readers of the *Corriere della Sera* took the story to be no more than a flight of fancy. It was even ignored by the agents of the British police, who were working diligently to thwart illegal immigration via Italy—all of which seemed to prove that the Lord watches over fools.

Be that as it may, after my talk with Moshe over apple tea, I went off to review the files on Lebanon and Syria so that right after flying back to Baghdad with the "Michaelberg" crew, I could leave for Beirut. But I never made that trip back to Baghdad, because, bursting with self-confidence after their successful flights from Iraq and Italy, "my boys" reverted to the American tradition of free enterprise and one fine morning left for Iraq on their own—without informing the Mossad and, naturally, without making a stop for me.

So it was that on September 20, 1947, a month to the day of our acrobatic departure from Haifa, Sammi happened to be driving over one of the bridges that crossed the Tigris, in the heart of Baghdad, when suddenly he noticed our two enterprising pilots walking in the opposite direction, bathed in sweat and looking bushed. Perplexed by their appearance, he decided to forgo caution and stop to offer them a lift. They were delighted to see him and gladly climbed into the car, informing him that *I* had ordered them to fly directly to Baghdad. When no one made contact with them, they had begun to search for a synagogue in the hope that the rabbi would inform his congregants of the opportunity to travel to Palestine and thus put them in business. They found the synagogue but not a sympathetic ear, and by the time Sammi lighted upon them, they were feeling pretty desolate.

The next day, we received an urgent wire from Baghdad reading:

To: Artzi
FROM: Berman
Pilots arrived last night but we lacked sufficient time to organize the shipment yesterday.

Flabbergasted, we wired back to ask what on earth they were talking about and received the following reply that same day:

To: Artzi
FROM: Berman
The pilots say they reached an understanding with you and Shammai about coming here. We fail to see why you've kept silent about it. At any rate, the shipment will leave at three in the morning local time, and if arrangements are not made for receiving it, the onus will be on you.

Arriving, as it did, at approximately 8:30 P.M., this wire created a difficult problem, because there was a curfew in effect at night, and we could hardly be expected to make the necessary preparations if we couldn't move about freely. But when we tried to get them to put the flight off till the next day, Baghdad replied that it was too late to postpone the departure. Left with no choice, within less than three hours, at 11:20, we again wired Baghdad announcing: "The preparations have been attended to. Happy landings!"

The plane left, arrived, and disembarked its passengers safely as before. By this third "Operation Michaelberg" (which, as matters turned out, was also to be the last, because the Haganah's arms people "expropriated" the method), it seemed as if nothing could be simpler. Reluctant as I am to admit it, at first I felt almost disappointed that the flights from Iraq could manage so well without me. One way or another, it seemed that the Iraqi chapter of my career had come to a close, so that I might as well try to do some good in Lebanon.

There were a number of details to be handled. First, I was to travel on my Iraqi passport again, under the pretense of returning home to Iraq via Lebanon. The problem was, according to the history of my comings and goings as recorded in the passport, I had left Palestine on August 20 but hadn't entered or left any other country, and I had certainly never returned to Palestine. The Iraqis hadn't bothered to stamp the passports of the "Michaelberg" crew—merely the plane's manifest—and obviously there were no officials on duty at the end of the runway at three in the morning or at the Yavneel airstrip at dawn. I was therefore told to avail myself of the services of Moshe Lichtenstein, whose specialty was creating such tools of the trade as suitcases with false bottoms and custom-tailored identity papers. Lichtenstein was not particularly concerned by my problem. "You'll get your passport back tomorrow with a fine entry stamp," he dismissed me curtly—and so I did.

In the meanwhile, I read all the Mossad's files on Syria and Lebanon but did not feel very much enlightened for the experience. I did learn, however, that "our man in Damascus," a local Jew named Eli Zagha, could make contact with the "Lords of the Desert," that there were three or four contacts I could call upon in my work, and that my exchange of letters with Tel Aviv would be effected through the offices of the H. T. Transport Company, which maintained a taxi service between Haifa and Beirut.

Now I had to conceal these names and addresses, along with phone numbers in Palestine and a substantial sum in cash for my various needs. Following the Mossad's standard procedure, I intended to stuff all this material into condoms and insert them into large tubes of toothpaste and shaving cream. But, for that purpose, I had first to go into a pharmacy and obtain the proper raw materials. After blushing a deep red and mumbling something obviously unintelligible, the shy kibbutznik in me finally managed to whisper my request for condoms into the pharmacist's ear—and received full understanding. But when I went on to ask him for Kolynos toothpaste—without, of course, explaining that I was about to embark on a secret mission to an Arab country—his understanding turned to indignation.

"Our local brands aren't good enough for you?" he huffed. "A young man like yourself should be able to get along without foreign imports!" And as I turned to leave, thoroughly chastened, he continued to mutter just loud enough for my benefit, "The snobs that have sprouted up in this

country!'' Fortunately there were other pharmacists in Tel Aviv less im-
bued with Zionist zeal, so that I was able to purchase products without any
Hebrew words on them and solve the problem of concealment.

The date for my departure was set as October 7, and the means of
transport from Haifa to Beirut was to be simply a bus or a taxi, the two
modes favored by the students from Palestine attending the American
University, as well as the merchants and tourists frequenting this route. On
the appointed morning, I left the kibbutz with Temima, who was to see me
off in Haifa and return home later that day. But at the travel agency in
Haifa, we encountered a crowd of irate travelers and discovered that all
the taxis and buses heading for Beirut had been turned back at the frontier. The Lebanese Government had unilaterally closed its border with
Palestine for "security reasons," due to the session of the Arab League
Council set to open that day in Beirut. The main subject on the agenda was
the Palestine problem, and the presence of prime ministers from a number
of Arab states and the Grand Mufti of Jerusalem (who had been exiled
from Palestine by the British) was undoubtedly the reason for the heightened caution. When we saw that the protests of the stranded travelers did
them no good, it seemed pointless to stand around waiting, so I suggested
that we might as well exploit this enforced vacation to enjoy ourselves a
bit. I expected at least a raised eyebrow from Temima, who was always
super-conscientious about her work. But this time even she readily agreed
to postpone her return home so as not to leave me abandoned and lonely
on the eve of my journey. That much settled, we took a room in the
Carmel Court Hotel—where I had first met the "Michaelberg" pilots a
few weeks earlier—and headed off for a good meal.

Unfortunately, I was in anything but a holiday mood. After having been
immersed first in "Michaelberg" and then in preparations for this latest
mission, the unanticipated "lockout" had jolted me back into the harsh
reality of the times. We seemed to be moving inexorably closer to a critical
point on three fronts: the struggle between the Royal Navy and the phantom fleet of immigrant boats sailing to Palestine; a decision by the United
Nations on the country's political future; and the relations between the
Jewish and Arab communities in Palestine in light of the policy of the
surrounding Arab states (which were already blustering about an armed
struggle and even outright war).

On the immigration front, the hushed attempts to steal past the British
blockade had given way to a brash struggle for the right to immigrate—
and, essentially, over the right to establish an independent state in Palestine. It was apparently having some effect, because on the political front
the British Colonial Secretary had reported to UNSCOP that his country

was prepared to relinquish its mandate and withdraw its forces from Palestine. Yet the Arab League remained determined to block a political settlement, and to make that point incontestably clear, it issued both transparent hints and blunt threats to plunge the Middle East into turmoil by means of strikes, demonstrations, and convening the Arab League Council. That was precisely what was happening now—and the reason I found myself stuck in Haifa.

The next day's headlines did not augur any improvement in my chances of traveling, especially as the declarations aired on the first day of the conference consisted of open threats to go to war if the UN decided on the establishment of a Jewish state. At the same time, the general obsession with security reached new heights, so that one wire service reported that the cloak of secrecy surrounding the Grand Mufti of Jerusalem was designed to prevent him from being "captured by British or Jewish terrorists." Just before noon, I bought the Arabic dailies, tucked them under my arm (as part of the image I was hoping to create), and again tried my luck at the travel agency. But the picture hadn't changed there, either. So I returned to the hotel in something of a funk and again asked Temima to stay with me, promising "just this once." To my surprise she was completely amenable, probably because she saw how depressed I was. Once you've agreed to take on a sensitive mission, there's nothing worse than repeatedly postponing it. You work yourself up to it for days, weeks perhaps, trying to stay composed; wrapping yourself in a cloak of humor (often black humor) to conceal your anxieties; and warding off such demoralizing questions as: "Has everything been prepared properly?" and, worst of all, "Is there really a point to all this?" And then, just when you've managed to quash such heretical thoughts, the trip is postponed for a day, and then another, and another, with each new day pitting you against the same old demons all over again.

In an effort to escape them for a while, I sat down in our hotel room to peruse the Arabic newspapers, finding little to gladden the heart, until suddenly my eye came upon something oddly incongruous. A Lebanese airline was proudly offering its services on the Haifa–Beirut run for a modest two and a half Palestine pounds. It invited the public to visit its agents, Shakhib and Elias Hal, at 126 Kings Street, Haifa. I actually chuckled at the sheer simplicity of the solution and wondered if it really was possible to fly off to Beirut just like that. Could it be that the Lebanese had closed the land border and completely overlooked the air connection? Absurdities of that kind were not uncommon in this part of the world.

"What's so funny?" Temima asked, picking her head up from the book she was reading.

I showed her the ad and told her that it brought to mind an anecdote my father used to tell about the country bumpkin who rushed into a police station shouting that he had caught a thief and demanding that the constable come along to arrest him.

"What have you done with him in the meantime?" the constable asked.

"I've tied his legs to a tree," the peasant replied with a look of self-satisfaction.

"Idiot!" laughed the policeman. "If his hands are free, he has probably untied his feet and is long gone by now."

The peasant looked perplexed, thought about it for a moment, and replied confidently, "No he hasn't. If I didn't think of that, neither has he."

So the two went off together and, sure enough, there was the thief still tied to the tree!

Bearing in mind the possibility that the Lebanese had simply neglected to think of the air connection, I waited impatiently for four o'clock, when the offices of Messrs. Hal were to open after the long Mediterranean lunch break. Then I walked in and inquired in Arabic when I could take the next flight to Beirut. The definitive reply was "Tomorrow, at 3 P.M."

"Can I buy a ticket now?" I asked.

"That's why I'm here," the young clerk said, smiling obligingly.

Indeed, within minutes I was equipped with a round-trip ticket (on the assumption that it wouldn't hurt to have a ticket back to Palestine right at hand), and things were beginning to look up. There was, however, one more obstacle to overcome.

The next day, at Haifa's small airfield, the policeman at passport control asked the routine questions about my place of residence and so forth before duly stamping my passport. But then, contrary to the usual procedure, he put it aside, saying that it would be returned to me shortly. In the meanwhile, he suggested that I wait in the airport cafeteria. I felt a stab of alarm at that departure from convention—particularly in light of the stamp crafted by Moshe Lichtenstein—but I decided to behave with pronounced indifference. Slowly I walked over to the cafeteria, ordered a bottle of beer, and sat drinking it insouciantly until my plane was called.

Upon boarding the small aircraft I found, to my astonishment, that I was the only passenger. I couldn't help thinking of the crowd of frustrated travelers who would undoubtedly have been delighted to join me had they only bothered to read the ads in the Arabic papers. The plane followed its usual procedure to the end of the runway, but after warming the engines, rather than pick up speed for a takeoff, it taxied slowly back toward the terminal.

"What's happened?" I asked the steward.

"The control tower has asked us to return," he told me politely but not very informatively.

As usual, my imagination filled in the rest, and I anticipated the worst. But fortunately there wasn't much time for self-torture. Through the window, I saw a British policeman running toward us, and when the plane came to a halt the steward opened the door and the policeman climbed in. But instead of barking "You're under arrest!" he gave me a reproving look and said in a rather scolding tone, "Sir, how do you expect to go anywhere without your passport?"

I had been concentrating so hard on acting nonchalant that I had forgotten the reason why! It took a few minutes for my heart to stop thumping, but then the pounding started all over again each time I imagined what would have ensued had I reached Beirut without a passport.

As it was, I was received most cordially at Beirut airport—as befits a lone traveler coming from afar—and everyone seemed free to take care of me. When the policeman at passport control asked where I would be staying, I asked him in turn to recommend a good hotel.

"The Saint George," he said. "It's definitely the most beautiful."

"Put down the Saint George," I told him, to his obvious satisfaction.

He hadn't exaggerated. The hotel, situated at the edge of the clear, blue, tranquil waters of Beirut Bay, was stunning. The prices left me rather stunned as well—especially by our standards at that time. But since I intended to be there for only a few days, I decided to splurge and, for the sake of appearances, to set up shop in the best hotel in town.

Beirut was Beirut, a bustling, bubbling, colorful city and mischievous port replete with flickering neon lights, bars, and sailors from every corner of the earth who streamed to its boisterous, tantalizing, but unquestionably vulgar entertainment quarter. After settling in at the Saint George, I immediately began (in penance perhaps) to plot my next move. Gazing out over the bay, I constructed the details of my new persona as a wealthy tourist who had come to Lebanon to rest, and, almost reflexively, I found myself asking the barman to bring me a pack of Players cigarettes—a duplicate of all the packs that had been emptied by my friend Yunis during our time together in Baghdad.

Until that moment, I had never smoked in my life. On the contrary, when the effect of smoking on the kibbutz budget was raised at one of our general meetings, I proposed (in what was considered outrageous extremism) that we forbid smoking for the sake of thrift. But now I remembered Yunis's retorts whenever I urged him to kick the habit. A man working under cover must smoke, he argued, for then he always has some leeway if he finds himself in a tight spot: he can divert a policeman's attention to a pack of cigarettes or a lighter or even hide behind a smoke screen. So on the dubious premise that it would enhance my desired image to be seen relaxing in a chic restaurant or café with a cigarette, I opened the pack and lit up my first. It tasted awful (my immediate association was burnt straw), and fortunately I didn't grimace or dissolve into a coughing fit. Yet even though I soon felt dizzy, I kept right at it. In fact, I continued to smoke for the next twenty years.

To clear my head, as the strip of red at the edge of the horizon grew steadily darker, I decided to take a walk along the Corniche, Beirut's lovely strand following the contour of the shore. Despite my decision not to try to contact any of my liaisons for a few days, so that I could firmly establish my cover and be quite sure no one was tailing me, I found myself walking in the neighborhood where one of our contacts, Madame Renée, lived. When I had asked my Mossad colleagues how I would recognize Renée, I was told, "You can't miss her. She's the size of a house." Indeed, when I sauntered by her address and furtively peeked through the window, just below street level, I saw her immediately. Slightly taken aback by her girth, I continued walking slowly on before deciding to retrace my route to the hotel. But when I passed by her house a second time, I heard an unmistakable "Pssst" followed by a woman's voice asking in Arabic, "Who are you looking for?"

"I'm not looking for anyone. I'm just out for a walk," I replied rather lamely.

"Aren't you the new one?" she pressed. "Come in quickly."

I lingered for a moment, calculating the wisdom of establishing contact so soon.

"Well, don't just stand there," she snapped, "come in!"

So much for caution and code words and all the other accoutrements of undercover work in enemy countries, I thought. Nevertheless I obeyed. As I walked down the steps and entered her room, she shut off the light—presumably to prevent anyone from seeing in—though I managed to get a glimpse of the worn robe decorated with Chinese motifs that encompassed her huge body. I remember thinking, in kibbutznik stereotypes, that this must be the "classic look" of *mesdames* the world over, and I half expected a bevy of garishly attired women to appear from behind a beaded curtain.

"You were supposed to come yesterday," she groused. "Where have you been?"

I explained about the closed border and asked after Givoli, my predecessor, but he had already left Beirut.

"Don't worry, though," Madame Renée assured me, "I'll explain everything."

When she stood up to make coffee, I could see folds of fat rippling under her stained and shabby robe and felt a sense of dismay at the thought that if anything went wrong, I would be wholly at the mercy of this woman's influence—at least in the first instance. As if she had read my thoughts, when she returned with the coffee, Renée commented that it was a pity Akiva Feinstein was being held in Damascus, because she didn't know anyone with clout there.

"Here I know everyone: policemen, judges, ministers," she boasted, oblivious to the skeptical expression that had settled on my face in the near-total darkness. "I can turn them all around my little finger," Renée added, twisting the ring on her pinkie as she spoke, while I mused that evidently these were men of less than impeccable taste.

"What we have to do is get the government to demand Akiva's return from Syria for the purpose of interrogation. Once he's back here, getting him out will be like plucking a strand of hair out of dough."

"If that's so," I challenged, "how come he was arrested in Beirut in the first place? How come he was tortured and sentenced to more than half a year in prison?"

"That's because I wasn't consulted or called upon to help," she retorted indignantly. "Everyone thought he knew better than the next guy, and Akiva's the one who's paying for that now."

Returning to my hotel, I slipped into a dull depression, undoubtedly brought on by the meeting with Renée. I also became practically obsessed about my cover, and the need to be fastidious about my appearance and behavior intensified in the days to come as I began to size up the atmosphere (which was close to war fever) and read the local papers. The letter I sent back to Tel Aviv on October 16 put it this way:

The mood here is turbulent. The papers are full of atrocity propaganda, creating the feeling that a war is already in progress. Every day, the press carries items about the massing of armies and reports that the Jews [in Palestine] are already fleeing outlying settlements, leaving their worldly goods behind. The papers are filled with wild speeches by Fawzi Kaukji* and others promising, "Soon we'll be drinking coffee in Tel Aviv!" and that if the Arabs of Palestine are patient a bit longer, "Soon they'll be rid of the faces they so despise."

* Head of the irregulars in Palestine known as the Arab Liberation Army.

To "post" this letter I gingerly made my way to the offices of the H. T. Transport Company, my liaison with Tel Aviv, and sat down for an introductory chat with the office's managers. Ostensibly I had come to look into travel arrangements back home to Iraq. But while we were waiting for the youngsters from the adjoining café to bring over the standard fare of Turkish coffee, sweet pastries, and cold water, I raised the idea of turning the office into an agency for processing immigrants who would leave Iraq with tourist visas. My offer included a fee of twenty-five Palestine pounds per head and was accepted with alacrity. This arrangement would open another, albeit narrow, channel for immigration from Iraq, for in principle Iraqi Jews could obtain passports and exit visas to Lebanon for the purpose of medical treatment or recuperation. The system was not problem free. Such passports not only cost a modest fortune in bribes, they were issued to individuals only—never to whole families—and whoever received one was obliged to deposit a king's ransom with the government as a guarantee of his return. In addition, the document was stamped with the caveat "For Lebanon Only" and sometimes with a second injunction: "This Passport Not Valid for Palestine." But neither of these restrictions was the obstacle to Jewish immigration via Lebanon. The real problem was that, at the end of 1946, as a result of Akiva's arrest, the liaison network we had established for immigrants passing through Beirut began to fall apart, so that "Berman" was told not to send any more tourists to "Ruthie." Now I believed I had found an appropriate and trustworthy address for our Iraqi tourists, and I hoped that our comrades in Baghdad would exploit it to the hilt.

That was one aspect of my mission. The next order of business was to arrange a trip to Damascus to begin dealing with the Feinstein trial and make contact with the "Lords of the Desert." The journey between Beirut and Damascus should have been a short and simple affair. A regular taxi service ran between the two capitals, and the border between the two countries was little more than a symbolic one. Anyone holding a Syrian or Lebanese identity card could cross it without a passport, and the bearers of foreign passports with a visa for one of the two countries could cross without a visa for the other, though they had to go through a slightly involved procedure whereby a border guard would inquire about the purpose of their trip, ask exactly where they were headed, enter their names and passport numbers in the station's large register, and then either stamp their passports or not.

All this I learned on the first of my many trips to Damascus, as a polite young Syrian officer scrupulously recorded my particulars. Since I assumed that I would be traveling this route often, I feared that having my name crop up repeatedly would turn me into an object of suspicion. So when the time came to return to Beirut, I planned the journey carefully. First I bought all the illustrated monthlies with interesting or enticing covers. Then I chatted with the other passengers and generously shared my pile of reading matter with them. Finally, as we neared the border, I dropped off into a heavy sleep, punctuated by conspicuous snores and sighs, and when the taxi pulled to a stop and the border guard asked for identity cards, I slept right on, despite his repeated demands. Eventually one of the other passengers took pity on me, as I had hoped, and vouched for my credentials.

"Let him be," he urged the border guard. "Can't you see he's exhausted? And anyway, there's no problem. He's one of us."

With one notable exception toward the end of my stay, when the inspection at the Syrian border was particularly strict, this system worked like a charm on each of my trips along the Beirut–Damascus axis. To insure myself against loose ends, I also avoided returning to any hotel I had been in before. Of course it meant that each time I shuttled from Beirut to Damascus or vice versa, I had to register anew, down to the last detail. But it was reasonable to assume that the forms I filled out at the various reception desks were scattered through piles that were gathering dust in some corner of the Police Ministry or Secret Police headquarters and were never sorted or compared. Consequently, I got to know most of the hotels in Beirut and Damascus, from the staid and dignified to the less exclusive but more convivial variety.

On this first trip to Damascus, I immediately sought out Eli Zagha, who was handling Akiva Feinstein's affairs and could also be my liaison with the "Lords of the Desert." Through him I made contact with Munir Assas, the local lawyer handling Akiva's case, with whom I was supposed to devise a line of defense and negotiate a fee. He told me that he was defending Akiva for political and moral reasons, as he regarded himself as an opponent of the government in every way—none of which prevented him from demanding (and receiving, for lack of choice) an exorbitant fee for his services.

I asked Assas to arrange for me to visit Akiva in prison and was told that it was no simple matter, since visiting rights applied only to relatives and "Surely you would not want to claim that you are his relative, recently arrived from Palestine. Otherwise," he said sardonically, "I can start preparing to handle your case too—at the same fee." Still, I insisted that some way be found, and he finally agreed to take me along to the prison the next day.

"How will you get me in?" I asked, out of more than idle curiosity.

"Leave that to me," was all he would say. "I'll see you tomorrow."

The next day, as we made for Damascus Central Prison, Assas explained that I must pretend to be his assistant and do whatever I was told. When we reached the fortress that had been converted into a prison, I saw that the guards were well acquainted with Assas and treated him with politeness and respect. When they heard through the gate that Maître Assas had arrived, they called for "Akiva from Palestine" to be brought out. Then the heavy iron door opened before us, Assas entered, and I followed behind him, carrying his briefcase.

The iron door creaked on its hinges and slammed behind us with an ominous thud. I was keenly aware of the heavy key turning no fewer than three times in the lock and of a twist of discomfort that stopped just short of a shudder as I followed "His Honor" into the attorney's room. A few moments later Akiva joined us there. I had not met him before, but I had certainly heard a lot about him and knew that he was regarded as one of the Mossad's bravest and most successful emissaries. As soon as he entered the room, I recognized him on the basis of the photograph I had seen in Tel Aviv. Short and broad shouldered, he sported a wide mustache whose pointed ends swept upward, in the style of the heroes and notables of the past generation in the Middle East. Everything about him bespoke pride and self-confidence, and were it not for his convict's uniform—a loose shirt and baggy pants made of rough cloth and wooden clogs on his feet— together with the prison backdrop and the guard standing at the entrance to the room, one might have taken Akiva for a pillar of the Damascus community.

After speaking with Akiva for a few minutes, Assas removed a large pad and pencil from his briefcase, thrust them at me, and announced loudly, "Selim, summarize what he has said." Then he turned toward the door, took out a pack of cigarettes, extracted one for himself, offered another to the guard, and proceeded to engage him in a lively conversation, while taking pains to position himself between the warder and me. Obviously this was my opportunity to speak with Akiva and try to encourage him, but I was so nervous that I barely managed to murmur that all his comrades in the Mossad send their regards. Akiva instantly understood who this new assistant was and tried to encourage me! "Don't worry," he said softly, "I feel fine. Eli Zagha takes care of supplying me with food, and the lawyer is doing his job." The rest of the meeting was spent whispering about the problems I wanted to clarify, especially the line of defense to be taken at Akiva's trial. I promised to give Eli Zagha whatever sum was necessary to continue caring for Akiva's needs and handle the trial, and when I saw that the guard was not looking, I managed to stuff a wad of bills into Akiva's hand—to pad his stay in detention—and saw it instantly disappear into the folds of his clothing.

At that point Assas began prodding me impatiently, "Come on, Selim, we don't have all day." We left Akiva and returned to the main gate. The big key turned three times in the lock, the door squeaked open on its hinges, and we were outside again, walking down the streets of Damascus —which now felt to me like the height of freedom and safety.

I did not see Akiva again before the trial, but once the proceedings began I made a point of coming to Damascus and attending every session, talking to Assas and visiting with Akiva. It seemed the least I could do— other than continue to nurse the hope that we would get him released in the end.

It was the end of October before I finally succeeded in arranging a meeting with the "Lords of the Desert." I awaited it impatiently, because I was all but obsessed with finding out why the operation that had begun as such a promising vision ended in tragedy, betrayal, and frustration. After an uneventful ride from Beirut to Damascus, I registered in a nondescript hotel and was careful to be prompt for my audience with Emir Sha'alan, whom I had last seen in Baghdad in the spring. It took place in the pastoral Café Qasr Shamia, in the town of Dummar, just outside Damascus, on the bank of a cool stream that flowed through the café's garden. I found the emir in traditional dress sandwiched between his two aides, the Kuzbari brothers, dressed in the latest Paris mode. Even in the most strained atmosphere, ceremony prevails in the East. A servant nimbly served us small cups of dark, sweet tea and brought in a narghile for the emir, who drew deeply on the mouthpiece in obvious enjoyment and then invited me to share in his pleasure. Before I could decline, the servant had produced another narghile and fussed over it silently, drawing repeatedly on the pipe until the embers glowed, the water bubbled, and a distinguished gentleman like myself could get straight down to the business of smoking. Considering that I had taken up cigarettes just a short while before and barely tolerated sharp, savory Virginia tobacco, the taste of the Turkish narghile struck me as acrid. Nevertheless, out of courtesy and in an attempt to place myself on a symbolic par with my host, I continued to draw on the narghile like a practiced smoker until I felt distinctly nauseous, whereupon I switched to toying with the pipe instead.

As the servant left, I bid for an edge by opening the conversation with the comment that I happened to be in Damascus on my way back to

Baghdad and did not want to miss an opportunity to greet my friends with a blessing of peace.

"Peace and Allah's blessings be upon you," replied Mahmoud Kuzbari, whom I was meeting for the first time and who turned out to be my sole partner in the conversation from that point on, the emir confining himself to an occasional nod as a gesture of support.

"Undoubtedly you also wish to know what happened in Baghdad," Mahmoud continued, forestalling an offensive by raising the subject first.

"I must tell you," I interjected, aware that my voice was shaking with anger despite my resolve to remain thoroughly businesslike, "that to this day I fail to understand what happened, though I have devoted no little thought to the matter. In fact I still find it difficult to believe that it happened at all. Is that your idea of honor, gentlemen? Vanishing without so much as a word? Leaving us with one hundred and twenty people in peril of their lives? We suffered great injury, to say nothing of grave insult. I simply do not understand."

"You are quite right to be angry," Mahmoud soothed, moving to defuse my ire with seeming understanding. "That is why we are glad you came here, so that we may explain the matter. The truth is that we averted a terrible tragedy."

My expression must have registered skepticism or impatience, because I saw consternation flash across his face before he resumed his démarche.

"Do you recall that we asked you to postpone the departure by one day? It was because rumors had reached us and we wanted to establish their veracity. A friend informed us that the Iraqi authorities knew the reason for our presence in Baghdad and were massing a force to block our exit. We are not afraid of such vermin, and if we had been alone I assure you we would have taught them a lesson they would remember. But we were concerned about your people. Imagine if any of them had been killed after we had given our assurance that no harm would befall them. What would you have thought of us then?"

"Then why didn't you leave at least one man behind to tell us? Why haven't you attempted to explain yourselves since it happened?"

"If we had anything to hide, if the emir's conscience were not clear, would we have agreed to meet with you now?" he parried, leading me to wonder whether we had been wrong about them after all. Perhaps we had accused them unjustly.

In the meantime, a bowl of pears and crisp, shiny red apples had been placed on the table, leading me to recall the tasty fruit I had eaten on my visit to Damascus as a child and arousing in me a sense of closeness, almost of belonging.

"And what happens now?" I asked, moving beyond recriminations.

"We have isolated the problem and solved it. You can depend on that," he said confidently, as the emir slowly nodded his assent.

The conversation went on for a while longer, but we had stopped raking over the past and shifted to planning the future, as I reported in my letter of November 4:

I have made contact with the "Lords of the Desert" and they are prepared to cooperate, even to work off the debt. I have reached an understanding with them whereby we will pay them the full price for the first shipments (on delivery, of course) and afterward we'll deduct their debt in installments. By the end of this week they will have all the arrangements completed, and I will set a date with them for a rendezvous in Baghdad. . . . On the first trip they will take twenty-five crates [immigrants], of the sturdiest kind only, and transport them with the buttons [soldiers] from Evri [the Jordanian Army]. The price is 55 Palestine pounds, and I have agreed to pay them here. Please forward the necessary sum to me in the coming days so that I won't be without means when it comes time to pay.

I met with the "Lords" again in mid-November and was treated to another dose of promises plus the demand for an advance, which I adamantly rejected. A few days afterward we met for the third and last time, and on November 26 I sent the following brief message to Tel Aviv:

. . . The "Lords of the Desert" are evidently worthless. They continue to ask for "a little money" to get the work going, but it's evident that there won't be any work.

Many years later, I found a description of Emir Sha'alan written by His Majesty's consul in Damascus in March 1937 and preserved in the archives of the British Foreign Office. It presented quite a different picture of the desert prince who had so impressed me in Baghdad:

He spends much of his time in the Damascus cabarets. Tends to consumption, not without qualities. Enjoys strong following in Ruala [his tribe]. Treacherously slew his rival and cousin . . . in April 1935.

His political allegiance depends on his pocket or his vanity. Sometimes both. He too is for sale.

In my innocence it would appear that I took a considerable risk in summarily breaking off talks with a man who had no compunctions about killing his own kin. We had to write off the sum advanced to the "Lords" in Baghdad, but at least we were not drawn into throwing good money after bad. Nevertheless, after severing my ties with Sha'alan and the Kuzbaris, I returned to Beirut at the end of November so steeped in disappointment that I was practically oblivious to the significance of the vote scheduled to take place at the UN on the partition of Palestine into a Jewish and an Arab state.

Toward the evening of November 29, however, I began to pick up signs of the approaching drama. The evening papers came out with a special second edition on the last-minute, behind-the-scenes efforts by the Arab delegates at the UN to thwart the plan, quoting their emotional speeches and truculent warnings that they would prevent the partition of the country by force, if necessary. Few were the times in my life that I felt as lonely as I did that evening—isolated, confused, and even uncertain as to whether partition was to our advantage or our detriment. After all, it meant slicing the country in two; not even Jerusalem would be in our control. Equally disagreeable was the thought of what was likely to happen if the resolution was voted down: a continuation of British rule, probably compounded by a considerable escalation of the fighting between Arabs and Jews.

The more I dwelled on the paradox and the fact that there was no one I could talk to, other than the waiters in the restaurant, the more I could feel myself sinking into gloom. To ward off the blues, I went to see a film—my private method for exorcising the demons that attack in hours of loneliness —but this time it didn't work. Returning to my hotel in the heart of Beirut, I fell asleep with a book, and when I awoke late the next morning, it was to the sound of an uproar outside.

Through my window I could see a crowd of a few dozen young men marching down the middle of the street, waving their arms belligerently and shouting wildly at the top of their lungs. The only word I could make out of their chaotic shouts was "Palestine, Palestine," but that was reason enough to be interested. I squinted to read the headlines from the newsstand across the street, but all I could see was that the front pages of all the papers were set in a thick black border. Suddenly it hit me that something good must have happened to us, and my mood immediately turned bright. In great anticipation I shaved, threw on fresh clothes, and practically bounded down to the street to buy the papers and celebrate—whatever the good news turned out to be—with a leisurely breakfast in one of the cafés.

The news was, of course, that the partition resolution had been passed by the UN, and as a result the peaceful, elegant, sophisticated city of Beirut was working itself into an all-out frenzy. Cars mounted with loudspeakers drove though the city announcing that a mass march would leave from the Place des Martyrs, Beirut's main square, at 3 P.M. Crowds milled around the newsstands, and here and there someone would read out items for those who couldn't get close enough or were illiterate. Radios were on at full volume in the cafés and restaurants, piping out military marches and emotional prayers. As the hour of the demonstration drew near, I found myself drifting toward the rallying point, having convinced myself that it would probably be the safest place in the city. Shortly thereafter, together with thousands of others, I was listening to the speeches of incitement blaring over loudspeakers. Then the march began, and this huge block of humanity edged slowly forward, echoing the rhythmic chant of men being carried on the shoulders of their friends. Each time they called out *Falastin biladna w'al-yahud klabna* ("Palestine is our country and the Jews are our dogs"), thousands of voices clamored in reply, the only break being an occasional "Down with the Zionists!" or "Kill the Jews!" Still, the process remained orderly to the end, and upon dispersing at nightfall we were informed that a general strike would be in effect the next day and another demonstration would be held at ten in the morning near the Ministry of the Interior.

Back at my hotel I saw Philip, one of my closest associates in Lebanon, sitting in the lobby looking conspicuously distraught. Philip was without question the most amiable smuggler I have ever met, and during my short stay in Lebanon we had become fast friends.

"Where *were* you?" he asked at just below a shout.

"Come on, let's get something to eat," I said and quickly ushered him outside, for fear that he would continue his exhibition of nerves in front of the staff and guests. By this point I, too, was alarmed, but I waited until we were a safe distance down the street before arranging my face in an incongruous smile—for the sake of passersby—and asking him anxiously, "What's happened, Philip? Why are you so upset?"

"You have no idea how worried I was about you! I've been to the hotel ten times today, and each time they told me that you'd gone out in the morning and hadn't returned. I was sure something terrible had happened!"

"Philip, get hold of yourself. And lower your voice!" I rasped, feeling more vulnerable now than I had all day.

"What did you think you were doing roaming around on a day like this?" he scolded. "I came over to invite you to stay with me, or to offer to stay with you in case anything happened. And what do I find? You're gadding about town in the middle of a near riot!"

"I wasn't wandering about," I said softly in the hope that he would follow suit, "and it wasn't a riot. I was at the demonstration, and I assure you it was the safest place in Beirut."

Philip stopped dead in his tracks and grabbed my arm more for support, I thought, than to stop me. "Good Lord," he croaked, "you must be mad!" There was no way I could convince him of the merit of my approach; I could barely placate the poor man.

I did not take up Philip's invitation to move in with him until the uproar died down. Neither would I let him baby-sit me at the hotel. Instead, the next day, I followed my logic to its natural conclusion and went off to join the second demonstration, though it occurred to me that Philip might have been right about my state of mind. The longer I stayed the clearer it became that the orderly disposition of the previous day's march was not going to hold until the end of this rally. Within the mass that closed around the Interior Ministry, one group of young men seemed particularly worked up and bent on getting control of the crowd. I moved toward them and joined in their shouts, which had risen to a pitch of near frenzy by the time their leader called out, "Let's go to Wadi Abu-Jamil!"—meaning the Jewish quarter of Beirut.

A lone voice counseled restraint, for the government would acquiesce in the demonstrations only as long as they remained peaceful. But it was countered by the overwrought leader, who egged his followers on with the cry "The government is with us!"

With that, the boisterous group started moving in the direction of the Jewish quarter, drawing parts of the larger body in its wake. Carried along by the press of people, I, too, was heading toward what I knew would be the object of violence when suddenly I found myself facing mounted policemen waving their clubs menacingly and shouting, "Get back!" I needed no further persuasion—and neither did the more zealous protesters, for soon the police had driven the entire mob back to the site of the demonstration, where speeches were in progress. Then, as we stood listening to the harangues, a high stone fence collapsed under the weight of the demonstrators crowded on it, and I barely avoided being injured. I knew that had I been hurt, even slightly, I would have been subject to some very uncomfortable questions. Meanwhile, the speeches came to an end and the crowd began to move on to a larger demonstration in the streets. We marched past the city's foreign embassies, shouting fierce denunciations of their vote at the UN, and soon I could hear the swish of stones flying on every side. By then I had had my fill of adventure and deserted the field of battle at the first opportunity.

That day, the Reuters correspondent in Beirut reported that ten thousand students had been involved in the demonstration and that stones were thrown at the U.S. Information Office and the French legation. Quoting official sources, the *Palestine Post* (today the Jerusalem *Post*) stated that "the government took steps to protect the Jewish quarter of Beirut by placing armed guards around it." Indeed, I could attest that in this instance the measures were truly effective. But the same could not be said throughout Lebanon; word of the provocation and harassment of Jews came in from various cities and towns, and the situation in Syria was appreciably more grave. In Aleppo, Jews were assaulted, dozens of shops and homes were looted and destroyed, and the historic synagogue was set ablaze. Rumors made the rounds that eight Jews had been killed in the course of the rioting, prompting countless others to flee to Lebanon. Feelings were running especially high in Damascus, where most of the demonstrations turned violent, and it was only by chance or providence that the Jewish quarter was spared. It seems that before an incited mob reached the quarter, it clashed with a group of Communists, a number of people were killed and injured, and the police intervened to halt the violence.

The turmoil all around me made me doubly intent on finding new ways to get Lebanese Jews—as well as the scores of others fleeing to Lebanon from Iraq and Syria—over the border into Palestine. The most logical way was through the services of my smuggler friend Philip, who was known to have close and reliable ties with police and army officers stationed nearby the border. On December 6 I wrote to Tel Aviv:

. . . I have arranged with Philip to carry out an experiment. His approach seems a good one: a car of local buttons [policemen] with one accompanying crown [major]. The price is 20 [Palestine pounds] for the large size, 10 for the small. We have many opportunities to work now and can operate on a broad scale. The first run will be made with ten laborers. . . .

Before making that attempt, however, I wanted to assess the system for myself. So Philip took me on a tour of the border area, and I was impressed by the relatively favorable conditions, Philip's contacts, and the respect he commanded at the various checkpoints we passed on the way. Satisfied that the plan was viable, I okayed the first run for December 21, and our people arrived at their destination safely. Delighted with the results, I threw myself into organizing other groups until I received an inconceivable message from Tel Aviv: "Stop further shipments for now." The rider "for now" seemed inane; I was, at any rate, returning home in a matter of days. After three months of running myself ragged, all I had to show for it was frustration and anger that almost all my attempts to deal with immigration had hit a dead end. The "Lords of the Desert" were charlatans, and now, when I thought that I had at least found a way over one border, I was ordered to hold off "for now." Also, my frustration and disappointment were compounded by the fact that, at the end of December, Akiva Feinstein's trial ended in disaster.

The verdict was to be handed down on Saturday, December 27, and on the day before, I made my way to Damascus to attend this final session, hoping that, despite the hostile atmosphere, I would be able to join Akiva in celebrating his release. I entered the taxi equipped with the usual stack of illustrated papers, offered them to my fellow passengers, and pretended to fall asleep as we approached the Syrian border. But the system that had worked so perfectly on every other occasion failed me now. The border guard just kept poking and shaking me until I had no choice but to respond (lest he take me for dead), and he herded me into the border station together with all the other passengers. Walking toward the building, I wondered whether I hadn't overdone it by traveling back and forth and changing hotels so often. It occurred to me that I might be walking right into a trap, and I tried to concentrate on what I would say. I even considered the possibility of remaining silent and refusing to answer any questions at all. But when I entered the border station, practically cringing in expectation of the worst, I discovered that the passengers were merely being asked to present vaccination certificates to show they had been immunized against cholera. There had been another of the periodic outbreaks of cholera in the region, and the Syrian authorities had decided to deny entry to anyone who was not properly protected against the disease. Yet hardly had I calmed down when I realized that, whereas all the other passengers were able to produce these certificates and continue on their way, I could not. When pleading and cajoling proved worthless, I approached the major in charge of the station and explained that I had to continue on to Baghdad that very day and had no intention of remaining in Damascus. But he, too, stood his ground, forcing me to adopt a more creative approach.

"Sir," I implored him just above a whisper, "perhaps you will nevertheless find a way to help me. Please!" And so saying I stuffed my hand demonstratively into my inside jacket pocket—the one that usually holds a wallet.

Seeing the menacing glint in his eye, I knew that the gesture was a mistake and that I might be in big trouble.

"What did you say?" I heard him growl.

"Nothing. Nothing at all. I was just thinking—"

"Thinking what?"

"I was just thinking that perhaps I could get the shot in Damascus. But I see that wouldn't solve the problem."

"You see right. Now get out of here and don't let me see you again."

I returned to Beirut crestfallen. How would it look if I reported that I had missed Akiva's trial just because of a cholera shot? I'd be the laughing-stock of the Mossad! After all, it was to attend the trial that I had been sent here in the first place, and now I was stuck in Beirut!

The next day, I woke to the sound of taxi drivers hawking their services and announcing their destination as Tripoli, not far from the Syrian border, in northern Lebanon. I conjured up a map of the country and realized that from Tripoli it was not very far to the Syrian city of Homs and from there to Damascus—assuming, of course, that the Syrians had contented themselves with closing the border only on the Beirut–Damascus road and hadn't bothered to seal the circuitous route via the north. Certainly it was worth checking out. I shaved and dressed in a wink, rushed down to a cab whose driver was calling "Tripoli!" and set off northward. The scenery on the coastal road was exquisite as we drove past the highest mountains I had ever seen to the east and the blue sea to the west. In Tripoli I changed my form of transport, boarding a bus to Homs—and crossing the border without a single question—then taking another bus southward to Damascus. The latter was an ancient vehicle that trundled along with great effort and seemed to stop at every village and hamlet on the way, mercilessly packing in passengers and their bundles, live fowl, and other appurtenances. Fortunately, having boarded at the first stop, I had the advantage of a window seat and could occupy myself with taking in the scenery, rather than be drawn into the goings-on inside the bus.

I reached Damascus after nightfall, exhausted after eleven hours on the road (instead of the usual two-hour journey). From my hotel I phoned Akiva's attorney and heard the grim news: Akiva had been found guilty and sentenced to three years imprisonment, the maximum penalty for the charges brought against him. All our hopes of getting him off with a light sentence, or even an acquittal—hopes that had been nurtured by Assas—had been completely vain. I made no attempt to hide my anger from Assas.

"I am sorry," he replied. "I did the best I could. But considering the political atmosphere these days, he didn't really stand a chance of an acquittal. We're lucky he wasn't convicted of forgery, too. That would have earned him a far longer sentence."

"I want to visit Akiva tomorrow," I snapped.

"I'm not sure that's advisable," he cautioned. "Conditions are not auspicious—"

"I insist," I told him curtly.

"All right," he said after a brief pause. "I'll come for you before noon."

We met with Akiva in the prison waiting room, and as he walked in I again noted the great respect accorded him by guards and prisoners alike. When he saw me, Akiva squinted as if in astonishment.

"When did you get out?" he asked.

"Out of where?" I questioned in return.

"Weren't you arrested yesterday in the courtroom?"

My expression evidently showed that I had no idea what he was talking about, because Akiva explained that, just before his trial opened on the previous day, the police had arrested everyone in the courtroom and interrogated them about why they were attending the trial.

"Afterward they announced that they had arrested three spies from Palestine, and I was sure one of them was you. When I didn't see you at the trial, I was sure you were in a worse position than I am."

I shook my head in disbelief as I related what had happened at the border. But rather than dwell on the miraculous twist of my own fate, I moved on to talk of Akiva's, asking whether he thought there was any point in appealing the verdict. He answered in the negative. "Nothing will help," he said with resignation. "I am a casualty of the establishment of a state for us, and that's all there is to it. Don't worry. I'll manage here."

My eyes filled with tears and I had difficulty speaking as it occurred to me that I was standing in the presence of a genuine national hero. In the little time left to us, we spoke about practical arrangements. I passed Akiva some cash and told him that I would leave more money with Eli Zagha to be held for him until he needed it.†

The end of Akiva's trial also marked the end of my mission, and I booked a reservation on the January 2 flight to Haifa. Before leaving, however, I took the trouble to find a young man in the Beirut Jewish community who would keep an eye on our affairs in Lebanon and take care of the various requests that came in from Palestine until we could send another emissary. He decided to give me a proper send-off by inviting me to celebrate New Year's Eve in one of Beirut's more exclusive and expensive cabarets. The kibbutznik in me sniffed at the notion of indulging in such bourgeois behavior, but my prospective host made such a nuisance of himself that I finally gave in. So it was that I welcomed in 1948 in truly surrealistic circumstances, with a glass of champagne in hand, an attractive French dancer at my side (liberally displaying her "greatest virtues"), and a trio of Gypsy violinists moving from table to table taking special requests in return for generous gratuities. When they arrived at our table, I asked for Grieg's "Solveig's Song." I had loved that melody ever since first hearing it emerge from my teacher's concertina and, despite its distinctly

† Akiva served his full sentence and did not return home until the middle of 1950.

Norwegian provenance, somehow I had always imagined it to be a typically Jewish outpouring of feeling. I also knew that a song like that
wouldn't give me away, and in any event I assumed that these three
wouldn't know it. But I was wrong. No sooner were the words past my
lips than the three Gypsy fiddlers began to play it, with eyes closed and
bodies swaying for dramatic effect, as though all evening they had been
waiting for just this request. Upon hearing those lyric strains (coupled
with the "mellowing" effects of the champagne), I turned instantly maud-
lin, stricken with longings for home and practically teary-eyed, until suddenly I remembered that the situation at home—and especially in Haifa,
my initial destination—was not exactly inviting.

The civil war that had been simmering just beneath the surface while
Palestine's political future remained in doubt had now erupted in full
force. A few days earlier, two grenades had been tossed at the crowd of
Arab day laborers gathered outside the main gate of the city's oil refineries, killing four of them and injuring forty-four others. This attack, apparently mounted by the dissident Irgun Zvai Leumi, under the command
of Menachem Begin, counteracted the efforts of the national and munici-
pal Jewish councils to maintain relative quiet in Haifa. It also set off a
vicious spiral of violence and retaliation that began with the two thousand
Arab workers in the refineries running amok and assaulting the four hundred Jewish workers with tools, iron clubs, and axes. By the time their
rage was spent, they had brutally slaughtered thirty-nine people and
wounded seven others, while the soldiers of Transjordan's Arab Legion—
stationed in Palestine under British command—looked on passively and in
some cases even blocked attempts to save the victims. The following night,
a Haganah unit mounted a reprisal operation by infiltrating two Arab
neighborhoods and retaliating against dozens of the rioters who had massacred the Jewish refinery workers.

Since echoes of these events—often in a distorted and exaggerated form
—had reached as far as Beirut, I assumed that life was severely disrupted
in Haifa. I therefore betook myself to Beirut's Central Post Office and
risked a phone conversation with the Mossad to ask that I be picked up at
the Haifa airport. When I landed, however, there were no familiar faces in
the terminal. A taxi from the Shakhib and Elias Hal Travel Agency—which
I remembered fondly from my trip to Beirut in October—offered to take
me into the city, but I announced confidently that a car would be coming
for me. Minutes passed and no one came. The airport had emptied out
when a policeman inquired about my plans, and I informed him—somewhat less confidently—that I would be picked up shortly. But still no car
arrived, and eventually I realized that it was pointless to go on waiting.

The remaining taxi drivers at the airport were Arabs, but for lack of choice I finally approached one of them and asked him in Arabic to take me into town.

"Whereabouts in town?" he inquired prudently. "You know that things are pretty ticklish in Haifa now."

I recalled what I had heard about the lower city, near the port, being divided between Jewish and Arab sectors, with the main thoroughfare, Kings Street, now two-thirds Arab and one-third Jewish—the Jewish section being fenced off and sandwiched in the middle. I also remembered what I had heard about skirmishes breaking out between the different sectors and the grim fate awaiting any Jew who had the misfortune to find himself in an Arab area. Evidently the driver was having similar thoughts about his own safety.

"Kings Street," I told him, but being as clever as myself he first wanted to know the exact number.

"I don't recall," I waffled, "but I can recognize the house. Drive along slowly and I'll show you."

On our way to town, I asked the driver about the state of affairs in Haifa and, as might have been expected, he carried on about the barbarism of the Jews, the outrage they had perpetrated, and the need to teach them a lesson. In the course of this outpouring, we entered Kings Street, and he began asking with mounting concern if we weren't approaching our destination.

"A little farther," I coaxed him until I could see the barbed-wire fence dividing the street between the Arab and Jewish sectors. I kept urging him forward with promises of "just a bit more"—and felt his resistance growing—until we had practically touched the fence. Then I shouted "Stop!" (quite unnecessarily by that point), jumped out with my suitcase, and barely managed to stuff a bill in his hand—and hear him grumble, "Damn you!"—before making a dash for the barbed wire. Meanwhile, he turned the car around, floored the gas pedal, and shot off with a squeal of tires, while I proceeded to the Mossad's office on foot. But even the royal welcome there failed to assuage my anger.

"Why wasn't I met at the airport?" I fumed. "How did you think I'd get here?"

"Since the incident at the refinery, it's difficult to get gas," one of my colleagues explained. "Anyway, Shammai, we trusted that you'd make it somehow, and we were right!"

It was probably meant to be a compliment, but I responded with a most ungracious curse—even though I was in no position to challenge their judgment. Though I had been away for less than three months, I had come home to a very different country, now in the throes of war.

FIVE

The Winds of War

As ANY BEDOUIN can tell you, this, too, is one of the sights of the desert: you come across a powerful torrent of water roaring its way across the wastes and take it to be a swollen stream that will go on flowing year in and year out. But then, in the spring, when the dun-colored earth is covered with a carpet of brightly colored flowers that gladden the heart, the flow suddenly stops, its last drops soaked up by the hard desert soil, leaving nary a trace. Soon the world is parched and withered as far as the eye can see; desolation returns to rule over all.

That was the picture I saw upon returning from Lebanon in January 1948. Immigration from Iraq, which I had imagined as a steadily flowing stream—especially in light of the "Michaelberg" flights and a daring two-truck convoy that brought in seventy-seven people late in October—had abruptly dried up. The explanation for this reversal was supplied by none other than Sammi, who had accompanied the group of seventy-seven and was delaying his return to Baghdad for two reasons: first because he had become engaged to a young woman from Basra who had been one of my charges on the first "Michaelberg" flight, and also because he lacked the necessary papers to get back into Iraq legally. We could no longer smuggle him in on one of the trucks that had brought all our emissaries to Iraq in 1947–48 (with the sole exception of myself), for now these vehicles rarely traveled the desert route eastward. Besides, the surveillance along the road had become appreciably more stringent.

So Sammi remained in Palestine and became the local oracle on immigration from Iraq. Now he explained to me that due to the unrest following the November 29 UN decision to partition Palestine, the Arabs' preparations for war, and the massing of regular and irregular Arab forces in the desert between Iraq and Palestine as well as along the borders, it had been impossible for the Mossad to continue immigration via the desert. (This also explained the strange order I had received to "stop further shipments for now.") Since the convoy of seventy-seven that Sammi had led in October, none of our people had left Iraq. On December 28, however, a group of thirty Jews (including twelve children) that had formed on its own and hired a private smuggler reached Palestine undetected.

The phenomenon of "wildcat immigration," as we referred to it, was neither new nor widespread. It was resorted to by Jews who wanted to come to Palestine but had not heard about the Zionist underground, did not know how to get in touch with it, or were simply unwilling to wait their turn or defer to the movement's order of priorities (for example, by yielding the right-of-way to people who were being pursued by the authorities). As a result they sought—and had little trouble finding—police officers and government officials who were prepared to issue them passports and exit visas in return for generous remuneration. Neither was there a dearth of smugglers—especially the kind that was willing first of all to take their money and then either honor their commitments or not.

The demand for smugglers grew, along with the pace of "wildcat immigration," as it became increasingly evident that the Mossad's channels were sorely limited. In fact, not only did the exorbitant prices fail to deter those bent on fleeing Iraq, but more and more Jews now decided to risk going off with unknown smugglers on untested routes.

Still, the group of thirty that left in December 1947 was in a class by itself, both from the standpoint of its size—which was extraordinarily large for a "wildcat" operation—and because the smuggler was himself an Iraqi Jew by the name of Ezekiel Mashiah. I nodded knowingly at the mention of the name, for I had met Mashiah at the beginning of August 1947 after the Mossad received a strange message from Kibbutz Bet Ha'aravah,* on

* Not included in the Jewish state according to the UN Partition Plan, Bet Ha'aravah was abandoned just before the establishment of Israel and was completely destroyed by the Jordanians.

the northern shore of the Dead Sea. The kibbutz reported that a "suspicious" group of people who claimed to be immigrants had crossed the Jordan River and entered the settlement in broad daylight, without taking the least precaution. The kibbutzniks, who didn't know what to make of this unorthodox maneuver, politely detained their guests and asked us to enter the picture. I drove down to the kibbutz with Temima and could tell at first glance that this was indeed a group of bona fide immigrants from Iraq. And in reporting on the incident to the Mossad and to our people in Baghdad, I described Mashiah as follows:

He impresses me as being a man who knows his way around. . . . [But] I believe his work jeopardizes our ability to operate, because he isn't cautious. . . . Their journey was drawn-out because he had not coordinated on meeting places. They changed vehicles four times along the way and finally arrived in luxurious Jordanian taxis! He took 200 Palestinian pounds per person.

Despite his careless ways, I recommended that we hold a meeting with Mashiah to establish means of working together in the future. To the best of my knowledge, however, no such meeting ever took place. Even I let the matter drop, first because of my pique with the Mossad and then because I was busy with "Operation Michaelberg" and preparations for my trip to Lebanon. But now that I was back and heard Mashiah's name come up again, I was furious that he was still running his amateur operation while we had stalled into a state of paralysis. So furious, in fact, that I demanded an urgent meeting with the heads of the Mossad.

"Don't you think it's shameful that while we sit around nursing our qualms and pondering our options," I mocked, "a petty operator like Mashiah brings in a group of thirty people?"

"As usual, you're exaggerating," Moshe Carmil shot back in a rare display of anger. "You know we're doing everything we can."

"That's easy to say. But after I found a way to bring people in through Lebanon, you ordered me to hold off 'for now'—heaven knows how long that will be. And now I see the whole Iraqi operation has been put in abeyance. We might as well pack in the whole business and let everyone fend for himself!"

"The void we leave by not working, in a responsible and cautious manner, is being filled by private smugglers," Sammi added, "and that's certainly far more dangerous."

"Shammai," one of Moshe's defenders challenged, "are you really prepared to accept responsibility for endangering people's lives by sending

THE WINDS OF WAR 99

them across the desert now, when it's crawling with Mujaheddin† and units of the Arab armies training and deploying for attack? Haven't you seen the flood of reports about these concentrations? Do you have any idea what's likely to happen to anyone who falls into their hands? I'm not talking about arrests and trials now, or even about torture. Are you prepared to have that on your conscience?"

The question was certainly a valid one, but we also had to face the issue of whether we could stand aside and do nothing.

"It seems to me that the whole lesson of the war and the Holocaust in Europe is not whether we have the right to place people's lives in jeopardy, but whether we have the right *not* to take risks."

A thoughtful silence descended over the room as my colleagues suddenly became absorbed in the tips of their fingernails and their shoes.

"I don't think we have a choice," I finally broke the impasse. "The situation will only get worse, and unless we intend to give up altogether, we must do something."

No one argued about that. In fact, right after the meeting a wire went out to Baghdad ordering the resumption of "shipments" on condition that the groups be no more than fifteen people, all of them men armed with the appropriate weapons. But for all intents and purposes, that wire was the proverbial last gasp. No other groups were dispatched through the desert. A few days later, Jumah (who had been the backup driver of the truck that overturned in the desert and had also taken part in the October convoy) was arrested, along with some of his cohorts. They were caught hauling contraband sugar, but the police were quick to charge them with smuggling Jews, and it stood to reason that we would no longer be able to avail ourselves of their services. Even Ezekiel Mashiah went out of business. And worst of all, the last "wildcat" group led across the desert by a local Arab smuggler came to grief.

Perhaps the term "group" is something of an exaggeration, as it consisted of only two people, Avraham Kedoorie Alafi, a twenty-four-year-old bachelor, and Naji Yosef Menahem, a thirty-five-year-old family man. A few days after leaving Baghdad, the smuggler who took them arrived back at the Alafi home with a prayer shawl and phylacteries as supposed proof that Avraham had arrived at his destination safely and that the remainder of his fee was due. He claimed that he had brought the two men to the bridge that spans the Jordan at the foot of the Golan Heights. But at about the same time, we were informed by Haganah Intelligence that two Jews

† Volunteers from the Arab countries sent to fight in Palestine and encourage the local Arab population to perpetrate acts of terrorism as long as the British mandate remained in effect and the armies of the sovereign Arab states refrained from acting openly.

had been captured by Arabs while trying to cross the Jordan not far from Bet Ha'aravah. They told their captors that they had come to trade in sheep, but the claim was not very convincing, especially since they were found to be wearing four layers of clothing under their robes, including pants and pajamas. Alafi and Menahem were whisked off to Fawzi Kaukji's Jericho headquarters, and all trace of them was lost. A few weeks after the incident, an Iraqi officer associated with the Mujaheddin returned to Baghdad and called on the two families to extort money with promises that their loved ones would be safely deposited in Jewish hands. But that, unfortunately, was the end of the affair, and we could only assume that they had been killed by Kaukji's men. Like the great Moses, they were allowed to come within sight of the Promised Land but not to enter it, and no one knows the place of their burial to this day.

For all these reasons, it appeared that Razouk was our last and only hope of getting any more people through to Palestine. Razouk, an Assyrian who made his living by trucking cargo from Baghdad to Haifa and back, had been working for us for quite a while. This loyal and devoted man brought some boys along, hidden behind his cargo, on almost every trip to Palestine, and he was equally willing to take our emissaries back with him in the opposite direction. A few months earlier, Yunis had come up with an idea for streamlining our work by helping Razouk buy a new, larger trailer and building in a small hidden compartment capable of holding ten to twelve people in relative comfort. The task of building this compartment was assigned to a company in Tel Aviv and took longer than expected, so that it wasn't until mid-February 1948 that Razouk came for the express purpose of hooking it up. He entered the country over the only bridge that was still intact—the Allenby Bridge, near Bet Ha'aravah—and was hosted at the kibbutz while the truck was driven to Tel Aviv and found to be in such dreadful condition that its motor would have to be overhauled or replaced altogether. I was therefore sent to Bet Ha'aravah, via Jerusalem, to reach an understanding with Razouk about all the relevant details.

Such a trip was no longer a simple matter. Even we in the Mossad, who were completely immersed in the cause of immigration, could not fail to notice the still undeclared but very costly war that was raging all around us —already, without question, a war for survival. In December 1947 alone, the first month after the UN vote for partition, 216 Jews were killed in armed clashes or other forms of violence perpetrated by Arab irregulars, and 389 others were wounded—this out of a total Jewish population of 650,000. In January, while I was banging my fist on the table insisting that some way be found to bring another handful of people in from Iraq, the violence mounted and whole settlements found themselves under attack.

Intercity traffic was particularly vulnerable to assault, so that by the time I found myself bound for Jerusalem, on March 1, the vehicle I boarded looked more like a tank than a bus. Its sides and windows were covered with armor plating sliced at intervals with small chinks to accommodate the barrel of a gun, and its front pane was replaced by a sheet of steel, with only a narrow slit of window affording the driver a view of the road ahead. Upon arriving at the Tel Aviv bus station, I had met Moshe Carmil, who made it a habit of seeing us off on every journey, whether the destination was near or far. He came bearing a small paper bag with a few fresh rolls, a package of halvah, and some oranges.

"Moshe," I scolded him, "you're provisioning me as if I were embarking on the Exodus from Egypt! I'm headed for my sister's house in Jerusalem, and I'm sure she'll be thrilled at the opportunity to spoil me."

"These days, every trip is like the Exodus," Moshe fussed, pressing the bag on me. "Take it. You just might need it."

He turned out to be right, for we didn't make it to Jerusalem that day, and neither did we return to Tel Aviv. The bus made off for Kibbutz Hulda, the rallying point for the dozens of vehicles that made up convoys to Jerusalem: sealed buses, trucks laden with sacks of flour and other provisions to feed the beleaguered citizens of Jerusalem, and a number of pickup-type trucks that carried our armed escorts—Palmachniks in their distinctive stocking caps. About six miles from Hulda, however, a British officer stopped the convoy's lead vehicle and informed its driver that the road ahead was covered with obstacles and mines. Left with little choice, the entire convoy turned around and retraced its route to Hulda to try again the next day.

The following morning, after a very bad night's sleep on the bus's cold, bare seats, we repeated the ritual of orders and counterorders until the structure of the convoy met the inscrutable satisfaction of its commanders and we were ordered to move out. A short while later, the convoy drew to a halt, the door of our bus opened, and a stocking-capped head popped in to announce, "Ready the weapons." Within moments the bus's built-in cache was emptied, parts of Sten guns were produced from under skirts, magazines were fitted onto weapons, other pieces were loaded and cocked. Then the bus fell silent again until the motor started up and we resumed our journey by entering Bab al-Wad, the narrow pass that starts the ascent into the Judean Hills. Again we drew to a halt.

"The road is blocked," one of the passengers explained knowingly, though a few moments later we lurched forward again. And then it began —a deafening hail of gunfire that drowned out even the motors. The firing slits snapped open and the Sten guns spit out their fire in return. From the urgent cries outside, we understood that a vehicle had been hit and disabled. Above the din we now could hear the escorts shouting, "Drive around it. Keep moving!" Now we were at the focus of the ambush, and I could hear the dull tap of bullets hitting the bus's iron plating. Suddenly it was joined by frightened cries of "Help me!" and "I'm hit!" within the bus itself. Bullets were penetrating the unprotected roof and playing havoc with the passengers. Looking around anxiously, I noticed a young woman whose face was covered with blood. She was Leah Rakov, a vivacious Palmachnik of about eighteen with whom I had struck up a conversation the day before. By sheer coincidence, she, too, was going to Bet Ha'aravah, where her unit was stationed. Now she sat slumped over in her seat, mortally wounded. I sat there paralyzed, staring at her in shock until I felt a hand on my shoulder and heard a voice say, "Friend, are you prepared to help?"

I nodded distractedly, my eyes still glued on the girl.

"Do you prefer to shoot or tend to the wounded?"

"What?" I mumbled, suddenly aware that I would have to act, make a decision, opt to save or to kill.

"I'll shoot," I heard myself say decisively.

And so I did—with rage, with loathing, but most of all with frustration, for I knew that my shots were completely ineffective. The attackers were well hidden behind the boulders that dotted the hillsides enclosing the road, and I could barely see through the slit in the steel plating. Gradually the fire diminished until all we could hear were the motors and the anguish of the wounded as we climbed higher into the hills.

At the entrance to Jerusalem, the convoy stopped for the grim business of counting the toll. Leah Rakov was dead. Various others were wounded, including a rather cantankerous fellow who, just before we pulled out of Hulda, had insisted that I give him my seat on the grounds that he had gotten it first. I readily yielded it to him; one seat was as good as another, as far as I could see. But now, as I helped carry him out, I could not help thinking that fate works in strange ways, for had it not been for his obstinacy, he would be carrying *me* out on a stretcher now.

Next day, the trip to Bet Ha'aravah was far more peaceful, especially because I hitched a ride with one of the trucks going to the potash works on the Dead Sea. The company's stockholders were mostly British citizens, and in deference to their interests the mandatory government made a point of keeping the way to the Dead Sea safe. What's more, this was the only road to Jerusalem from the east, and the Arabs had an interest in keeping it open, because they used it too. In short, I reached Razouk with little trouble and brought him back to Jerusalem, where we joined another convoy to reach Tel Aviv. Naturally, I warned him that the trip might get a bit hairy. But our journey back was wholly uneventful—thanks to a Haganah action that had opened the road temporarily for our convoy to get through—and when I informed Razouk that we had reached Tel Aviv, he gave me a reproachful look and said, "Oh, Yusuf, you were just teasing me, trying to scare me!"

"No, Razouk," I said sadly. "I wish it were a joking matter."

The irony of the whole episode was that after literally risking our lives to reunite Razouk with his truck, when it came to deciding how to proceed, we found ourselves blocked yet again. Haganah Intelligence was flooding us with fresh information about the buildup of Arab forces— Mujaheddin and regular-army units—along the main roads in Transjordan and all along the river. Obviously every truck would be stopped and thoroughly searched along the way before reaching Palestine, while the passage over the border would effectively be impossible. And on the unlikely chance that a truck could get through, we would still have to get the immigrants from the Dead Sea to the coast, and under the present conditions even I had to admit that the prospect of getting them through was unrealistic. The most reasonable conclusion was therefore to keep the truck where it was and send Razouk home by plane. Even this last alternative for keeping a trickle of immigration going from Iraq was now closed to us. It was as if the last drops had been soaked up by the hard desert soil.

Nevertheless, as a sign of faith, on March 10 Sammi returned to Iraq to continue his work as coordinator of illegal immigration. (We solved the problem of papers for him by changing the picture on my passport, which now sported an array of stamps from Lebanon and Syria as well.) Back in Baghdad, he concentrated on refurbishing his connections with key people in the Border Police and officials at the airport. In the past we had managed to get some people out of the country on false or doctored passports. Reequipped with non-Jewish (usually Christian) names and new birth dates, they were joined together into new, wholly fictitious families that could travel on a single document. Naturally this method had its limitations, to say nothing of the fact that it was frightfully expensive, for it required bribes to a class of people whose rates were inordinately high. For that reason we usually saved it for particularly sensitive or urgent cases, such as people who were already being sought by the police. Now it seemed the only way to get anyone out.

Soon after Sammi's return, therefore, Iraqi immigrants began to filter in again, usually on Egyptian planes that made a stopover in Lydda. Yet their arrival at the airport was not yet the end of the journey or of the complications. The British were still running the airport and considered it their duty, even at this late date, to prevent any Jew from entering the country illegally. Neither was the drive to the airport, just outside Tel Aviv, a routine affair; there, too, we had to use armor-plated vehicles with armed escorts. And as if all that weren't enough, the need to dissemble up to the last sometimes presented problems of its own, for just as it would never have occurred to a Jew to travel to an Arab-populated area, it was equally illogical for an Iraqi Arab to be headed for Tel Aviv. So whenever a group (usually composed of two couples) was expected, I would be at the airport with an armored car, waiting to take the immigrants to their destination.

It was a labor of love, especially since many of the arrivals were leading members of the underground, and I was genuinely delighted to see them here on the threshold of freedom. Until they got out of the airport, however, it was still just the threshold, and more than once things went awry in a way that would have been amusing had we not had so much at stake. One of the first "shipments" at the end of March was composed of two couples who had been given strict instructions about what to say at Lydda. Yet apparently the heady sense of freedom that filled them when they stepped onto the soil of Palestine wiped those orders right out of their heads. Coming through passport control, they duly declared themselves to be Iraqi Christians. But when asked to state their destination in the country, they cheerfully replied: "Tel Aviv."

The British passport officer smiled tightly under his barbered mustache and patiently explained (in a heavy cockney accent they found difficult to understand) that surely they were unaware of the local situation: as Iraqis it was most unadvisable for them to go to Tel Aviv. Perhaps they would prefer Jaffa or Jerusalem?

"No, we must go to Tel Aviv," Giora, the group's spokesman, replied resolutely.

Soon the British officer was joined by a number of Arab clerks who tried to get through to the four visitors in a chorus in Arabic. "If you go to Tel Aviv," they warned darkly, "the Jews will slaughter you!"

But Giora would not be moved. "We want Tel Aviv," he insisted.

I stood nearby pretending to be engrossed in a newspaper but actually taking in every word of this mini-drama and becoming increasingly frantic with each protestation. I tried to signal the second couple, who glanced in my direction but seemed baffled by the mime I was performing off to the side. Meanwhile, Giora had become absolutely adamant about going to Tel Aviv when suddenly he paused and, I assumed, realized that he was working himself into a corner but didn't know how to get out of it. He couldn't agree to go to an Arab area any more than he could change his declaration and admit that he and the other members of the group were

Jews. There seemed to be no choice but to insist on having his own, wholly unreasonable, way.

To my surprise—and enormous relief—the British officer finally shrugged in capitulation, stamped the two passports, and let them move on. After all, he had done his best. How far was he expected to go to save the lives of these four Iraqis whose stubbornness was matched only by their stupidity?

So much for the first hurdle. As they exited the terminal, however, the two couples were assailed by a small mob of porters and taxi drivers, all of them Arabs. Fearing another disaster but equally afraid of destroying my own cover by approaching them openly, I dashed over to Shimon Levy—whose family owned the airport hotel and who was consequently in a position to move around freely—and appealed for help. There was no time to go into details like code names and messages. "Just get them out of sight for a while," I implored, and after nodding calmly Shimon approached the two couples with an intimidating swagger, pointed at them like a sergeant major, and barked in English: "You, follow me upstairs!"

Assuming that this gruff man was yet another British official, Giora tried to defend his little group by explaining, "We've already completed all the procedures."

"Come upstairs with me. Now!" Shimon snapped in a tone that put an end to further protest.

After ushering them into the airport restaurant, Shimon sat them down and, for lack of any other instructions, brusquely told them, "You may register at the airport hotel and remain here." But Giora just stuck to his old tune, repeating, "We want to go to Tel Aviv."

"You stay seated right here!" Shimon told him and then rushed back to me in a state of exasperation. "Your friends must be complete imbeciles!" he whined. "Whatever I say to them, they answer 'No!'"

I scribbled a note to Giora saying, "Welcome! Do what this man tells you," and signed it "Amo Yusuf." That did the trick. When Shimon brought it to the four newcomers—together with coffee and cake—they followed his instructions to the letter. A short while later, he led them through the kitchen, bundled them into the armored car (which I had brought around to the back), and gladly packed us off to Tel Aviv.

On another occasion, one of the immigrants was asked to carry a tube of shaving cream that contained our mail. When the young man entered the terminal and noticed me from a distance, he pulled the tube out of his hand luggage and began waving it in the air, shouting, "Amo Yusuf, Sammi asked me to give you this!" I tried to signal him to shut up, but he wouldn't take the hint. He just kept shouting excitedly, informing everyone in earshot that "Sammi said it's very important!" At that I simply made myself scarce—while I was still a free man—until he finally calmed down.

On the whole, however, these incidents were exceptions. Sammi briefed our people carefully, and all of them were schooled in the rigors of underground life. But even when one of these lapses occurred, the palpitations and drops of sweat that washed down me were promptly forgotten the instant I found myself sitting alongside the immigrants on our way to Tel Aviv. Listening to the latest news from Baghdad and receiving regards from friends, I could feel the sweet syrup of success ooze through me, and I would already be looking forward to the next "shipment."

But on April 22 even this last loophole was closed. We had to wire Baghdad:

TO: Berman
FROM: Artzi
The four reached Lydda safely. The road from Lydda to Tel Aviv is cut, and for the meantime they have remained there. . . .

Three days later we sent the following wire:

TO: Berman
FROM: Artzi
1. Lydda Airport temporarily abandoned by the Jews. In the coming days it is out of the question to pass through Lydda.
2. Stop sending people via Lydda until further notice.

No such notice was ever given. The key had turned one last time, locking the eastern gate for good. And all this had happened at a time when the prospects facing the Jews of Iraq were even bleaker than the outlook for Jews in other Arab lands. The harrowing *farhoud* was still fresh in their memories as the country buzzed with rumors of more of the same. Such rumors, moreover, were not easily discounted, for the Iraqi Government was caught in a particularly awkward position that did not augur well for the Jews.

Iraq had not known quiet and stability since the withdrawal of the Allied armies, in 1945. The country seemed torn between the extremes of Rashid Ali's pro-Nazi camp, which railed against any hint of British influence (to say nothing of Zionism and the Jews), and the aggressive Communist Party, which had been declared illegal and forced underground but still commanded considerable sway. It also gained the loyalty of a number of Jewish intellectuals who, especially in the wake of the *farhoud*, were attracted to its cosmopolitan ideology and shunned the Zionist solution to their plight. In fact, some of the leading ideologues and activists of the Iraqi Communist Party came from the ranks of these new converts.

The Communists were particularly adept at capitalizing on the double misery of rampant unemployment and hunger (made worse by successive years of drought) to make deep inroads among the country's students, industrial workers, and even civil servants. By 1947 they were able to get the masses out onto the streets in huge demonstrations and cripple the country by organizing strikes in the public services, focal industries, and most impressively of all in the large Iraq Petroleum Company. The government's attempts to break these strikes—inevitably leading to casualties —only fueled the flames.

The one point on which the ambitious Communists and frustrated pro-Nazis found common ground was their adamant and vocal opposition to Britain's special status in Iraq. A twenty-year treaty signed in 1930 (before Iraq was granted its full independence) accorded the British a preferred status in many spheres and was the basis for the creation of the Iraq Petroleum Company, an economic giant that was pumping out the country's wealth and had become an object of enormous resentment in Iraq.

Combined with this anti-British feeling, the postwar economic crisis inevitably left its mark on Iraq's political life. The national and local governments were riddled with corruption; tribal and sectarian clashes were commonplace; and governments rose and fell with astonishing frequency until, in a bid to ease the country's distress, the government of Saleh Jabr appealed to Britain for help. The British, though willing to comply, made their aid conditional upon the conclusion of a new Iraqi agreement to replace the one drawing to an end. There was nothing subtle about the way in which Whitehall maneuvered the Iraqis through every step of the process. They hosted the regent, the leading ministers, and even journalists as part of a softening-up process. But it wasn't until August 1947, after the main points of the treaty had been hammered out, that they began to free up the Iraqi currency reserves frozen in London so that their legal proprietors could finally use them to import food and other vital necessities. And it wasn't until November, when the details of the new treaty had been finalized, that their generous loans and other benefits went into effect.

By the end of November, "all was ready, it seemed, for the signature of a new Treaty," wrote the British historian Stephen Longrigg in his book *Iraq: 1900–1950*—all, that is, but the Iraqi public, whose mood was colored by the vigorous protests coming from left and right. Sensing the gathering storm, the government seized upon the United Nations decision to partition Palestine—the same decision that led to demonstrations and riots in Lebanon and Syria—as the ideal means of distracting the public's attention. It opened enlistment offices for the Mujaheddin—volunteers for the *jihad,* or holy war, against the Zionist infidels in Palestine—and saw to the establishment of the League for the Defense of Palestine as the leading propaganda and fund-raising organ, to which the threatened and intimidated Jews were forced to make generous contributions. But while inciting the public, on the one hand, Jabr's government took great care to forestall any kind of violent outburst against the Jews, for fear that once that genie was free, it could just as easily be turned against the regime.

Predictably, the Iraqi people closed ranks behind their government's courageous stand in taking the lead in the *jihad* and relegated the struggle against the new treaty with Britain to the back burner. Buoyed by this turnabout, at the end of December 1947, the Iraqi Government felt confident enough to go ahead with signing the new agreement. A delegation headed by Prime Minister Saleh Jabr departed for London to tie up loose ends, and on January 15, 1948, the new treaty between Iraq and Great Britain (known as the Portsmouth Treaty, after the venue of its signing) went into effect. For the politicians it was an occasion for celebration. Abdul Illah and King George VI exchanged exuberant cables of congratulation, while Jabr and his entourage—who felt entitled to a few days of rest after their great effort—extended their stay in Britain.

From that distance it was difficult for them to appreciate how far the mood had swung back home. When word of the terms and conclusion of the agreement got around, a storm of protest rocked Baghdad. Riding on the wave of pent-up anger, the Fascists and the Communists reestablished their control over the embittered masses. Once again the streets were filled with wild demonstrations that climaxed in bloody clashes with the police and claimed scores of lives and hundreds of injured. When the funerals of those felled by police bullets drew some hundred thousand people, a considerably sobered Jabr (who had returned to Baghdad to try to regain control) not only resigned but fled for his life. Soon "daring" new slogans and demands had found their way into the demonstrations, including the call for agrarian reform and the cry to release Kurdish political prisoners. Loudest of all, however, was the demand to punish those responsible for government corruption and the shameless capitulation to Britain.

The one way the authorities could see for coping with the explosion of fury was to transform it into the tried-and-true expedient of incitement against the Jews. Once again, the government began to play up the urgent need to save Palestine from the Zionists, planting its agents among the demonstrators against the Portsmouth Treaty to call out anti-Jewish slogans. After the police had opened fire at one such demonstration in Baghdad, killing and wounding many of the participants, someone cried out that Jews had shot into the crowd from Hakak's Emporium (Hakak being well known as a Jew). They instantly converged on the store, looting everything possible and destroying the rest.

Slowly the government that was formed after Saleh Jabr's resignation established control over the country. The regent announced that the Portsmouth Treaty would not be ratified unless far-reaching changes were made in it, and news of events in Palestine began to drive demonstrators into the streets demanding a war to salvage Arab honor. Bowing to "the will of the people," the government began to dispatch units of the Iraqi Army to the front with an orgy of emotional send-offs. For the present, the soldiers were being sent as far as Transjordan, where they were to wait along the Palestinian border until the British mandate officially ended, on May 15, 1948. However, about a thousand Mujaheddin were sent from Iraq directly to Palestine and placed under the command of Fawzi Kaukji, of the Arab Liberation Army.

Rather than sate the appetite of Iraq's inflamed citizenry, the departure of troops for Transjordan and Mujaheddin for Palestine sparked its imagination and encouraged demands for more vigorous action against the Zionists—which is precisely what the rulers in Baghdad had in mind. It wasn't long before these calls for action had turned into shrieks of "Kill the Jews!" The Portsmouth Treaty, the shortage of bread, the ubiquitous corruption in government, were never again mentioned at a demonstration.

The closer May 15 came the more frequent and troubling were the wires coming in from Baghdad. On May 5, we received the following report:

TO: Artzi
FROM: Berman
The past week has been filled with cases of incitement, incidents in which Jews have been attacked or accused of spreading poison. . . .
One of the injured died of his wounds today. The police have instituted searches and arrests among the Jews, as a result of which eleven Jews have been sent to a concentration camp. . . . They include teachers, lawyers, and the editorial staff of the Jewish newspaper *Barid al-Yom.* To the best of our knowledge, this is just one aspect of an extensive action. . . .

Even just hours before the proclamation of the State of Israel, our people in Baghdad remained somber. Their concern over the possible reaction in Iraq overshadowed everything else, as we could see from the cable sent on May 13:

TO: Artzi
FROM: Berman
The tension is similar to yesterday as fear reigns over all. The Jews will probably not go out to work on Friday, Saturday, and Sunday. Many Jews living in Arab neighborhoods have abandoned their homes and moved into the ghetto. We are taking precautions and trying to make contact with the community organization.

The most important news in that message was the attempt to open a dialogue with the official bodies of the Iraqi Jewish community. Until that point there had been no communication—to say nothing of cooperation—between the Jewish communal institutions and the Zionist underground in Iraq. Much to the contrary, the leaders of the Baghdad Jewish community chose to ignore the underground and treated the emissaries from Palestine as interlopers whose meddling was likely to bring disaster on everyone. The friction never reached the point of an open rift, and in a number of cities—particularly in the Kurdish area of northern Iraq—there was a close and fruitful relationship between the underground and the Jewish establishment. But in Baghdad and the south, no one could have imagined collaboration of any sort.

Now, however, in light of the unprecedented circumstances, the circle of hostility was broken. Haunted by memories of the *farhoud* and feeling the full weight of the responsibility they bore, the community's leaders agreed to recognize the underground and even meet with the emissaries from Palestine. The immediate result of this rapprochement was that on May 14, the day on which David Ben-Gurion was to proclaim the State of Israel, members of the Shurah (the armed self-defense organization of the Iraqi Zionist underground) were posted throughout the Jewish quarters in Iraq's main cities and a system of lookouts and guard duty was worked out. The Shurah also assembled a collection of primitive but effective weapons —a few revolvers and hand grenades, iron bars, knives, stones—in the event that it proved necessary to defend Jewish lives and property. For the first time since the *farhoud*, the Jews of Iraq could take heart in the knowledge that if rioters showed up again, this time they wouldn't have an easy time of it. It might well be that word of these preparations reached the potential rioters and dampened their enthusiasm. In any case, from then on the Zionist underground was a focal, if not the most influential, factor in the Iraqi Jewish community. From a handful of maligned youngsters, it was on its way to becoming the highest authority for the Jews of Baghdad and Iraq as a whole.

Friday, May 14, 1948, was a day fraught with rumors and tension in Iraq. As military convoys rumbled through the streets on their way westward, the country's Jews were understandably concerned about the fate of the nascent state that was the target of all this military might—and not just because they sensed that their own fate was inevitably bound up with it. On that warm spring afternoon, many of them closed their shutters against inquisitive eyes or descended to their cellars before huddling around their radio sets, toying with the dials, and straining to hear, over the whistles, sputters, and static, the broadcast from Tel Aviv. When the voice of David Ben-Gurion could be heard proclaiming the establishment of "a Jewish state in Palestine, the State of Israel," by the rivers of Babylon many of the House of Jacob sat down and wept yet again—for joy and out of fear; feeling privileged and feeling trapped. On that Friday evening, the Jews returned from synagogue early, speaking in muted tones, oppressed by a sense of dread. The next morning, we shared their deep disquiet when we read the following wire from Baghdad:

TO: Artzi
FROM: Berman
1. Martial law has been declared throughout the country.
2. It appears to be directed primarily against us and the Communists.
3. Yesterday and today a state of alert has been in effect in the police and the secret police. . . .
4. In response to the enormous tension and to information that has reached us from official sources, we declared a state of alert last night. Today all our people are in their positions. . . .

That same day, the Iraqi units camped in Transjordan crossed the border into Palestine, and Radio Baghdad exultantly informed its listeners that the great Iraqi Army had reached a point twelve kilometers from Tel Aviv, "conquering" Tulkarm, Nablus, and Jenin. The truth of the matter was that these cities and towns were in the sector of Palestine earmarked for an Arab state, and there was no "conquest," because there were no Jews living or stationed in the path of the Iraqi advance, so that there was no resistance. As a matter of fact, these troops were welcomed by the Arabs. Nevertheless, even though the Iraqis had yet to fire a shot, the very existence of a state of war with Israel was an ideal pretext for declaring martial law throughout Iraq. The government could now treat its opponents with a heavy hand and forgo even lip service to the rule of law. Before long, military courts were churning out judgments not open to appeal. Stringent censorship muzzled the press, strikes and demonstrations were prohibited, civil rights were suspended, and detention camps with a seemingly unlimited capacity were opened in southern Iraq.

With the courts no longer bound to honor standard judicial procedures —even for appearance' sake—any rumor or sliver of information or libel was enough to have a man arrested, interrogated, tortured, and held in protracted detention. Understandably, people were prepared to pay any price for their freedom, but the thriving commerce in bribes only whetted the appetite of the corrupt police to pull more and more people into custody. Neither did the payment of graft necessarily ensure one's release or exemption from punishment, and many a family was reduced to ruin while one of its members continued to languish in jail.

It goes without saying that the first to be affected by these draconian measures were the Jews, who immediately fell victim to mass arrests. Among the most infamous sources of "incriminating" evidence against them were the mail sacks generously provided by the British authorities. Until the end of the British mandate, standard postal ties existed between Palestine and Iraq, and families were able to maintain ongoing contact. But as their rule drew to an end, the British decided to delay and concentrate all the mail destined for Iraq in nine large sacks to be turned over directly to the Iraqi authorities. On May 20 we learned that these mail sacks had been passed on to the censor in the Defense Ministry, on the grounds that they contained proof of contact with the enemy during wartime—yet another pretext for arresting hundreds of people. The trials of these newest detainees dispensed with such bothersome details as evidence; that the accused had received letters from a country that had in the meantime become an enemy (because Iraq had violated the partition decision and declared war on it) proved their treason conclusively. Whenever names were mentioned in these letters, their bearers were added to the list of criminals. And since it seemed inconceivable that any Jew alive would write to another without asking after all his sisters and brothers, uncles and aunts, neighbors and friends, soon the prisons were jammed with dangerous "spies caught in the act" of maintaining ties with the enemy.

Perhaps the worst blow was that the new government formed early in the summer included Sadiq al-Bassam, a notorious pro-Nazi and anti-Semite, as Defense Minister. Bassam's appointment to the post during a period of martial law was rightly taken as a particularly ominous sign for the Jews. Indeed, immediately thereafter Iraq's criminal code was amended to place Zionism alongside communism as an outlawed political creed, so that anyone caught or accused of advocating or even condoning these wicked ideas stood to receive a long prison term with hard labor or, in extreme cases, even the death sentence. The Jews of Iraq were horrified, for experience had taught them that in their neighbors' eyes the line between Judaism and Zionism was fuzzy, at best, and would be especially so in a state of martial law with a man like Bassam setting the tone.

As if to confirm that the worst fears were no exaggeration, one of the prisoners hauled in under the new law was Shafiq Addas, an assimilated Jew *par excellence* who had never evinced the least interest in Zionism. Addas was known as an inordinately successful businessman who boasted Arab partners and close connections with the upper crust of Iraqi officialdom. Word had it that even the regent frequented Addas's home whenever he came to Basra. On occasion the press had carried items implying that Addas was a Zionist, a Communist, or both, but the charges were so preposterous that no one took them seriously. Even after his arrest, most people assumed that he was a victim of mistaken identity or some other fleeting misunderstanding. But even though he was flagrantly miscast in the role, Addas was chosen as the object of the first show trial to follow from the law that made Zionism and communism equally heinous as criminal offenses.

Brought to trial, Addas was charged with funding subversive Communist activities, organizing Communist demonstrations, and devoting the rest of his time to hatching a villainous Zionist plot and smuggling arms to the "Zionist gangs" (a popular epithet for the Jewish underground in Palestine). Witnesses for the prosecution—more than twenty in number—described the accused's exploits in a manner that put Sheherazade to shame. But when it came time for the defense to call its witnesses, the president of the military court announced that, as far as he could see, it was an open-and-shut case, so that it was unnecessary to waste the court's time with additional testimony. Addas's lawyers, among the most renowned in Iraq, promptly resigned in protest, making it all the easier to summarily convict him.

At the end of three sessions, the court did precisely that. Addas was found guilty of all the charges against him and was sentenced to death by hanging. The regent himself confirmed the sentence, and at dawn on September 23 the hapless Addas was executed on the gallows erected right in front of his home in Basra. Thousands streamed to the posh quarter to witness and celebrate the hanging in song and dance and with whoops of joy. One report added the particularly macabre detail that after Addas had been pronounced dead and was removed from the gallows, it was necessary to string his corpse up again to quell the chorus of protest from the crowd that had not had its fill of the gruesome sight. One chant kept on demanding that the body be fastened to a jeep and dragged through the streets of Basra, but the district governor drew the line there. (Ten years later, by the way, no similar defense was found for the king of Iraq and his uncle, the regent, who had confirmed Addas's sentence. In the midst of the revolution of July 14, 1958, their bodies were dragged through the streets of Baghdad as the city rang with exultation.)

The trial and execution of Shafiq Addas marked the climax of that particular wave of persecution against the Jews of Iraq. The whole affair had been handled so crudely that it left many Iraqis with the unsettling feeling that things had gone too far. In any event, four days after the hanging, Defense Minister Bassam was forced to resign. But although his departure softened the government's style somewhat, it did not change the essential situation. Martial law remained in effect; the amendment to the criminal code was not rescinded; the arrests, torture, and extortion not only continued but were stepped up again once the Army's setbacks in Palestine became public knowledge.

On another level, Shafiq Addas's trial became something of a turning point in the history of the Iraqi Jewish community, much as the Dreyfus trial had left an indelible mark on Jewish life in Europe. Even the particulars were alike: the choice of a Jewish scapegoat for a humiliating military defeat; the flagrant abuse of judicial norms; and, above all, the cries of an incited public demanding "Death to the Jews," while the ostensibly enlightened press did its best to keep the caldron at a boil.

Little wonder, then, that the Addas trial—and all the other tribulations that befell the Jews of Iraq in 1948–49—contributed to a growing identification with Zionism even among the class of intellectuals who had tended to blend into their surroundings and regard themselves as Iraqis in every way. Now even they were forced to admit that hostility toward Jews was not restricted to the poor, the ignorant, or to groups on the fringes of society. It had taken hold at the very heart of Iraqi life. "Shafiq Addas represents all the Jews of Iraq," one of these disabused intellectuals observed at the time, "so that the blow the government has brought down on him is a blow to us all."

The effects of that blow set the stage for my own odyssey to the East and the bold turn of events in the pages to come.

SIX

A Parisian Interlude

ON THE MORNING of May 14, 1948, the day on which the State of Israel came into being and one day before martial law was declared in Iraq, I quit the Mossad for the second time and informed Moshe Carmil that I was going to join a combat unit.

"You know I enlisted back in February," I reminded him, "but each time I get ready to leave, you pull another stunt to keep me in the Mossad. We're really at war now, and there's no point in staying on."

"Why not?" Moshe asked, as if I had just uttered a heresy.

"Because I'm not doing any *good* here," I whined, "and the Army needs people!"

"And what do you propose we do about our work in the Arab countries?" he went on. "Just forget it? Leave our emissaries to rot there?"

When I failed to reply, he put me off yet again.

"We'll talk about it some more, perhaps at the beginning of next week," he said, leaving me hanging. But then, seeing my look of annoyance, he added in explanation, "It may be a long conversation, and there's no time for that today. I've got to get to Tel Aviv Museum, where Ben-Gurion is going to proclaim the establishment of the state. And while we're on the subject, I suggest you come along. It won't hurt you to hear BG."

"I'll pass, if you don't mind," I begged off grumpily. "I'm not in the mood for proclamations and ceremonies right now." And while I didn't exactly stalk out, I did return directly to the kibbutz—and to this day have not forgiven myself for turning down the opportunity to say, "I was there" when the State of Israel was officially proclaimed.

But that is said with hindsight. On May 14—and those days in general— the prevailing mood was not exactly festive. Our excitement over the prospect of independence was tempered by sadness and no little anxiety. That morning, for example, we received the terrible news that the Etzion Bloc, five kibbutzim situated halfway between Jerusalem and Hebron, had fallen to Transjordan's army, the Arab Legion. Its defenders had put up a desperate battle that cost the lives of close to half its adult population, with the surviving 260 people taken off to Jordan as prisoners of war. We had also learned that Kibbutz Bet Ha'aravah, north of the Dead Sea—the way station for our immigrants from Iraq that was better known as an extraordinary attempt to turn an arid area with salty soil into a blossoming oasis— had been abandoned by order of the Haganah so that its inhabitants would not suffer a similar fate. The road to Jerusalem was completely blocked, leaving the city under siege. Worse yet, since the previous day, when the British high commissioner had left the city as the mandate drew to a close, Jerusalem had been subject to incessant shelling by the Arab Legion.

The State of Israel, on the other hand, did not have a single piece of bona fide artillery, for up until that point we had been under the mandatory administration, which had actively prevented us from deploying for self-defense. We were able to prepare some weapons and ammunition in the underground, but only small arms, not cannons, tanks, or fighter planes (though it must be said that by utilizing our "Michaelberg" technique, over the previous months the Haganah had managed to bring in some medium-sized weapons such as machine guns and mortars).

We had no illusions that once the British mandate formally ended, at midnight on May 14, we would be facing a massive attack from the thoroughly equipped regular armies of the surrounding Arab states. The Transjordanian Arab Legion, which was under British command and was deployed inside Palestine as part of the British garrison, was officially instructed to leave the country with the rest of the British forces. However, some of its soldiers failed to leave—or rather, managed to remain— and those who did go returned within hours, redeployed in many of their previous positions, and began fighting on familiar terrain. Even the Egyptians managed to deploy in a few strategic positions prior to the departure of the British forces on May 15.

To the Egyptians' credit, it must be said that, out of fidelity to the accepted "rules of conduct," they at least took the trouble to declare war on us. The UN archives contain a cable dated May 15, 1948, sent by Egyptian Foreign Minister Ahmed Khashaba Pasha to the president of the Security Council formally announcing: "Egyptian armed forces have started to enter Palestine to establish security and order in place of chaos and disorder which prevailed and which rendered the country at the mercy of Zionist terrorist gangs who persisted in attacking the peaceful Arab inhabitants, with arms and equipments [sic] amassed by them. . . ." The other attacking countries—Syria, Transjordan, Iraq, and Lebanon— did not even bother officially to declare war on us, though in coordination with Egypt they certainly mounted an overt assault against the State of Israel as it was being born.

It's hardly surprising that most of the world's military experts—including the British chief of staff, Field Marshal Montgomery (the famed "Monty," remembered for his valorous stand in repulsing the German army in North Africa during World War II)—assessed that Israel, with a total population of 650,000 people and months of costly warfare already behind it, did not stand a chance against the blitzkrieg of the five regular armies about to enter the fray fresh and full of vigor. In fact, the consensus was that the boast of the Arab chiefs of staff that they would meet in Tel Aviv within two weeks was a highly plausible one. Even President Truman, a staunch supporter of establishing a Jewish state, was influenced by the pessimistic outlook of the experts, for he counseled the leadership of the Jewish community in Palestine to refrain from proclaiming the state and to ask for an extension of the mandate instead.

In Palestine, too, there were people who believed that opting for political independence under such conditions was an ill-calculated risk, and it was only at Ben-Gurion's insistence that the state came into being when it did. He sensed that any postponement might mean forfeiting the historic opportunity that the Jews had dreamed of for two millennia. He was also confident that the motivation of the small Jewish community and its fighters would enable them to overcome the awesome odds—albeit at a heavy toll in lives. Still, in such a small community, where almost everyone seemed to know each other and the number of dead and wounded was considerable even before the outbreak of fighting with the Arab armies, everyone was touched by a feeling of sadness and great concern about what the future held.

That, more or less, was the atmosphere on May 14. In preparation for my next meeting with Moshe Carmil, which I assumed was going to be a fateful and final one, I began to write a memo summing up the subject that I had been handling and warning about for months. While my colleagues seemed geared up to celebrate the conclusion of the Mossad's operations (after all, we were now a sovereign state, so there was no longer any need to smuggle immigrants into the country), I was feeling more anxious and frustrated than ever. Back in March, I had submitted a detailed memorandum to the Mossad on "The Dilemma of the Jews in the Arab Lands," noting:

[When we] reach political independence, the problem of immigration from the European Diaspora will be solved. But the same cannot be said of the situation in the Oriental countries; the fate of the Jews there will only grow worse from day to day. And . . . the only possibility of emigrating from these countries will be by clandestine means.

Now that we had our independence and there was a general feeling that it had settled the problem of immigration from the Diaspora, I felt obliged not to allow the fate of Jews in Arab lands to be overlooked. So I picked up the thread of that earlier memo and analyzed the present situation:

Now that the Arab armies have overtly joined the war . . . I wish to turn your attention to the situation of the Jews in [the Arab] countries. On a variety of occasions, representatives of the Arab states have declared that they will retaliate against the Jews living in their countries if a Jewish state comes into being.* The reports of attacks . . . arrests, and the like over the past few days heighten the probability of retaliation, and we must assume that if we succeed in routing the invading armies, that probability will become a certainty.

For this reason it is imperative, as I see it, to treat the predicament faced by these Jews as one sector of our overall front. The Arabs lump them into the same category with us, and ignoring that fact won't make their lot any easier.

I couldn't imagine how to present the case any more strongly than to place the fate of Iraqi Jewry on an equal footing with our own war for

* For example, Heichal Pasha, Egypt's representative at the United Nations, warned that if the organization approved the partition proposal, "it might be responsible for very grave disorders and for the massacre of a large number of Jews. . . . Riots would spread through all the Arab States and might lead to a war between the two races. . . . The proposed solution might endanger a million Jews living in the Moslem countries." Iraq's representative, Fadhil Jamali, was more subtle and discriminating in his choice of words—warning that partition would "breed interreligious prejudice and hatred" in Iraq and "produce more chaos and disorder, not only in Palestine but all around it"—yet the threat implied in this message was the same.

survival. But, a few days later, as I was waiting for this latest memo to be typed, an air-raid siren began to wail, followed by the deep rumble of what I assumed were again Egyptian planes. (They had already bombed Tel Aviv a day or two earlier.) This time their target was the ever crowded central bus station, a few blocks away from our office. Later we learned that some fifty people had been killed and dozens of others injured in that raid. Yet even before the depressing statistics were known, as I watched the cars speeding wildly through the streets to deliver casualties to the city's hospitals, I felt the pendulum of my mood swing sharply again. I had played the waiting game long enough. After placing that memo on Moshe's desk, I would simply march out and join a combat unit forthwith.

Moshe outmaneuvered me again. After reading my analysis, he summoned me urgently to his office and handed me a sheaf of papers, mostly wires that had come in from Iraq over the past few days. I knew what they contained. I had followed the reports of fear and incitement, of wild accusations about Jews poisoning wells and rivers, and of the arbitrary arrests and incarcerations in a concentration camp. Recalling that it was Moshe's wont to emulate the barber who greeted his customers with a harrowing tale of murder and mayhem because it's easier to shave a man when his hair is standing on end, I assumed that this latest "softening up" meant he had a specific proposal to make. And I had a feeling I knew exactly what it was, too.

"Is it that you want me to go to Baghdad?" I said, more weary than angry by then. "What's the point of it, Moshe? What can I contribute there now?"

"We won't know that until you get there," he replied gently, trying to keep the conversation low-key. But seeing my disgruntled look, he took another tack. "Let me show you some interesting analyses I've read recently." As he drew some papers out of a file and began to leaf through them, I realized that they were the memos I myself had written.

"Here's a pertinent point," Moshe began to quote: " 'Even at the height of the war [meaning World War II], we tried to show our support for our brethren [in Europe]. Many of our comrades gave their lives for that cause, even though we knew all along that the chances of rescuing anyone were practically nil. . . . The fact that we already have people working [in Iraq] places a great responsibility upon us.' Shall I go on?" he asked.

I answered him with silence, my eyes averted.

"You won't forgive yourself if you don't go," I heard him say in a hoarse, sad voice. "None of us will forgive ourselves."

Those words hit a sensitive nerve, and Moshe knew it. The doubts about whether we couldn't have saved more people from the Nazis continued to gnaw away at all of us. And now there was this new crisis.

"How long do you want me to go for this time?" I asked, resigned to what had to be.

"I don't think it will be for very long," he soothed me. "Meet with the key people, exchange ideas, and work out a plan of action. In the meantime, we'll look for replacements for the emissaries there. You yourself suggested recruiting them among the immigrants who have come from Iraq, and it sounds like a good idea. Any other practical suggestions are more than welcome."

"That's all well and good," I told him sourly, "but it doesn't solve the problem of getting Jews out. If we can't find ways to save them quickly—even just a few of them at first—all the emissaries in China won't help. The whole operation will wither and die."

Moshe did not dispute the point. "Well, you've listed all the things that should be looked into," he said, moving a pencil over my memo on the subject. "I accept your suggestion that we return to getting people out by air, on special passports, and I'm prepared to investigate the possibility of renewing the 'Michaelberg' flights. As to getting through by boat from Basra, I must tell you frankly that it doesn't sound very practical to me. But I'm willing to check it. Now that immigration from Europe is perfectly legal, the people who have been working with us there will be only too glad to continue collecting the fees they've grown accustomed to getting from us. So if you want to keep thinking about it, that's fine. No one ever died of thinking. But first pack your suitcase."

A few days later I was able to tell Moshe that I had found a traveling companion who would remain in Baghdad after my return. Ya'akov Sitton, a member of my kibbutz who was a native of Syria and could therefore construct a reasonable cover, had volunteered to go to Baghdad with me. And to my great surprise, his offer received the enthusiastic support of the entire kibbutz. At the general meeting devoted to the subject, one of our members argued heatedly that the kibbutz could not just "abandon" me to the clutches of the Mossad forever, and clearly Carmil and company would not leave me in peace until someone was found to fill my shoes. Hence she proposed that Ya'akov be my replacement, and her point was well taken.

From then on the problems we faced were technical—above all, how to get to Baghdad. Obviously there was no longer any overland route to Iraq; neither could we fly directly from Tel Aviv to Baghdad. In fact, it was difficult to fly from Tel Aviv anywhere. Our sole air link with the rest of the world was through Sde Dov, a small airfield just north of Tel Aviv that was visited erratically by planes coming from Europe. There were no such things as scheduled flights, and certainly no flights to any of the Arab countries.

Considering that obstacle, our only choice was to reach Europe and try to get to Baghdad from there. But, for that purpose, we would need suitable passports and visas for each leg of the journey, and they were not readily obtained by the citizens of our young state. Moshe did his best to speed things up, but the fact is that everything in Israel was operating according to different priorities—and understandably so, since we were in the midst of a full-scale war. So, my distaste for delays notwithstanding, though I was resigned to going off once more, leaving the kibbutz, the family, and Temima, I found myself stalled again—much longer, in fact, than the last time. It wasn't until June 29, 1948, that, bearing well-worn and newly doctored Iraqi passports, Ya'akov and I left for France on a chartered plane. (No regular airline was prepared to fly to Israel then, because of the perilous situation, and El Al, Israel's national airline, did not yet exist.) During our stopover in Rome, when the pilot came across an opportunity to make a more lucrative flight, he hadn't the least compunction about abandoning us—at least for a while. But since we didn't have entry visas for Italy, we were forced to grit our teeth and settle into the airport lounge until the plane returned the next day.

Upon arriving at our destination, we were hungry and grumpy as bears. But our first sight of Paris changed all that. Paris was beguiling to two young men passing through on their way from one war of survival to another. The city's beauty and grace, the sense of stability, of balance, of sheer normalcy, in contrast to the stridency and strife that had framed our lives for close to a decade, was almost startling. Both of us felt an enormous, giddying sense of release, and in retaliation for the night spent stewing in the airport, we checked into a posh hotel, had dinner in its luxurious dining room, and took up every one of the waiter's suggestions: white wine, red wine, three full courses plus dessert and coffee—all exquisitely pleasing to the palate after almost two days of enforced fast.

The next day we had a rude awakening when we realized that we had polished off a whole week's allowance in a single night. In any case, wining and dining on that scale was considered an aberration by Ya'akov, who was a man of labor and principle, ramrod straight, and who reverted to character first thing the next morning. This was Ya'akov's first trip abroad, and even at home he rarely spent time outside the kibbutz. In essence, he had shot straight from our little collective outside Rehovot onto the streets of Paris, and evidently he believed that the same norms applied in both. That morning, he rose early, as usual, then washed, dressed, and made his bed just as fastidiously as he did at home. When I awoke and saw his handiwork, I credited it to innocence, or at least ignorance of the ground rules, and thought I would spare him the bother again.

"Ya'akov, in a hotel you don't have to make your bed," I said softly so as not to get his dander up. "There are chambermaids to take care of that."

"I don't need anyone to make my bed for me," he replied stubbornly.

"But no one makes his bed in a hotel!"

"For me it's a matter of principle!" he retorted starchily. "I will not have servants doing things I can perfectly well do myself!"

I was not about to fight with him, so I got out of bed and made for the bathroom, though not before dropping the casual comment, "Have it your own way. When the chambermaid arrives and sees your bed is made, she'll undoubtedly conclude that we spent the night in the same bed."

When I emerged from the bathroom, Ya'akov's bed was a wild scramble of sheets and blankets. Evidently the puritan had gotten the better of the egalitarian in him.

After relocating to more modest accommodations, as befit the emissaries of a poor nation, we reported to the Mossad's offices in the Passage de Lido, close to the famed cabaret. The Passage and nearby Champs-Élysées thronged with people of every color, making the area an ideal location for the Mossad's headquarters. The office itself was a hive of frenetic activity: typewriters clattered away in the background while phone conversations went on with the capitals of Europe and mysterious destinations in the United States—all in a Babel of languages peppered with code words like "knives" (for Messerschmitts), "nails" (for ordinary bullets), and the like. The object of all this hubbub was to acquire arms and get them to Israel. It seemed as though all the resources of the Mossad for Illegal Immigration —its ramified connections with shady shipping companies, greedy captains, and police officers whose palms and pockets were open to "suggestion," as well as with simply good-hearted people who were prepared to lend a hand—had been shifted over to the task of acquiring arms. That was an especially pressing problem, because the United States, like most of the rest of the world—with the prominent exception of Czechoslovakia—had imposed an embargo on weapons to the Middle East. Essentially, however, it affected Israel alone, as our army had just come up from underground, while the Arab countries had certainly had ample time to prepare for their assault. Yet contrary to the expectation that once the state was in existence there would no longer be any need for illegal immigration from Europe, it turned out that one of the terms of the cease-fire imposed by the UN in July was a prohibition on allowing young people to enter the country, lest the ostensible "balance of forces" be upset. Hence anyone of draft age who wished to come to Israel—a description that applied to thousands of refugees—had to resort to the tried-and-true methods and services of the Mossad for Illegal Immigration.

Just competing for the attention of the people running this show was a daunting prospect. Ya'akov and I were greeted cordially, of course, but then immediately given to understand that, as priorities went, our mission did not exactly head the list. The bureau was run by Oscar, whom I had never met before, and had I not known for a fact that I was in the office of the Mossad for Illegal Immigration, I would never have suspected that this man sitting opposite me was involved in anything in the least way illegal or clandestine. Smartly dressed, with his thinning hair fastidiously combed, Oscar looked more like someone you would expect to encounter in White-hall or Wall Street. Only the heavy bags under his eyes, betraying a combi-nation of sadness and sheer exhaustion, conveyed the feeling that his re-sponsibilities weighed heavily on him.

I assured Oscar that we would take a minimum of his time; all he had to do was get us to Baghdad quickly. Our passports, I knew, were a complica-tion, because they attested that their bearers had visited Palestine—an "enemy country" since May 15. And with martial law in effect, anyone entering Iraq with such credentials was liable to fall directly into the hands of the secret police. Originally we had intended to land at Basra, where the underground had a "solid understanding" with one of the officers at passport control. But before we left Israel, the Mossad received an urgent wire warning us that landing at Basra "will lead to disaster," whereas "We have reached an agreement to have Shammai land at Baghdad airport . . . [though] the officer does not agree to take the risk of having two people land."

That left us with the problem of getting Ya'akov in. Nevertheless, on the assumption that we would work that difficulty out somehow, I asked Oscar to arrange for us both to fly to Baghdad.

"On one condition," he said emphatically. "No stopover in any Arab country. I suppose I can trust your special arrangements for getting into Iraq, but with those passports, a stopover in any other Arab country will be your downfall."

Conceding the logic of his argument, I agreed—only to discover, a day or two later, that none of the flights to Iraq met his condition.

"What about going through Iran?" I asked him after making that discov-ery.

Oscar looked confused. "Is there a flight to Baghdad with a stopover in Iran?" he asked.

"In a manner of speaking," I said sarcastically. "What I meant was, how about flying to Iran and stealing over the border from there?"

"The point being?"

"The point being that Iran is not an Arab state and is not at war with us. Does that route meet your condition?"

Now he looked nonplussed. "What do you think?" he asked.

I really wasn't sure. Iran was pretty much *terra incognita* in terms of our complicated political situation. Though not an Arab state, it was a Muslim country, and I, for one, didn't know which side it was on. Yet from the little I did know, I tended to assume that the Palestinian stamps in our Iraqi passports would not present any special problem.

In any case, Oscar suggested that we pay a visit to the Iranian consulate and try to obtain entry visas. We promptly did so and came up against the standard Iranian foot-dragging that I would later come to know so well. If an Iranian gives you a polite smile and tells you, "We'll do our best. Come back tomorrow," it's a sure sign that your cause—whatever it may be—is quite hopeless. Today I know that I was right about the Palestinian stamps in our passports not disturbing the Iranians; the problem was the passports themselves. Considering the strained relations that traditionally obtained between Iran and Iraq (much the same for centuries as they are today), it was hardly surprising that the polite reply we received was merely an evasion. But we were still innocent of such matters and left the consulate buoyant, never suspecting that weeks would pass before we would realize that we never had a chance of getting those visas.

When we finally did get the picture, I approached Oscar and asked him to relent about the stopover, but he wouldn't budge. Then I demanded that at least he procure other passports for us, and he assured me that he would do his best. I was also assured that people were still working behind the scenes to obtain the cooperation of the Iranian consul, so that there was no need to be "so upset."

That was easy to say, but frustration was eating away at me. I felt like a fifth wheel on the heavily taxed wagon of the Mossad and began to ask myself whether I wouldn't be better off returning home, where I might at least do some good as a soldier. While trying to make myself useful in the office, I picked up snatches of conversations and glanced over the files of the Berichah, the illegal but persistent movement of Jewish survivors of the death camps, without papers or means, across the face of Europe to the boats waiting to take them to Israel. The tales buried in those files not only renewed my faith in the power of the human spirit but set me thinking whether we couldn't organize a similar flight from Iraq via an intermediate country.

A glance at the atlas sufficed to show what I already knew: that the notion was not very promising. Iraq was surrounded by other Muslim countries: Syria, Jordan, Saudi Arabia, and Kuwait to the west and the south; Turkey to the north; and Iran to the east. The latter two, Turkey and Iran, were at least not Arab states. But Turkey was an unlikely route of escape, because its border with Iraq passed through forbidding mountain terrain. Besides, it lay far from the centers of Jewish population in Iraq, which meant we would have to organize a trek across the country, and under conditions of martial law, that was out of the question.

That left Iran—to which all roads seemed to be leading—and a very different kind of border. It begins in the mountainous region of Kurdistan, in the North, but the farther south you go, the more the topography becomes level and negotiable, until the land border gives way to the frontier running down the middle of the Shatt-al-Arab, the broad channel created by the confluence of the Tigris and the Euphrates. It was over this section of the border that contraband had found its way from time immemorial. Even I had once crossed illegally from Iraq to Iran and back again —during my days as an emissary in Iraq—and I assumed that, since barely a year had passed since then, the system was still the same.

I hardly had to strain my memory to remember the details: I had been led from Basra to a shallow, palm-covered cove where a smuggler who worked the waterway had his "headquarters." He ran his operation like a nonscheduled ferry. Whenever a few "passengers" had gathered in his palm grove, performed the mandatory bargaining ritual, and made their payment, the smuggler pulled a tin boat out of its hiding place among the palms, invited his passenger in, and proceeded to row across the channel to the shah's realm. On my trip across, the strong current carried us well downstream, and I recalled—with no particular pleasure—stories about the sharks that were rumored to roam this sector of the waterway. More than once I had noticed someone in Basra with an arm or a foot missing and remembered the whispered explanation: "Shark."

We, however, were destined for a different fate. Halfway across the channel, we were spotted by an Iranian police boat, which came speeding at us with its siren emitting an indignant howl. With the last of his strength, our smuggler rowed us almost as far as the opposite bank, and all the other passengers—who seemed to be veterans at this game—folded up the hems of their caftans, jumped out of the boat, and took off at a run. Naturally I followed suit, but to no avail. The police caught up with us all,

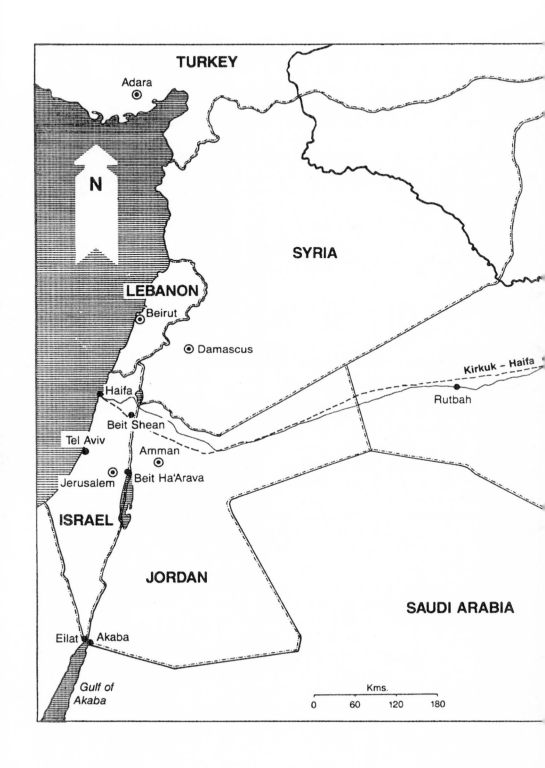

TURKEY

Adara
⊙

N

SYRIA

LEBANON

⊙ Beirut

⊙ Damascus

Kirkuk – Haifa

Haifa

Beit Shean

Rutbah

Tel Aviv

Amman
⊙

Jerusalem ⊙

Beit Ha'Arava

ISRAEL

JORDAN

SAUDI ARABIA

Eilat

Akaba

Gulf of
Akaba

Kms.

0   60   120   180

Ayn Diwar

Mosul

Kirkuk

r. Tigris

Khanagin

Qasr–e Shirin

Kermanshah

Hamadan

Qazvine

Teheran⊚

IRAN

Ba'qubah

pipeline

r. Euphrates

Baghdad

Ramadi

Karbala

IRAQ

Ahwaz

Shatt al-Arab

Basra

Khorramshar

Abadan

Persian Gulf

KUWAIT

deciding (no doubt because of the conspicuous difference in my dress) that I was the choice catch in the group and promptly placing me under arrest.

Under different circumstances I would probably have been faint with fear. But I knew that the border was so porous here because the local police were of a particularly venal variety. Since I was ignorant of the Persian language, it took a while for me to make myself understood. Soon enough, however, through a combination of hand and facial gestures and by simply shrugging my shoulders, I managed to communicate that I had nothing more to offer than the sum to be found in one of my pockets. The policemen relieved me of it and let me go. The return trip, made a few days later, was quite uneventful, leading me to the conclusion that crossing the river border illegally was practically a pedestrian affair.

Thinking back on it, I also recalled my surprise at finding that in Muslim Iran the Jews were in no way subjected to persecution—and certainly they were not living in terror. Zionist activities and the study of Hebrew were perfectly legal pursuits. After my long stay in the Iraqi underground, I felt high on the freedom. I could walk the streets of Abadan and Khorramshahr without looking over my shoulder. I could speak Hebrew with my companions out in the open in a normal tone of voice. We even sang Hebrew songs right out there in the street!

As all these details came back to me now in Paris, I suddenly realized that our problem was that we had been thinking backward. We had always regarded Iraq as a way station for people coming to Palestine from Iran, rather than the opposite, for the simple reason that Iraq was geographically closer to Palestine. Now we had to reverse our perfectly logical thinking and get it through our heads that if we could get Jews over the border in the opposite direction, even if they were stuck in Iran for a while, they would still be halfway to salvation—or at least out of immediate danger.

Inordinately pleased with myself, I took my thinking straight to Yosef Barpal, who happened to be in Paris. I was eager to win his approval because of Barpal's special standing in the Mossad. He was much older than the rest of us—well over fifty at the time—and we tended to think of him as the "grand old man" of the Mossad. When I presented my idea, at first he didn't respond at all. I tried to read his reaction from the expression on his face, but as he peered at me through his thick glasses set in heavy dark frames, his eyes did not betray a thing. One of his hands slid over his bald pate as if he were trying to slick down a patch of fly-away hair, while the other turned a fountain pen round and round as he considered the notion. Finally he remarked in a deep, fatherly voice, "Well, Shammai, that's a fine idea. You can take it up with the comrades when you reach Baghdad."

"I can see that you're not very impressed," I pouted, "and maybe it isn't the ideal solution. But what other way is there? The desert route is closed. We're not getting anywhere by air or by sea. So what else is left? Why is the Berichah possible from Europe and not from Iraq?"

"Because Iraq doesn't have neighbors like Holland and Denmark," he said a bit snappishly—and then thought better of his tone. "Look, Shammai, you're an enterprising young man, and that's fine," he resumed patronizingly. "I admire your work and appreciate that you come in every day with new ideas and fresh demands. But don't go around carrying the world on your shoulders. You're willing to go to Iraq, and that's a lot. Quite a lot. Your very presence will encourage our people there, and that's important for morale, regardless of how many Jews you manage to smuggle out. There are times when the most important thing is just to hold out and not lose heart."

But I had more ambitious designs, and I left Barpal's room simmering with resentment. I tried to raise the idea before other people in the office, but the most I got was a bemused smile or perfunctory nod before they plunged back into their own affairs. Eventually I dropped the subject, tired of being the office nag and beating a dead horse. Until I met the abbé again.

I had first met Abbé Alexander Glasberg in Palestine at the beginning of 1948, when Moshe Carmil asked me to take him around. Moshe explained that he was a French priest who had done much for the cause of "illegal" immigration, especially during the affair of the *Exodus 1947*. I had heard the two of them speaking Russian, so I assumed that the abbé was fluent in many languages, and as I led him to the car I asked in my halting French whether he spoke English.

"No," he replied, "I don't speak it, and I don't like the language. But we can talk in Yiddish."

"Don't know a word of it," I reciprocated.

"How come a Jew doesn't speak Yiddish?"

"How come a French priest does?" I thought to myself but refrained from asking. Instead I explained that I had been born in Iraq, and the Jews in the Arab lands don't speak Yiddish; it's strictly a European tongue.

"Sorry," the abbé said sheepishly, "I didn't know."

I decided to indulge my curiosity after all. "And how is it that you understand Yiddish?"

"You'll probably laugh: for me, it's *mama loshen,* my native tongue," he said without batting an eye.

I assumed he was pulling my leg but had his reasons for evading the subject, so I respected them. Steering the conversation in a new direction,

I began telling him about myself, and in the many hours we were to spend together, I spoke about life on the kibbutz, my mission to Iraq, and my "interlude" in Lebanon. It wasn't until after the tour that I learned from Moshe Carmil that the abbé's explanation for his familiarity with Yiddish was no joke at all. Alexander Glasberg had been born in 1902 to a Jewish family in the Ukrainian city of Zhitomir. He studied in a *heder,* the traditional Jewish elementary school, and acquired a rudimentary knowledge of Hebrew, but the language he grew up on was Yiddish. At some point along the way he converted to Catholicism—the circumstances for this dramatic step being unknown to Moshe—and in 1932 he emigrated to France, enrolled in a theological seminary in Paris, and was subsequently ordained a priest. In September 1939, just after the outbreak of the war, Glasberg was appointed a junior clergyman in the small town of Moulins, not far from Paris, and after the German invasion he moved to Lyons, in Vichy France, and was appointed a curate there.

Glasberg began to devote all his time and energy to aiding the many refugees passing through the area, and he also established contact with the French Resistance. At first he was moved by a general humanitarian impulse, but in the course of his work, as he encountered more and more Jews fleeing the brutal persecution of the Nazis, childhood memories of pogroms in his native city drove him ever closer to the anti-Nazi Resistance. Though the lot of the French under the occupation was a bitter one, the worst agonies were suffered by the Jews, who were systematically hunted down and slaughtered. Wittingly or otherwise, Glasberg soon found that his energies were focused on rescuing Jews, the very people whose fate, like a latter-day Jonah, he had once tried to escape. He was especially active in saving Jewish children, whom he hid in churches or with Christian families so that he could later smuggle them into safer areas. Among his other accomplishments, Glasberg succeeded in rescuing, at virtually the last minute, 108 Jewish children from the town of Venissieux who were about to be deported with their parents to one of the Nazi death camps. He continued this work—through an impressive show of boldness and resourcefulness, at no little risk to himself—even after the Germans entered Lyons, in November 1942. Sentenced to death in absentia, he went underground and continued to operate in the ranks of the Resistance until the end of the war.

By the time I met Glasberg, he had been decorated by the French Government and was the vice president of the national organization of French Resistance fighters, a position he held until his dying day. After World War II he returned to Paris and established the Centre d'orientation sociale des étrangers to aid refugees from Franco's Spain, Salazar's Portugal, and the

Iron Curtain countries, laboring tirelessly at the head of a small and dedicated staff to ease the lot of countless victims of fear and persecution in their native lands. Over the years, he also developed contacts with various Socialist figures in France, and it was the latter who interested him in Israel's cause and placed him in touch with the Mossad people in Paris, who often availed themselves of his good offices.

In 1948 Glasberg came on a trip to the Holy Land (when we first met). Moved by what he witnessed there, he returned to France an ardent supporter of the Zionist enterprise and was eager to help in any way possible. He also became a denizen of the Mossad's Paris office, where I ran into him one day just as I was about to give up and head home. The abbé extended me such an enthusiastic welcome that one would have thought we were long-lost friends.

"Shammai," he cried out across the room, "what's an Asian like you doing here in Paris?"

"I'm on my way to Baghdad," I told him, as if apologizing for my presence so far from the line of fire.

"Well, then, why haven't you called to say hello?"

"I didn't want to bother you," I said for lack of any other excuse.

"Bother me? Nonsense! I want you to come over to my office tomorrow and tell me what's happening to the Jews in the Orient as a result of this war of yours. Let's have lunch."

The abbé's offices were near the famed Les Halles, the city's central produce market in those days and a magnet for tourists, who found a special fascination in watching a fleet of trucks deliver mountains of fresh fruits and vegetables from all over the country. The area was dotted with restaurants that ranged from cheap and simple, for the farmers and drivers, to expensive and luxurious, for the tourists. Some, however, catered to true French gourmands, and it was to one of these that the abbé took me for lunch. Obviously this was not his first visit there, for when we entered, the proprietor came forward to greet him and ushered us to a quiet and comfortable corner.

As a novice at the rite about to be performed, I followed it closely, both for the sake of broadening my education and to get a better sense of this strange man of paradoxes sitting opposite me. Lifting the large menu up to his myopic eyes, the abbé studied it thoroughly and consulted with the waiter on the most appropriate choice. When the wine list arrived, I could see that he took the selection most seriously. No sooner had a vintage been agreed upon when the wine steward appeared and produced a bottle, handing it smartly over to the abbé, who peered at it at close range, read the label carefully, and proceeded to interrogate him about the details of the vintage. Then the steward removed the cork with measured grace and flourish, poured a bit into the abbé's glass, and stood looking on solicitously as Glasberg raised the glass to his nostrils, savored its aroma, tasted it in a few small sips and, after a few seconds of tense silence, finally pronounced, *"C'est bon."*

Now the steward filled both our glasses and the abbé raised his in a toast, but I beat him to it.

"À votre santé!" I announced, my sole contribution to the rite.

"L'chaim!" the abbé reciprocated with a mischievous wink. "Now, tell me, what's happening in your Orient and what are your plans?"

I wasn't in a position to speak about what was going on in all the Arab countries, but the situation in Iraq was clear—and frightful. I told him what I knew about the civil unrest, the declaration of martial law and the terror it cast on the Jews. I explained about the mail sacks from Palestine, the arrests, and the relentless fear of being hauled off to prison, or worse.

"And what are the chances of getting your people out of there?" he asked.

"None," I replied bluntly.

"None at all? But how can that be?"

I told him of the little we had managed to accomplish until Lydda Airport was taken over by the Arabs, of the desert routes that were completely blocked now, and of feeling at an utter loss about how to break the blockade.

"Then why are you going there?" he asked with impeccable logic.

"To be with our people," I explained. "To encourage them. After all, we can't just abandon them there."

"That sounds very noble," Glasberg remarked with more than a hint of sarcasm, "but it's not good enough. Isn't there anything that can be done? Or at least tried?"

We lapsed into an uncomfortable silence during which I made a detailed study of the glass in my hand.

"Well?" he pressed, as though he sensed I was holding something back.

"I had one thought," I said, barely above a mumble. "Perhaps it might be possible to smuggle people into Iran and then find a way to transfer them on to Israel, via Europe if necessary."

As soon as those words were out, I regretted raising the same senseless notion that had already been rejected by everyone else.

"Shammai, that's a capital idea," he exclaimed, "absolutely marvelous!

You claim that you don't know any Yiddish, but I see that you have a *Yiddishe kop** on your shoulders.''

Glasberg had come to life, and through his thick lenses I could see his eyes fill with an impish sparkle. As he ran his chubby fingers through his sleek gray hair, it was clear that his mind was working in high gear.

''There are still a few unsolved problems,'' I added, embarrassed by his praise. ''First we have to smuggle the people into Iran, though I believe that can be handled fairly easily. The real question is whether Iran will be prepared to treat our people as refugees and not ship them back over the border. Then we'll have to find some way of maintaining the refugees in Iran till we can move them on. And above all—'' I added, but then stopped, sensing that I was about to divulge a piece of information that was best kept inside the organization.

''Yes?'' Glasberg egged me on. ''Above all . . . ?''

I looked into the abbé's eyes, seeing more concern than mere curiosity, and decided that I could truly trust this man.

''Well, the truth is that my colleagues are not very enthused about the idea.''

''Are you saying that the Mossad is against it?'' he asked in astonishment.

''Not actually against it,'' I qualified for the sake of accuracy. ''They just don't believe in it.''

''Well, they're wrong,'' the abbé pronounced with such decisiveness that I was intrigued about what he knew that the Mossad didn't. ''We can get help from IRO,'' he assured me, referring to the International Refugee Organization. ''I work with it all the time, and I'm sure it will accord your people the status of refugees. Then the Iranians won't be able to send them back. In fact, IRO will probably maintain refugee camps for them. That's why it exists. I'll tell you what: I am prepared to go to Iran on IRO's behalf to investigate this idea of yours.''

By now I was becoming infected by his confidence and enthusiasm.

''And I have another idea,'' he pressed on, ''though it will have to be checked out. We may be able get help from the Assyrians in Iran. Do you know who the Assyrians are?''

''As a matter of fact, I do. I remember how the Iraqis persecuted them and how they were massacred in 1933.''

''Well, then, you know only half the story,'' he explained. ''Since World War II, their situation has changed for the worse in *Iran*—where they're

* Literally a ''Jewish head'' (in Yiddish), the connotation being a clever, imaginative mind.

suspected of collaborating with the Russians—and today they're trying to return to Iraq."

"The wandering Assyrian," I quipped to Glasberg, an erstwhile Jew.

"Yes, quite," he murmured back. "At any rate, I have some good contacts with the heads of their church, and they have a few monasteries along the Iraqi border that may be of help to us. It's worth pursuing."

"Absolutely," I chimed in.

"And if you have no objection, I'd like to talk the whole matter over with Oscar and Barpal. I'm sure they'll change their minds."

"Be my guest," I told him, thinking that he would surely get a better hearing than I had—though I never dreamed he would do such wonders within the Mossad. Glasberg's upbeat assessment of the idea engendered a dramatic change in the Mossad's attitude toward it—and toward myself as its author. Soon we were grappling with the question of finances. To solve them, Barpal raised the entire subject of Jews in Arab lands before some members of the Political Committee of the World Jewish Congress. In fact, he proposed a plan for saving fifteen thousand such Jews and asked the organization to allocate $4–5 million to fund our operation. Nothing was settled at that session, but on the strength of the preliminary response, I got Barpal to underwrite the transfer of two hundred people from Iraq to Iran.

With that promise to cover the costs of a "trial run," moral support from Glasberg, and the general turnabout in attitude, I felt that at least I wasn't going off to Baghdad empty-handed. But the problem was still how to get there. The officials in the Iranian consulate continued to treat us politely, with smiles and assurances, but never produced visas. A further investigation of ways to get to Iraq directly also came to naught. By the end of July my patience had run out, and I demanded that a clear-cut decision be made: either we were going to Iraq or we would return home. That ultimatum finally resulted in some movement to break the deadlock. Oscar's experts on "preparing papers" recommended that we abandon our efforts to get visas on the Iraqi passports we had brought along with us, and on August 8 I was able to cable Moshe Carmil that Ya'akov Sitton and I would be traveling to Baghdad, via Teheran, on French passports—to be supplied by Oscar's experts—and that the date for our departure was set for August 23. Then, at the last minute, there was another delay. I was so miffed by the sloppy handling of our trip that I set down the whole story in a snappish letter to Tel Aviv:

It wasn't until [Oscar] left that I had an opportunity to look at the passport that was prepared for me, and I discovered that it had expired.

A new passport was readied for me (within a day), but then there was another foul-up. Before leaving, [Oscar] made a point of obtaining a letter of recommendation for me so that I could get an Iranian visa. But he left no indication of where he had placed it or who had written it for him. After a great to-do, by sheer luck we managed to get another letter, and of course it's already too late to get the visa today. If I manage to get it tomorrow morning, I can still make tomorrow's flight; if not, it means a delay of another week.

I did not get the Iranian visa the next morning and fumed and fidgeted through most of that extra week. In the end, I didn't leave for Teheran until August 31—two whole months after arriving in Paris. And even then I went alone, without Ya'akov. Originally we assumed that he would join me in a week or so, after his papers had been arranged, but that proved to be wishful thinking. After waiting in Paris for three more months, he decided to do the only useful thing and moved on to another front: working with the Zionist youth movements in North Africa. Instead, the abbé and his secretary were to join me in Teheran.

After stopovers in Rome and Istanbul, I arrived in Teheran in fine form. At passport control I confidently presented my new French-Moroccan passport (Morocco being a French protectorate) to the duty officer. Selim Hillel, alias Shlomo Hillel, alias Amo Yusuf, had been transformed overnight into one Maurice Perez, the representative of Gasoline and Sitex, two French companies with offices on the Rue de 4 Septembre, in Paris. (The director of these companies, Emanuel Racine, a veteran of the French Resistance—who, incidentally, emigrated to Israel in the 1950s—readily complied with the request from his good friend Abbé Glasberg and appointed me his agent in the Middle East.) I had various identities and passports both before and after (especially after) that one. But never again would I have a passport that served me for so long, so far and wide, and so faithfully as this French-Moroccan document. And never again would I feel so perfectly at home with a cover as I did with the engaging, enterprising, and energetic Maurice Perez in Teheran.

SEVEN

Monsieur Perez Goes to Teheran

COMPARED TO PARIS, Teheran was small and lacking in elegance, like most Middle Eastern cities. I had imagined it would be a replica of Baghdad, but it bore not the least resemblance to my native city, primarily because the surrounding scenery was so starkly different. Instead of the flat, dun-colored desert that bore in on Baghdad from all sides, Teheran was couched among high mountains; and in place of the sluggish river that cut Baghdad in two and was the city's hallmark, through the heart of Teheran went a broad, arrow-straight, tree-lined boulevard. When I expressed surprise at finding such a long, ruler-straight road in the heart of an ancient city, I was told that the boulevard was hardly ancient and that "ruler-straight" was exactly its secret. It seems that the former ruler of Iran, Reza Shah Pahlavi—a man who was used to getting his way—wanted to accord his capital a modern look by adding a boulevard. So he called for a pencil and ruler, drew a straight line across a map of the city, and ordered the destruction of every building in its path. And since it didn't pay to argue with Reza Shah, within a few days his decree was carried out with precision, and the boulevard was paved.

Yet my strongest and most lasting impression of Teheran came from the older part of the city: the huge, crowded bazaar whose high, arched ceiling protected shoppers from the sun, so that even at the height of summer the market remained cool and damp and the sharp scent of the oriental spices hung in the air in their full potency, never dissipating. On my first visit to the bazaar, after recovering from the assault of the spices and adjusting to the dim light, I stood agape at the countless Persian carpets, in a profusion of colors and exquisite designs, thrown carelessly one on top of the next in stacks the height of a man, and I felt almost insulted by the way these magnificent creations were treated with indifference.

Above all, however, Teheran was unfailingly gracious to me. After weeks of marking time in Paris, it felt good to begin focusing on the chances of doing some fruitful work—which looked very promising indeed. Naturally my first days in Teheran were devoted to establishing contacts with a whole new gallery of personalities. I quickly discovered that two Israelis were stationed in the city in official capacities and two others had been living there for quite a while, developing business interests. Of the former, I came to rely heavily on Eliyahu Ben-Yitzhak, the representative of the Jewish National Fund, whose help in financial matters was to become the cornerstone of my entire operation.

My closest associate in Teheran, however, was Dov Adiv, a Palestinian Jew who had been living in Iran for years (and was subsequently appointed one of El Al's senior managers). A native of Poland, Adiv had immigrated to Palestine in 1936, at the age of fourteen. As an individualist *par excellence,* he was not cut out for life on the kibbutz he had joined right after graduating from high school, so he went off to work in the oil refineries in Haifa. Ultimately, that brought him to Iran, for during World War II he was transferred to Abadan to oversee the automated equipment in the huge refineries there. When the war ended, Dov found that he was in no hurry to return to Palestine. Instead he moved to Teheran, where he tried his hand at business and, incidentally, married Helen, the daughter of one Professor Asch, who had reached Iran in flight from the Nazis.

I went to see Dov (on the recommendation of a friend) and I found a man of about my age with thick sandy hair and large, alert blue eyes that expressed a mixture of wit and playfulness. We met in his small travel agency, Iran-Trans, where he greeted me cordially and promised to do whatever he could to help. "And I think I can do quite a lot," he added without much modesty. "I'm familiar with local conditions, and I have connections with many people of influence. My office, its POB, cable address, and yours truly are all at your disposal."

Even at first glance, I had the impression that his expansive self-appraisal was probably well founded. In short, Dov instantly won my confidence, and I decided to tell him all about my plans. As I did so, he went into action almost reflexively, reserving rooms for the abbé and his secretary in the Park Hotel, the finest in Teheran. When I meekly inquired about the prices there, implying that I was on a shoestring budget (which was putting it mildly), he rebuked me for even contemplating lodging so distinguished a figure as the abbé in anything but the best accommodations. I liked his forcefulness and felt that Dov and I would go far together.

Having located the Israelis in town, my next move before Glasberg's arrival was to seek out the leaders of the local Jewish community, especially the circle of Jews of Iraqi extraction who had been living in Iran for many years and were economically well established. I assumed that their network of contacts with the authorities was highly developed, for without such connections they probably could not have cultivated their commercial interests. I also assumed that they continued to maintain ties with their relatives in Iraq and were thus likely to know reliable smugglers who worked between the two countries. What I was looking for was smugglers who could be trusted with human lives.

When Dov mentioned the name of Mualem Zion Edri ("Master Zion"), I nodded vigorously in recognition, though I was surprised to hear that he was now living in Teheran. Mualem Zion was a native of Baghdad who had devoted himself to religious studies and moved to the Iranian city of Khorramshahr, on the Shatt-al-Arab, to serve the Jewish community as a teacher and a ritual slaughterer (required for practicing the dietary laws). While tending to his religious duties, however, he also dabbled in commerce—at which he proved extraordinarily adept, so that within a short time he had developed a reputation on both sides of the border as a man of wealth, status, and connections. I had first met him in Khorramshahr during my brief foray into southern Iran while working in the Zionist underground, and I came away from that meeting with the impression that his reputation was well deserved. In his Khorramshahr house, the lush green garden of the inner courtyard, the ornate furniture, the servants who seemed to walk on tiptoe, and the many visitors who waited quietly and patiently to be received by the master had all bespoken a man of both means and considerable influence.

Mualem Zion's Teheran home was a more modest affair, though still a very comfortable apartment whose dimly lit drawing room was decorated with fine Persian carpets, huge vases, trays, samovars, and silver teapots decorated with Persian figures and designs. The maid served us sweet, cold rose water, and as I sipped it I had the distinct impression that there were no other servants. Certainly there were no other visitors waiting to be received. Mualem Zion had decided to cut back on his activities, and apparently that is why he had moved to Teheran. I had understood from Dov, however, that he was still a very active man whose connections were as widespread and powerful as ever. Dov also confirmed that Mualem Zion had remained wholly loyal to the Zionist cause.

Based on those assumptions, I began our talk by saying that I had had the honor of meeting him a few years back in Khorramshahr, though I didn't know whether he remembered me.

"Of course I remember," he said, "except that then you weren't called Maurice."

"Ah, yes," I mumbled, embarrassed about my multiple identities. "The people in the movement called me Yusuf then."

"Not Yusuf, Amo Yusuf," he corrected me, as if to signal that although he had retired from business, his memory had not betrayed him and he was not a man you could diddle on details. Having taken his point, I decided to approach my problem directly.

"Mualem Zion, I've come to ask for your advice and help."

"I know the war in Israel is a hard one," he broke in, "and you un-doubtedly need financial aid. But to my regret business has been very bad lately, especially for the Jews here. And on top of that, we are caring for Jews who have fled from Iraq. We have to support them, and that's a heavy burden on our small community."

"I haven't come to ask for money," I told him, noticing that his face remained impassive at that announcement. "We need to smuggle some Jews over the border from Iraq as soon as possible, and I was hoping you could recommend a reliable man to bring them over."

Now his face darkened, and instantly I realized that my directness had been a mistake. Indeed, Mualem Zion's negative reply came swiftly.

"I don't have any connections with *katsajtzia*.* I don't even know any," he said dourly. But seeing the disappointment on my face, he quickly added, "I suggest you go see Salman the Driver. I believe he can help you."

"Who is this Salman?" I asked skeptically. "Mualem Zion, I have come to you because I need the help of someone serious, someone I can trust."

"Don't worry," he assured me. "He is one of us"—the last words being said in Hebrew, as was the custom in the patois of the Iraqi Jewish commu-nity. "You can trust him, and I'm sure he will help you."

Hearing the accent on the word "sure," I understood that the subject was closed, so I returned to a comment that had intrigued me earlier.

* A Turkish word commonly used in Iraq and Iran meaning "smugglers."

"Tell me, who are these refugees from Iraq you spoke of? When did they arrive?"

"They've been coming over in dribs and drabs for the past few months," he explained, "even after the imposition of martial law. Usually they are people with relatives here and aren't a problem. But recently a few Jewish Communists have come over, and they don't have any family here. We're doing our best to help them, because we're afraid that if the authorities catch them, they'll be sent back to Iraq to face imprisonment—or worse. They can't work. They hardly dare to leave their hiding places. We provide them with the essentials—food and clothing—but I honestly don't know how long we can keep it up. Soon winter will be setting in, and then they're really in for difficulties."

Suddenly his lips formed a half smile, as if the solution to this predicament had come to him as he was talking.

"Why don't you take them with you to Israel," he proposed. "You're always eager to get people there."

Indeed, getting persecuted Jews to Israel was my business, so to speak. But in this case, I had to explain that if they were Communists, they probably wouldn't want to go. "You know, the Communists in Iraq were vigorously opposed to Zionism. They hate us. When they had the opportunity, they even persecuted us."

Mualem Zion gave out a snort of laughter. "Not any more, my son. Now they'll be overjoyed if you take them. They're not such big shots now that they're in hiding and afraid to even show their noses. They stand to be arrested here, both because they entered the country illegally and because they're Communists. They fled from Iraq because they were persecuted both as Jews and as Communists. And the irony is that, at the same time, they're accused of being adherents of Zionism, which you claim they hold in the greatest contempt.

"Look what's happening to poor Shafiq Addas," he continued.† "Little good it does him that he always regarded himself as an Iraqi of the first order, that he associated only with Arabs, and that he had Arab business partners. They haven't said so much as one good word for him. Now the Jewish Communists are beginning to realize that they have no business in Iraq either. The fact is that they're fleeing here. And who do they come to for help? Their Arab friends? The local Communists? No! They come to their Jewish brothers, who hide them and provide for their needs. So you see, my son, if you can get them out of here, they'll kiss your hands. Because only in Israel can they be Communists to their hearts' content!"

† Shafiq Addas was then being tried in Basra.

His argument made eminent sense. Yet even if I had chosen to make these problematic refugees a priority, I still had no way of getting them from Iran to Israel. On September 16, two weeks after arriving in Iran, I had sent off the first immigrant in the hope that, like the first swallow, she would augur the arrival of spring. Actually, her dispatch was a rather simple affair and had only indirect bearing on the complex problem of getting people from Iraq to Israel. My "swallow" was a middle-aged nurse who had reached Iran on a valid Iraqi passport that was about to expire and could not be renewed in Teheran. When it did run out, so would her visa, making her presence in Iran illegal. By chance I had had occasion to meet the Italian consul, and I struck up a friendship with him. When the nurse entered the picture, I asked him to grant her a visa for Italy on humanitarian grounds, adding my assurances that upon reaching Rome she would be placed in the care of our people there and would be sent on to Israel. His willingness to cooperate led me to hope that it might be possible to utilize this route again in the future. It also provided me with a courier to take out my first report on what I was doing in Teheran. Until then it had been necessary for me to confine myself to oblique hints in open cables, but now I wrote forthrightly to our people in Paris:

It's clear that there are many possibilities for working out of here, in terms of both the Iraqis and the locals. . . . There's a chance of reaching up to a few dozen a month. . . . Dozens of Iraqi refugees are already here, and a spontaneous flow (of rather small proportions) continues all the time.

Backing these assessments was Mualem Zion's story about the Jews who had come in from Iraq and the assessment of "Salman the Driver"—whom I had met in the interim—that it was definitely possible to smuggle people from Iraq into Iran. But the main question was whether the Iranians would be prepared to grant them refugee status and allow us to proceed with their organized transfer to Israel. It seemed to me that this—rather than the difficulties of stealing over the border, which Abbé Glasberg hoped to solve with the aid of his Assyrian friends—was going to be the greatest hurdle.

Nevertheless, we now turned to investigate the Assyrian connection. A week after my arrival in Teheran, I was followed by Abbé Glasberg and his charming secretary, Nino Weill, who worked for him with loyalty and devotion from the time of the Resistance to his dying day. Nino, whose delicate features were contrasted by a look of astuteness, came from Alsace. She was the daughter of an assimilated Jewish father and Christian mother but had been raised as a Christian in every way, to the point where she hadn't the vaguest notion about any Jewish customs or rituals—all of which added yet another piquant detail to the strange trio we made.

Our first meeting after their arrival was at the Assyrian church in Teheran, where we met with Monseigneur Thuma, a frail-looking, polite man whose strongest features were his well-tended black beard and crisply ironed dark robe. Glasberg introduced me as his personal assistant but did not reveal the real purpose of our mission. He merely explained that word had reached Paris about the difficult condition of the Assyrians, and especially the state of the monasteries along the border, and he was interested in knowing whether any Assyrians were fleeing over the frontier into Iraq. Thuma's reply was predictably evasive, but after some subtle coaxing he finally came through with the suggestion we had been fishing for: that we visit the monasteries and assess the situation for ourselves. He even recommended an Assyrian taxi driver who spoke a bit of French.

So a day or two later, the abbé, Nino, and I made off for the border in the Assyrian's taxi. Our first trial was to cope with the condition of Iran's roads, which had evidently not had any maintenance work since the departure of the foreign forces at the end of World War II. Slightly the worse for wear, we bumped our way into the city of Hamadan and almost immediately set about tasting the delicacies of the local cuisine—at the insistence of the abbé, who was not one to forfeit a meal.

"In the Park Hotel, in Teheran, we get European cuisine," he complained as justification for the present indulgence. "They take us for snobs."

After asking the driver for his recommendation, Glasberg ordered *tchello kebab*, a huge mound of white rice served with slabs of butter, raw egg yolks, and skewers of meatballs, lamb, and venison (from the deer hunted in the surrounding mountains). It was served with ice-cold bottles of a thick white liquid called *dogh-ab-ali*, yogurt mixed with seltzer or water, which is believed to be an aid to digestion and without which no meal is complete. But here the abbé's resistance broke, and he insisted that we all drink vodka, explaining in absolute seriousness, "It's very important for hygienic purposes."

Later that afternoon, we reached the district capital of Kermanshah and shortly thereafter our destination, the Assyrian monastery, where we received a warm and moving reception. The resident monks and priests from all over the area, dressed in festive attire, had been waiting for us for hours, together with children of all ages from the local Assyrian community. As we emerged from the car, our wrinkled clothing covered with dust, we were met by a brief speech of greeting and were invited to walk between the two rows of excited children. The abbé led the way, followed by Nino and myself—in that order—and the children crowded around us to kiss our hands, one after the next. Instinctively I knew that I must not allow them to kiss me. Sooner or later my true identity would come out, and I didn't want any of the Assyrians to feel peeved that I had permitted the children to kiss my hands under false pretenses. I therefore maneuvered myself to receive every child who approached me with a hug and a pat on the shoulder or the head, so that my hands were not available for their displays of reverence.

After washing with the aid of a large pail of water and a ceramic basin, we all revived somewhat, and our appearance became more acceptable for the festive dinner held in our honor in the refectory. Seated around the long tables laden with food—and, to the abbé's delight, bottles of vodka—were leading figures from the local Assyrian community, who had awaited us patiently. When we entered the refectory, they all stood up and applauded enthusiastically until we took our seats. This ovation was followed by a series of welcoming speeches in florid French, to which Glasberg replied in brief, thanking our hosts for their warm reception and expressing the hope that during our stay we would get to know their problems and needs. At the close of this speech, the abbot rose to say grace, and to my astonishment I understood most of it, because the blessing was chanted in Aramaic, which is also the language of many ancient Jewish prayers. Hearing familiar words and phrases like *ha lachma* ("this is the bread") and *de-shemaiya* ("in heaven") repeated in the blessing brought back memories of my Talmud class in high school and of our family's traditional Passover seder, because of the many Aramaic passages woven into the text of the *Haggadah.* I stole a look at Glasberg and saw him beaming back at me. Evidently he had similar memories!

The meal ended well after dark, and when it came time to retire, each of us was assigned to a narrow cell furnished only with an iron bed, a chair, and a rickety wooden table bearing a bowl and pitcher for washing. Above my bed was a large wooden crucifix, and the walls bore a number of depictions of Jesus as a babe and on the cross. I was truly exhausted that night, but nonetheless I found it impossible to sleep. As I lay on my back and watched the flickering light of a kerosene lamp cast weird shadows on the ceiling and walls, I felt almost as though I were caught in a surrealistic play. There I was, spending the night in an Assyrian Catholic monastery on the Iraqi-Iranian border with an assumed identity as the personal assistant of a Catholic priest of Jewish origin. Christian children pressed forward to kiss my hands, and the abbot was saying grace over bread in the tongue of my forefathers. Was all this really happening? And could these Assyrians really be the missing link in bringing Jews from Iraq to Israel?

These thoughts gradually gave way to an uncanny sense of déjà vu, and I realized that, once before, the Assyrians had been a link to Jewish emigration from Iraq to Palestine—the emigration of my very own family. For undeniably it was the victory procession of the Iraqi Army through the streets of Baghdad in August 1933, after the massacre of the Assyrians in northern Iraq, that had tipped the balance for my father. We watched that parade through the shutters of our house at the corner of Al-Rashid Street, Baghdad's main thoroughfare, and the alley known as Bab al-Agha. A military band heralded the appearance of troops carrying bayoneted guns, with mule-drawn field guns bringing up the rear. Far more memorable than the procession itself, however, was the deafening roar "Long live Ghazi!"—Ghazi being the fervidly nationalist crown prince who had supported the massacre, in contrast to his father, King Feisal I, who was regarded as a liberal, moderate man reputed to have been dismayed by the slaughter.

Watching this spectacle from behind the shutters, my father seemed pretty dismayed himself. "If that's what they do to the Christians and the world fails to react," he brooded, "what do *we* have to look forward to? We no longer have any life here."

I was a child of ten then—the last in a line of seven sons and four daughters—and strange as it may sound at first, I was overjoyed to hear those words. In an attempt to turn them into action, I rushed over to my father, kissed his hand as an act of respect, and asked, "Papa, are we going to Palestine? When will we go?"

"With the Lord's help, we shall all leave here," he replied more diffidently than I would have liked. "But it's best not to talk about it. I don't want anyone talking about it. The walls have ears."

In which case they had certainly gotten an earful, for that was not the first time the question of emigrating to Palestine had come up in a family discussion. We were a traditionalist family, like most of the Jews in Iraq, and believed ourselves descended from the Judean exiles who had been led off to Babylon after the destruction of the first Temple, in 586 B.C., or eleven years earlier, when King Nebuchadnezzar exiled Jehoiachin, king of Judah, and "carried away all Jerusalem, and all the princes, and all the mighty men of valor, even ten thousand captives, and all the craftsmen and smiths; none remained, save the poorest sort of the people of the land" (as related in II Kings 24:14). Thus we were the heirs of a community that had remained faithful to the Land of Israel in the spirit of its ancestors' lament: "How shall we sing the Lord's song in a strange land? If I forget you, O Jerusalem, let my right hand wither!" (Psalm 137:4-5).

Yet even within this community, which was Zionist almost by nature, my family was among the few whose ties to Palestine were concrete. The Hebrew teachers who came to Baghdad in the mid-1920s frequented our house; we studied Hebrew and read books and newspapers from Palestine; and my brother Eliyahu, eight years my senior, was among the founders of the Ahiever Zionist Society. Still, until the early 1930s, the notion of actually moving to Palestine was never seriously considered. We were comfortably off. My father's import-export business continued to thrive, and as my brothers completed their studies, each in turn made off for one of the world's commercial centers—India, Japan, England—to further the family's far-flung commercial interests in cloth and tea. The center of this network remained in Baghdad, under my father's direction, and it looked as though it would remain that way for some time to come.

In the autumn of 1932, however, Iraq received full independence after centuries of domination by a series of foreign conquerors (the last of whom were the British, who took the country in 1917), and this period of independent rule was far from a golden age for the Jewish community. Until then, pressures and harassment from the Arab population—often in the form of slapping a Jewish child's face as he returned home from school or insulting an older Jew in the street—were all too common. From time to time, violent anti-Zionist demonstrations were also known to balloon into attacks against the Jews per se, because the fine distinction between Zionism and Judaism was soon lost on the incited crowd. Yet as long as the British held the reins in Iraq, in the form of their mandate, these outbursts of hostility were not allowed to get out of control and pose a real danger to the Jewish community—particularly because the British were dependent upon Jews to help them run the country in the financial and economic spheres. But when Iraq reached full independence, all that began to change. The frenzy that marked the independence celebrations reminded the Jews of their essential vulnerability; they wondered whether the independent Arab regime would always take care to afford them the necessary protection. And the ardently nationalist and pan-Arab mood, together with the growing tension over the clashes in Palestine, only intensified their fears.

Before long, another warning light began to flash. Hitler's rise to power in Germany, at the beginning of 1933, was received with expressions of unabashed delight by the Iraqi press and public at large. Two elements in Nazism spoke to the Iraqis: the anti-British sentiment and anti-Semitism—to the point that Hitler's particularly virulent brand of anti-Semitism began to take root in Iraq, with its most enthusiastic proponent, German Ambassador Fritz Grobba, becoming a highly popular figure in government and intellectual circles.

My brother Eliyahu was the first member of our family to read the handwriting on the wall and decide that he had no future in Iraq. In the middle of July, 1933, he left for Palestine to study in an agricultural school and work the land, as commended by the Zionist doctrine of the day. Not that it was an easy decision, especially as my parents constantly implored him not to go.

"If you want to help the Jews there, start working like your brothers," he was told again and again. "Become a man. Stand on your own two feet. Make a good living, and then you'll be able to help them. Why must you insist on ruining your life?"

But Eliyahu stood his ground, retorting that he wasn't interested in going into business and didn't care about earning a good living. The important thing was to build a Jewish homeland in Palestine, and to do that one had to become a man of the soil. After repeated bouts of temper, sulking, and tears, he did what he had to do. One afternoon, Eliyahu simply left, a small suitcase in hand. The rest of us dissolved into tears, not realizing that his departure had tilted the scales even further in the direction of Palestine for us all.

Not a month had passed when the massacre of the Assyrians took place in northern Iraq—in a sense, the very event that ultimately led to my being in this narrow, eerie cell in a monastery on the Iranian-Iraqi border. For generations, the Assyrians had lived in the mountainous region in the vicinity of the Iranian, Iraqi, Syrian, and Turkish borders. Their origins are more a matter of myth and tradition than recorded history. Some of them claim direct descent from the ancient Assyrians and explain that when Nineveh, the capital of the Assyrian Empire, fell in 606 B.C., many nobles fled to the north, where their descendants continued to live for the next two and a half millennia. Others trace their ancestry to a less exotic source and believe they are the progeny of the tribes that fled to the northern mountains from the plains of Iraq after the Mongol invasion in the thirteenth century A.D. One way or another, the latter-day Assyrians were a small, veteran Christian community that prayed in the same Syrian-Aramaic dialect spoken by the inhabitants of Babylonia in ages past.

This small Christian sect was closed in on all sides by a sea of Muslims: Turks, Kurds, Persians, and Arabs—both Shiites and Sunnis—who were often in conflict among themselves but invariably hostile to these unusual Christians. The life of the Assyrians had therefore never been a blissful one; hardship, persecution, massacres, and wars were their standard lot.

Fated to live by the sword, they grew into tough, merciless fighters—which only intensified the enmity toward them.

Their condition deteriorated drastically with the outbreak of World War I, when Turkey, attacked by the Christian states of Europe, took the war to be a kind of *jihad* against the Christian "infidels." Soon friction erupted between the Turkish authorities and their Assyrian subjects, to the point of an Assyrian uprising. A number of scholars hold that the Russians (and probably the British, as well) encouraged this revolt by promising the Assyrians autonomy or full independence after the defeat of the Turks. It is beyond question, however, that the insurrection cost the Assyrians dearly. Initially they succeeded in repulsing a number of attacks by government forces assisted by units of Kurds (who had been the Assyrians' sworn enemies since time immemorial). But soon afterward they found themselves under siege and had to fight their way out to move their entire community—from infants to the elderly, a total of some seventy thousand souls—through sub-zero weather over the snow-covered mountains to Iran. For a while thereafter, they enjoyed the patronage of the Russians, who provided them with weapons for self-defense. With Russia's withdrawal from the world war (following the Bolshevik Revolution) and the subsequent stabilization of British rule in Iraq, His Majesty's Government extended its protection to the Assyrians and brought to Iraq those who had survived the sword, disease, the hardships of exile, and their journey—altogether some thirty-five to forty thousand people. Then the British recruited fighting units among the Assyrians, using them to quash sporadic rebellions within the country and in border clashes with the Turks. Taking full advantage of the Assyrians' loyalty and eagerness to please, they also cultivated the illusion of a "common fate" and went so far as to dub the Assyrians "our smallest ally"—an expression that bespoke both affection and contempt. Neither were the British above nurturing their "ally's" hopes of settling in the mountainous region of northern Iraq, where they felt at home.

Such illusions were shattered one after another as the British mandate drew to a close. For although the Anglo-Iraqi Pact of 1930 referred to the status of the various minorities in Iraq, including the Assyrians, when the mandate came to an end the Assyrians found that all they had to show for their loyalty were vague promises. Worse yet, when they realized that they were unwelcome in independent Iraq and some tried to return to Turkey, the Turks greeted them with machine-gun fire. And when they tried to enter Syria—in the hope that the French mandatory authorities there would allow them to settle in the country's broad plain in the north—they were turned back at the border.

On August 4, 1933, a group of Assyrians who had been refused entry into Syria clashed with a unit of Iraqi troops manning a position near the Turkish border. Following this exchange of fire—which some say was provoked by the Army—Iraqi soldiers (who had conveniently been concentrated in the area ahead of time) launched an assault on the Assyrians. As part of this action, the four hundred Assyrian inhabitants of the town of Sumayyil were ordered to report to the police station and turn in their personal weapons. Upon doing so, they were taken out to the courtyard and summarily shot in cold blood. This was the signal for the start of a mass slaughter, with soldiers killing indiscriminately and civilians (both Kurds and Arabs) looting everything within reach. The massacre continued for days, and even the most conservative estimates spoke of hundreds of dead and wounded and thousands of people left homeless.

In the strife-torn Middle East, the action was in itself not a particular cause for surprise. But the response to it spelled more evil to come. Not only were the perpetrators of the crime never brought to justice, they were actually decorated by Crown Prince Ghazi. Their commander, General Bakr Sidqi—who was known for his sadism, blind hatred of the Assyrians (and minorities in general), and readiness to slaughter them at any opportunity—was promoted and even granted the title of "pasha." The bloodletting was celebrated by victory parades—first in Mosul and then in Baghdad—and supported by cheering crowds. No less alarming was the response of the world at large. In October the League of Nations Council expressed regret at the use of "excessive and unjustified means" and even established a committee of representatives of Britain, France, Italy, Denmark, Mexico, and Spain to find a place of refuge for the Assyrians. The committee duly met a few times and discussed various possibilities, from Brazil to the banks of the Niger, in the heart of Africa, but nothing ever came of these schemes. The Assyrians remained scattered between Iran, Iraq, Syria, and the southern part of the U.S.S.R., nursing their wounds and roaming from one territory to another.

About three weeks after that harrowing slaughter, the minorities in Iraq suffered another blow, and this time it was clear to anyone with the least bit of sense that the alarm signals had escalated to piercing sirens. On September 8, King Feisal I died, and his son Ghazi ascended the throne. The new king was a young man (twenty-eight) with a reputation for being corrupt, hotheaded, irresponsible, a radical nationalist, and an earnest disciple of the Nazis. His ascension left my father quite determined to leave Iraq for Palestine. Thus the idea born after the terrible slaughter of the Assyrians had fully matured in the space of less than a month, and the course of my own life changed radically. Now, fifteen years later, in September 1948, I found myself lying on a narrow cot in a monastery near Kermanshah because, once again, my life had crossed paths with the Assyrians. They were looking for ways to get people from Iran to Iraq, and I was hoping to utilize them to smuggle my people in the opposite direction. Is it any wonder that sleep eluded me that night?

The next morning, I left my room at the hour set for breakfast, honestly not realizing the rules were so strict that I had been expected to join the monks for matins. But apparently the abbot thought otherwise.

"We missed you this morning, Monsieur Perez," he greeted me in French and in a distinctly reproving tone.

"I didn't sleep well last night," I explained, punctuating that brief statement with an embarrassed cough as I realized that I was in a fix.

After breakfast, we all went out on a tour of a number of Assyrian institutions and one of their schools. In the course of the outing, we also reached one of the many rivers in the area, whose water, as cold as ice even in the summer, was swarming with fish. The monks produced simple fishing rods, cast their lines, and took in quite a haul. But the prize catch was an eel, which could be transformed into dishes fit for a king. On our way back to the monastery, we passed through Kermanshah and caught the attention of some Muslim children, who ran after us shouting, *"Misihian, Misihian"* ("Christians, Christians") and grimaced at the sight of the eel, as if they were retching. Abbé Glasberg followed the children's reaction with an amused expression, and when I finally found myself walking beside him, I murmured, "I see that sometimes it's almost as difficult being a Christian as it is being a Jew."

"You know, Maurice," he replied, only partially in jest, "the worst of all is to be both."

Then he changed to a businesslike tone. "How do you feel?"

"Very uncomfortable," I admitted.

"I can imagine!" he said sympathetically. "Be patient just a bit longer."

When we reached the monastery, I went directly to my cell—to stay out of harm's way—and left Glasberg and Nino in the company of the abbot. Half an hour later, one of the monks appeared at my door and invited me to join them.

"I've explained everything to the abbot," Glasberg told me assuringly, "and you don't have to report for prayers. This afternoon you can sit with him and hear all about his work. You can trust him implicitly. Also, I've promised him that we'll buy the monastery a pickup truck to bring the

Jewish refugees over from Iraq, whenever they appear, and for their own use the rest of the time. I'm sure you'll have no objection to that."

"Of course not," I said, lying through my teeth, for in fact I wasn't particularly happy about the outlay. What's more, when I had an opportunity to talk with the abbot that afternoon, my doubts that we would ever derive any benefit from the truck grew stronger, for he led me to understand that because of the bad blood between the Assyrians and their Kurdish and Arab neighbors, they refrained from working with local smugglers. This did not cramp their activities in any way, because they had people of their own who were familiar with the area and could easily reach the Assyrian villages on the other side of the frontier. But they were unable to penetrate as far as Iraq's urban centers—Baghdad, Mosul, and Basra—where most of the Jewish population was concentrated. In short, I saw that our salvation was not likely to come through the Assyrians, and for a moment I felt a strong pang of disappointment—though the good news that came out of our talk was confirmation of our suspicion that the border was porous here, in the center of the country, as well as in the South. Yet even though we would not be using the Assyrians' good services, I had no choice but to honor the abbé's promise, and as matters turned out it was a solid investment in goodwill. Admittedly, no Jewish refugee ever set foot in the truck. On the other hand, a few months later I was saved from disaster by the courage and decency of the abbot—and the value of having such virtues on your side cannot be measured in dollars and cents.

But I am getting ahead of myself, for I was still in the exploratory stage then, and when we returned to Teheran I tried to draw up a realistic assessment of whether we could get an operation going via Iran. First of all, I noted the fact that there were definitely opportunities to cross the border into Iran. That was attested to by both "Salman the Driver" and the abbot at Kermanshah. The real problem, it seemed to me, would not be getting our emigrants into Iran, but getting them from Iran to Israel. One option was to do so illegally—for example, by the "Michaelberg" method—but that was clearly not desirable. For logic dictated that in addition to bearing all the risks of a smuggling operation, we would undoubtedly incur the wrath of the Iranian authorities, once they discovered what we were up to. The natural course was to strive for an understanding with the government whereby the fleeing Iraqis would be recognized as refugees. Unfortunately, the chances of reaching such an accord seemed very slim indeed. As I had learned when the abbé arrived in Teheran, even Glasberg's confidence that IRO could recognize our people as refugees had not been borne out—for technical reasons having to do with its charter—and how could we possibly expect that Iran would be willing to do more than the international family of nations?

While struggling with this paradox, it occurred to me that we could also waive a formal agreement and content ourselves with a tacit understanding that the refugees coming from Iraq would not be sent back over the border, because they were only passing through and would be quickly sent on to Europe. When I talked this over with Glasberg, he was quick to see the merits of such an arrangement.

"My contribution to the scheme will be to obtain French visas," he offered, explaining that many of his friends from the Resistance now held senior government posts, especially in the Ministry of the Interior. "I will give them my personal assurance that none of the refugees will remain in France—and my word is still worth something!"

"If this works," I enthused, developing the idea as we talked, "they won't even reach France. What we've got to do is find a special airline that will work for us and fly them directly to Israel!"

And eventually we did. But in the early stages, Glasberg's influence in getting the visas proved to be critical. Initially I considered using the good services of the Italian consul, who had displayed considerable understanding. But soon I discovered that this channel was highly limited, for the consul was reluctant to issue a large number of visas. Moreover, his grasp of the situation was sometimes very loose. On one of my visits to his office, he told me that he had decided categorically not to issue any more visas to Iraqi Jews. In response to my surprise and disappointment, he explained that the Iraqis had recently refused an entry visa to a member of an Italian trade delegation because he was a Jew. The indignant consul had therefore decided to retaliate by refusing entry visas to Iraqi Jews. It took all my patience to explain why, under the circumstances, his plan for retribution was most inappropriate.

That left us totally at the mercy of the abbé's contacts in high places. Glasberg returned to France in the middle of October bearing a list of fifty families—over 250 people—who were candidates for French visas. It was a work of minor fiction that I prepared by letting my imagination run wild. I couldn't possibly know in advance who would be dispatched—and who would get through—to Iran, so I chose names at random and joined them together into families. The names, it later turned out, were not a problem; our people arrived without papers anyway, so we could give them any names we wanted. The challenge was to create families by matching the arrivals with the particulars of the family members listed on the visas.

Of course these visas had to be attached to an appropriate travel document, so that at first I sent people to Italy and France on slightly "doctored" expired Iraqi passports. When the Iraqi consul refused to renew them, I simply found a way around his obstructionism. Through rather primitive means, I managed to create a highly convincing replica of the Iraqi consulate's stamp and blithely went about imprinting it on passports. My stamps fell somewhat short of being works of art; then again, neither the French and Italian authorities granting the visas nor the Iranians working in passport control ever took the trouble to clarify the reason for the unusual blurriness of these Iraqi stamps. As a result, a small stream of immigrants made its way to Europe by what the Mossad referred to as "Shammai's arrangement." Yet this, too, was a highly limited system, because of the need for Iraqi passports, of whatever vintage.

Then Zion Ezri entered the picture. Ezri was a middle-aged, educated Jew from the city of Isfahan who spoke fluent French and had a wealth of contacts in the police, having served in its ranks as a translator (with the rank of inspector). Fortunately for us, he was also a staunch Zionist and was willing to help us in any way possible. For Ezri, that meant coming to a financial arrangement with a few senior police officers whereby refugees who made their way to Teheran would report to one of the specified police stations, turn themselves in, and declare before Ezri's associates (or their subordinates) that they had fled from persecution in Iraq. They would be duly tried for entering Iran illegally but would be punished with only a token fine. And once they produced entry visas to another country, the authorities would issue them *laissez-passers* and allow them to leave Iran.

Upon hearing this news, my only fear was that I might be hallucinating, for who could hope for anything more. I decided that it was imperative to put this new arrangement to the test immediately and, with luck, create a precedent. The problem was that we hadn't actually begun smuggling people in from Iraq yet, and the chances that we would do so in the immediate future were still unclear, as I had not yet established contact with our people in Iraq.

Then I remembered my talk with Mualem Zion about the Jewish Communists hiding out in Teheran who would "kiss your hands if you take them to Israel." They certainly met the criterion outlined by Ezri, and I decided to see if we could help each other out. There were seven of them, all highly educated men (one, I recall, was a doctor), and their communism derived from idealism—though by that point they sounded sorely disillusioned.

"We've come to the conclusion that it's impossible to live in Iraq as we've known it," one of these young men explained to me. "After the pogrom in 1941, your conclusion, as Zionists, was that the Jews had no future in Iraq and should therefore go to Palestine. We Communists believed that the answer was to change the quality of life in Iraq by effecting a fundamental change in the regime."

"Then how come you don't go back there?" I asked him. "Perhaps you intend to stay holed up here until someone else changes the regime for you?"

"Because if we return now," another answered me angrily, "the Iraqis will simply execute us!"

"Then why don't you go to Russia?"

"What are you talking about, Russia? We're Jews!" one of them blurted out.

"They don't want our kind in Russia," a fourth grumbled. "The gallows there are just as high as they are in Iraq."

Seeing the depth of their disillusionment, I continued to meet with them, and at one point I told them that I could help if they genuinely wanted to emigrate to Israel. They rose to the challenge and immediately pledged their loyalty to the state. But when I went on to explain that, to make the plan operative, they would have to go to the police and declare that they had just arrived from Iraq as refugees, they seemed stunned. Finally one of them broke the silence.

"Maurice, we thought that you were truly our friend and wanted to help us. Now we see that you want to bury us," he said with such bitterness that I was truly offended. "Since coming to Teheran we haven't dared to poke our noses out the door. Now you tell us to turn ourselves in? What if they don't act according to your plan?"

"I admit there's a certain risk involved, but there's a risk in continuing to hide out, too. The difference is that from the moment you agree to go to the police, we will consider ourselves responsible for you."

"In other words, you want us to be guinea pigs for your Zionist scheme," one of them spat.

"I'm sorry you see it that way," I told him. "To our way of thinking, people aren't used as guinea pigs. If it's necessary to take risks—and essentially there's always some risk in everything we do—we see that as pioneering. If you're prepared to take that risk, we'll consider you pioneers—and I believe you'll succeed. If not, we'll stay friends just the same."

On the day they went to the police station with Zion Ezri, I stood outside sick with anxiety, smoking one cigarette after the next, so that by the time they emerged from the building I had finished off a pack. That first, decisive test went smoothly. The seven men were fined and ordered to leave the country forthwith, but due to the usual Iranian procrastination, it took quite a while before they were issued the papers that enabled them to leave.

Meanwhile, I sought a way to make direct contact with our emissaries in Baghdad so that we could start bringing people into Iran. I also wanted to overcome the barrier of misunderstandings that had plagued my mission ever since I left Israel and particularly since my arrival in Teheran. The roundabout system that required me to communicate with Baghdad via Paris had caused not only delays but considerable (superfluous) anguish all along the way. While the abbé and I were laying the groundwork for getting our people out of Iraq via Iran, our emissaries in Baghdad were reporting to the Mossad on a deterioration in the situation there:

. . . Dozens of youngsters have been arrested and sent to detention camps . . . all on the basis of letters sent from Israel. . . . Part of the library and [educational material] has been confiscated by the police.
. . . In Mosul an entire family has been arrested, including the coordinator of our branch there, who was badly burned while trying to destroy the [educational] material. In short, the situation grows grimmer every day.

Following that preface, their letter went on to present the unequivocal challenge that "We must concentrate on the only immediate solution: emigration. No amount of emissaries will do any good [here] unless there is a way to get people out."

Unfortunately—and incredibly—Baghdad was never apprised of the fact that getting people out was precisely what I was working on in Teheran. Apparently our people in Paris (to say nothing of Israel) did not deem my proposals, plans, or even the purpose of my trip to Teheran and the Assyrian monastery worth reporting to the movement in Iraq! I was not aware of this "oversight," and although I was searching assiduously for a way to establish direct contact with Iraq, it wasn't until the latter half of November that I managed to get a letter through with one of our people from Abadan. Only then did Baghdad discover what was actually going on, and the reaction—wired to Tel Aviv on November 23—was predictable:

To: Artzi
From: Berman
. . . Shammai informs us of what is going on in Teheran and of the unlimited opportunities to get people from Iran to Israel. He also asks us to get people to him as soon as possible to be sent on to Israel.
1. Let us know if the above-mentioned opportunity is feasible so that we can quickly arrange to get people into Iran.
2. If it is feasible, we can't understand why you've kept this from us. . . .

The astonishing reply to this cable—and its muted criticism of the wasted time—was sent out from Tel Aviv promptly the next day:

1. We haven't heard from Shammai about unlimited opportunities for getting people from Goldman‡ to us here.
2. We will ask Shammai for clarifications. . . .

And following the ironclad rule of bureaucratic life that criticism should be answered by countercriticism, the wire added:

4. [Your transmission] implies that you are able to get people into Goldman. If that is true, how come you haven't done so, even if it proves impossible to transfer people directly here? . . . Elaborate upon these possibilities quickly and in detail.

This was an astonishing complaint, for our people in Baghdad had never been told that they should be sending immigrants to Teheran. Moreover, they were unlikely to entertain such an idea on their own, because no one had any reason to consider Iran a jumping-off point for Israel. As to the Mossad's innocence about the chances of getting people out via Iran, over a month before this exchange of cables, right after Glasberg's return to Paris, Yosef Barpal had sent a long cable to Tel Aviv stating:

The abbé is back. According to the attached report . . . we can bring in at least a hundred [immigrants] a week. . . . Details are in the letter. It is necessary immediately to send Goldman one man to administer activities there, one to handle [emigration], and [a wireless operator]. . . .

Yet the critical contents of this cable—the assessment that "we can bring in at least a hundred a week"—were never relayed to Baghdad either.

Meanwhile, I had despaired of attaining fluent, two-way communication with our people in Baghdad, so I decided, rather than wait to work things out in coordination with them, I would simply present them with a *fait accompli* by dispatching smugglers over the border with written instructions to send immigrants back with them. "Salman the Driver" put me in touch with two smugglers recommended as highly experienced and reliable; among their other virtues was a small motorboat in which they easily negotiated the Shatt-al-Arab between Abadan and Basra. We agreed on a price, and I entrusted them with a short note to be delivered to the Philips outlet in Baghdad, which was owned by Selim Sweri (the same Selim who had met me at the airport on my first trip to Baghdad). The note, written

‡ The Mossad's code word for Teheran and Iran in general.

in Hebrew, stated that the bearers were friends of mine and instructed Selim to send "samples" back with them. I trusted that he would get the point and refer them to the appropriate parties, which he promptly did. The result was that on November 28, Tel Aviv received the following cable:

To: Artzi
From: Berman
Tell Shammai that his two agents have arrived and tomorrow we shall send people with them as a test.

Everything went like clockwork from then on, and a few days later I wired Paris—openly—confirming that I had received "the two samples" and requesting that Baghdad be informed of their arrival.

I no longer recall who these two "samples" were, and naturally I have no idea what became of them after they reached Israel. If we had been less preoccupied with mundane details and had had a stronger sense that we were making history, we probably would have been more meticulous about documenting the particulars of these two forerunners who opened the eastward route out of Iraq.

As it was, we were far too busy shifting our operation into high gear. By the end of November, Baghdad informed me that they were sending over Sammi and a wireless operator and would even let me have their reserve wireless set. Such willingness to forgo the reserve set was decisive—and very daring. But by then everyone was convinced that without direct, coded wireless communications between Baghdad and Teheran, the whole operation would deteriorate into a farce—if it ever got going at all.

Sammi and the wireless operator, Eliyahu Shina, crossed into Abadan in mid-December. I met them there, and together we waited for the wireless set to arrive the next day. It was being brought in by a reliable smuggler (one of Sammi's contacts) who was known to be costly but had a special "arrangement" with officers from both the Iraqi and the Iranian security services stationed on both sides of the river—meaning a generous bribe, due in advance. Still, considering that the object in question was as vital and sensitive as a wireless set, in this case money was no object.

At the appointed hour on the following evening, we were waiting for him at the home of Ya'akov Eitan, one of the leading movement activists in Abadan. The smuggler was late, and as the minutes passed, the tension became almost unbearable. At one point I found myself pacing the room and literally wringing my hands, like a caricature of nervousness. Sammi tried to ease our distress by telling us how he had persuaded the smuggler to take on the job and admonished him to be particularly careful with the package because it contained—or so Sammi would have him believe—an unusually large jar of a rare drug that would save human lives. Finally, when our package turned up around midnight, the air all but vibrated with a collective sigh of relief. Yet as we celebrated its arrival with strong, sweet tea and wonderful pastries baked by Ya'akov's mother, the smuggler seemed oddly uneasy. After a while Sammi came right out and asked him what was troubling him.

"I hope you won't be angry with me, but I thought the matter over carefully and decided not to tell the officers what you said about the contents of the package," he confessed apologetically—though I honestly couldn't see what difference it made what he told them. "I was afraid that if I mentioned a jar of medicine, the bastards—you know how they are—would think that I was trying to smuggle in liquor, and that would be very bad. So I told them it was a radio. Simply a radio."

"Simply a radio," Sammi echoed, half choking on a most uncharacteristic giggle.

By then the rest of us were doubled over, and the only answer the smuggler received was our hoots of laughter. Just a radio, indeed! Out of politeness, we refrained from asking whether he had peeked at the contents of the package or his choice was just a wild guess. Either way, the incident reminded me of my high school mathematics teachers explaining how two mistakes—or two erroneous leads—could produce the right answer, and I decided to use the smuggler's story to move the radio on to Teheran, past the customs inspection designed to foil smuggling from the south. The next day, we went to a radio shop owned by one of Ya'akov's friends and asked for a large packing carton and a letter to RCA's main branch in Teheran asking to have the radio checked out because its owners were complaining of consistently poor reception. I also managed to pry the glittering RCA emblem off one of the radios in the shop and placed in a prominent spot on our set. Then we packed the radio in the box and I took it, together with the letter, to the airport in the neighboring city of Ahwaz, where I had booked a flight to Teheran. The small package I carried by hand contained the telegraph key to transmit code and a set of crystals to make the radio operational.

When asked at customs what the carton contained, I whipped the letter out of my pocket with perfect aplomb. The customs inspector perused it but wasn't particularly impressed, either because he wasn't one to believe everything he read or because he couldn't read at all. In any event, he insisted that I open the carton and even volunteered to hold the small package for me so that I could apply myself to untying the rope with both hands. As I bent over to do so, I was sure that the pounding of my heart could be heard right through the layers of heavy clothing that I wore, it being the height of winter. But the inspection proceeded without further incident, and once the customs man was satisfied that the radio was indeed just that, I was allowed to tie the carton up again. To make doubly sure that this was really the end of the matter, however, before I extended my trembling hand to retrieve the small package he was holding for me, I decided to repay the courtesy with one of my own. Removing a bill of a large denomination from my pocket, I told the inspector, in my most dulcet tones and finest Persian (which I was picking up at a phenomenal rate), "May your hands never tire." He was only too glad to exchange the small package for the large bill, while I was suddenly aware of the sweat trickling down my back despite the bitter cold.

When I reached Teheran and told Dov Adiv about the journey, highly pleased with the way things had gone, he caught me off guard by teasing me caustically.

"Idiot, when are you finally going to learn that you give them the money *first,* not after everything's over. You could have saved yourself the trouble."

And upon consideration I had to admit that he was right.

The arrival of the wireless required us to set up a high antenna on Dov's roof, while making sure that it wasn't too prominent. Though Dov's experience served us well in this area, we suffered a series of frustrating failures before regular wireless communications were finally established with Baghdad, on January 26, 1949—and the reception was excellent. While Dov was struggling with these technical problems, I was busy persuading Sammi to stay and work with me in Iran. His usefulness in Baghdad was at any rate dwindling, because some of the officers with whom he had dealings were now under arrest, and there was reason to believe that sooner or later the trail would lead to him. He had therefore planned to return to Israel, but when I revealed my own plans to him, Sammi agreed to team up with me in Teheran. First, though, he returned to Baghdad to wind up his affairs, and I exploited the opportunity to get a long message through directly to Tel Aviv. Everything that I had tried to convey in hints, open cables, and letters via Paris, I now laid directly on the line:

After wasting three months, I have finally met with [Sammi] in Goldman and proved that there are great possibilities here. In a single week, fifteen people were transferred in the south [over the Shatt-al-

The author's grandfather, Salman, and grandmother, Aziza Hillel, in Baghdad, 1923.

The author as a child with his mother and brothers, 1928.

An alley in the Jewish quarter of Baghdad.

A *guffa,* the typical ferryboat crossing the Tigris River.

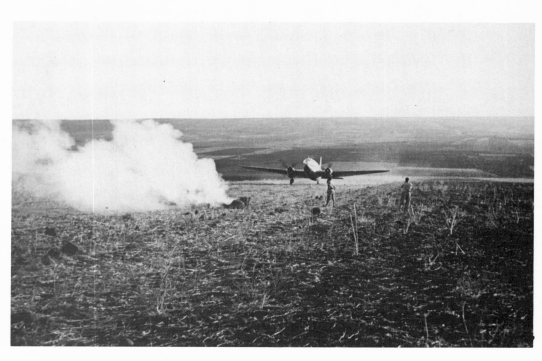

"Operation Michaelberg": the plane bringing the author and a group of immigrants from Baghdad lands in a watermelon field in Palestine, 1947.

The famous Haganah ship *Exodus 1947* in Haifa Harbor before being forced to sail back to Hamburg with its cargo of "illegal" immigrants.

Meeting of the underground pioneer organization of Iraq following the disaster in the desert, Passover 1947. (The author is front, far left.)

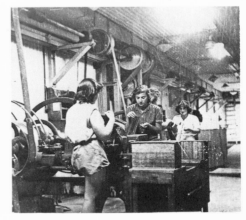

Workers in the underground arms factory. At left, back to camera: Temima, the author's future wife, 1946.

Thousands of Jews crowd the courtyard of a Baghdad synagogue when registering for immigration, 1950.

New immigrants from Iraq—arriving at a transit camp in Israel.

Scene in a ma'abara—a camp for the housing of new immigrants during the early days of their arrival in Israel.

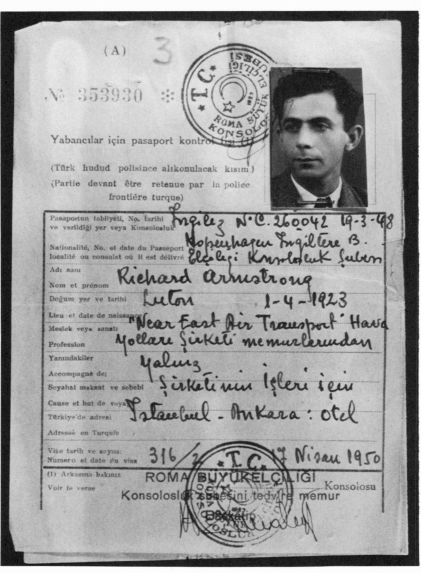

This Turkish *laissez-passer* was added to the author's forged British passport issued in the name of Richard Armstrong, 1950.

Arab] just as an experiment. The prospects look good in the center of the country too [the region of Qasr-Shirin and Khanaqin], but without enough staff to organize the operation here, money will simply be wasted without achieving results. . . . If you cannot or do not intend to send five people here immediately for Mossad work, there's no point in starting in on the groundwork. . . . [And] how do you imagine I'm supposed to work here without some arrangement about funds? . . .

To tell the truth, had it not been for Eliyahu Ben-Yitzhak, I probably never would have gotten anywhere at all with my plans. Eliyahu was a native of the Iranian city of Meshed who had emigrated to Palestine as a child, immediately adopted the country's ways, and subsequently filled a number of public posts. He had been in Teheran for about a year as the representative of the Jewish National Fund and was one of the Israelis I had looked up soon after arriving in Iran. But it wasn't until later, after we had formed a close friendship, that I appealed to him for help. My problem was that the Mossad in Tel Aviv and Paris neglected to forward me any money for quite a while—due either to a short circuit in communications or to a lack of faith in my ability to turn Iran into a way station for emigrants from Iraq. Needless to say, I nagged for money endlessly. When repeated appeals remained unanswered and the flow of immigrants into the city continued at a steadily rising rate, I approached Eliyahu in near desperation and asked him to help out with the money that was in his keeping for the Jewish National Fund.

"Maurice," he replied in a guarded tone, "close as we are, I can't give you money earmarked for the Jewish National Fund without official approval. This isn't my personal bank account."

"Well, I have that approval," I told him.

"You have the approval of the Jewish National Fund?"

"No, but I have power of attorney from the government of Israel, and I hope that bears no less weight with you than the approval of the Jewish National Fund."

Eliyahu looked unabashedly skeptical. "What do you mean by power of attorney? I'm talking about something formal, something in writing. It's not a question of personal trust. I know you're an honest man. But when it comes to public funds, one must be meticulous about formalities."

Silently I reached into my pocket and produced an envelope that contained a letter bearing the heading "Provisional Government of the State of Israel, Paris Legation" and under it the following typewritten statement:

To Whom It May Concern

The bearer of this paper, Shammai, is on an important mission on our behalf. We would be grateful for any aid extended to him in fulfilling his mission.

Respectfully,

The signature was impressive, if quite unintelligible. It happened to be Oscar's, and he had equipped me with the letter for just such a contingency. Ben-Yitzhak gazed at it for close to a full minute and finally asked suspiciously, "And who is this Shammai?"

"That's me," I told him brightly.

After a shorter silence he again asked, in quite a different tone, "Maurice, do you really think it's all right?"

"Eliyahu, I would never do anything that would compromise your position," I assured him. "Whenever I take money from you here, I'll immediately send off an order to have the equivalent transferred to the Jewish National Fund in Israel."

"Will you give me a receipt?"

"Certainly."

"How will you sign it?"

"I'll sign it: Shammai, on behalf of the government of Israel."

He squinted, as if pained by the decision he knew he would have to make. Then his face set into an expression of resolution and he asked in a thoroughly businesslike tone, "How much do you need now?"

I mentioned a sum, received a check, signed a receipt, and for a while my financial problems were solved. From then on, whenever I ran out of money, I went back to Eliyahu Ben-Yitzhak and always received a fresh infusion of funds just for the asking.

I suppose one could argue that the money was used for a noble cause, thereby justifying this rather dubious system. But, in retrospect, I admit it was an irresponsible approach, practically bordering on fraud. All I can say in my defense is that in addition to the good that was achieved with those funds, back in those days, right after the establishment of the state, we still hadn't weaned ourselves of the informal and even underhanded ways of getting things accomplished. It never occurred to me that formal procedures should take precedence over doing whatever was necessary to save lives. Every time I took money from Ben-Yitzhak, I truly did write to Paris and asked to have the Mossad in Israel deposit the equivalent with the Jewish National Fund. What's more, I was assured that this was being done —though I couldn't attest to how *quickly* it was being done. In any case, a few months after this arrangement began, when Ben-Yitzhak sent the pile of receipts signed by "Shammai, on behalf of the government of Israel" to his home office, all hell broke loose. The officials of the Jewish National Fund, who evidently lacked the least sense of humor, were in no way impressed by my title or my cleverness. Thus I was forced to wire Israel:

TO: Artzi
FROM: Goldman
The representative of the JNF here has received telegraphed instructions from the main office . . . forbidding him to give me money without express permission [from Jerusalem]. . . . Soon I shall have to leave here for lack of funds.

And in a subsequent letter, I raised the problem again, with growing exasperation:

As to the matter of money, I have repeatedly asked you to come to an understanding with the JNF so that I can receive funds. . . . Why don't you answer? . . . Are you testing our patience, or is this your way of economizing?

The grief of having taken money from the JNF continued to haunt me for long afterward. Even after the matter was settled in principle, a disagreement broke out over the exchange rate by which the payments should be calculated. Dour accountants sat on both sides of the barricades, and I was called upon to explain again and again the arrangement I had with Ben-Yitzhak and the exchange rates at the time of the transactions.

But even these difficulties and the eventual mess over money could not detract from the fact that in December 1948 we smuggled some forty people from Iraq into Iran! And no less important, we sailed through our first attempt to send on to Israel the first Jews who had entered Iran without papers. They were the seven Communists who were hiding out in Teheran when I arrived—the "guinea pigs" by their definition, "pioneers" by mine—and our system passed the test with flying colors. The cable sent from Paris via Tel Aviv confirming the arrival of the seven in Marseilles (and the subsequent arrival of seventeen other immigrants in Paris) even departed from the usual dry style of such communications and ended with a hearty "Congratulations!"

At the end of December, Oscar sent me a long letter that tried to make amends for all the misunderstandings and the months of frustration it had taken for me to prove my point. "We follow all your activities closely and even understand [your complaint] that not enough is being done," he wrote. "This letter comes to let you know that there are good chances of improving the situation and expanding your activities. I want to tell you that I, personally, am full of admiration for what you have managed to do up to now under such difficult conditions. And I can assure you that your work is fully appreciated by all the comrades." He then went on to detail all the matters then on the agenda; even the sensitive problem of finances was covered in this letter—under the heading of "candies"—with the comment: "We have wired you . . . that we are prepared to deposit any sum here so that it will be available to you there." And finally, the cherry on the cake, as it were: "The most important thing: additional people [emissaries to Iraq and Iran] are definitely available. . . ."

Oscar's letter was dated December 31, 1948, and I couldn't help but regard that date as symbolic. Presumably I could start off the new year satisfied with myself and my accomplishments. All my demands had been or were about to be met. There was appreciation and even admiration for the work I had done. And the idea of a breakthrough via the east now had both full support and the necessary funding.

Nevertheless, I cannot recall feeling particularly gratified in those days. On the contrary, I was consumed by anxiety and felt more like a mountain climber who was sure that the next peak was the summit only to discover when he got there that he was surrounded by even higher, more rocky peaks with no way around them. Now that my demands had been fulfilled, I knew I could make no more excuses. Now we faced the real test and were about to find out whether the glint of light I had seen so clearly was a figment of my imagination or a sign that we were approaching the end of the tunnel.

EIGHT

"Can These Bones Live?"

AT THE END OF 1948, while we were struggling to chisel a few cracks in the wall closing in around Iraqi Jewry, so much pressure was building up inside Iraq that when the first chink opened, the outward flow of Jews threatened to become a deluge. The first to steal over the border were the youngsters of the Zionist movement, who had long dreamed of emigrating to Palestine out of idealism and now found their imaginations fired by the young state's valiant war and victories over the invading Arab armies. Others found themselves on the wrong side of the law, either because they had been caught trying to leave the country illegally and were out on bail or because they had put up the bail and had to be rescued along with their beneficiaries. Also in this broad category of "criminals" were people mentioned in the letters sent from Palestine before May 15, including a few senior officials and other Jewish civil servants who appeared to be prime candidates for show trials on the model of the Shafiq Addas farce.

Yet beyond all those who were forced to flee to safety were ordinary Jews who had simply resolved to leave Iraq. Drawing up a balance of the year's events—from the street demonstrations and the cries of "Death to the Jews" to the sporadic arrests and torture of Jews, the extortion that followed the affair of the mail sacks, and finally Shafiq Addas's trial—they could easily make out the direction in which things were going. The martial law declared on May 15—on the grounds of Iraq's participation in the war in Palestine—was an instrument for governing with a high hand in an atmosphere of terror. And that certainly did not bode well for the Jews.

For all the power it enjoyed, Muzahim al-Pachachi's government still proved unable—and essentially unwilling—to contend with the country's severe economic problems, which were again threatening to cripple Iraq. Its much touted decision to send the Iraqi Army off to fight in Palestine, over six hundred miles from Baghdad, placed an even greater strain on the state's already dwindling coffers, with some 40 percent of the national budget now going to the war treasury. Then the war went sour too. After the first days' enthusiastic reports of the Army's advance on "the suburbs of Tel Aviv," rumors of setbacks in battle began filtering back to Baghdad. After the first truce (which went into effect on June 11, 1948), the Iraqi Expeditionary Force ceased to function altogether. Still, the rulers in Baghdad preferred to keep their soldiers as far as possible from their own capital, for fear that their return would only aggravate the unrest in Iraq. Yet that solution held for only a short time. During the final days of 1948, violent demonstrations in Baghdad called for "a renewal of the fighting," making it painfully clear that keeping the Army in Palestine was both leading Iraq to bankruptcy *and* aggravating the domestic ferment.

It was in these circumstances that, on January 6, 1949, Muzahim al-Pachachi's government reached the end of its road, and that experienced old fox Nuri Said was called upon to form a new government. Presumably there was reason to believe that in the intervening months the crisis born of the Portsmouth Treaty had been completely forgotten (for Nuri had been one of the treaty's leading architects). But a man like Nuri Said was not one to depend on assumptions. To distract the public's attention from his own dubious record and the difficult problems at hand, he quickly produced two familiar "rabbits" from his hat. The first was the old vision of the Fertile Crescent, which would provide Iraq with an outlet to the Mediterranean. The second was that comfortable fallback known to do its job without fail: persecuting the Communists and the Jews.

At first Nuri contented himself with publicizing the death sentences that had been passed (in absentia) on some thirty Jews. To a man, the "condemned" were people who had long left Iraq, legally or otherwise; in fact, most of them were full-fledged citizens of Israel. But in its eagerness to dazzle the public, the Iraqi Government took care to omit that detail, so that the whole world believed that these Jews had already been or were about to be executed. So convincing was this sleight of hand that at one point Israel's Foreign Minister, Moshe Sharett—known as a moderate and cautious man—warned the Iraqis that if reports of the execution of Jews for Zionist activity were confirmed, Israel would regard these measures as "an aggressive act by Iraq in her war against Israel and [would] respond accordingly."

Only after that ominous monition (and a scrupulous check of the names of the condemned, in consultation with our people in Baghdad) did it emerge that the Iraqi executioner was quite idle at that point. Still, that discovery was barely reassuring, for the arrest, brutal interrogation, and pronouncement of harsh sentences on Jews accused of Zionist activity continued apace. And soon thereafter, when the Iraqi hangman was allowed to prove his mettle by dispatching four Communist leaders (one a Jew) in a single day, it appeared that the execution of Jews *qua* Jews, on any number of charges, was only a matter of time.

Given this increasingly hostile atmosphere, it is not surprising that when opportunities arose to flee to Iran—and particularly when word got out that Jews who reached Teheran would be able to continue on to Israel—there was no dearth of candidates for emigration, despite the hardships and dangers of the journey. And dangers there were aplenty, for our system suffered from one major drawback: once our immigrants reached Teheran, we could approach the police and invoke our understanding with them; but on the long journey through Iran to the capital, our "arrangement" did not hold, and it was every man for himself. The first of our groups was caught in mid-January 1949 on its way from Khorramshahr to Ahwaz to catch a train for Teheran, and the four boys were held in custody in southern Iran under unspeakable conditions. At first we feared that they would even be deported back to Iraq, but after they had spent more than two months virtually rotting in jail, we managed to get them out on bail and bring them to Teheran. When the second group (comprising two girls) was caught in the Ahwaz train station, Sammi rushed there to handle the matter personally—though he himself was in Iran illegally and didn't know a single word of Persian. Afterward, when I asked how he managed to persuade the police officer to let the girls go, he merely shrugged and explained contemptuously that it wasn't necessary to speak the language; he just kept stroking the officer's hand with an envelope containing a wad of crisp bills, and that got all his humanitarian arguments across very clearly. "No florid speech of yours would have been any more convincing."

Despite occasional hitches and alarms, however, we soon had our hands full not only with our own immigrants but with people who had reached

Iran by their own devices but nevertheless knew about us and came knocking on our door. All of them were most welcome, but I had to admit that I had run into a very serious snag: while the pressure to flee Iraq was mounting daily, the rate of obtaining the documents needed to move these escapees out of *Iran* was far slower than I had expected. That left me facing a problem I had not foreseen: what to do with all the refugees who were stuck in Teheran under the severe winter conditions of snowstorms, temperatures hovering around zero Fahrenheit—in short, a climate that bore not the least resemblance to what they were accustomed to. And now we were no longer dealing exclusively with strong young men and women but with whole families, from toddlers to the aging and ailing.

I started out in a very magnanimous mood, renting hotel rooms for the new arrivals. But at the rate they were coming in, had I continued with that method, within days I would have filled all the hotels in Teheran—and emptied my anemic bank account. I consulted with Dov Adiv, Zion Ezri, and his son Meir, who had joined our operation with great drive (and, incidentally, was to become Israel's ambassador to Iran in the 1970s), but they merely confirmed that I had indeed worked myself into a predicament. When I asked for their advice on solving it, all three of them seemed to draw a blank. There was no hope of speeding up the formalities, they said, and no place to lodge an appreciable number of people. Hence I would have to decelerate the pace of our rescue operation. When I absolutely refused to slow down the exodus from Iraq—to the degree that I still had control over it—they pointed out gently and patiently, but quite firmly, that the alternative might be the need to bring the operation to a total halt.

"And what if we simply moved into one of the Jewish institutions in the city?" I asked.

"First of all, there aren't very many institutions, other than synagogues," the elder Ezri explained to me. "And invading them would only cause an uproar and draw attention to the problem, which is the last thing we need."

"There's only one institution where there's no danger of being thrown out once you get in," Dov added with characteristic cynicism, "and that's the cemetery."

Choosing to ignore that comment, I asked him to arrange for me to meet with the leaders of the Teheran Jewish community.

"It won't do you much good," Dov remarked sourly, "but if that's what you want, nothing could be simpler. They're good people, really. And you should get to know them in any case."

I dressed as respectably as possible to cover up for my main weakness—

that I was only twenty-six—and made off to meet with the pillars of the Jewish community at the home of Moussa Tov Pastour (who till the end of his days regarded himself as the head of the Zionist movement in Iran). As Dov had suggested, they were all kind and upstanding men but a bit lacking in imagination and perhaps, too, somewhat fearful that my enterprise would end up wreaking havoc in the local Jewish community. I talked to them at length and with great emotion about the fate of Iraqi Jewry, and in return I received generous quantities of tea and sympathy, a warning that there were rumors afoot about "hundreds of Iraqi Jews" living in Teheran illegally, and the regretful clarification that they had no idea where to lodge my immigrants.

"Is that really to be the end of it?" I thought gloomily. After all my talk, cables, and angry letters, would I really have to inform my comrades in Tel Aviv, Paris, and, worst of all, in Baghdad that no more people should be smuggled out to safety because I had nowhere to lodge them? In my distress I remembered Dov Adiv's sarcastic gibe and suddenly heard myself saying, "There's one place I can put my people up without disturbing anyone."

"And where is that?" Moussa Tov asked curiously.

"In the old cemetery near Teheran," I said, hardly believing that I actually had the nerve to say it.

A long, oppressive silence descended on the room until one of the other notables asked in an injured tone, "Mr. Perez, why have you come here to offend us? And how can you show such disrespect for the dead? We have explained the situation to you in all seriousness."

"Heaven forbid that you should misunderstand me!" I gasped while actually warming up to the practicability of the idea. "The last thing I would wish is to offend anyone. And I am sure that the saintly souls who have found their final resting place in that hallowed ground would consider it a great privilege to help save the lives of other Jews."

I knew that the danger of antagonizing these men had passed when their objections shifted to pragmatic considerations.

"Have you any idea how cold it is?" one of them asked.

"Do you know how high the snow drifts can get?" another chimed in.

"Where are you going to put your people so that they won't freeze to death?"

"Surely there must be a mortuary there," I reasoned. "We can fix it up to suit our needs and install heaters."

"But won't your people balk at staying in a mortuary?" someone asked. "Who could sleep in a place like that?"

"I'm sure they'll prefer a mortuary above ground to graves below it," I replied—a bit sharply, perhaps, but intent on driving home the urgency of the situation.

Silence filled the room again as each man followed his thoughts to wherever they led. Finally Moussa Tov revealed where his had taken him.

"Do you know the meaning of the cemetery's name, 'Bahashtia'?" he asked.

"No," I admitted. "Could it be the name of the place where it's located?"

"*Bahashtia* means 'paradise,' " he said with an encouraging smile, "and that is a good sign. For my part, you are welcome to use the cemetery. And I wish you the very best!"

The other gentlemen followed his lead, and we parted on excellent terms. By the next morning I was already getting the place ready for lodgers—cleaning, scraping, disinfecting, boarding up windows, and putting in kerosene heaters and coal stoves for cooking. In a matter of days, the old Jewish cemetery in Teheran had become a camp through which more than twelve thousand immigrants would pass in the course of the following twelve months. Not long after that fateful meeting in Moussa Tov's house, hundreds of "tenants" were already crowded onto its grounds, and we had little choice but to add additional structures for sleeping quarters, cooking, and sanitary needs.

The task of maintaining this hostel proved so complex that I doubt whether I would have taken it upon myself had I gauged it properly from the start. Problems cropped up everywhere, but I concentrated on the basics: supplying and storing food, obtaining blankets and clothing, and providing medical care. Many of the immigrants required immediate medical attention either because of the rigors of their journey—to say nothing of the tension and excitement—or because of the radical change in climate and the fact that Teheran is almost 4,000 feet above sea level, which makes some people feel alarmingly weak. Yet beyond tending to their physical needs, we had to keep the immigrants busy, so I soon found myself immersed in organizing study groups, sports, and other activities. I was aided enormously by Ya'akov Sofer, an Iraqi Jew who had lived in Palestine for many years before moving to Teheran. In response to my call for help, Ya'akov assumed responsibility for all the logistics of maintaining the camp. He worked absolutely tirelessly, and we became fast friends.

Even with that burden lifted, I found myself spending every free hour in the camp, primarily to ensure that morale remained at a reasonable level. For the same reason, I joined in all the camp activities, from volleyball (on the court we cleared not far from the graves) to communal singing. Often I just sat talking to the impatient immigrants, who were sometimes forced to wait for weeks at a stretch without word on when they would be able to embark on the second leg of their journey. And more than once I joined them as they sat through a long, cold winter night in the mortuary, wrapped up in woolen blankets around a glowing coal stove, singing the somber, monotonic songs of the wandering Bedouin.

But usually we managed to keep the mood upbeat, and we also shared many times of gaiety and laughter. Spirits were especially high on the days when the police were scheduled to visit the camp, accompanied by a photographer, to check and photograph the families applying for *laissez-passers*. Whenever that happened, we had to match up our camp residents with the visas issued by the French consulate, so that all our theatrical and artistic talents were given free rein. We turned girls into boys and vice versa, altered people's ages, and made other "adjustments" in appearance, so that, each time the police came, we celebrated a kind of mini-Purim* in the land of Queen Esther and her cousin Mordecai. At times like that, my comrades took great pleasure in observing wryly that Bahashtia was surely the merriest graveyard in the whole of the Middle East!

But I was struck by another biblical parallel: the symbolism of the rundown Jewish cemetery in Teheran coming to life with the echoes of children chattering away in Hebrew, singing songs of Zion, and dancing their way to their salvation and the vision of the Valley of the Dry Bones, in which, the Bible tells us:

. . . there was a noise, and behold a shaking, and the bones came together, bone to his bone. And when I beheld, lo, the sinews and the flesh came up upon them, and the skin covered them above . . . and the breath came into them, and they lived, and stood up upon their feet, an exceeding great army . . . [for] Thus saith the Lord God; Behold, I will take the children of Israel from among the heathen, whither they be gone, and will gather them on every side, and bring them into their own land. . . . (Ezekiel 37: 7–10, 21)

Musings of that sort aside, I knew that the pressure on the Jews of Iraq kept building. So once we had the Teheran camp established as a going concern and we felt that the southern escape route over the Shatt-al-Arab was working more or less satisfactorily, we decided to try to open up the northern route through Khanaqin (on the Iraqi side) and Qasr-Shirin (in Iran, about 130 miles west of Kermanshah). To do so, at the height of the winter I traveled to Qasr-Shirin to meet with representatives of the move-

* Holiday commemorating the rescue of the Jewish community of Persia and Media from the threat of annihilation. One popular custom is to hold costume parades and parties.

ment from Iraq and make all the necessary decisions and arrangements. I also decided to use this opportunity to deliver the pickup truck to the monastery near Kermanshah. My partner on the journey was Benik Pinhasi, a clever, spunky young man who was wholly devoted to our cause and was to serve as driver, escort, guide, and especially as friend. Benik, who today lives on a *moshav* in Israel, was born in Russian Armenia to a family that had migrated there from Iran many years earlier and returned to Iran when he was a child. He spoke a number of languages and was well versed in the ins and outs of life in Iran—which was very fortunate, since I would soon be in need of all his talents.

The trip to Kermanshah, which had taken about eight hours when I made it with Abbé Glasberg and Nino in September, took over two days this time because of the miserable weather. None of the snow had been cleared off the roads, and for miles at a stretch it was impossible to discern that there was a road at all. To negotiate segments like that, convoys would band together and wait until a man equipped with a long stick, for checking the depth of the snow, came along to lead them. Added to this limitation was the problem of the windshield, which was constantly being conquered by a layer of frost, so that our vision was completely blocked. Since the pickup lacked the modern convenience of a defroster, we had little choice but to resort to more primitive methods of fighting the frost, such as scraping it off with knives and even pouring vodka over the windshield in an attempt to melt it—albeit with an enormous sense of (noble) sacrifice. Benik's high-pitched protests over the extravagant waste of good vodka did him no good; I chose to pamper the window, rather than the driver.

After an exhausting day, we stopped for the night in Kazvin, about halfway between Teheran and Hamadan, at a hotel whose Armenian owner was one of Benik's acquaintances. Our rate of progress the next day was no better. And in the afternoon, when we were already pretty close to Kermanshah, the police halted the convoy altogether, informing us that armed highwaymen were operating in the area and we would be wise not to go any farther until sunrise. Left with little choice, on the recommendation of the police we stopped at the nearby *tchai huneh* (literally a tea house but actually closer to a pub or an inn) to pass the time till morning. The *tchai huneh* was essentially a mud hut, one of the many along the roads in Iran where a traveler could allay his hunger and rest his weary bones. That evening it was crowded with customers, some of them travelers like ourselves, others farmers from the vicinity or peddlers and smugglers of various kinds. Most were dressed in heavy, warm camel's-hair robes over layers of colorful rags that were patched together in often weird combinations. Each robe was held closed by a broad sash with a dagger protruding from it—obligatory equipment in those parts for every self-respecting male who cared for his life.

After we entered and seated ourselves on the upended logs in one of the corners, we were approached by the owner bearing a copper tray with small cups of strong, sweet tea that helped revive us. Following the local custom, a series of toasts ensued between Benik and our host, each wishing the other the best of health and the like in such grandiloquent phrases that I had some difficulty following the Persian. In the meantime we were approached by a boy (evidently our host's son) carrying a tray laden with blocks of white goat cheese and homemade yellow butter in one hand and a bowl of creamy yogurt in the other. I clearly remember the exquisitely carved wooden spoon standing in that bowl that was to serve both Benik and myself—as if a spoon apiece were an extravagance. On his head the child carried two enormous pitas—the flat bread ubiquitous in the Middle East—that completely covered his wild, curly locks and flopped down over part of his face. When he reached us and unloaded his cargo on the clay floor, we were instantly apprised of the fact that he had not come in contact with soap and water for many a day. But by then I had already overcome some of my more finicky inhibitions, so that the meal we ate in that *tchai huneh* tasted like a feast fit for a king. The wholesome country atmosphere, the warmth within the hut, and the genial hospitality had rendered me quite mellow—until I found out about the sleeping arrangements.

The *kursi* is, to the best of my knowledge, an original Iranian invention. Essentially it is a very broad, low table with a round opening in the middle and is usually set up in the center of a room. A coal heater is placed under this opening, and then the table is covered by a sheet of canvas or blankets that drape down to the floor. To sleep in a *kursi*, you crawl in and lie with your feet pointing toward the center, so that only your head remains exposed. The heater provides warmth to all comers—and the more the merrier.

There was no way I could live with that arrangement, especially after I saw who my neighbors to the left and right were to be. The rules of conspiracy be damned: nothing was going to get *me* into that lice-breeding contraption. Seeing the look of mortification on my face, Benik came to my aid by persuading the proprietor to set up a wooden bed for me on the side of the room. Actually, it hardly proved necessary, for I wasn't destined to get much sleep that night anyway. At the end of the meal, a friendly game of backgammon got going by the light of sooty oil lamps and lasted till the wee hours of the morning. After each game, the loser was obliged to order a round of arak for the whole crowd. This custom gave me an opportunity to make up for the poor impression I had created due to my excessive individualism, and within a short time I had won a respectable reputation among the denizens of the tea house as a good drinker, at least. Fortunately, they were all tucked cozily into the *kursi* and blithely snoring away when I exited into the freezing night and, unobserved except by the distant stars, delivered myself of the arak that was swiftly eroding my gut. Just as the price of the drinks in that establishment was "popular," so was their quality, and my aristocratic stomach simply rebelled with a vengeance. For years afterward I couldn't bear the smell of arak.

The meeting with my comrades from Iraq took place in Qasr-Shirin in the home of Eliyahu Mualem, who was soon to become dedicated to our cause and help us considerably. The two boys arrived before dawn, having stolen over the mountain border in the dead of night and then crossed one of the tributaries of the Sirwan River, whose raging, icy waters had overflowed its banks. Then they waited for us in Mualem's house for hours without knowing, of course, that highwaymen had held up our progress (though mercifully not our convoy). That extra wait only heightened their tension and excitement—and, I must admit, my own, especially because I knew that one of the people coming to this meeting was Shneur, whom I had last seen at the end of the runway in Baghdad.

When we entered Mualem's house, Shneur swung around to face us at the far end of the hallway (which he had evidently reached in the course of pacing) and bounded toward me. For a few seconds we just hugged one another mutely, and when he finally did speak, he was practically stuttering with emotion.

"I can't believe you're here!" he exclaimed.

"Do you recall the last time we saw each other?"

"Of course," he said. "It was in the airport. At night."

"And do you remember what you said to me then, when we parted?"

He looked back at me sheepishly as he confessed, "I don't recall a thing. It was a very unsettling moment."

"Ah, but *I* remember," I reported proudly. "You said, 'Amo Yusuf, come back to us.' Well, here I am!"

That seemed to call for another round of embraces, which lasted until we were called into the dining room for a light meal. As we ate, I listened carefully to the description of the route the boys had taken through the boulder-strewn mountains and over the swollen river. Clearly it was unsuitable for anyone but young, strong, and adventurous men—at least during the winter months. But it was passable, and so there was no reason not to begin using it. I therefore gave the boys the names of a few more smugglers, received Eliyahu Mualem's consent to utilize his house as a way station, and settled the financial arrangements regarding lodging for the immigrants, their journey to Teheran, and the "hush money" that would undoubtedly have to be shelled out at the many stops along the way. We also devised a system of communication between Qasr-Shirin and Teheran and settled on appropriate code words for letters, cables, and even phone calls if necessary. Then, after an emotional parting with the young men who had to pick their way back over the forbidding terrain to Iraq—and the grim situation awaiting them there—Benik and I returned to Kerman-shah late that night.

We were scheduled to visit the Assyrian monastery toward noon the next day and deliver the pickup truck, as promised. But rather than drive it to Qasr-Shirin, we decided to leave the truck in Kermanshah for servicing, after the difficult journey from Teheran, and continue westward by taxi. It was in that same taxi that we returned to a rather shabby hotel in Kerman-shah and, after the tiring ride and all the excitement of the past few days, instantly flopped down onto our beds and plunged into a deep sleep from which we did not emerge until late the next morning. Benik went to the barbershop for a shave, but I decided to waive that indulgence and wash up in the room. Hence I was alone when, soon thereafter, I heard some-one rapping insistently on the door.

"Who's there?" I asked as a matter of habit.

"Open up! Police!" came the terrifying reply.

The rapping now turned into pounding that pressured me to open the door quickly, before I had time to plan how I was going to explain my movements in the area. And as soon as I had the door open a crack, a strapping man in civilian dress burst into the room.

"Your papers!" he barked, in sharp contrast to the exquisite manners I had grown accustomed to in all my dealings in Iran. Silently ordering myself not to panic, I removed a driver's license from my pants pocket and held it out to him. He looked it over disdainfully and continued in a no-nonsense tone, "I mean an identity card. Or a passport."

"My French passport is in Teheran, and I haven't got any other papers," I explained with the best approximation of calm I could muster—not real-izing, of course, that in so saying I had revealed the major part of my problem. I had arrived in Iran in August 1948 on a visa good for one month only. At the time, I thought it would suffice, since I was planning to go on to Iraq; and when it turned out that I would be staying in Teheran after all, I tried to extend the visa but got absolutely nowhere. Even the ties I had developed in the course of my immigration work did no good.

Getting visas to stay in Iran and visas to leave it were two entirely different matters, handled by two distinct, rival departments that spent more time foiling one another's plans than tending to their own. So I simply despaired of extending my stay legally and decided to take out a driver's license (which was valid for a year) on the off chance that it would serve as satisfactory identification in an hour of need—though I really didn't believe that if anything went awry or I was subject to a genuine investigation, a driver's license would be of much avail. Moreover, I knew that falling afoul of the law in Iran could be a most unpleasant affair. Descriptions of the conditions in the country's jails and of the methods of interrogation were not in the least encouraging. And I was keenly aware that if an investigation were to branch out—in our case, reach my place of residence, which also housed a wireless station and a wireless operator without any papers at all—the odds of getting off easily (or even with our lives, for that matter) were not particularly promising.

At that point, however, the detective seemed to content himself with my driver's license, for he moved on to the next subject.

"Where is your friend?" he asked gruffly.

"Which friend do you mean?" I parried. "I have many of them."

"Now see here, I'm not playing games with you," he roared. "Where is the man you came with? The one who's sharing this room with you?"

"Oh, *that* one," I said, beaming over our breakthrough in communication. "He went out to buy something in a clothing shop"—this being my way of gaining time to plan out my moves.

"All right, let's go look for him," the detective ordered. So I put on my coat and accompanied him out into the brisk morning air.

"Do you prefer to walk or take a carriage?" he asked.

"I'd prefer the carriage."

"You'll have to pay the driver, you know."

"Chashm," I replied in my best Persian—meaning, approximately, "My pleasure."

Upon settling into a carriage, I stuck my hand into my coat pockets to fish out my gloves and, to my horror, was reminded of their contents. In one I felt a small and highly incriminating piece of paper that I knew contained names and phone numbers; the other held a neatly folded newsletter from my kibbutz that had reached me just before I left Teheran. At the first opportunity I feigned a coughing fit so that I could stuff the note into my mouth and swallow it, but the newsletter was another matter entirely. On the one hand, it didn't contain any secret or dangerous information; from what I had managed to read, I knew that it reported an increase in milk production, in the number of eggs gathered from the chicken coops, and other details attesting to the kibbutz's flourishing economy. On the other, all this fascinating if wholly innocuous information was given in Hebrew, and the obvious question was how the supposedly French-Moroccan Maurice Perez would explain his presence in and around Kermanshah, near the Iraqi border, without papers but with a detailed report in Hebrew on agricultural produce in Israel? Clearly, my first priority was to relieve myself of that albatross.

Fortunately, my predicament reminded me of an old joke about a thief who was caught in the act and pleaded with the policeman who was hauling him into the jailhouse to let him stop at a bakery and buy some bread, promising to bring the policeman a tasty cake in return. Touched by compassion, the policeman consented and waited outside while the thief, predictably, entered the bakery through one door and promptly fled through another. Some time later the same policeman caught the very same thief, and when they passed a tobacconist on the way to the jailhouse, the thief begged to be allowed to buy some cigarettes. By then the policeman was wise to him and replied, "Oh, no. You won't make a fool of me again. This time, you stay out here and *I'll* get the cigarettes."

As we traveled in the carriage from store to store, going to all the shops where I knew Benik would not be found, I decided to try my luck with the same strategy. Alongside one of the shops I suggested to the detective that I would go inside and see if my friend was there. "Absolutely not," he snapped. "You stay here in the carriage while I go in and have a look." Unlike the thief in the story, I saw no point in trying to make a getaway. But I did have enough time to unravel a corner of the upholstery and stuff the newsletter inside. And unless that carriage has been destroyed by now, it probably still contains undeniable evidence of my kibbutz's startling progress.

In time the detective gave up on finding Benik in any one of the stores and decided to deposit me with his superior at the station house while he waited for my friend at the hotel. The superior, an inspector seated behind a broad, polished desk in a heavily starched uniform, asked me to take a seat and began a systematic interrogation: name, address, birthplace, date of entry into Iran, residence, and so on. I gave him as little information as possible, and he wrote it down. The fact that I had managed to dispose of the incriminating newsletter and suspicious slip of paper was a great source of relief but still left me with the problem of accounting for my movements.

"What brings you to Kermanshah?" the inspector asked.

"I've come to visit the abbot of the Assyrian monastery," I replied, for lack of any other reasonable explanation. But then I immediately regretted having said it, for the inspector pressed the call bell on his desk, and when a soldier entered the room, he placed a note in the young man's hand and dismissed him. I assumed that they were going to confirm my alibi with the abbot, and that set me worrying. What would I do if he denied ever having met me?

"And what were you doing in Qasr-Shirin?" the inspector continued in the same tone of mild curiosity that I found particularly suspicious.

"I heard that the drive there is lovely and the scenery breathtaking," said I—not very convincingly, I fear.

"Indeed," the inspector retorted. "But did you not in fact go there to smuggle something? My guess is that you're smuggling goods or people."

Fearing that I might have reddened at the accuracy of his analysis, I quickly assumed an injured expression in the hope that the blush would pass for anger.

"I regret that you have that impression, sir. I am the representative of a highly respected French company," I said as pompously as I could, "and I firmly protest your insinuations. Is there a French consul in this city? I wish to speak with him immediately."

"A Frenchman, are you?" he said skeptically. "Well then, how come you speak Persian? Don't tell me you've managed to learn the language fluently during the four months you've been here, as you claim."

"Thank you for the compliment," I said coyly. I had indeed picked up Persian easily because many of its words are identical to their Arabic equivalents, and others, from an Indo-European source, were also easy for me to remember. I made grammatical mistakes, but they didn't prevent me from speaking fluently.

Yet the subject was soon forgotten, for at just that moment the detective returned with Benik, who entered the room like a cyclone, loudly complaining that these country bumpkins had dared to offend a distinguished gentleman like myself and warning that he did not intend to allow such behavior to pass unnoticed. On the contrary, he would protest it vigorously in the proper quarters in Teheran. As a matter of fact, he insisted on speaking with his friend General Sartip Safari, the chief of police, and demanded that he be phoned immediately. The inspector, who impressed me as being far from a country bumpkin, seemed genuinely taken in by this exhibition of self-importance and ordered the phone operator to connect him with police headquarters in Teheran. When the call came through, he quickly passed the receiver to Benik.

"Is the chief of police in?" Benik shouted into the mouthpiece, adding after a second or two, "When is he expected back?"

Benik covered his free ear with his palm and strained to hear the response from the capital.

"Well, the minute he comes in, please tell him that Benik called. Yes, B-e-n-i-k. I must speak with him urgently. I'm in Kermanshah. Ker-man . . . This is impossible!" he fumed at the inspector, as if he were personally responsible for the poor connection. "Can you hear me?" Benik shouted back into the receiver. "I'll call him back. Yes. Fine. God bless you," he concluded with the traditional Persian phrase of parting.

The inspector spoke more softly now and was quick to explain that he meant no offense. The city was rife with rumors about strangers, and he was obligated to check us out—especially after he learned that we had hired a special taxi to take us to Qasr Shirin, on the Iraqi border. And in such weather, no less! I, too, changed my tone, commending him on his alertness and assuring him that there was no need to apologize. "You were only doing your job," I said with a broad smile, "and I appreciate that." Whereupon I stood up and extended my hand in parting.

"One moment, please, Monsieur Perez. Won't you be good enough to take your seat," he said more solicitously but just as firmly as before as he again rang the bell on his desk. When a soldier entered, the inspector said brusquely, "Show him in."

I almost choked on my own breath. In the doorway stood the Assyrian abbot, and I could see in his eyes that he was surprised to see me seated in the inspector's office. Now came the moment of truth, the face-to-face meeting—the confrontation, in professional jargon—an effective if odious method of demolishing an alibi. Three little words from the abbot—"Never met him"—were all it would take to place me in deep trouble and destroy our whole carefully constructed operation.

"Do you know this man?" I heard the inspector ask curtly.

"I certainly do, Inspector," came the definitive reply.

"Is he an honest man? Can you trust him at his word?" the policeman continued.

"Mr. Perez has been invited to join me for dinner today, and I would hardly invite a man to dine with me were I not sure of his rectitude and good intentions."

No man could ask for more. Indeed, the inspector was satisfied enough to release us immediately. Yet, to this day, I continue to wonder how many people in that situation would have spoken as he did. After all, the abbot did not know why I had been taken into custody or what suspicions hovered over me. His own position was precarious enough, and yet he took a great risk that could have been avoided merely by saying, "I don't believe we've met" or "I don't seem to recall." My annoyance with Abbé

Glasberg for having promised the Assyrians the truck had been transformed into undying gratitude before I had even stepped out of the room.

It was the promised truck that now carried us to the monastery, where the monks served us a meal—though I was still not up to feasting. A few glasses of vintage vodka helped put me back in shape, however, and soon I was ready to face the long bus ride over snow-covered roads to Teheran. When we took leave of the abbot and could finally speak in privacy, I shared my amazement with Benik.

"I had no idea that you knew the chief of police!"

"Who doesn't know the chief of police?" was his flip reply.

"But you told the inspector you wanted to speak with him."

"Really, Maurice! What was the alternative? To let you rot in jail?"

"And you left a message that Benik called."

"Let them go find out who Benik is."

"But what would you have done if he had been in just then?"

"What do you mean? Do you think the chief of police has nothing better to do than sit around in his office all day waiting for cranks to call? Actually, I didn't even hear what they were saying at the other end. I just said what I had to and hung up, so stop badgering me with questions," he snapped, embarrassed by his own audacity.

At first I thought the northern route was jinxed, for in addition to our brief contretemps in Kermanshah, a group of six immigrants dispatched by that route were caught on the Iraqi side, shipped back to Baghdad, and held in detention (our people in Baghdad believed they had been betrayed by a police officer in Khanaqin). And later that year, in October 1949, three young men disappeared and were apparently murdered for their money by the smuggler who was to have led them from the border to Qasr-Shirin. But even so, we didn't give up. The Qasr-Shirin route was important to us, even if fewer people utilized it, because it enabled us to vary our movements and forced the Iraqi police to deploy along a very long border, rather than concentrate solely on the south. Moreover, although the northern route was genuinely difficult and required great physical stamina, it was much shorter for our members living in northern Iraq, who could thus avoid traveling hundreds of miles south to Basra only to continue hundreds of miles north again to Teheran.

Meanwhile, the stream of immigrants in the south continued almost without a hitch. Directing the operation from the field, Sammi tried to expand it, so that by the end of February 1949, a hundred twenty of our people had crossed the border (in addition to twenty others who had made it to Iran on their own), and our immigrant camp in Teheran began to swell and throb with life.

The visas for Europe were also obtained regularly, enabling us to assure the Iranian authorities that our "customers" would leave the country just as soon as they were provided with *laissez-passers*. Yet despite all the palms we greased and pockets we stuffed—and all the promises we received in return—the rate of departure from Iran continued to be agonizingly slow. And when the people who received *laissez-passers* finally did reach Europe —Paris or Rome—they were again placed in immigrant camps and were told to wait their turn to sail to Israel. This system involved a large financial outlay, to say nothing of the extended displacement of people who had already experienced considerable discomfort in our makeshift accommodations in Teheran. As long as we were dealing with isolated individuals, we had no choice but to work through Europe, and neither was the problem particularly irksome. But from the moment we began handling groups of dozens and then hundreds of people, the indirect route no longer struck me as being logical. In January 1949 I wrote to both Paris and Tel Aviv about instituting a more efficient arrangement, and my correspondents replied that as soon as a greater number of people had been issued *laissez-passers* and exit visas, it would be possible to charter flights directly to Israel. In fact, Air France had already agreed to the idea in principle.

Their condition was met at the beginning of March 1949, when the Iranians issued 102 *laissez-passers*—an appreciable number by all accounts and proof that we had graduated out of the experimental, episodic stage of our program. On March 3, therefore, I cabled Tel Aviv to ask whether Air France's offer still stood, estimating that our immigrants would be able to fly out of Teheran within a week. Five days later I received the answer that "Air France's offer is still concrete, but only to [France]. The price [to France] is £83, after a discount. . . ." But the whole idea was to avoid having to fly via Europe, and the notion of sending over a hundred people by this circuitous route seemed a waste of time, energy, and cash. Worse yet, I discovered that Air France's regular flight out of Teheran made a stopover in Damascus, which was quite out of the question for Jewish refugees from Iraq who had left their country illegally and had no documents other than *laissez-passers*. I expressed my disappointment the next day in a wire to Tel Aviv and immediately began to make my own inquiries about how to get our people out promptly, before their *laissez-passers* expired.

When we approached other airlines flying to Europe, in the hope of finding a flight without a stopover in an Arab country, we immediately came up against the problem of money. Until then I had assumed that arrangements for special flights would be made in Paris, so that the payments would also be made abroad. Now that I had to send my immigrants by regular commercial flights, I would have to pay in Teheran. And if one ticket on Air France cost £83 (at a discount!), the price of 102 tickets would be close to £8,500 (about $35,000 at the exchange rate of 1949)— a veritable fortune for us in those days. I asked Tel Aviv and Baghdad to transfer £5,000 to me and proceeded to check the possibility of alternative flights.

It was Dov Adiv who came up with the suggestion of seeing whether we could fly to Israel on Iran's own national carrier, Iranian Airways. He was well acquainted with the manager of the company, Gholam Ibtihaj, and believed him to be not only talented and influential but a man one could do business with—and specifically a man who would agree to charter flights to Israel. Actually I myself had thought about Iranian Airways a number of times but had always dropped the idea. The company boasted a total of five two-engine Dakotas that flew mainly domestic flights and had no regular international route. Having flown with it, I could attest that almost every flight was marred by some technical or other sort of snafu, and it was common for a plane to reach its destination on one engine. Considering my predicament, however, and in the absence of any other solution, I agreed to meet with Ibtihaj.

The fellow who turned up was an elegantly dressed, middle-aged gentleman whose girth was matched only by his ego. Educated in the West, he spoke fluent English and was very candid about his political ambitions. In fact, he made a point of detailing his good connections—including the fact that his brother-in-law was the chief of police, Sartip Safari. Dov was quite right about his commercial instincts. After hearing our introductory remarks, Ibtihaj got right down to business, declaring, "I'm ready for a deal. It's good for you and it's good for me." To which he quickly added with a broad smile, "It's even good for Iran."

I responded by making any deal conditional upon a solemn commitment that the planes would not fly over Iraq—or any other Arab country, for that matter. Together we studied a map and traced a route that would take the flights north over the Turkish border, then due west toward Adana, and finally south over the Mediterranean to Israel. The price Ibtihaj quoted was reasonable—much lower, at any rate, than the cost of a flight to Paris—and as my resistance faded I began to see the advantages of establishing ties with the Iranian national airline and building contacts with local commercial factors.

Since the Dakotas were capable of taking twenty or twenty-two people, at this stage we were talking about five flights and hoped to start the series on March 17. To do so we had to work at a frenetic pace, shuttling to and from the French consulate for the visas, collecting the money transferred from Baghdad and then converting it to local currency, briefing the pilots and the prospective passengers—and all this in addition to our routine work of maintaining the camp and meeting the new arrivals from Iraq. But the prospect of sending our first large group from Teheran straight to Israel was such a tonic that we never seemed to tire.

The flight scheduled for March 17 was canceled due to bad weather. Two days later, we discovered a problem that we hadn't foreseen and that forced us to make a risky decision. Despite my agreement with Ibtihaj, the planes would not be able to fly over Turkey, because the Turks refused to approve the flight route we had sketched out—or at least would not permit any stopover for refueling, without which a fully loaded Dakota could not make it from Teheran to Tel Aviv via Turkey. The one possibility that remained was to take a direct route, as the crow flies, over Iraq and Syria— precisely the course I was trying to avoid.

Still, time was pressing, so that when I wired Tel Aviv to explain the situation and spell out the Iranian proposal about the direct route, I stressed that "If your answer is negative, you must contact Air France immediately and get the 102 people out of here." Again I reminded them that Air France's regular flight from Teheran was via Damascus, and "If you settle with [the French], you must emphasize that they cannot fly over or land in any Arab country."

Though I was obliged to wire Tel Aviv and consult with the heads of the Mossad, I honestly did not place much hope on a solution coming forth from Zion: if the usual pace of things held in this case too, I could expect many a day to pass before Tel Aviv settled the matter with Air France. Neither did I believe in the chances of persuading the French to change their standard flight route. So, rather than wait idly for salvation, I applied myself to solving the problem on my own. Dov Adiv arranged an urgent meeting with Ibtihaj and the pilot who was to take our flights, and I opened it by broaching the somewhat unorthodox idea that had taken shape in my mind. Since the risks involved in flying over Iraq and Syria applied only to a passenger plane whose destination was known to be Israel, if there were some way we could conceal these two facts—that is, if the control tower in Teheran would announce that the plane was empty and was destined for Beirut, say, or Cairo—presumably there was no danger that it would be forced to land in an Arab country somewhere along the way.

"That's just brilliant," pronounced the captain, a Frenchman, with such heavy sarcasm that Ibtihaj literally winced at his lack of diplomacy. "And what am I supposed to do with the people? Teheran will announce that we're leaving with an empty plane and then we reach Beirut or Cairo with twenty people inside. What will I say then? That they were all born along the way? And what do you think they'll do to your people in Beirut or Cairo? Aren't Lebanon and Egypt Arab countries, in your book?"

"You'll reach Beirut or Cairo with an empty plane," I explained patiently, "just as the control tower announced. All you have to do is diverge from your standard flight path to let the people off in Israel along the way. Then you'll take off again and continue the flight as planned."

This was essentially a variation on the tried-and-true "Michaelberg" plan, but I was not at all sure how it would go over with Ibtihaj and the French pilot, who did not impress me as the adventurous type. Ibtihaj was the first to react.

"All right," he said, "I'll take it upon myself to arrange for the control tower to announce the departure of an empty plane."

This contribution was critical, for without the collaboration of the control tower the plan was worthless, and Ibtihaj was the only one who could ensure it.

Now we both turned to the pilot.

"Well," he began in a tone that suggested something short of firm resolve, "if that part is arranged, I suppose I can carry out the rest of the plan without any special difficulty."

"And the others in the crew?" I asked, taking nothing for granted.

"You can depend on them. They're all absolutely first-class."

"Well then, gentlemen, are we in business?"

We were. So when no word came from Tel Aviv about an understanding with Air France, I wired the plan that we had settled on in Teheran. In point of fact, the Mossad people neither approved nor rejected it. They merely cabled back laconically that we would have to land in Haifa, rather than at Lod Airport† (which was bustling with activity that precluded any hope of secrecy), and provided such details as the width of the air corridor, the altitude and point at which the flight should cross the coast, and the warning that "you must not fly over the port or any ship. . . . Communications over the same wavelength as with Lod." I chose to take all that as their sanction to go ahead.

In a subsequent conversation the pilot explained to me that after giving the matter much thought, he had come to the conclusion that Beirut was preferable to Cairo as his presumed destination, because the distance was shorter, and with more than twenty passengers aboard he was limited in

† The Hebrew name given to Lydda Airport, today Ben-Gurion Airport.

the amount of fuel he could take on. For this first flight, however, I insisted that he declare his destination as Cairo, since that way he could exploit the fact that a cargo flight out of Cairo was already on order. This required us to take certain special measures, to which I agreed only on condition that the entire plan remain secret. I even kept the matter from our local activists, and when I cabled the details to Israel I insisted they maintain total secrecy.

Finally, on the evening before the first flight, I invited all the members of the crew (along with Dov Adiv and his wife) to dinner at the Park Hotel. I wanted to become acquainted with all of them personally. I just couldn't see my way to place the lives of twenty-two human beings in the hands of nameless, faceless people, and I wanted to try to instill in them something of our sense of mission. The crew consisted of four men: the captain and the copilot, both French; a Greek communications officer; and an Iranian steward. After spending that evening together, and meeting them again many times thereafter, I found that they fully deserved the pilot's assessment of them as truly fine and responsible people. Toward the end of the meal, when I steered the conversation to the operation that lay ahead, I tried to sound composed and businesslike but could barely conceal my emotion, and I'm sure they sensed it. I explained who their passengers would be, why they had fled their native land, and what was likely to befall them if their plane landed in an Arab country—at best torture and perhaps even execution.

"I understand you perfectly, Monsieur Perez," the pilot assured me gravely. "You can trust me that even if it means placing lives in jeopardy, I will not land in an Arab country."

The other three crewmen nodded their heads in assent, and that was reason enough to refill our glasses and drink a toast to success—this time with a sense of fellowship that had been forged around that table.

The rest, as they say, is history. Before first light on Friday, March 25, a group of twenty-two people stood huddled in the cold of the Bahashtia camp clutching their meager belongings as they waited for the bus that would carry them to the airport. Despite the early hour, all the residents of the camp gradually emerged from the buildings to give them a hearty send-off. Some of these people had come to Bahashtia three months earlier and had known moments of severe doubt about whether they were not indeed doomed to live out their days among those tombstones. Even now they had no idea that they would be in Israel within hours; for security reasons we continued to let them believe that the plane's destination was Paris. Only the head of the group knew the truth, because he was given an envelope containing the first twenty-two Israeli visas issued in Teheran.

He was ordered to conceal it and not remove it from its hiding place until the plane had landed in Haifa. The visas were improvised, of course. Told that equipping the immigrants with papers would facilitate their registration upon entering the country, I decided to keep these documents spare and typed up notes stating:

I, the undersigned, a representative of the government of Israel, hereby confirm the entry of —————— to Israel as an immigrant.

SHAMMAI

Everything went smoothly at the airport, so that within minutes of the immigrants' arrival, the Dakota lifted off the runway and Dov Adiv descended from the control tower with his thumb pointing upward as a sign that the announcement had been issued as planned. I told Mansour, one of the local activists, to remain at the airport, follow the communications coming in from the plane, and report back to me. Then we drove back to town, but, rather than return home, I went out for a walk in the crisp spring air. I needed to be by myself a bit to grapple with my awful sense of helplessness. Until an hour before, I was still in a position to make decisions, change plans, even scrap the whole operation if I chose to. Now the process I had set in train was going on its own, beyond my control. All I could do was fret and hope for the best—though logically I knew that even if I were on the plane, I probably couldn't change whatever fate had in store.

Actually, I was supposed to have been on that flight. I had made up my mind to "drop in" on Tel Aviv and discuss the things that were troubling me face to face with my superiors. For the most part, these were the same old issues: finances and personnel to supplement or replace the emissaries in Iraq and Iran. "I wish to inform you," I was soon to write sourly (in a letter that went out with the second flight), "that neither [the Mossad emissary] in Berman, nor [Sammi], nor I can go on working." And I explicated:

As for me, I've already explained to you that my residence permit expired long ago and I can't seem to get it renewed. I might be served with a deportation order any day, and in a situation like this, with dozens of [Iraqi Jews] here, that could lead to disaster. And besides, all three of us have long overrun the period set down for our missions. I don't know whether it's quite clear to you what conditions are like here at this time. . . . We feel that our productivity is steadily waning. The only thing that keeps us going is a reluctance to leave our posts before replacements arrive, because it will take years to rebuild the organization and reestablish our contacts. Still, there's a limit to everything. . . .

I also spoke of problems with the aging wireless and the fact that, delighted as I was over the deal with Iranian Airways, clearly it was only a stopgap measure. Sooner or later we would have to reach an understanding with an airline that had larger and more reliable planes if we wanted to cover long distances without refueling—which was the only way to avoid flying over Arab countries. At any rate, as soon as I had resolved to go, I applied for the exit and entry visas that would allow me to leave and return to Iran legally. But despite repeated promises, they still hadn't materialized, and now I decided that if I didn't receive them soon, I would take one of our future flights illegally.

These were the thoughts that buzzed through my head as our first flight was in the air and I was walking the streets of Teheran to get a grip on my nerves. By the time I returned home, the plane had been in the air for five and a half hours and I had all but forgotten about Mansour, still stationed at the airport, until the phone rang and I heard his voice crack with anxiety at the other end.

"Maurice, something bad has happened," he wailed, "something very bad!"

"Getting all worked up won't help, Mansour. Tell me exactly what you've heard. But *exactly.*"

"It's not good. The Beirut control tower says that the Iranian plane WF.AAK en route to Cairo has reported one of its engines is gone. Maurice, that's our plane!"

"It happens to them often," I told him in a soothing voice. "Let's hope everything will turn out all right. Find out exactly where the plane is located right now and call me back."

"I've already checked. It's over the Mediterranean, near the Lebanese coast. Maurice, you know what will happen if it's forced to land in Beirut!" He was wailing again.

"Let's hope that won't be necessary" was all I was prepared to offer. "But don't stand there by the phone. Go back and find out what's happening."

A few minutes later he called again, even more shaken than before.

"The situation looks terrible, Maurice. The whole airport is in an uproar. The plane has just announced that its second engine has conked out and it's losing altitude. Oh, Maurice, it's awful!"

"Mansour," I comforted him with my immutable reply, "we must hope for the best. Go back and find out what the plane is reporting now."

A few more minutes passed before the phone rang a third time, and now Mansour sounded very different. "Maurice, it's all right!" he crowed. "The plane has announced that it's making an emergency landing in Haifa."

"Excellent, Mansour," I said in the same neutral tone as before. "Now you can return here."

I should add that the commotion was equally great at the airport in Haifa, where fire engines and ambulances stood waiting at the ready and the entire airport staff, from baggage handlers to airline officials, had gathered outside the terminal to watch as the drama unfolded. Much to everyone's relief, the plane made a faultless landing. The French captain and Iranian steward were the first to disembark, and the whole crowd was amazed at their perfect composure, as if nothing out of the ordinary had happened. Their cool was matched only by that of the two Mossad men who had come to meet the plane, for they alone knew that the whole drama had been staged. This flourish had been cooked up by the pilot and myself to cover for the fact that the plane would not reach Cairo. (Obviously we couldn't repeat so elaborate a ruse, so that subsequent flights simply made unscheduled—and unannounced—stops in Haifa before going on to Beirut.) In any case, while the crowd dispersed quietly outside, the plane's passenger cabin had turned into the scene of bedlam, for the head of the group had informed his fellow passengers that they were in Israel.

"But Maurice said we were going to Paris first!" one of the immigrants insisted, as if the group leader had made an incredibly stupid mistake. It took a few seconds for our immigrants to grasp what had happened, but once they did the mood became wildly jubilant. First the passengers burst into applause. Then they began to descend from the plane in a hubbub of singing, whooping, dancing on the tarmac, and embracing each other in a joy still bordering on disbelief.

Rather than continue on to Cairo, the empty plane was "repaired" overnight and returned to Teheran the next day. On March 28, when we brought the second group to the Teheran airport, I told the pilot, "On your next flight you're going to have a stowaway."

"Anyone interesting?" he asked with a teasing grin.

"To the degree that I am," I said with a short bow of the head. "I must make a brief visit to Israel. Will you agree to have me along?"

"Only on condition that you promise to return," he quipped.

"You needn't worry about that. But I must tell you that I have no visas, for leaving or returning."

"I'm no policeman, and I'm certainly not an Iranian stoolie," the captain informed me obligingly. "I'll get you out of here. You can count on that."

So on March 30, the date of the third flight, I reported to the airport early. The terminal was crawling with policemen, but it no longer fazed me, for by that point many of them were greeting me like an old friend; a few even snapped to attention and treated me to a smart salute. Their pay was so low that they were glad of any "subsidy" they could garner from the more fortunate and benevolent of the world, and I was evidently considered a prime sample of that species. Consequently I was able to enjoy not only respect and attention but comfortable conditions, such as the ability to come, go, and otherwise move freely about the airport without being followed. I arrived without baggage (lest my "silent partners" be alarmed about the loss of such a lucrative source of supplementary income), and when the pilot arrived I joined him in a stroll out to the plane, parked not far from the terminal. We then returned to the main building and retraced this route a few times, but during the last of these walks I remained in the cockpit while he walked back to the terminal alone. Within minutes the plane had filled with our immigrants, taxied onto the runway, identified itself to the control tower as a flight to Beirut without passengers, received permission for takeoff, and made its way aloft.

About two hours later, we crossed the border and proceeded to fly over the barren plains of Iraq, so strikingly different from the green, mountainous terrain of Iran. I was in exceptionally good spirits that ebbed for only a few minutes due to a curious incident. Coming toward us at one point was the Iranian Airlines plane marked WF.AAK, which had made the first Teheran–Haifa run and was now on its way back from Cairo with the cargo that our crew had failed to take then. Its pilot contacted us over the radio and warned that the Egyptians knew about our little caper and were determined to arrest our crew if they ever showed up in Cairo.

"Pay no attention to him," our pilot said good-naturedly. "He's just pulling my leg out of envy."

Thus assured that all was well, I stopped worrying and walked into the passenger compartment to meet with our immigrants, who were surprised but delighted to see me. I had become very friendly with many of them during the weeks we spent together in the camp, and now I took special pleasure in teasing them about their plans to paint the town red once we arrived in Paris. Then I returned to the cockpit and immediately sensed that something was wrong. Before I could even ask what the matter was, the plane's port wing dipped sharply and we began making a 180-degree turn. I barely managed to stop myself from falling, but as soon as I got my balance (and my breath) back, I demanded to know what was going on.

"We're returning to Teheran," the pilot said curtly and handed me a piece of paper on which the radioman had written the following message from the Teheran control tower:

Do not fly over Syria. There's a danger your plane will be shot down. Suggest you return to Teheran.

I actually felt faint and noticed that the hand holding that paper had begun to tremble slightly. "They must have found out about us," I thought. "The game's up." I recalled the message we had received from the pilot of WF.AAK about an hour before, and now it appeared to be far from a joke.‡

"What do you intend to do?" I asked the pilot.

"Well, we're already heading back to Iran, as they suggest. I intend to fly this plane as far back as it will go, though we don't have enough fuel to make it to Teheran."

"How far are we likely to get?" I prodded.

"We'll try to land in western Iran. Maybe we can make it to Kermanshah."

"*Maybe?*" I said, giving vent to my growing alarm. "And what if we can't? You promised me that under no circumstances would you land in Iraq!"

"I believe we have enough fuel to reach Kermanshah, perhaps even Hamadan. Do you have a better suggestion?"

I sat there feeling stunned but still enough possessed of my wits to know that I had to think fast, for every passing minute brought us farther eastward. If we returned to Teheran, and certainly if we landed in Kermanshah, it would be impossible to keep our operation secret. Much to the contrary, we would have a major scandal on our hands if the plane that had left Teheran presumably empty a few hours before were to return with twenty-odd passengers. All the details of our stratagem would come out, and all the people who had helped us—Jews and non-Jews—would find themselves in very difficult straits. Worst of all, it would mean the end of everything we had built up in Iran—not just the immigrant camp, but the entire fabric of relations with government and commercial elements.

And if we did not return to Iran? If we kept on flying to Israel, despite the warning? We would imperil not only the operation but the plane and all its passengers. I reread the note in my hand. The message was unequiv-

‡ The remark, we later learned, was prompted by the fact that the Egyptians noticed in its log that WF.AAK had landed in Haifa, and they asked for an explanation.

ocal: "Do not fly over Syria. There's a danger your plane will be shot down." Once again I sensed the dull, heavy feeling that came over me when the lives of many people were in the balance and I had to make a decision. I alone was responsible for those people sitting behind me in the passenger compartment believing that finally they were safe. Any decision I made could be fateful for them. We seemed damned if we returned and doomed if we didn't, and I could not know which was the greater peril.

I was, however, able to distinguish what brought us closer to our goal and what moved us farther away from it. Returning to Iran definitely meant destroying the one outlet we had from Iraq. On the other hand, if we continued to fly westward, we might be taking a terrible gamble, but at least we stood a chance of making it to Haifa. The odds may not have been the best, but at least there were odds. So I replied to the challenge of coming up with a better suggestion by saying that I thought we should make for Haifa anyway.

The pilot didn't even bother to respond; he just kept on flying eastward. Now I not only had to persuade him, I had to do it quickly, and that meant resorting to something a bit more drastic than reasoned debate.

"What I can't understand," I began in an almost chatty tone, to keep him off his guard and not betray my ploy, "is why you're so scared of the Syrians. Our boys were not afraid of them during the war."

"You read the transmission, Maurice," the pilot replied, somewhat puzzled by my obtuseness. "The Syrians might shoot us down."

"Well, maybe our boys were just better or braver pilots," I commented offhandedly. "They weren't afraid of the Syrians."

"How can you compare me to your pilots!" he retorted, anger creeping into his voice now. "They're just kids. What kind of experience do they have?"

"Actually," I kept chattering, completely ignoring his replies, "I'm beginning to suspect that your problem has more to do with—how shall I put it? . . . timidity, perhaps."

I said this while studying my upturned palms, so as to avoid his gaze, but when I peeked out of the corner of my eye I could see that he had flushed a deep crimson.

"You really have a helluva nerve talking to me like that," he growled. "Do you know how many air battles I fought during the war? Do you know how many ribbons I was awarded?"

"Then explain to me," I continued, deliberately provocative now, "how come you lose your nerve when it comes to a bunch of puny Syrians! You have nothing to fear from the ground, and if their planes try to intercept us, you can always duck past the border into Jordan or Israel. So who are you afraid of?"

"I'm not afraid of anyone!" he bellowed. Then he paused to compose himself, and when he resumed speaking it was in a deliberate, measured rhythm. "I am responsible for the passengers on this aircraft, and I do fear for *their* lives."

"Well then, I will assume full responsibility for the lives of the passengers," I declared.

"It's not as simple as that. I am the captain of this aircraft—"

"But these are *my* people and they are in *my* care," I informed him sharply. "It has to be *my* decision, and *I* say we turn around and continue on to Haifa."

The pilot looked to his copilot for aid, but when the latter shrugged as a sign that he could offer no counsel, he simply relented.

"You should have put it that way in the first place," he said by way of retreat. "If you take responsibility, I'm prepared to fly to the ends of the earth if you want."

To this day I'm not sure why he gave in. As captain he unquestionably had the last word. And if we had been shot down, my declaration of responsibility would have been meaningless anyway. Perhaps it had dawned on him that the consequences of turning back would be as disastrous for him personally as they were for the broader operation. Or perhaps he was so incensed by my aspersions on his manhood that he was itching for an excuse to prove his prowess. In any event, the port wing dipped down again, the pilot executed another 180-degree turn, pointing the aircraft westward, and we flew on in a pensive silence. I didn't have the courage to visit with the passengers for whom I had just declared myself fully and exclusively responsible. All I kept thinking was that I should be sending up a prayer of earnest supplication pleading, "Lord, please let everything turn out all right. Just this time, Lord. Just this once. . . ."

A while later the pilot tapped my shoulder, pointed through the starboard window, and informed me gravely: "Damascus." Not another word was spoken, as if we feared they would hear us below. But I strained to see out as far as I could into the blue. Nothing happened. No plane was visible anywhere in the vicinity. The sky remained vacant and tranquil as Damascus fell behind us and we continued flying westward, unmolested, until the blue above blended in with the azure of the sea and we found ourselves out over the Mediterranean Sea. Then, once again, there were smiles in the cockpit and jokes at the Syrians' expense. Once again, there was boisterous laughter—perhaps excessively boisterous—and within a few minutes we had landed in Haifa and quickly dispatched the passengers. I shook the pilot's hand firmly and, rather than explain or apologize, simply said, "Thanks." He smiled so warmly that I knew all was forgiven. I then took leave of the rest of the crew, and we agreed that I would return with them on the fifth—and last—flight. The plane took off immediately for Beirut and reached it empty, just as the Teheran control tower had announced.

Meanwhile, I learned the meaning of the urgent transmission sent us from Teheran. There had been a military coup in Syria that morning—the first of a series that was to rock that country—and General Hosni al-Za'im had dispersed the parliament, ousted the president and the government, and wrested control of the country. In reporting the takeover, Radio Damascus announced—for good measure, as it were—that Syrian airspace was closed and any plane entering it would be summarily shot down. Teheran's efficient control tower duly passed the warning on to us without regard for the agitation it would cause.

Having received that briefing on the *haute politique* of the Middle East, I was now to get a taste of the exercise of power on another level. After all my charges had passed through immigration in perfect order, I proceeded to follow in their wake but was stopped by the border policeman standing in the aisle.

"Passport," he snapped.

"I haven't got a passport," I told him, "and I'm not an immigrant. I come from here."

"But I saw you come in with them," he insisted.

"That's right. I arrived together with them, but I'm an Israeli."

"Do you have an identity card? A passport? A *laissez-passer?*"

I shook my head in the negative each time, whereupon he pronounced, "If you haven't got any identification, stand over there on the side and wait."

"But—"

"No buts. Wait."

So I moved off to the side to consider how I would identify myself. I had left the country as one Ya'akov Munir and had since become Maurice Perez but had left the passport bearing that name in Teheran. As the policeman walked back toward me with another man in civilian dress, however, I suddenly remembered the document that had stood me in good stead in much tighter spots than this one, and I proudly produced my Iranian driver's license. The civilian took it from me, glanced at it, and turned it over, as if something on the other side would be more illuminating than the first.

"What is this?" he finally asked.

"A driver's license. Can't you tell?"

"Say, are you trying to make a fool out of me? A visa. Do you have a visa for Israel?"

Now I saw my opening and proposed to him in all seriousness, "You know what, since I'm the one who issued the visas for all those immigrants, if you let me use your typewriter, I'll draw up another one just like it for myself."

It had not been my intention to anger him, but I evidently did so, in spades, for he turned red as a beet and railed at me, "Don't be such a smart aleck. Without a passport and a visa, you don't enter the State of Israel. This isn't no-man's-land!"

For a moment I thought he was going to arrest me, and that was the first time I realized that I really had a problem on my hands. It had never occurred to me that I would be barred from entering my own country because of a travel document. The Israel I had left nine months earlier was like one big family; it was enough for you to speak fluent Hebrew to prove that you "belonged." But the intervening months had turned us from a family into a state, with the standard bureaucratic rules and formalities that could not be winked at. So there I stood at an impasse with an irate servant of the state who was determined to save his country's honor by keeping me out of it! Once his anger subsided, however, he allowed me to call our people in Haifa, and Shmuel Vardi, the Mossad's devoted driver, came to my rescue by bringing the incident to a close with smiles and handshakes.

Afterward I mused that this was probably just a warm-up for the real confrontation awaiting me in Israel. After months of exchanging angry letters and cables and feeling a lack of responsiveness from Tel Aviv, I had come prepared for bitter arguments. But much to my surprise and satisfaction, meeting face to face put an end to all the misunderstandings and actually stepped up the decision-making process. Even the most pressing problem—finding alternate ways of bringing immigrants from Iran to Israel—was solved. We decided to hire Trans-Ocean—an American charter company through which the Mossad was bringing people in from Bombay on larger, four-engine planes—to fly the Teheran–Lod route as well. I even had a long meeting with Ronnie Barnett, a British Jew who had volunteered to work in the cause of illegal immigration and was serving as a kind of liaison officer between the Mossad and Trans-Ocean. So it was with a solid achievement that I could return to Teheran (after an unscheduled delay) with the Iranian Airways plane that had carried out some supplementary flights for us.

After taking off from Beirut, unbeknownst to the control tower there, the plane made a short, unscheduled stop to pick me up in Haifa, and we headed back into Lebanese airspace. While the plane was still over Lebanon, the Beirut tower contacted us and asked the pilot to note his exact location. When he complied, the puzzled voice of the air controller came back over the plane's radio.

"You left Beirut more than an hour ago. How come you're where you claim to be?"

The question was indeed an embarrassing one. In the interim the plane had flown to Haifa, landed, taken me aboard, and taken off again—that's how come. The pilot didn't lose his head, though. On the contrary, he handled the problem as if he had been waiting—and rehearsing—for it for weeks.

"After leaving Beirut I thought I had something wrong with an engine," he said quietly and steadily into his microphone. "So I decided to turn back. But now I see it's fine, so I've turned round again and I'm heading for Teheran."

The radio remained mute for a few seconds that seemed like an eternity before the voice from the Beirut tower returned with the assurance, "Okay. Good luck!"

"Phew!" the pilot exhaled loudly as he wiped an imaginary film of sweat off his brow. The incident was a minor one, but it proved to me that we had exhausted this particular ruse for getting our people to Israel, and the understanding with Trans-Ocean hadn't come a minute too soon.

I still had one more hurdle ahead, however: to get back into Iran unnoticed. Before leaving, I had arranged with Sammi that upon reaching Teheran I would follow the Michaelberg method in reverse, namely, jump out of the plane at the end of the runway and sneak out of the airport (though this time in broad daylight). So when we landed I asked the pilot to turn the aircraft around slowly, thereby concealing me from the control tower's line of vision. That part of the maneuver worked beautifully, and I managed to get off the tarmac and lie flat in an open field alongside it. But just as the plane began to taxi over to the terminal, I saw a police jeep coming straight toward me. There I lay, completely exposed, without anywhere to go. The truth is that there was no point in trying to flee, because the police in the jeep certainly would have caught up with me. Instinctively I tried to make myself as scarce as possible, rolling myself into a fetal-style ball and pulling my brown gabardine jacket over my head in a desperate attempt to approximate a large lump of earth. I lay there paralyzed, waiting for a hand to clutch my shoulder and pull me up on my feet, and in my mind's eye I could already see myself bound hand and foot, taking blows in the infamous torture chambers of the Iranian Secret Police.

Even the sound of the jeep's motor as it passed right by me could not drown out the pounding of my heart.

I waited a long moment, then another, then a third, until curiosity got the better of me and I lifted a corner of the jacket to peek out at the jeep as it moved steadily away from me. Surveying the rest of the field in the same manner, I began to crawl slowly in the direction of a familiar black Buick that was standing on the main road, far from the terminal. It was Ya'akov Sofer's car, with Ya'akov and Meir Ezri standing beside its open hood, tinkering with an array of tools as though carrying out some complex repair. When they saw me coming, the repair job promptly ended, I quickly ducked into the vehicle, and the three of us literally zoomed off into the city.

Dov Adiv, who was waiting in the terminal, later related that he practically had a stroke when he ran into the pilot and heard him exclaim, "That was organized beautifully! The moment Maurice jumped out, the jeep came along and picked him up!"

"What are you talking about?" Dov spluttered. "What jeep? Where did it take him?"

"Perfect timing! As soon as he got out, the police jeep was ready and waiting."

Dov blanched, turned on his heel, and rushed home in a panic. He knew he would have to consult with Sammi before taking measures to deal with my arrest, but he was afraid to risk talking over the phone. When he arrived to find me serenely sipping a cup of tea, he broke out into a string of Russian curses ending with the exclamation, "I almost went out of my mind, and you're sitting here and drinking tea!"

After we calmed him down, I briefed him and Sammi on the deal with Trans-Ocean and told them exuberantly that we were entering a new stage of our venture in Iran. What I did not know, but would soon find out, was that it would be a new phase in more ways than one—and not all of them were going to be pleasant.

NINE

In the Shadow of
the Gallows

OUR DECISION to use Trans-Ocean's planes made it possible to transport a substantially larger number of immigrants directly to Israel in safety. Thus the time had come, I believed, to exploit this breakthrough to the maximum by trying to open up a new channel and bring Iranian Jews to Israel as well. As soon as I returned to Teheran, I decided to discuss the matter with Gholam Ibtihaj, on the assumption that the mutual success of our first joint venture had whetted his appetite for more. By April 25, four days after my return, I was able to wire Tel Aviv that, at my request, Ibtihaj had phoned the Prime Minister and the chief of police (his brother-in-law) and proposed that they allow Iranian Jews who wished to emigrate to Israel to do so, on condition that they travel with the Iranian carrier or through an arrangement with it. This "arrangement" was a reference to the fact that although we would no longer be flying on Iranian planes, I had come to an understanding with Ibtihaj whereby Iranian Airways would act as Trans-Ocean's local agent and provide all the necessary ground services for its planes.

Their response, as Ibtihaj reported it, was "positive and encouraging," the one condition being that the emigrants renounce their Iranian citizenship. About a week later, I reported on another meeting with Ibtihaj in which we framed the final agreement. It stipulated that, for its services, Trans-Ocean would pay Iranian Airways the standard rate set by IATA (the International Air Transport Association) and that an additional fee (which Ibtihaj set at $25 per person) would be charged for handling the immigration papers, including the obtaining of exit visas and other formalities. "Ibtihaj says," I added in my wire, "that an unlimited number of Jews will be permitted to leave."

By the end of the month we had signed a formal and legal agreement with Iranian Airways—and a very special agreement it was, considering the fact that Muslim Iran did not yet recognize the State of Israel and no diplomatic relations existed between the two countries. This contract was composed of ten clauses, one of which effectively made Zionist activity openly legal by establishing that:

Iranian Airways will make all necessary arrangements with the Iranian government, police, and customs authorities to obtain exit visas for the passengers as detailed below. . . .

1. Permission in writing from the Iranian government and police openly to recruit volunteers among the Jewish residents of Iran who are prepared to renounce their Iranian citizenship in return for exit permits to Israel.

Gholam Ibtihaj signed on behalf of the Iranian company and Dov Adiv signed on our side as the representative of Peltours Ltd., the Israeli travel agency whose interests he represented in Iran. Yet at Ibtihaj's insistence, I was no longer able to evade involvement of some sort, so that this historic document also bears the signature of "Maurice Perez, Witness."

The Iranian Jews who took advantage of this arrangement—known as the "Big Deal" in the Mossad's code—were, above all, members or graduates of the Zionist youth movement. But there were Jews who were attracted to the idea of building new lives in the young state as a way out of the poverty they suffered in the Jewish quarter of Teheran. Graver still was the condition of the Jews in the provincial cities, for most of their wealthier brethren had moved to the capital, leaving the Jewish communal institutions in the provinces without sources of support and the impoverished members of these communities with little hope of improving their lot.

Particularly pathetic, however, was the condition of the Jews from Meshed who wandered the streets of Teheran without any means of livelihood but were afraid to return to their native city, where they had lived as Marranos for about a century. The history of the Meshed community is a singularly sad one. In 1839 a rumor swept through the city that the Jews—whom the Shiite Muslims regard as *nijis,* or impure—had touched the sacred grave of the Imam Reza, a popular site of pilgrimage for the Shiite masses. The inflamed pilgrims and many residents of the city, who were known for their religious zeal, rampaged through the streets and butchered Jewish men, women, and children in a frenzy of slaughter. For lack of choice, most of the surviving Jews converted to Islam—but only as far as the eye could see. For generations they continued to maintain their Jewish ways in secret, living in constant fear that they would be discovered. Their condition improved during the reign of Reza Shah, who ascended the throne after the 1925 revolution and tried to institute reforms in Iran, overcome the country's social and economic retardation, and free the regime from the influence of the fanatic clergy. As part of this attempt to transform Iran into a modern society, the Jews of Meshed were permitted to practice their religion openly, and presumably all was well again. But after World War II the situation reversed itself. Once the Allied armies (which had conquered Iran in 1941) withdrew from the country, the new shah, Mohammed Reza Pahlavi, failed to command the same degree of authority as his father, so that the religious fanatics were able to regain some of their influence. Consequently, the Jews of Meshed again found themselves under pressure, and many fled to Teheran in the hope of reaching Israel. The contract we now had in hand enabled us to accommodate them—as well as anyone else who wanted to go. The fact is that from 1949 through 1951, the years in which we were working in Iran to facilitate the escape of Iraqi Jews, 24,805 Iranian Jews also emigrated to Israel.

So there we were, admiring, if not exactly resting on, our laurels, when on June 17, 1949, we suffered a stunning blow and found ourselves transformed into pawns to be sacrificed in a gambit to improve Iran's relations with Iraq. It all began a few days before, when a group of thirteen of our immigrants was arrested in southern Iran and twenty-two other Jews who had crossed the border on their own were likewise taken into custody. At first we did not realize that we were up against a special problem, for arrests of this sort had happened before, and we usually had no difficulty working the problem out: the detainees were transferred to Teheran, tried and sentenced to a token fine, and allowed to stay in the immigrant camp until they received their *laissez-passers.* Nevertheless, since this was a particularly large group, Zion Ezri went to Khorramshahr to meet with Lieutenant Colonel Mir Jahangiri, the commander of the Border Police in Khuzistan (whose brother Ezri knew from his own service in the police), and make doubly sure he would honor the existing arrangement. Ezri's efforts succeeded insofar as the colonel agreed to release the detainees on bail and put them up in the Khorramshahr synagogue, under police guard, until instructions arrived to transfer them to the capital. But then came a bolt out of the blue: an order arrived from Teheran, signed by Foreign Minister Ali Asghar Hekmat personally, instructing Jahangiri to deport the detainees to Iraq forthwith.

There was never any question but that this deportation order was directly related to the state visit of the Iraqi regent, Abdul Illah—a visit on which both countries had placed great hopes. Before long, it also became clear that the Iraqi consul in Khorramshahr, who had been working tirelessly to block the flight of Jews from Iraq and demanded that the refugees be extradited, had brought the matter to the attention of the visiting Iraqis. As fate would have it, one of the members of the regent's entourage was Ali Haled al-Hijazi, Iraq's chief of police and a notorious anti-Semite whose malevolence was fed by a pique over the fact that so many Jews had managed to flee Iraq, thus making a mockery of his force. Hijazi was thus particularly eager to explain to his hosts that these self-styled refugees were in fact dangerous criminals and "subversive elements"—a euphemism for Communists, whose extradition was ensured in a treaty already drafted by the two countries. And not to be outdone by his chief of police, Abdul Illah was quick to make the continuation of his visit contingent upon the prompt return of the prisoners in Khorramshahr.

The irate Iraqi officials were placated by Hekmat, who was authorized by law to order the deportation. It was only reasonable that in his capacity as Foreign Minister, Hekmat (who, ironically enough, was the descendant of a Jewish family that had converted to Islam a generation earlier) would do his best to make the regent's visit a success. Yet we later discovered that, beyond his official duty, Hekmat had his own ax to grind with us. At any rate, during this period he absolutely refused to see any of the people who tried to intercede on our behalf, including his own close friends. Thus we had good reason to be alarmed, and in my mind's eye I was already conjuring up the devastating sight of dozens of Jews—the "dangerous criminals" who would be extradited to Iraq—being strung up on gallows in the main squares of Baghdad and Basra. I knew that the Iraqis were quite capable of such barbarity and, worse yet, of hanging not only the hapless fugitives but the other members of their families as well.

Every enterprise suffers setbacks from time to time, and one would think that I would have been steeled to them by that point. But I took this setback very hard and very personally. Suddenly I felt as though I had lost my footing in Iran, and I was gripped by terrible forebodings of disaster, fearful that we were about to lose everything: the camp, the flights, the whole kit and caboodle. As the hours passed, I could feel myself sliding into a state bordering on despair as I launched into an orgy of self-re-proach, blaming everything on my own *hubris*—that quality of arrogance that inevitably tempts the fates. Every last misgiving my colleagues had expressed along the way—and that I had swept aside or even ridiculed—came back to haunt me now. Left to my own devices, I might have wallowed in this misery indefinitely. But fortunately I was surrounded by people like Sammi and Dov, who had little patience for this kind of self-indulgence and expected me to act. And at their prodding I soon wrenched myself out of the shock and dismay that threatened to cripple me and plunged, instead, into a round of activity as the best antidote to despair.

I began by summoning our leading activists for an urgent consultation and mapped out a two-pronged strategy. Naturally it called for enlisting the aid of our friends in high places and putting all possible pressure on the Iranian Government to reverse Hekmat's decision. Still, attaining that objective could take time, and time was a commodity we emphatically did not have, because the deportation might be carried out at any moment. Thus, above all, we had to find a way to postpone the execution of the order, and if we could not delay it we would have no choice but to sabo-tage it by dispersing the immigrants and hiding them until it was safe to go on.

I estimated that it would take a week or more before the pressure we could apply through various quarters would bring about the revocation of the expulsion order. Moreover, once the regent's visit was over, our chances of succeeding would improve considerably. Zion Ezri, who was our adviser on the legal and judicial side of the affair, explained that while the Foreign Minister was empowered to sign the deportation order, it could be implemented only by the Border Police—and that, he believed, was the direction in which we should turn to obtain a postponement.

A quick investigation showed that Lieutenant Colonel Jahangiri, whom Ezri had met a few days earlier when trying to obtain the release of the thirty-five on bail, was in Teheran that day. His deputy was known to us as a genuinely villainous character, making it imperative to find Jahangiri and appeal to him for help before any irreparable damage was done. After making a number of frantic phone calls, we finally located him, and I accompanied Ezri to make an emotional plea for our cause. Jahangiri agreed to grant us a few days' reprieve but warned, "The time at your disposal is very limited. If the order is not fully rescinded, sooner or later I'll have to carry it out."

"How will you ensure the postponement?" I asked.

Ezri flashed me an angry look, suggesting that I had muffed everything

by seeming to question his authority or abilities. But Jahangiri took the
question kindly.

"That's a military secret," he quipped. "You just leave it to me."

We thanked him profusely, adding that by saving the lives of innocent,
defenseless people, he was doing a great and honorable deed that would
surely be requited. Afterward we learned how he managed to postpone
the deportation, and his system was really quite elementary. First of all, he
sent his deputy a cable stating that, due to the importance of the matter
and the risk of complications, he had decided to return to Khorramshahr
and handle the affair personally, so that no action should be taken until he
arrived. Upon reaching Khorramshahr the next day, he cabled Teheran to
ask whether he should merely transport the detainees up to the border or
actually turn them over to the Iraqi police. And when the answer arrived,
he cabled back that some of the people were ill and asked whether he
should deport the rest or wait until it was possible to expel them all together. And so it went on, with Jahangiri using his gifts of imagination and
resourcefulness to pose question after question and consequently gain us
the time we needed to get the order repealed.

Our line of persuasion was also kept simple and to the point. We argued
that the Iranians had proved willing to help the Iraqi Jewish refugees out
of loyalty to a long and deeply ingrained tradition of humaneness. It was
therefore inconceivable that they would now bow to the dictates of the
Iraqis and reverse their policy in response to pressure of the crudest sort.
Having settled on that straightforward approach, we drew up a schedule of
meetings with leading personalities, and I was able to report to Israel: "We
are trying to get the order rescinded in the capital. In the meantime
[Sammi and Zion Ezri] have flown south to check out the possibility of
sneaking [the immigrants out of the synagogue] if necessary." That was a
relatively simple operation. It was no problem to dispose of a policeman or
two stationed outside the synagogue—whether by bribery, guile, or force
—and disperse the thirty-three immigrants among the homes of Jews living
in Khorramshahr, Abadan, and Ahwaz. On the other hand, by resorting to
an action of that sort we would clearly damage the relationship of trust that
we had labored so hard to establish with the authorities. I therefore told
Sammi to deploy for a rescue action but not to carry it out unless there was
absolutely no other choice—meaning that the deportation was imminent—
and even then not without my express approval.

Matters never reached that point, however. Instead, the next day Tel
Aviv cabled back to ask: "Will our intercession from here . . . via France
or the United States . . . help or do harm?" I, who hadn't thought about
using such channels, now forgave my colleagues back home all the frustra-

tion they had caused us throughout the year, and suddenly I appreciated the power and importance of an experienced center of operations. I wired back immediately that it would be most desirable to receive help from the American ambassador in Teheran, clarifying that he alone could make a tangible contribution, for "the others here are worthless." Abba Eban, then Israel's ambassador to Washington and the United Nations, had a talk first with Nasrollah Entezam, Iran's ambassador to the United States, and then with a number of American officials. Meanwhile, inspired by the idea, Dov and I approached the American political attaché in the Teheran embassy, who displayed "a very supportive and understanding attitude" that was soon translated into concrete action.

The Iranians were particularly sensitive to public opinion in the United States just then, for Congress was debating arms sales to Teheran and a loan of $250 million, in addition to which the shah was scheduled to visit Washington at about that time. Fortunately, Israel's stand against the aggression of the Arab states, coming so soon after World War II and the systematic annihilation of European Jewry, created a climate in which anyone turning his back on Jews in distress, or worse yet turning them over to ruthless executioners, could hardly expect a sympathetic hearing in the West. Therefore we placed great stock in a broad hint coming from the Americans, while back in Iran there wasn't a stone we left unturned. Through sheer persistence we eventually got through to Colonel Kiya, the commander of the Border Police; General Sartip Safari, the chief of police; Ali Razmarah, the chief of staff; and a number of cabinet ministers, including Minister of the Interior Manuchehr Eghbal, Minister of War Ahmadi (one of the most powerful and influential men in Iran), and Minister Without Portfolio Khalil Fahimi.

At the same time, Sammi signed the detainees in the synagogue on cables appealing to practically everyone who was anyone in Iran. The small Jewish community of Khorramshahr, which did all it could to ease the immigrants' discomfort by bringing them food and trying to encourage them, declared a day of fasting and sent wires to members of parliament and the government, as did the leaders of the Jewish community of Teheran. In my reports from that period, the only criticism I voiced was of the leaders of the small Iraqi-Jewish community in Teheran, who continued "to fawn horribly before the Iraqi delegation and ignored the fact that this delegation wished to send their brothers back and execute them."

Especially touching among this symphony of appeals was Manya Fanahi's effort to intercede on the refugees' behalf. Manya was the daughter of Boris Monosohn, the treasurer of the Ashkenazi synagogue in Teheran and one of the more prominent members of the small community of European Jews who had settled in Iran. She herself had converted to Islam and married Habib Fanahi, the scion of one of the most wealthy, distinguished, and influential families in the country. Dov knew her well and suggested that we try to utilize her contacts and easy access to the ruling circles in Teheran. So he arranged for us to meet at her comfortable and tastefully furnished home, and with barely a preamble I laid the entire affair out before her. Manya Fanahi was visibly moved by the predicament, to the point where tears stood in her eyes and she had trouble speaking. Finally she composed herself enough to declare, "I swear to you that I shall do everything in my power to save the lives of those unfortunate people."

Manya Fanahi was a woman of her word, in the most literal sense possible. From what I was later told (and had confirmed by several sources), she went straight to Ashraf Pahlavi, the shah's twin sister and a long-time acquaintance. Telling her of what the Jews had endured in Europe (and mentioning that members of her own family had perished in the Holocaust), Manya declared that she wanted to regard Iran as her home but could not bear the thought that the people with whom she had chosen to bind her fate would lend a hand to the murder of innocent Jews. Whereupon she did something incredible: removing a small container of darkblue liquid from her purse, she informed the princess that it was a vial of poison and threatened to drink it right there on the spot if her hostess did not promise to help save the hapless, hounded people whom Manya considered as her brethren. Whether startled or touched by the firmness of her friend's resolve, Ashraf promised to speak with the shah immediately. She was certain that the matter had not reached his attention, for it was inconceivable that her brother would lend his support, even tacitly, to so heinous a crime.

In a curious way, the story seemed like a modern reenactment of the biblical tale of Queen Esther in the very same country, if not quite in the same setting. Manya Fanahi did not follow the original script exactly; neither was she in a position parallel to that of the young queen. But while it is impossible to know which of all the many leads we pursued actually tipped the balance, the fact is that the decision to rescind the deportation order was made with the knowledge and express approval of the shah, and Manya definitely had a hand in that.

Thus on June 23, 1949, I was able to wire Tel Aviv:

To: Artzi
From: Goldman
1. Thanks to the great pressure we have worked up here, the
   government met last night and decided to cancel the deportation

order, which was signed by the Foreign Minister. The people will be transferred to the capital. . . .

I might have added that despite the heavy pressure exerted by the Iraqis right up to the last minute, that decision came while Abdul Illah was still in Teheran and on the very same day that a Treaty of Mutual Assistance and Good Relations was signed pledging cooperation in fighting "Communism and Zionism," for example by extraditing fugitives who crossed the border illegally. Hence the threat to deport people caught stealing over the border remained in force. The immediate danger had passed, but we would indeed face it again in the future.

At the end of June, for example, when King Abdullah of Jordan visited Teheran, the peeved Iranian Foreign Minister found a pretext for signing a new deportation order for yet other refugees caught crossing the border. We mobilized our Iranian and American friends and managed to foil his design, but other orders were issued in August and yet again in September. In the latter case, Iranian Ambassador Entezam, who happened to be in Teheran just then, came to our aid. The day we raised the problem with him, Entezam announced at a private party attended by leading government figures—so we were told by one of the participants—that if the captured Jews were deported to Iraq, "there would be no point in his returning to America and the UN." The others present were left to infer that he was not speaking only of himself. The shah was about to depart on a visit to the United States, and if his ambassador had no business being there, presumably he, too, was better off staying home.

Like a team that deals in stamping out brushfires, time and again we were able to neutralize the threat posed by one factor or another in Iran. But the general trend was not encouraging. At one point we began to sense what I characterized in one of my reports as "a very alarming phenomenon, namely, that our Iranian friends are growing tired of helping us." Fortunately, however, the Iranians grew even more tired of the Iraqis. The joint committee established to settle the border problem between the two countries met once, found itself at a stalemate, and never reconvened. Soon thereafter the Iraqis reverted to their familiar ways and began to harass the tens of thousands of Iranian citizens living in Iraq. In return, the Iranian Government decided to take the stringent measure of deporting all Iraqi citizens from Iran. Ironically, however, the latter were for the most part Jews, and one could assume that Baghdad was not grieved by that decision. As a matter of fact, to this day I am not at all sure that the whole affair was not some demonic scheme dreamed up by Foreign Minister Hekmat, who missed no opportunity to vex the Jews and retaliate for each

of his setbacks. In any case, through the vigorous action of the Iraqi community in Iran—with our aid and encouragement, plus the efforts of some
prominent Iranian Jews—this order was likewise reversed.

Still, we had gotten the message that the mounting tide of refugees was
emphatically not to the Iranians' liking. Even Chief of Police Sartip Safari,
unquestionably a friend who had proved his support for us on a number of
occasions, approached the Iraqi minister in Iran—on his own volition and
independent of the regent's visit—to demand that the Iraqis intensify their
guard along the border because the flood of refugees had become a genuine nuisance. And in a talk with one of our own people, Safari argued that
fully half the Iranian police force was tied down by the refugee problem.
He even went so far as to appoint a board of two senior officers to go to
the south and trace the routes of flight. On August 24 this board submitted
a four-page top-secret report containing a detailed description of the
routes used to reach Iran and the points at which the refugees usually
crossed the border. Clearly the police had the subject down pat, as we
could see from the copy that reached our hands thanks to our special
connections:

. . . Both banks of the Shatt-al-Arab are lined with many date palms
that make it easy for people to infiltrate and for smugglers to operate.
. . . They work as follows: during the day, they ready the people for
the journey and keep them hidden in the palms, and at night, when the
guard is lighter, they transfer them over our border. . . . The
smugglers receive large sums—evidently paid by the board of the
Jewish community—and so they are prepared to take any risk.

Later on in the report, we were surprised and gratified to find the following very Zionist-oriented, and not unsympathetic, explanation of the reason for the exodus from Iraq:

As I stated above, the Jews of the world are partners in the
establishment of the State of Israel and they are involved in it because it
is their primary objective. They are prepared to give body and soul for
it, and they are determined to help one another reach their objective.
. . . They work for the State of Israel, which is the Promised Land for
the Jewish people and its historic homeland. It is quite clear that all the
Jews of Iran agree with this outlook, which is why they are aiding the
Jews fleeing from Iraq.

The operative part of the report called for a series of measures that
boiled down to a major increase in manpower, the number of vehicles,
spotlights, and other sorts of heavy equipment, and the construction of

guard posts at regular points along the border. Finally it warned—as police forces the world over have a way of warning—that "As long as the police lacks such apparatus, it cannot act effectively to correct the situation."

And since the Iranians were not about to make that kind of major investment in sealing their border, the statistics continued to rise. By the end of 1949, hundreds of Jews were arriving, where only dozens had come through before. The Iraqis tried to block up the loopholes on their side but failed miserably. Taking another tack, in mid-August their Foreign Ministry submitted a formal complaint with the State Department protesting that the planes of an American company, Trans-Ocean, were violating Iraqi airspace on their flights from Teheran to Israel. When Trans-Ocean sent a representative to Baghdad to negotiate the matter, he was treated to a "stern warning that combat planes will be sent up if their airspace is violated again" and was put on notice that "Iraqi combat planes have been placed on alert and have begun to carry out regular patrols along the borders."

That was a whopping threat, but a threat is all it was. At any rate, it was not enough to stop the flow of refugees to Iran or our flights to Israel. The first Trans-Ocean plane had left Teheran, with seventy immigrants, on June 22, at the height of the flap over the first deportation order, and thereafter they just kept on flying—Iraq's bluff and bluster notwithstanding. As a matter of fact, rather than feel daunted by the whole experience, at one point I tried to cheer up my comrades in Baghdad by writing that we were actually better off for it:

. . . We now have an opportunity to renew our labors on a grand scale. We have emerged from the crisis even stronger. Today our connections here are more powerful and ramified. As I see it now, the moment the people cross our border they are no longer in any danger. And the greater the number, the easier it makes things for us. . . .

Still, if anyone could be classified as a casualty of this hard-won achievement, it was I. Considering the wider circumstances, perhaps casualty is too strong a term, but after the months of tension and relentless activity, I was completely exhausted. Zion Cohen had already been chosen as my replacement, and during my visit to Tel Aviv in April I had received a solemn promise that his dispatch was receiving all due attention. After returning to Teheran, I had asked about him from time to time, but my questions and angry cables on this subject either went unanswered or elicited vague assurances that the matter was being handled. All I knew was that Cohen and his family were in Paris waiting for a North African passport and that the continuation of their journey was repeatedly delayed.

Finally I was informed that Zion Cohen had become Aristide Callas, and on July 13 I was able to cable Tel Aviv, with an enormous sense of relief, that "Zion Cohen and his family arrived safely this evening." It was only then that I began to believe that my "brief mission" was finally coming to an end.

The changing of the guard in Teheran took longer than I had planned, for despite all the contacts we had cultivated over that year, I had to work hard to obtain a legal exit visa. Thus it wasn't until mid-September, after standing trial for remaining in Iran on a lapsed visa and paying a hefty fine, that I finally received the necessary papers. In the meantime, additional emissaries (including a new wireless operator) began to arrive and start working in Iran and Iraq. The tasks that had been handled by three of us— Sammi, Eliyahu Shani, and me—during the difficult period of building our operation in Iran were now divided among a far larger number of people, and we looked upon this improvement with a considerable degree of satisfaction.

I returned to Israel on September 30 on one of three Trans-Ocean planes that left that day filled to capacity. There was something symbolic about the fact that on the final day of my mission, a mini-airlift had begun from Teheran. It was backed by a firm, broad base of operations, a large staff of emissaries, a bustling immigrant camp, and above all a steadily mounting flow of escapees from Iraq. A single year had passed since I had arrived in Teheran. It had been a difficult, nerve-racking year, a year of crises, anxieties, and disappointments. But it had also been a year of breakthrough and new hope.

So I felt that finally, unquestionably, I had earned the right to go back to my kibbutz, settle in with Temima (if she would still have me), and get used to the feel of soil between my toes and under my nails—in short, to lead a normal life for a change! Glancing around during takeoff, I saw the familiar signs of tension and excitement on the faces of my fellow passengers, most of whom were flying for the first time. I had forgotten what that felt like. How many flights had I been on in the past three years? *No matter,* I thought, *this is going to be the last one for a long time to come.*

"What are you grinning about, Maurice?" asked Eliyahu Shani, our radio operator, who had also been replaced and was on his way to Israel beside me. "Do you get a kick out of flying?"

"Not really," said I, the blasé world traveler. "I don't mind it either. But I'll tell you this much: once we land in Israel, I'm going to stay earthbound. Mark my words: many a new day will dawn before you catch me on a plane again!"

The thought actually kept me grinning halfway to Tel Aviv.

TEN

Nuri Strikes Again

THURSDAY, APRIL 27, 1950, dawned to find me slumped in a seat next to Ronnie Barnett on a night flight from Amsterdam to Baghdad. We had met at the Amsterdam airport the evening before, I having flown in from Paris with a brand-new identity that was to be put to its first test on neutral ground. Silently I had presented my British passport to the Dutch immigration official, who studied my particulars, glanced up at me, and broke into an inscrutable smile. Then he walked over to a colleague in the adjoining booth, showed him the passport, murmured something in Dutch, and joined him in a short burst of laughter.

By then I was feeling distinctly uncomfortable, but fortunately the consultation did not go on for long. A second or two later the officer returned, still chuckling, and asked in fluent English, "Do you play the trumpet?"

"No," I replied in puzzlement.

"Are you at least related?" he continued with a broad smile, obviously pleased with himself.

My own laugh then was of relief. "Considering the state of my finances," I quipped, "I wish we were!"

He tossed his head slightly and comforted me with the standard "Have a pleasant stay in Holland!'' as he stamped the passport and slid it back toward me.

This spurt of mirth had been prompted by the name of Richard Armstrong, which graced my passport and reminded the Dutchman of the famed Satchmo. I was not particularly happy about the name, for the reason illustrated here. Throughout my service in the Mossad, I had always gone for the gray, eminently forgettable alias that would slip softly by passport officers and the like. Neither did I know then—and still don't know now—whether I had been christened Richard Armstrong out of necessity or because the "fixer" who prepared the document was simply enjoying himself at my expense.

The choice of a British passport for this trip was also of dubious wisdom. After all, the Iraqis were well acquainted with the British, and it stood to reason that many a good Englishman was still to be found in Iraq—all of which did not bode well for an impostor like myself. Nevertheless, since Ronnie and I were traveling together, it was decided that we should be of the same nationality. That way he could also pose as an old friend and serve as my advance man, as it were, explaining away the many discrepancies between my appearance and demeanor and that of a true son of Albion.

The tangled web we wove around the figure of Richard Armstrong, Jr., was designed to explain two blatant features—his relatively diminutive size and dark skin tone—as well as his permanent residence in Copenhagen, rather than the British Isles. Richard Armstrong's history was no ordinary one, Ronnie was to relate in muted tones, and often with a smirk. His father, Richard Armstrong, Sr., had been a colonial official in India and returned from the East with a swarthy-skinned son whom he adored. Heaven only knows why the child was raised in Copenhagen, but the fact is that the young Armstrong still preferred living there. His tastes and mien might therefore be more "cosmopolitan" than strictly British. "But good breeding always shows through," Ronnie was to assure anyone who would swallow this romantic hogwash—while I, for my part, was expected to at least approximate some typical British mannerisms.

And so, while waiting for Ronnie in one of the bars in Schiphol Airport, I began to occupy myself with the pipe that came along with Richard Armstrong's "breeding." After dismantling and cleaning it, I packed it again with fragrant tobacco, lit it with my trusty Ronson, and proceeded to fill my surroundings with a cloud of light blue smoke. I wanted to continue smoking cigarettes as well, but Ronnie insisted that even the most eccentric Englishman, if a true devotee of the pipe, would never need anything more.

"But you smoke both cigarettes *and* cigars, and you never touch a pipe!" I pouted.

Then again, he could afford to. His "persona" was not bound up with the exploits of some salacious sahib. All Ronnie had to do to pass as a loyal subject of the king was be himself, while I had to forfeit the comfort of cigarettes (at least when I was in company) and cultivate that blasted smokestack, which burned my tongue and lips.

As these thoughts churned through my head—and I was evidently puffing away furiously—I failed to hear my tormentor approach.

"Hello, Dick!" Ronnie greeted me loudly, in the best old-boy fashion, then switched to *sotto voce* and implored me to "Take it easy! You're polluting the whole bloody airport with that thing!"

I spat one last billow of smoke in his direction before laying the pipe aside and licking my lips for relief.

"What will you have to drink, Dick?"

"Coca-Cola," I said instinctively, anticipating the feel of the sweet, bubbly liquid sliding down my parched throat.

"Don't you *ever* let me hear you say that again!" he whispered hoarsely. "You'll drink whiskey and soda or gin and tonic."

We compromised on a good Dutch beer, and I resolved to stop giving Ronnie such a hard time. In all fairness, the Armstrong pose wasn't his idea, and I knew that the only motive behind his fussiness was to save my skin. Besides, no one was forcing me to go to Baghdad. I had volunteered for the mission of my own free will—all my talk of "retirement" notwithstanding—because a succession of events had climaxed in March 1950 in a unique opportunity to save the battered and terrified Jews of Iraq. Having invested over three years in that cause, I wanted to see things through to their proper conclusion. And if that meant going to Baghdad under yet another identity—pipe and all—so be it.

Paradoxically, the man responsible for my change of plans was none other than Prime Minister Nuri Said. To understand how, in spite of himself, he engendered such a dramatic turnabout in the flagging fortunes of Iraqi Jewry, we must go back to the beginning of 1949, when he returned to power after a twenty-two-month hiatus. At that time, I was in Teheran desperately seeking a way to accommodate the surge of refugees who were arriving in the city (and finally had to be put up in the cemetery). The pressure that was driving them to flee Iraq in growing numbers—and that would mount relentlessly in the months to come—was being generated by Nuri Said's malicious and often irrational behavior when it came to the Jews.

When Nuri returned to the premiership on January 6, 1949, it was his tenth term in that office and not one particularly remembered as being of benefit to Iraq or its Jews. I would even venture that Nuri himself did not derive much satisfaction from the office, though at first his government did appear to be enjoying success. The state of martial law accorded him broad powers that he used first to trounce the Communists, arresting hundreds of them and even sending some to the gallows.

That much accomplished, he decided that the path to glory in the inter-Arab arena lay in taking a radical position on the Palestine question. While the other combatants were negotiating armistice agreements to end the 1948 war, Iraq announced that it would not conduct talks or agree to any armistice with Israel. Instead, after summarily withdrawing his troops, Nuri published a unilateral plan for solving the Arab-Israel conflict. Ironically, its main feature was the division of Palestine along the very lines that had been proposed by the UN partition plan and rejected by the Arabs in November 1947 (and thereafter superseded by Israel's gains on the battlefield). But over and above that, he called for the complete disarmament of Israel, Arab sovereignty over Jerusalem, the reconstitution of Haifa as an international zone, and the return of all the Arab refugees.* Frankly, it was absurb to believe that the Israelis would accept these demands. But when Nuri saw that Israel was less than receptive to his offer and that the Arab states were unwilling or unable to unite behind it—or any other plan, for that matter—he succumbed to a fit of rage, and the Jews of Iraq became the object of his rancor.

Nuri's unpredictable behavior when it came to the Jews was attested to not only by our sources in Baghdad but, as I would later discover, by various British diplomats who feared that their protégé would fly off the handle and embarrass His Majesty's Government. In reconstructing the course of that year's events, I have had the benefit of access not only to memoirs but particularly to the archives of the British Foreign Office, which are a gold mine of information and explain a number of enigmas that plagued us at the time. For example, it emerges from a perusal of this archival material that at the beginning of 1949, as revenge for the drubbing his army took in Palestine and in response to the fact that hundreds of thousands of Palestinians had become refugees as a result of the war that

---

* Over half a million Palestinian Arabs left their homes in 1948 for the neighboring Arab states or those parts of Palestine under Arab control. Some of them fled in panic; others had to go because of the war; and yet others left on the recommendation of the Arab leaders, who asked them to evacuate the area "temporarily" so that their armies could overrun the prospective Jewish state without any obstacles or delays.

the Arab states had started, Nuri thought up a diabolically clever way to crush the nascent State of Israel. His idea was to gather together all the more than 120,000 Jews of Iraq, load them onto trucks, drive them to the Israeli border, and force them over it—thereby swamping Israel with destitute refugees and, presumably, bringing about its swift collapse.

When the British Foreign Office got wind of this idea (which was never aired publicly) and relayed it to all its legations in the Middle East for comment, it touched off a curious episode that was to linger in the background for much of 1949 and, as we shall see, serve Nuri's designs in conducting a systematic campaign of harassment against the Jews. The initial flurry of British correspondence centered on the question of whether Nuri would indeed expel the Jews from his country and what the consequences of such an action would likely be. Sir Hugh Dow, Britain's consul general in Jerusalem, observed ironically, "Nuri Pasha's threat to expel the Jews from Iraq would probably have a very different effect from what he intended. It would be welcomed by the Jews here . . . and [they] would insist on Iraqis taking displaced [Palestinian] Arabs in return." But Sir Henry Mack, the British ambassador in Baghdad, tended to pooh-pooh the seriousness of the suggestion, and he was evidently correct in judging that Nuri's proposal was less a full-fledged plan of action than a scheme for unnerving the Israelis.

Nevertheless, the men of the Foreign Office—who persisted in regarding themselves as the guardians of Iraq's best interests—were taking no chances. They ordered Mack to act promptly to forestall any such move—not, I must add, to avert additional human suffering, but because "the expulsion of the Jews from Iraq would provide the Israeli Government with the perfect excuse for refusing to pay compensation for the property of Arab refugees." To which Ambassador Mack replied, "I shall do my best to dissuade [Nuri] from any action along these lines if it appears that he is seriously intending it."

And that, it appeared, was that. The entire subject vanished from Britain's diplomatic correspondence until some six months later, toward the end of the summer, when Said apparently raised the notion again with the local British diplomats. This renewed talk of expulsion was probably what prompted the rather intriguing September 5 letter from the Foreign Office's Middle East Secretariat to Ambassador Mack, in Baghdad, expressing a definite change of heart about how to deal with Nuri's latest rumblings:

. . . It occurs to us that Nuri Said's threat to expel the Jews from Iraq
. . . is worthy of further thought. . . . If the threat could be

transmuted into an arrangement whereby Iraqi Jews moved to Israel, receiving compensation for their property from the Israel Government while Arab refugees were installed in the property in Iraq there would seem to be something to commend it. . . . Iraq would be relieved of a minority whose position is always liable to add to the difficulties of maintaining public order in time of tension. For its part the Israel Government would find it hard to resist an opportunity of bringing a substantial number of Jews to Israel. However much it disliked the idea of assuming this extra burden public opinion in Israel would probably force it to do so.

Any idea of expelling Jews from Iraq should obviously be discouraged. A reasonable proposal for an exchange of population (with suitable arrangements for compensation) might on the other hand have something to recommend it.

. . . You should not say anything to the Iraqis at present.

Of course there is no way of knowing whether Ambassador Mack and his staff in Baghdad really did refrain from discussing this variation on the theme with the Iraqis. Yet it is an extraordinary coincidence that within a few weeks, on September 29, 1949, in reporting on a talk with Nuri Said, the Baghdad embassy credited *him* with a suggestion regarding "a compulsory exchange of about 100,000 town Jews for Arab refugee townsmen. . . . The whole or a portion of the Iraqi Jews' property should be taken as compensation for what the Arabs lost in Palestine and it would be up to the Israeli Government to give the Iraqi Jews an equivalent amount when they got to Palestine from what had been confiscated from the Arabs."

Was this really Nuri's own idea and true intent? And was there any chance whatever of translating it into action? All I can say is that there was ample reason to doubt Iraq's readiness to accept Palestinian refugees. At the height of the war against Israel, Transjordan's King Abdullah appealed to the Iraqis to admit one hundred thousand of the refugees crowded into his country, but Baghdad would not hear of it. Various UN committees seeking a solution to the Arab refugee problem likewise recommended Iraq as an ideal place for them—by virtue of its abundance of good soil and water and its need for manpower—but they, too, were ignored. Hence there were probably never grounds to believe that Nuri Said was in the least concerned about solving the plight of the Palestinian refugees. Moreover, it is a matter of record that on October 31, 1949, after word of the idea leaked to the press, the New York *Times* published a letter to the editor by Abdullah I. Bakr, the minister and chargé d'affaires of the Iraqi embassy in Washington, vigorously denying reports of Iraq's interest in a population exchange. And if any illusions still lingered, Fadhil Jamali, Iraq's ambassador to the UN (who also served as his country's Foreign Minister), again repudiated the idea in a newspaper interview published in February 1950, thus finally putting an end to all the diplomatic maneuvers surrounding the subject.

It therefore seems reasonable to conclude that Nuri Said never intended to release the Jews of Iraq, either by summarily throwing them out or by negotiating an exchange of populations. What he did do throughout 1949 —and with increasing vigor beginning in the autumn, just as these diplomatic maneuvers were reaching their height—was relentlessly harass the Jews by turning them into a collective whipping boy for his army's ignominious performance in Palestine. Their intolerable position brings to mind La Fontaine's fable of the hungry wolf who was looking for a pretext to polish off the lamb he met by a stream.

"You cursed me here a year ago," the wolf accused the terrified lamb.

"Oh no, sir," his prospective victim replied, "that cannot be. I wasn't even born a year ago."

"Well, then," the wolf rationalized, "it must have been your brother."

"I have no brother," the lamb replied with great relief.

"Then it must have been another one of your relatives!" the wolf snapped—whereupon he gobbled up the hapless lamb.

By the same reasoning, the Jews of Iraq were being punished for the insult their relatives had caused to Iraq's pride by repulsing its army and driving it to defeat.

Yet they were blamed not just for the defeat per se. Since the war had aggravated Iraq's economic difficulties and the grave shortage of basic products, it was easy to blame the Jews for these troubles as well. And for good measure another absurd claim was added to the indictment against them, namely, that the Jews leaving Iraq illegally were selling their property at a fraction of its worth, thereby fostering economic "stagnation"— the word on everyone's lips in those days. Indeed, the Jews who had decided to leave the country, like those who remained, had great difficulty disposing of their real estate and were forced to settle for as little as a tenth of its value—if they were fortunate enough to find a Muslim buyer with the clout to overcome the formal obstacles and conclude a deal at all. Yet this situation existed by government design. And even though it touched upon only a few hundred people per month, at most, and certainly had no tangible effect on the Iraqi economy as a whole, a distorted version of its impact was making the rounds.

On top of all this, the Iraqi authorities were riled by their failure to stem the wave of Jewish flight from the country. Especially infuriating, from their standpoint, was the publicity this flight was receiving abroad, making it look as though the Iraqi Government was at a loss to keep the country's borders sealed even under conditions of martial law!

The police let out some of their frustration by torturing the luckless people they caught, the relatives of those who got away, and anyone so much as suspected of association with the Zionist movement. Even a purportedly disinterested observer like the British ambassador felt constrained to report (after it had been going on for months): ". . . There is no doubt that the persecution of members of the families of the Iraqi Jews who have made their way to Palestine has continued." The accounts that came in from our people were far less reserved. On August 24, 1949, for example, we received the following cable on events of the previous few days:

The persecution of the Jews intensifies. Leading figures in the community have been arrested in Hilla [a small town south of Baghdad]. The head of the community in Khanaqin, the ritual slaughterer [who died a few days later as a result of torture], and other notables have been placed under arrest on charges of abetting the flight of Jews. The state of the prisoners is appalling. They are being punished by hard labor. . . . Some of the prisoners have been transferred to Badra [a remote settlement near the Iranian border] . . . where it is difficult to visit them.

Similar reports flowed in throughout September. In Basra people were caught while attempting to flee to Iran. In Kirkuk, Salah Efraim—an elderly man whose daughter was one of our youth-group leaders and had been smuggled into Iran—was tortured and then beaten to death by his warder. In Baghdad the police raided the Ottoman Bank, arrested the eight Jewish clients on the premises, and charged them with attempting to smuggle money to Israel. Precisely the same charges were made against three Jewish merchants in Mosul. But the worst catastrophe struck when the police found a Jewish informer who helped them direct their blows in a more precise and thus damaging manner.

Said Halaschi, a thin, swarthy-faced, seventeen-year-old Jewish youngster whose most memorable feature was his prominent dark-brown eyes, was one of the many young people who joined the Zionist movement in Baghdad. Within a short time, however, the leaders of his cell became aware of his tendency toward capriciousness, and at the beginning of 1949 they expelled him from the movement for his "low moral standards." Months later, toward the end of the summer, the police came to Halaschi's house looking for his brother, who was an active Communist. In the brother's absence, they took Said into custody and turned him over to the Secret Police. Whether out of terror or the lure of financial reward, he agreed to work for them and began proving his worth by divulging the names and addresses of all the members of the Zionist movement known to him—with stress placed on the youth-group leaders. In the autumn he joined the police units on their raids to identify the people in question. (In January 1950 Halaschi was even sent to Iran, in the company of a Secret Police officer, to spy on our activities there.) Our people in Baghdad were so incensed and alarmed that they actually asked the Mossad for permission to eliminate him, but were firmly refused.

The movement deployed quickly to deal with this perilous situation, first by halting all its activities and sealing its arms caches, then by ordering all its leaders to hide in the homes of other members believed to be above suspicion. The most vulnerable people were transferred to other cities or even smuggled out to Iran and from there to Israel. During this period the Qasr-Shirin route was in heavy use, for although it required a physically trying journey that often took three or four days of trudging through deep valleys and up high mountains, the police control was less effective there. On the other hand, the police efforts to halt the flight of Jews in the south went into high gear. The Basra train station, for example, was crawling with spies and undercover agents, and many of our people were indeed caught there. Within days, however, the police hit a dead end and were no longer able to snare the people they sought. Unfortunately, this proved to be something of a Pyrrhic victory, for in response to the abrupt end to their string of successes, the police began to run amok.

An experienced hunter knows that sometimes he must lie in wait silently for hours until his frightened prey believes the coast is clear and emerges from its hiding place. A poor hunter is liable to lose patience and begin firing blindly in every direction but hasn't the least chance of scoring a hit. That is precisely how the Iraqi police reacted when they realized their quarry had outfoxed them. Having grown used to sure hits on every raid, they lost their heads and began to strike out wildly, with all their might and barbarity. If the police came to a house and failed to find the person they were looking for, they arrested the entire family and savagely tortured them—though always to no avail, because these poor people honestly had no idea where their sons or daughters were to be found. The fruitless interrogations only stoked the fury of the thwarted policemen, so that soon the arrests spread to Jews who were in no way connected with the Zionist movement or the flight from Iraq, and night after night blood-

CARNEGIE LIBRARY
LIVINGSTONE COLLEGE
SALISBURY, NC 28144

chilling shrieks could be heard echoing through the Jewish quarters of Baghdad. As the capital's prisons filled with Jews, the police began to transfer their inmates to concentration camps that had been set up in Badra and in Abu Gharib, south of Baghdad, at the start of the military regime.

I was apprised of this situation early in October, when I reported to the Mossad's offices after a short vacation with my father in Tel Aviv and with Temima on the kibbutz, and thereafter I followed the cables coming in from Baghdad daily. One of the more infuriating of these reported that on October 3, in the midst of Yom Kippur, the Day of Atonement—the holiest day of the Jewish calendar—the police had surrounded the synagogue in Amara, a pathetic little town on the Tigris between Baghdad and Basra, and arrested a number of worshipers including the head of the local Jewish community. This move was so outrageous and unprecedented that even the British historian Stephen Longrigg cited it in his book *Iraq: 1900–1950* as symptomatic of "an increase of hostile pressure on the . . . Jews" and observed that "the sight of the terrified [Jewish] community . . . aroused in some the worst instincts of spite and bullying."

The wire reporting this incident was soon joined by harrowing descriptions of the arrest and torture of various other people. Considering all this, I was understandably fearful for the fate of the movement and the Jews of Iraq as a whole. Suddenly I was flooded with memories of the slaughter of the Assyrians in 1933, and my colleagues advised me to see Foreign Minister Sharett and tell him just how serious I thought the situation was. As soon as I could, I told Sharett—and anyone else who was prepared to listen —that we could no longer afford to settle for clandestine action; we had to work openly, making every possible effort and exerting every pressure on the Iraqi Government to bring the excesses to a halt before the situation got completely out of hand. Clearly our comrades in Baghdad believed the same, especially in light of their cable of October 12:

TO: Artzi
FROM: Berman

. . . .

4. We have no way of dealing with the situation.
5. We have brought all the activities of the movement and the Shurah to a halt.
6. The signs indicate that it may be a mass phenomenon, and the arrests and torture will affect hundreds if not thousands of Jews.

And if that weren't chilling enough, the following wire arrived on October 21:

To: Artzi

FROM: Berman

Dozens of searches have been conducted in the homes of leaders and commanders [of the Shurah]. Three girls and one boy have died as a result of torture. Teachers and students have been arrested in schools. The Secret Police are resorting to brutal torture:

1. They fetter the prisoners' hands with chains, string them up, and whip them.
2. They dip their hands and feet in boiling water.
3. They burn them with hot irons all over their bodies. People have reached a state of hysteria, and some are hardly recognizable as a result of the torture. . . .

The campaign we organized to bring these events to the world's attention—with the aid of our diplomats and Jewish institutions in a variety of capitals—proved to be a double-edged sword. For it exposed some of our sources and, more to the point, proved the existence of clandestine communications between Baghdad and Israel. When Foreign Minister Sharett declared that we had a list of the names of 250 Jews arrested in Iraq, the Iraqi newspaper *Al-Yakzhah* responded: "We neither confirm nor deny it, but the public should know that the Jews in Iraq have a secret means of conveying information." Nuri Said himself told the Iraqi parliament that the authorities were sure the Zionist underground maintained wireless contact with Israel.

Despite the risk of exposure, however, the campaign appeared to be paying off, for the facts we publicized aroused a surprising and gratifying degree of interest. American papers such as the New York *Times* and the *Herald Tribune,* almost all the important French papers, and many other responsible news media in Europe—though not in Britain—gave prominence to the reports coming from their correspondents in Tel Aviv and told of the measures being taken by the Israeli Foreign Ministry and Jewish organizations the world over. Soon the Iraqi legation in Washington and the delegation at the United Nations were taking the trouble to respond, usually by publishing long letters to the editor denying Israel's claims. Yet that actually gave us hope, for their very need to deny our accounts seemed to indicate that the Iraqis were concerned about world public opinion and might abate their persecution of the Jews.

Unfortunately, the media's interest was not long-lived; after a while, new arrests and instances of torture—to say nothing of the missions by Israeli diplomats—ceased to be "hot news." Fearing that this decline of interest would lift the pressure off Iraq, I went to see the late Moshe

(Moish) Pearlman, then the army spokesman and head of the Government Press Office in Tel Aviv, who heard me out and pronounced, "You're right, Shlomo. There's a chance that the subject will become routine. But to change that we need solid facts, real proof. Publicity is like a bonfire: the flames can start out high, but if you don't keep feeding them with new logs, they'll die out."

This demand for proof was already a very sore point with me, for I had encountered it repeatedly in the cables coming in from our ambassadors abroad.

"What other facts do you want?" I raged at Moish. "The transmissions from Iraq give dates and places, the names of the people who have been arrested, seriously injured, or have died under torture. Do we have to bring them here to testify?"

"Don't get sore at me!" Moish protested quite rightly. "I don't make the rules; I'm just trying to help. Perhaps the thing to do is send a foreign journalist to investigate the situation. Or maybe we *can* bring witnesses from Iraq to provide firsthand testimony. Unfortunately, Shlomo, there aren't many other choices."

I left Moish's office feeling thoroughly disheartened. Sending a journalist to Iraq was a fine idea, but who says the Iraqis would let him in? And the idea of bringing a witness straight out of Iraq was adding insult to injury. Moish probably thought it was as simple as bringing someone over from England or France: you just send a cable and the man turns up!

I was still grumbling to myself when I returned to the Mossad's offices and ran into Sammi, who was eager to hear the latest news from Baghdad. When I told him about my disappointing talk with Moish, to my astonishment I heard him lilt, "Shlomo, what's the problem? If all he needs is a witness, we'll give him a witness!"

"But how?" I asked in a whine of frustration.

"I'll be the witness," he declared as if nothing could be simpler. "Look, a lot of people know you, but no one knows me. So I'll do it."

"But Sammi," I insisted, "it has to be someone who's come out of there recently. You left Baghdad ten months ago."

"Tell me, Shlomo," he practically sneered, "what did they do to you on the kibbutz during your week there? Pickle your brain?"

I stopped to consider his proposal and began to appreciate its virtues. In fact, I began to savor it. "You're right," I conceded begrudgingly—but then, seeing the mock scowl on his face, I finally broke down and confessed with a shout of delight, "All right! So you're a goddamned genius!"

For decency's sake, I waited two days before phoning Moish to report that a man who had left Baghdad less than a week earlier had arrived that very morning.

"Great!" Moish exclaimed. "How'd you do it?"

"We got in touch with our people in Teheran and asked them to send someone who had come out recently," I said, outlining a logical but wholly fictional scenario.

"Good," said Moish, getting into gear, "I'll organize a large press conference. We'll invite all the foreign correspondents, and your man can address them and answer their questions."

"It's not that simple." I feigned apprehensiveness in the hope of sounding more convincing. "There's a problem."

"What's that?" he asked.

"He doesn't speak any communicable language."

"What?" Moish barked in a mixture of puzzlement and alarm.

"I mean he doesn't know Hebrew, English, or French, and essentially he barely knows Arabic. He speaks only the Arabic dialect of the Jews of Iraq. He's just a simple shopkeeper, you see, and he lacks an education."

"That's no problem," Moish said in a tone of relief. "You'll translate what he says into Hebrew and English. You *can* do that, I hope."

"I'll try," I replied modestly.

The next afternoon, I ushered Sammi into the press conference in the Ritz Hotel on the Tel Aviv seashore. When we entered the hall I was taken aback; never had I seen so many journalists. They virtually packed the room, which was thick with smoke from their cigarettes, pipes, and cigars. Sammi was dressed somewhat oddly—befitting how he thought his audience pictured an Iraqi Jewish refugee—and wore dark sunglasses to complete his getup. Moish was briefing the journalists but promptly stopped to introduce me and "a Jewish refugee from Iraq who arrived yesterday and wishes to remain anonymous because his family is still there." In the midst of this introduction, Sammi suddenly dissolved into a fit of rage, spat out a string of curses, and began to stomp toward the door. Mystified by what had set him off, I ran after him—and, fortunately, remembered to address him in Arabic. He explained in agitation that he had seen the journalists' cameras but under no circumstances would he agree to be photographed.

"It will place my family in danger," he railed. "You promised that I would be safe, and I believed you. But now I'm leaving."

It took all I could do to calm him down, whereupon I explained the problem to Moish, and he asked the journalists to put away their cameras. Only then was I able to cajole Sammi into sitting down by the dais. Moish, meanwhile, informed the journalists that the Israeli Government stood behind this man's statement, and I thanked heaven that he stopped there and did not go into any details about the "refugee" himself. Deep inside I felt uneasy about the way we were bending the rules, though I told myself that there are times when the end really does justify the means, and this was surely one of them.

In his inimitable way, Sammi related everything we knew from the wires, embroidering the bare facts with some rather colorful descriptions and personal impressions I thought entirely superfluous—until I remembered that he was supposed to be a petty Jewish merchant from Baghdad. When it came time for questions, he began to balk and once or twice almost stalked out in anger, so that again I had a hard time pacifying him. I also had quite a time translating his every word and the many colorful idioms and proverbs that pepper the Iraqi-Jewish dialect—which I never suspected he commanded so well.

When the press conference ended, one of the Israeli journalists came up to me and remarked, "I never imagined that there were such primitive people there. He was like a wounded animal."

"Don't judge others until you're in their place," I recited an ancient Hebrew proverb, "and don't forget what he's been through these past few days." But though I spoke reprovingly, inwardly I was exulting, because I knew that if a sharp-eyed, seasoned Israeli journalist was impressed, we had accomplished what we had set out to do.

Indeed, on October 25–27, the papers in Israel and around the world gave prominent coverage to the story of the "Jewish refugee from Baghdad." The New York *Times* headlined its article "Anti-Jewish Drive in Iraq Described," while the *Herald Tribune* headlined its piece "Iraqi Pogrom Charge Laid to Jew Who Fled: . . . Israel Studies Plan to Ask U.N. Sanctions." The subhead was a reference to the fact that, spurred by this new wave of publicity, Israel's diplomats were working feverishly on their own front. On October 21, Foreign Minister Sharett cabled Eliyahu Elath, Israel's ambassador to Washington, a list of the actions that had been decided upon in talks with the Mossad—including demonstrations at the Iraqi embassy in Washington and the Iraqi mission in New York—in addition to formally raising the matter at the United Nations.

On November 4, Elath reported on a talk with Assistant Secretary of State for Middle Eastern Affairs McGhee in which the latter stressed that the State Department "strongly recommends not raising the subject of Iraqi Jewry at the U.N." since "a debate in the General Assembly would stir up feelings and do Iraqi's Jews more harm than good." But although our Foreign Ministry was disposed to accept that advice, the threat to bring the matter before the General Assembly remained in force and kept the Iraqis looking over their shoulders—that is, until Terence Shone, one of the members of Britain's UN delegation, almost ruined everything. On November 8 he reported to the Foreign Office, in London, about a conversation he had had with the head of the Israeli delegation, Abba Eban, about the time the General Assembly was taking to get through its agenda. "[I] then asked him whether he was going to add to its labours—by bringing up the treatment of his compatriots in Iraq. He laughingly replied that his delegation had no such intention, but that he trusted that we would not tell the Iraqis." Such trust was, I fear, misplaced; the British evidently told the Iraqis that the General Assembly would not be called upon to debate the problem. Even so, the members of the Iraqi delegation could not help but sense the gist of the activity going on in the UN's corridors and committee rooms. And although we could not have predicted it then, a few months later the chairman of the delegation, Tawfiq Suweidi, was to become Iraq's Prime Minister, and we may reasonably assume that the "softening up" he got at the UN had something to do with the policy he adopted immediately upon entering office.

As for the reaction in Europe, the French seemed to know the facts for themselves, as a memorandum sent to the Quai d'Orsay by the head of the French legation in Baghdad on October 28, 1949, spoke of "arrests carried out in the best Gestapo fashion," "brutal kidnappings," and "talk that the buildings of the Center for Criminal Investigations sometimes echo with the screams of those being put to various systems of torture." But the British were intent upon regarding these developments from a completely different perspective. Since the Foreign Office felt bound to keep Nuri and his regime under its protective wing, it chose to treat Israel's complaints of a brutal anti-Jewish policy as malicious propaganda. At the beginning of November, Mordechai Eliashar, Israel's minister in London, was crisply informed by Michael Wright, the head of the Eastern Department in the Foreign Office, that his government had investigated Israel's allegations of mistreatment and found that the Iraqis had arrested a number of Jews, including four women, but that they were being detained for "Zionist activity, which is a criminal offense." And well over a month later, on December 12, Britain's ambassador in Baghdad cabled Prime Minister Clement Attlee the soothing message: "I have no doubt that 'third degree' methods current in all oriental and some occidental police forces were used but not a single specific case of torture has been brought to my notice."

Not content with merely fogging over—or refusing to see—the facts, the British seemed intent upon slandering us for trying to expose them. Eliyahu Elath cabled Moshe Sharett on November 4, 1949, that "persons in the British embassy here [in Washington] are spreading the story that

Israel has fabricated the persecution of Jews in Iraq to increase the collection by the [United Jewish Appeal]."

Yet even the British could not deny reality for long, and at the beginning of December, when Prime Minister Attlee felt it necessary to demand a full report from his ambassador to Baghdad, Sir Henry Mack found it impossible to avoid the assessment that:

> . . . The condition of the Jews in Iraq has deteriorated since May 1948. . . . Martial law has been grossly abused to the detriment of Jewish individuals and the Jewish community does not enjoy such equality of economic opportunity as it did in the past. . . . Heavy sentences were inflicted for such offences as making fun of volunteers for the Arab Liberation Army. It is not possible to obtain complete details of these cases, since the hearings were held in secret.

After again denying the "untrue" reports of abuse and torture that had been circulated by the World Jewish Congress, charging that they were "clearly designed to create prejudice," the ambassador nonetheless conceded that "the treatment of the Jews of Iraq is not creditable to the Iraqi Government, and [it] cannot be defended against charges of discrimination. . . . It is, I fear, inevitable that the Jewish community in Iraq will live in some insecurity, and it seems probable that this ancient community will decline in numbers and influence." Yet he continued to insist that "It does not seem to me . . . that the suggestion of the World Jewish Congress that they will be totally destroyed has any foundation whatever."

The Jews of Iraq were in no mood to debate whether the peril they faced was a decline in the size and influence of their community or its total annihilation. They knew only that their state was desperate. So much so that the same Jews who had failed to react publicly after the *farhoud* in 1941, the mass arrests in May–June 1948, or the hanging of Shafiq Addas, now clamored for action. The official head of the Jewish community, the Hakham Sassoon Kedoorie,† a staid, submissive, and gentlemanly septuagenarian who had been appointed by the government, found himself parrying strident demands to confront the authorities and take demonstrative measures. Day after day, the parents of youngsters who had been arrested in the dead of night gathered in his office and gave him no rest until he finally yielded and agreed to declare Tuesday, October 25, a day of fasting and prayer. By then, however, he had simply lost control of the commu-

† Hakham is a title of respect for a rabbi used by Oriental Jewry and literally means "sage."

nity. On October 23 the mothers and sisters of the detainees gathered outside Kedoorie's office and demanded that he join them in a protest demonstration in front of the regent's palace. When he refused, they barged into the room and left it a shambles. Even his tremulous capitulation did not mollify the women, who went on to topple his miter (the symbol of his position) and hurl abuse at him before curious passersby. We do not know who called the police; it might have been one of Sassoon's frightened aides. We do know, however, that the law arrived in record time, dispersed the demonstrators with unusual force, and set about making arrests. Then the police proceeded to haul in Jewish males found on the surrounding streets—most of whom hadn't the slightest connection with the demonstration—and the vicious circle gathered greater momentum.

The fast set for October 25 surprised everyone—and none more than the Jews themselves—because the strike that accompanied it shut down the Jewish community to a man. Not a child appeared at school; shops and businesses remained shuttered; and even the Jews employed in government service stayed out of work that day. The police—who regarded the strike as a provocation if not an outright insurrection—responded by escalating their violence. As the head of the Jewish community, Sassoon Kedoorie did all he could to obtain the release of the detainees and persuade the authorities to let up on their persecution, but the community no longer believed in him. On the contrary, it took to blaming him for everything that went wrong. His repeated denunciations of Zionism and Israel (made to placate the authorities) and his willingness to assure foreign journalists that all was well left him looking like a Quisling.

Kedoorie either realized that he was incapable of leading his flock during such turbulent times or felt that the community failed to appreciate his efforts. In any case, at the height of the uproar he tendered his resignation to the regent, and the post of acting head of the Jewish community was conferred upon Ezekiel Shemtob, who was as different from Kedoorie as black is from white (and who, it just so happened, was my mother's cousin). A suave, affluent Jew who had studied in Constantinople and then in Geneva, Shemtob was a man of the world and secular in his outlook and lifestyle. He was also a proud and forceful leader (as one might expect of a man of his wealth, education, and station) and was known to associate with a number of leading government figures—most prominently Tawfiq Suweidi, who was soon to become Iraq's Prime Minister. All these qualities were to make quite a difference in the months to come.

As one of those quirks of fate, the day after Kedoorie resigned, the regent also accepted Nuri Said's resignation and charged Ali al-Ayubi

Jawdat with forming a government. Nuri's departure was prompted not by his policy toward the Jews, of course, but by his failure to solve Iraq's economic problems, make up for his government's disastrous episode in Palestine, and boost Iraq to a position of leadership in the Arab world. His successor held the post less than two months, but during that period he did manage to relieve the pressure on the Jews in one way: on December 18, 1949, barely a week after taking the oath of office, he lifted the martial law that had been in effect since May 15, 1948. Yet, rather than diminish the flight of Jews from the country, the repeal of martial law acted like a spur. Police officers and smugglers who had earlier kept a prudent distance from the Jews now stepped forward to offer their services, and the following statistics attest to the results: in January 1950, the Mossad transferred 1,058 Iraqi Jews to Iran; in February, 1,020 people were brought over; and by March, the number was up to 1,700—and these figures do not include the people who fled on their own!

The other side of this coin was that the number of people caught while trying to flee also rose dramatically. Foiled in their efforts to seal the border, the police began to arrest anyone "suspected of fleeing" at critical transfer points, such as the general vicinity of the Basra railway station. This was a serious complication, because every Jew in Basra—including the city's permanent residents—fell into the category of "suspect" and was therefore liable to arrest. They also became easy prey for gangs of hoodlums and other common criminals, and this new element of wanton violence only compounded the Jews' sense of vulnerability, prompting a flood of cables from Baghdad that conveyed new depths of despair. Again and again they called for some action that would force the Iraqi Government to reverse its policy; again and again they were told that the Iraqis were unlikely to bow to world public opinion, so that there was little more we could do. The best advice Tel Aviv could offer was to "keep working on getting out as many people as possible," for at least the flight of Jews to Iran was receiving worldwide media coverage that portrayed Iraq in a very negative light. Early in February 1950, for example, the New York *Times* took the trouble to send one of its correspondents all the way to Khorramshahr, just over the Iranian border, to document the exodus in an article headlined "Jews Leaving Iraq in a Steady Flow."

More important, however, the mood in Iraq itself had begun to shift as more sober-minded Iraqis sensed the dangers of the mounting violence. If hoodlums were allowed to attack Jews in broad daylight, with complete impunity, they might soon train their sights on other citizens. The whole situation could spiral out of control and end in the collapse of public order. The specter of anarchy in the streets began to concern the Iraqis increasingly just as our movement people were at the point of giving up hope. In a way, the situation paralleled the case of the two armies that had been fighting a long war of attrition over a narrow river. One day, quite independent of each other, their commanders reached the identical conclusion that it was pointless to go on, so that the next morning first light showed the banks of the river to be deserted: both the armies had withdrawn.

Almost the same thing happened in Iraq. Just as it seemed that the Zionist movement was about to break under the relentless pressure, at the start of 1950, with Nuri Said far from the helm of state, his successors concluded that their war of attrition against the Jews was doing the country more harm than good. Thus quite abruptly on January 27 we were informed from Baghdad that Ezekiel Shemtob had gone to see Prime Minister Jawdat and received assurances not only that the Jews would again be issued passports but that the sentences passed in October through December, the period of the worst persecutions, would be reviewed.

Ironically (or so it first appeared), within days of that communication Jawdat was forced to resign. But rather than halt the process he had set in motion, his departure actually accelerated it. For in his place came Tawfiq Suweidi, a one-time Foreign Minister and chairman of Iraq's delegation at the UN and thus a man more sensitive than his predecessors to public opinion abroad. Suweidi also bore the unique (and little-known) distinction of having studied at the Jewish Alliance Israélite Universelle school in Baghdad, once regarded as the finest educational institution in Iraq and thus the choice of a number of aristocratic Muslim families for their sons' education. Perhaps that was why the new Prime Minister displayed an unusually fair attitude toward the Jews. At any rate, on February 15 Baghdad wired us that Suweidi had told Ezekiel Shemtob (his friend since childhood) that the government would grant Jews *laissez-passers*. On the twenty-seventh we received word that Shemtob had demanded that the Jews wishing to leave be issued passports, not just *laissez-passers*, and believed the matter would be settled within a week.

Yet less than a week later, the unbelievable happened—and on a date that could not have been more appropriate: Purim. I say appropriate because Purim celebrates the dramatic reversal in the fortunes of the ancient Jewish community of Persia, which was about to be put to the sword in a nationwide pogrom ordered and organized by Haman, the king's chief minister, but was saved at the last minute by the intervention of Esther, the king's new bride. Perhaps because of their geographical proximity to the stage on which this ancient drama had taken place, Iraqi Jews had always held Purim in special favor and observed it with great relish, throwing masquerade parties, indulging in practical jokes, and generally enjoying themselves. Above all, they scrupulously followed the custom of sending home-baked goods to relatives and friends, filling large platters with the delicacies traditional to the day: *hadji-bada,* the star-shaped cookies of sugar and almonds; mouth-watering *zangulla,* pastries filled with honey; deep red *luzina,* made from quinces and covered with chopped almonds; and the sweet, pure white *man-il-samma* ("manna from heaven"), whose name says it all. They also kept the custom of giving their children "Purim money," usually no more than loose change that the youngsters would use in playing cards and other games of chance that were *de rigueur* on Purim, for they symbolize the "casting of the lots"—or sudden turn of fate—that the holiday commemorates.

And so it was on Purim that the lots were cast again. Just when it seemed to the frightened, weary Jews of Iraq that all hope was lost, on Thursday, March 2, 1950, as they gathered in their synagogues to read the Book of Esther and recall the remarkable deliverance of their ancestors from official persecution, they learned that Minister of the Interior Saleh Jabr had introduced a draft law permitting Jews to leave Iraq "for good" in return for renouncing their citizenship. The bill was passed that very day by a large majority in the Chamber of Deputies and was sent on to the Senate, where it was hotly debated—with no few swipes at Israel and the Jews—but was finally enacted two days later.

By then I was back on my kibbutz—renamed Ma'agan Michael and relocated on the coast south of Haifa—trying to settle comfortably into one of the branches of its economy. I fully believed I had completed my work in the Mossad, though headquarters continued to relay cables and reports to me "for your enlightenment," as Moshe Carmil put it. That was how I became privy to the urgent cable sent from Baghdad on March 2 informing us of the exciting development. It caught us completely by surprise and opened with the emotional and touching statement: "We are entitled to weep with joy upon seeing the fruit of our labors and the labors of those who preceded us. Here is the salvation of these poor, tormented Jews." Until then we had reason to hope that the Iraqis might ease the pressure a bit and perhaps grant a few people travel documents, if only to take some of the wind out of our sails. But no one dreamed that such a radical change was in the offing—certainly not the opportunity to save all the Jews of Iraq.

Moreover, in all due modesty, it must be said that the law itself, and particularly its preamble, makes it absolutely clear that this change of heart came about as a result of our success in organizing the illegal emigration via Iran—whose dimensions grew from day to day. At the time, we ourselves failed to appreciate the impact our work had made, but once the law was published it was plain to see that the Iraqis felt it keenly. The preamble put it bluntly:

It has been noticed that some Iraqi Jews are attempting by every illegal means to leave Iraq for good and that others have already left Iraq illegally. As the presence of subjects of this description forced to stay in the country and obliged to keep their Iraqi nationality would inevitably lead to results affecting public security and give rise to social and economic problems, it has been found advisable not to prevent those wishing to do so from leaving Iraq for good, forfeiting their Iraqi nationality. This law has been promulgated to this end.

In short, despite the brutal pressure placed on the Jews and in contrast to what we, in our frustration, regarded as our sorely inadequate rescue program, the fact of the matter is that the Iraqi Government broke first. Yet it is equally clear (from a perusal of official documents and memoirs that have been published since then) that the Iraqis—and not only the Iraqis—never imagined that almost all the Jews in Iraq would respond to this opportunity and relinquish their citizenship to emigrate to Israel. The reports of the British ambassador in Baghdad, for example, show that Tawfiq Suweidi and Saleh Jabr estimated that only between seven and ten thousand people would opt to leave.

Looking back, it's possible that we inadvertently contributed to this miscalculation by the upshot of the so-called Big Deal we had concluded with the Iranians a year earlier. For it really wasn't such a "big deal" after all, either in terms of its repercussions or of the response of the Iranian Jewish community. On the one hand, here was Iran, a Muslim country, allowing its Jews to leave freely for Israel (on condition that they renounce their citizenship) and not a single one of the Arab states raised so much as an eyebrow. At the same time, only about one quarter of Iran's Jews took advantage of this opportunity, and, other than the hard-core Zionists, they generally comprised the poorer elements of society. Thus perhaps the Iraqis expected the same response if they offered similar terms: given their freedom, the Jews of Iraq would undoubtedly get over their panic, return to their usual ways, and find plenty of reasons to stay put. Those who did leave would be the Zionists, who were at any rate a disruptive element, and the destitute, with naught to contribute to the country's economy. As long as relatively few Jews left, the arrangement was unlikely to cause any more of a stir than its Iranian precedent.

If the truth be told, when it came time to estimate the number of Jews who would choose to come to Israel, a few of the veteran observers in Tel Aviv came to much the same conclusion. It was precisely at times when the

Jews were free to emigrate from a country, they argued, that they were least likely to go—and the history of Jewish life in the Diaspora provided numerous examples to back them up. Others believed that the Jews would be loath to renounce their Iraqi citizenship for fear of being stuck in Iraq as stateless persons. Yet others assessed that the Jews would think twice and twice again before forfeiting their property and other assets (since it was at any rate impossible to sell anything at more than 10 percent of its value) and would prefer to wait for less troubled times. All in all, the various experts offered estimates that ranged from ten to twenty thousand people.

I participated in the meeting at which these estimates were aired, because as soon as I had received details of the law, I caught the first bus to Tel Aviv, made straight for the Mossad's headquarters, strode into Moshe Carmil's room, and announced in a voice trembling with emotion that I was prepared to go to Baghdad immediately or do whatever else was necessary to help organize this new exodus. Don't ask me why, after all these years, I expected Moshe Carmil to jump up, slap me on the back, and exclaim "Welcome on board again!" What I heard instead was, "That's good, Shammai, because we've already sent Baghdad a cable that you're on your way."

It wasn't quite that simple, though. First we had to answer a number of questions about the degree of cooperation we could reasonably expect from the Iraqi Government. Would it agree to hold direct—albeit secret—talks with an authorized representative of the State of Israel to arrive at an arrangement for transporting the emigrants out of Iraq? Would it at least agree to speak to a representative of one of the large international Jewish organizations, such as the World Jewish Congress or the Joint Distribution Committee? And what was to become of the Jews' property? There were also a few highly practical problems related to absorbing the immigrants in Israel. That's when the question of numbers came up.

When it came my turn to express an opinion on how many Jews would leave Iraq, I felt obliged to offer a maximalist reading and spoke in terms of seventy thousand people—over half the Jewish community. I believed that as soon as some real movement began, a kind of mass phobia would set in, and whoever saw his neighbor leaving would join the stream of emigrants for fear of remaining behind alone. But I did not imagine that even such "maximalism" would make me appear as lacking in imagination, for what actually ensued was beyond our wildest expectations: over a hundred thousand Jews—fully 95 percent of the Jewish community—were to leave everything behind them and emigrate to Israel.

A few weeks later, as I was making the final preparations for my mission,

I was invited for a talk with Levi Eshkol, who was to become Israel's Prime Minister in 1963 but was then treasurer of the Jewish Agency, the body responsible for immigrant absorption. I had met Eshkol before, at party conferences and the like, but this was the first time I actually had a chance to talk with him, and I considered it quite an honor. Barely had I entered the room when he boomed at me, *"Yungeman,‡* I hear you're going to Baghdad."

"Indeed I am!" I replied proudly, and to make an even better impression immediately added, "I'm leaving in a few days to help our people there organize the mass immigration." That, I was sure, would earn me a generous dose of encouragement and compliments. But instead his tone turned inexplicably gruff.

"I'm told you think seventy thousand will come within a year."

"I hope even more will come," I replied enthusiastically and began to hold forth on my theory of "infectious phobia." But Eshkol cut me off sharply.

"Now listen to what I have to say. What's your name, anyway? Hillel or Shammai? Sometimes you appear as one and sometimes as the other." Rather than wait for my reply, however, he went on at the same breathless pace. "Tell your good Jews that we'll be delighted to have them all, but they mustn't rush. Right now we lack the ability to absorb them. We don't even have tents. If they come, they'll have to live in the street."

At first I was so taken aback that I didn't know what to say and thought perhaps the best idea was to take a humorous tack. Having noted that the Public Works Department was working on the street just below Eshkol's office, I quipped, "I guess that's why they're widening the street here."

"Don't hand me wisecracks!" he bellowed. "You don't know what you're bringing these people into. You must make it absolutely clear to them that conditions are very difficult, downright primitive. Otherwise they'll be bitter—and rightly so. I don't want them protesting outside my window; I'll send them to demonstrate outside Ma'agan Michael!"

Unwilling to abide any more of this sacrilege, I stood up to leave, frostily thanked him for inviting me, and added that I had no intention of going to Iraq just to tell people to stay put until we could ensure for them the amenities of gracious living. If they didn't get out quickly, the perils awaiting them there were far greater than the difficulties of settling in Israel. And if those were his terms, I was not prepared to go at all and would duly inform the head of the Mossad that I was withdrawing from

‡ "Young man" in Yiddish.

the project. Whereupon I marched toward the door, reaching it just in time for his parting shot: "Just don't say I didn't warn you!"

Shaul Avigur, the chief of the Mossad, was ill, so I vented my outrage to Moshe Carmil, who tried, as was his wont, to smooth things over.

"You must understand the terrible responsibility he bears," Moshe reasoned. "He's the treasurer, and there's no money in the till. Since May '48 we've brought in all the people who were in the British detention camps on Cyprus, the refugees from the DP camps in Europe, all the Jews of Yemen, and more keep coming in from Eastern Europe and other places. You yourself worked like a madman to step up the flights from Iran. I don't have to tell you all this. And there really *aren't* any tents. At first we bought up army surplus from the British in India, but even that has run out.

"Go out to the immigrant camps and have a look for yourself. Don't you know that we already have a hundred thousand people crowded into them? And there's no prospect of getting them out any time soon, because there's no housing available!"

I tried to interrupt this litany, thinking that perhaps Moshe, too, had to be reminded of the terrors stalking the Jews in Iraq. But he wouldn't yield.

"It's not just a problem of housing, either. There's no food! The Minister of Finance has already threatened to tighten the rationing, and he'll certainly want to cut back on the milk-powder and egg-powder ration. The food inspectors have been armed with pistols to protect themselves. Do you realize what that means?"

"Moshe, I don't want to underrate your fears or the gravity of these problems—"

"And worst of all, there's not even any work," he interrupted again. "Did you know that in addition to the people living in the camps—most of whom are unemployed, of course—there are about *thirty thousand others* out of work? That's a veritable army of unemployed people! Haven't you read about the demonstrations for 'Bread and Work'? Haven't you heard about the violence in the labor exchanges, the demonstrations by unemployed Arabs in Nazareth, the clashes between the police and Communist demonstrators? Tell me, don't you read newspapers there in Ma'agan Michael?"

"Moshe, we're talking about a basic question of principle," I snapped. "Am I to encourage the Jews of Iraq to come here, or am I to tell them to sit on their fannies and wait until 'further notice' from some stodgy bureaucrat?"

Moshe flushed but held his temper. More to the point, he seemed unwilling to commit himself on the issue. "Listen," he said, "I have to go see

Ben-Gurion. Why don't you come along, present the problem to him, and hear what he has to say? That will be the authoritative answer."

So on March 27 I was taken to see Ben-Gurion and began by explaining the dilemma. But he, too, cut me off and pronounced with his clipped, high-pitched speech, "You're going to bring Jews. Tell them to come quickly. What if the Iraqis suddenly change their minds and rescind the law? Go and bring them quickly."

And so I did. But much later, when I began my career in public life and was confronted by complaints about the conditions these immigrants had to endure during their first years of "absorption" and the grudges that remained festering as a result, I would often recall those two conversations with Eshkol and Ben-Gurion and wonder which of them had been right. Eshkol wanted all the Jews to come—and come quickly—no less than Ben-Gurion did, but as treasurer of the Jewish Agency he was intimately acquainted with the circumstances in the camps and appreciated the resentment of the immigrants who arrived with such great expectations only to become soured by the intolerable conditions. His caution was unquestionably legitimate. But Ben-Gurion's answer was the Zionist answer, the answer demanded of the Prime Minister in those historic days when the gates of salvation had suddenly swung open and no one knew how long they would remain that way.

By then, too, some of the anxiety stirred up by the emigration law had subsided. Those of us who tended to fear that the Iraqis were setting a trap to see who would renounce their citizenship, so that they could be punished for disloyalty, were satisfied that this was not their intent. Yet we still didn't know what would become of the property of the Jews who registered to leave. Neither did we wish to create a population of "stateless" Jews before there was any way of transporting them out of Iraq in numbers. For these reasons, we asked our emissaries to try to delay the start of the registration for emigration, and it wasn't until April 4, 1950—over a month after the law was passed—that Tel Aviv wired Mordechai Ben-Porat, the Mossad's chief emissary in Baghdad: "Shammai is leaving for Europe today, and we hope he will reach you within two weeks. . . . Do not make any commitments or [transport] agreements until he arrives." Further on in that transmission, with some reluctance, the Mossad conceded: "Agree with you that the registration should be initiated. Take care that only a few people are registered at first and, for the present, only young people and others without property."

It turned out, however, that the Jews of Iraq agreed with Ben-Gurion.

Within less than two weeks of receiving the green light from Ben-Porat and our other emissaries, over ten thousand men and women had registered to renounce their citizenship and leave Iraq—and the lines were growing longer each day.

ELEVEN

Miracle on the Tigris

"Miracles do happen, but you have to work hard for them."

Dr. CHAIM WEIZMANN, 1941

THOSE LINES OF IRAQI JEWS were the reason Ronnie Barnett and I—or, rather, Richard Armstrong, Jr.—were traveling to Iraq. Ostensibly we were two officials of the American charter company Near East Air Transport and were going to Baghdad to obtain the franchise for transporting Jews out of the country. It must be said that the only genuinely counterfeit element in this façade was Armstrong. Near East Air Transport really did exist (albeit under a slightly different name); Ronnie Barnett was indeed employed by it in a senior administrative capacity; and the airline was very much interested in winning the franchise. The owner of Near East, an American by the name of James Wooten, was an experienced, dynamic, even adventurous businessman who, as the head of Alaskan Airlines, had overseen the transport of Jews from Yemen to Israel a year earlier. Thereafter Wooten established another company, Near East Air Overseas, in partnership with El Al (which had come into being in November 1948). We hoped that the slight alteration in its name ("Air Transport" instead of "Air Overseas") would suffice to cover the traces of the Israeli connection so that the company could successfully bid for a monopoly on flying the Jews out of Iraq.

The groundwork of this plan was laid by Ronnie Barnett, who had moved over from Trans-Ocean to Near East and quickly became one of the company's leading lights—especially in the area of establishing the contacts necessary to secure agreements with the Iraqi authorities. Ultimately Ronnie's high-living ways, particularly his proclivity toward gambling and extravagant wheeling-dealing, proved to be his undoing. But in the days we were working together in Baghdad, he was a sharp-witted, creative, and resourceful man who took to complex situations like a duck to water and had a flair for endearing himself to almost everyone he met.

One of the men whose trust he had won, thus setting our present mission underway, was Abdul Rahman Raouf, the managing director of the Iraq Tours travel agency. The two had first met when Ronnie was handling a flight of Muslim pilgrims to Mecca for Trans-Ocean, and they hit it off so well that when we began contemplating an airlift of Jews out of Iraq, Ronnie invited Raouf to Rome (where he was living at the time) to discuss a deal. I, too, was in attendance at this meeting, but since it was my debut as Richard Armstrong, I let Ronnie do most of the talking. What he talked about—and offered Raouf—was the "deal of the century": collaboration with Near East Air Transport in flying Iraqi Jews to Israel. He made a great point of stressing that if Raouf could "fix things" with the right people in Baghdad and secure an exclusive for Near East, he personally stood to turn a tidy profit.

Clearly that prospect appealed to Raouf. In responding to the proposal with enthusiasm, he let Ronnie in on the fact that none other than Prime Minister Suweidi just happened to be on the board of Iraq Tours and was, moreover, a close personal friend. Not that the Suweidi connection could solve all the questions Ronnie had raised. For example, Raouf seemed highly skeptical about getting the government's official sanction for flights from Baghdad directly to Israel. Everyone would know the truth, of course, but for appearance' sake it would probably be necessary to state that their destination was elsewhere. Yet this was a fairly minor point, he believed, and at any rate the whole scheme would have to be negotiated by the Near East people in Baghdad.

Since matters had come that far, we had little choice but to find out whether the man was all he claimed to be. On April 11, 1950, I therefore cabled the following request to Tel Aviv for relay to Baghdad:

Check out the standing of Abdul Rahman Raouf, a director of Iraq
Tours . . . who claims to be authorized to draw up and sign a contract

on behalf of the company and the government. Also that Tawfiq
Suweidi has an interest in and derives benefit from dealings of Iraq
Tours.

So far, so good. But then the plot began to thicken. Two days later, our
emissary in Baghdad, Mordechai Ben-Porat, sent the following reply:

Abdul Rahman Raouf works for Iraq Tours. . . . He is a negative
character. In my view and that of many transport experts, one should be
wary of him.

This wire troubled me greatly, less because of the downbeat assessment
of Raouf than the reference to the "transport experts" with whom Ben-
Porat was in contact. I knew that he had been looking around on his own
for a travel agent, and I feared that as a result we might find ourselves on
some very slippery ground. In mid-March Ben-Porat reported that while
on a trip to Basra he had taken a "daring step" and, introducing himself as
a representative of the Jewish community, had called "the manager of the
British travel agency A. H. Fuller and Company, Major T. A. Caton."
Further on in this wire, he added the startling detail that Caton was employed not only by the travel agency but also as a member of British
Intelligence and had spent many years in the British Army in Iraq, Iran,
and Egypt—all of which did not necessarily commend him.

Since we had no better agent at the time and Ben-Porat had made no
binding commitment to Caton, we let the matter ride. But now that Iraq
Tours had entered the picture, I feared that we would end up working at
cross-purposes. If Ronnie's man Raouf was indeed in cahoots with
Suweidi, and Ben-Porat's man was moonlighting for British Intelligence,
we might soon be up to our necks in a bitter struggle for what promised to
be a very lucrative contract. There was nothing like the sweet smell of
sterling to bring out the grimmest determination in men, and that kind of
competition could sabotage our whole scheme. I therefore decided that we
were best off gambling on Raouf and that we had better get working as
quickly as possible. So on April 26, 1950, Ronnie and I—that is, Dick
Armstrong—were on our way to Baghdad determined to close a deal and
put Near East Air Transport in business!

My first sensation upon stepping out of the plane was that someone had
slapped me in the face, but it was only the effect of the heat and blinding
light of a Baghdad noon after hours in the plane's dim, air-conditioned
cabin. It took me a few seconds to recover my senses, but then I saw our
man, chubby Mr. Raouf, waving to us from the bottom of the steps. As we

reached the tarmac, he hugged each of us tightly in turn, and I clearly recall being assaulted by the pungent odor of sweat.

"Welcome, my friends!" he cried in English as he grabbed my arm in one hand and Ronnie's in the other and marched us off to the terminal. After seating us at a grease-stained table, he asked for our passports and plane tickets, so that he could clear the formalities, and suggested that we have something to drink in the meantime.

"I'd like a whiskey and soda," said I, mindful of Ronnie's strict instructions.

"Ah, I am most regretful, Mr. Armstrong. We cannot get whiskey here at this hour. I'll call for a cold lemonade. I am so sorry," he repeated, not noticing that I was anything but annoyed by the inconvenience. "You can have your whiskey afterwards at the hotel."

"I hope you've booked us at a good one," said Ronnie in genuine concern.

"Just as I promised, it's the Regent Palace Hotel. Absolutely the finest in the city. Right on the river."

"What river is that?" I asked, stretching my innocence perhaps a bit too far.

"The Tigris," Raouf replied brightly. "In Arabic we call it the Dijla. A very mighty river."

Minutes later, the formalities completed without my having to look a single passport officer in the eye, we were off in Raouf's car, traveling into the city over the route that I could once have driven blindfolded but hadn't covered since "Operation Michaelberg," in August 1947. The Regent Palace was also a throwback to the Michaelberg days (our pilots had stayed there), and for a brief moment I felt a pang of fear that someone might recognize me. But that, I immediately understood, was just paranoia brought on by my return to native ground, the strain of maintaining my cover, and the enormous sense of pressure to get moving on the right track quickly. In any case, we parted with Raouf, and when he had finally gone, Ronnie remarked conspiratorially, "So far, so good. I had no idea you were such an *artiste*. You almost had *me* convinced that you'd never set foot in Baghdad before!"

I smiled wanly at the compliment, for my mind was rushing ahead. I could barely contain my impatience to make contact with our emissaries, get an update on developments, tie up loose ends, and put an end to the Caton connection. The first problem—how to establish contact safely—had already been dealt with. On the assumption that we might be followed (as was the practice regarding many foreign visitors), before leaving Israel I had cabled Baghdad that I would be in the bookstore attached to the

Regent Palace Hotel every day at six. I was well acquainted with this shop (whose owner was an Indian) from my previous stay in Baghdad. It sold books in English as well as foreign newspapers and magazines, making it a particularly fitting place for Dick Armstrong to frequent. It also afforded conditions for passing notes (between a book's pages), holding brief conversations with ostensible strangers, and other seemingly innocent ways of making contact.

The next question was when to initiate that contact. For safety's sake, I had agreed not to communicate with our people in Baghdad on the day of our arrival. But by the time Ronnie and I had finished our "five o'clock tea," my patience had run out, and I casually remarked that I had neglected to pack the book I had been reading and was going down to buy another copy.

"Dick," Ronnie chided me, "you're not sticking by our agreement. Are you sure it's all right?"

"Look," I said just above a whisper, "I admit that I'm impatient. But what guarantee do we have that it will be any safer tomorrow, or the day after? Meanwhile, every day that passes without nipping off this Caton thing only makes matters worse."

Seeing that I was determined to go, Ronnie decided that it was wisest to accompany me. We both strolled casually into the Indian's bookshop, and while Ronnie spoke to the proprietor about getting the London *Times* sent to his hotel room daily, I turned to browse at the shelves. Seconds later I found myself standing beside David Shukhor, one of the commanders of the Shurah, whom I recognized from my last mission to Iraq. Flipping through an art book, he mumbled almost without moving his lips, and certainly without looking at me, "A taxi is waiting outside with Habib* at the wheel. Get into it when you leave here." Then he replaced the art book, turned around, and walked placidly out of the store. I continued browsing, glancing around surreptitiously until I saw that Ronnie and I were the only customers in the shop. Then I approached the proprietor and paid for two books I had chosen. Ronnie quickly followed suit for his illustrated weeklies, and as we walked out the door together I commented rather loudly—for the benefit of anyone who might be interested: "Ronnie, why don't we take a taxi and do a quick round of the city, just to see what it looks like." Whereupon I opened the door of the cab parked in front of us, pushed a rather startled Ronnie inside, and sat myself next to him. Mordechai Ben-Porat started the motor, and we lurched off toward nowhere in particular.

* One of the names by which Mordechai Ben-Porat was known in the underground.

I had first met Mordechai Ben-Porat in Israel before he left for his mission in Iraq in the autumn of 1949. He was one of a new breed of emissaries that the Mossad was sending to Iraq in response to my suggestion that we use veterans of the Zionist underground who had come to Israel in recent years. They knew their native ground inside out and had less of a problem establishing a convincing cover. It's true that because they had a history in Iraq and some of their acquaintances even knew they had fled the country illegally and settled in Israel, they ran the risk of being recognized and turned in by someone nursing a grudge. Then again, everyone working undercover in Iraq ran the risk of exposure, and it was reasonable to believe that because of their personal connections and deeper familiarity with the country, these native Iraqis would, if worse came to worst, have a better chance of wriggling out of a tight spot.

Ben-Porat had been in Israel longer than his fellow emissaries serving in Baghdad at that time, having come to Palestine in 1945. He immediately joined the Haganah underground and remained in the military after the Haganah was reconstituted as the Israel Defense Forces. By the time he was discharged, in 1949, just before leaving for Iraq, he had reached the position of company commander, with the rank of captain. When I was asked to brief him, I came away with the impression that his dynamism and assertiveness made him an excellent choice as an emissary.† Now we met again in the rather dilapidated taxi that the underground had managed to borrow or pinch, but it was hardly a grand reunion, since all three of us were literally rigid with tension and afraid to utter a word. Ben-Porat kept glancing into the rearview mirror to make sure we weren't being followed, while Ronnie and I peered nervously out the side windows for the least sign that something was amiss. Only when we had thoroughly satisfied ourselves that no one was tailing the car did we loosen up and begin talking freely.

The conversation began as a duet, with Ronnie eager to broach the matter of disengaging from Caton, and Ben-Porat offering to fill us in on what was happening in Baghdad. I motioned to Ronnie to let Mordechai speak, and he proceeded to tell of the incitement campaign by the radical nationalists against the new emigration law. One Shiite religious leader had even issued a *fatwah,* or religious ruling, forbidding his followers to purchase property from Jews, because "by buying from the Jews you are destroying the markets and undermining the economy." As the atmosphere turned ugly, the threats against Jews escalated. On April 8 a bomb had been thrown into the Al-Baiza café, on Abu Nuwas Street—most of

† Mordechai Ben-Porat subsequently pursued a career in public service and was both a member of the Knesset and a government minister.

whose patrons were Jews—wounding four people, one of them seriously. But despite these attempts to sow panic among the Jews and keep them cowering in their homes, the registration to renounce citizenship continued in a calm and orderly manner—especially after the Interior Minister was persuaded to allow experienced Jewish officials to handle all the paperwork on behalf of his ministry. That the Jewish-community organization fudged a bit on this point—the "experienced officials" turned out to be young people from the Zionist underground, who carried out their work in a disciplined and efficient manner—did not seem to bother the authorities. The Masooda Shemtob and Tweig synagogues became the central registration points, and long lines extended beyond their gates every day.

"And this Caton character," Ronnie asked brusquely, determined to clear up the issue of the "competition."

As Ben-Porat detailed the history of his contacts with the major, I saw Ronnie's expression darken. I, too, felt sure that unless we brought this flirtation to a halt, we would find ourselves in the middle of a minefield. Caton, we knew, was serving more than one master, and if forced to choose he surely would not put our needs first. Of course, that was only my inkling about him. But we felt we had reason to shy away from the major. And if we refrained from ordering Ben-Porat to break off all contact with him forthwith, it was only because we were concerned about not actively antagonizing Britain's official representatives in Iraq. I knew that we might yet need their goodwill to iron out some of the technical aspects of getting our immigrants to Israel, such as obtaining permission to fly via Cyprus (which was still a Crown Colony) or, preferably, *purporting* to fly to Cyprus while actually going directly over Jordan (which was under strong British influence).

After being approached by Ben-Porat, Caton also thought of using Cyprus as only a cover while flying directly to Israel—which was the most natural and economical route. Unfortunately for him (and quite surprising for a man of his experience), he went about broaching this idea in an amazingly forthright letter to the Iraqi Minister of the Interior proposing that Jews be flown "from Baghdad and Basra direct to Lydda [airport in Israel], where the passengers will be disembarked. The aircraft will then be flown to Cyprus, where the papers will be cleared and the aircraft returned to Baghdad and Basra to pick up fresh loads." In closing, Caton asked for the minister's consent to this plan. Needless to say, he never received the courtesy of a reply, for even if the Iraqis could be persuaded to wink at direct flights to Israel, they certainly could not be expected to give their consent in writing!

Still, it was not clumsiness or cheek that cost Caton and the other British transport companies the lucrative deal they were vying for. Much to the contrary, it was their very British propriety, civility, and methodicalness in going through all the proper channels. In the course of time, when a few of these companies complained that the Baghdad embassy was to blame for the fact that the whole deal had fallen into the lap of an American firm, Ambassador Mack countered that the Americans had won through lack of fair play. For while "the British firms had submitted applications to the Director-General of Civil Aviation [in Iraq], who had forwarded them to the Ministry of Communications and Works for further action, which, the latter told us, could only be authorised by the Minister of the Interior," the American firm had bypassed this whole bureaucratic rigamarole "and had gone 'right to the top.' "

That we certainly had. In fact, a mere five days after their sudden appearance in Baghdad, Richard Armstrong and Ronald Barnett, two parvenus representing what by any respectable British standard could only be described as a fly-by-night airline, were already being received by the Prime Minister—and in his home, no less! Whether or not the British ambassador knew of Suweidi's connection with Raouf and Iraq Tours, the swift access we acquired to the Prime Minister must have stuck in his craw. Ironically, however, this prompt invitation to Suweidi's home resulted from the fact that one of the British companies had stopped playing strictly by the rules. When Raouf appeared in the hotel dining room at breakfast that day, his tie pulled open over a shirt that was soaked with sweat even at that early hour, he informed us excitedly, "The Prime Minister wants to see you at his home this afternoon, because he is under heavy pressure. Some British company has contacted Colonel Sabah Said, who is the director of Iraqi Airways *and* the head of the Civil Aviation Authority, and has offered him a partnership in a charter deal, or at least some kind of benefit from the profits."

"Does this Said have more of a say in the matter than the Prime Minister?" Ronnie asked skeptically.

"Sabah is Nuri Said's son!" Raouf exclaimed, adding for the benefit of his two foreign partners, "Nuri is an important and very strong political figure. He was even Prime Minister until a few months ago. He's a great friend of the British, and he's not very happy about the fact that your company is an American concern."

Ronnie and I exchanged wary looks.

"So you see," Raouf continued almost breathlessly, "the Prime Minister is afraid that the franchise may go to another firm altogether. That's why he has invited you. If you can persuade him to close a deal, everything else will fall into place."

I could not have imagined a more encouraging and unsettling piece of news. It was wonderful for Richard Armstrong, of course, but for Shlomo Hillel, the home of the Prime Minister of Iraq was a veritable lion's den. I honestly felt rattled and knew that I needed some time to prepare myself for the next act in this brazen masquerade of ours. So after seeing to it that cables were sent off to Tel Aviv reporting this latest development, I returned to the hotel and found myself heading automatically to the shaded veranda overlooking the river. The waiter placed a glass of whiskey and soda in front of me—a drink I had begun to imbibe with enjoyment by then—and I gazed out on the Tigris, whose turbid waters flowed southward in a brisk current that sent waves smashing up against the hotel's protective wall. The water was especially high then and had already caused heavy flooding throughout Iraq. It certainly made things difficult for the *guffas* that came floating past. (The *guffa* is an institution on the Tigris. A small, round boat, about ten feet in diameter, made of braided reeds and ropes covered with a layer of tar, it serves for fishing and transporting goods.) As these *guffas* tried to make their way across the river that day, they spun around almost wildly, despite the efforts of their "captains" to control their movements with long, thin oars.

Bodies of water—lakes and seas and especially water flowing in a river —have always held an almost hypnotic fascination for me. But as I sat on the veranda of the Regent Palace Hotel that afternoon, even the sight of the turbulent Tigris could not deflect my thoughts from our forthcoming meeting with the Prime Minister. I tried to follow the hallowed tradition of the Mossad and retain my equanimity under all circumstances, yet I couldn't help but feel that I was approaching a very dramatic occasion. After all, it wasn't every day that a young man from Israel was invited to the home of a Prime Minister of an Arab state. There was something quite unreal about it. Here was I, the youngest child of Aharon and Hanini Hillel, of Bab al-Agha Alley in the Jewish quarter of Baghdad, about to meet the Prime Minister to discuss ways of bringing my long-exiled people back to their homeland. The whole idea was almost overwhelming.

For a moment, I also considered whether I wasn't carrying my audacity too far in accepting the Prime Minister's hospitality in his own home under an assumed identity. Thinking back now, I find it hard to avoid the feeling that both the risk and the chutzpah bespoke a touch of madness. Imagine the political repercussions, to say nothing of the screaming headlines, that would have ensued had an Israeli agent been caught red-handed practicing his trade in the home of the Prime Minister of Iraq!

"Dick," Ronnie called from behind me, bringing me out of my reverie.

"Shall we have lunch now? The PM will be expecting us promptly, you know."

Appetite had I none, but I did join Ronnie in the dining room to pick at my food while we recapped the points we would be raising at the meeting. Then Raouf turned up, ushered us to his car, and off we went—perhaps to make history.

Accompanied by two aides, Tawfiq Suweidi received us in the beautifully tended garden of his home in Karimat, a section of posh villas west of the Tigris, with the scent of blossoming roses creating a pleasant, informal atmosphere for our talk. Suweidi, a diplomat and statesman who was then in his late fifties, had studied law in Constantinople and completed his studies at the University of Paris. With his beer belly, full face, thinning gray hair, and large nose straddled by heavy, dark-framed glasses, he inspired a sense of trust and sympathy, in addition to the respect that went along with his title. We seemed to make a similar impression on him—or at least he was concerned about salvaging his country's image in the eyes of the two Englishmen seated in his parlor—for he addressed us, in English, in a somewhat apologetic tone, confessing his distress over the situation in which his government found itself. The problem, as he framed it, was that Jews were leaving Iraq and crossing the border illegally into neighboring Iran, thereby causing their country considerable economic damage.

"When a man leaves illegally, you don't know what he's smuggling out with him," Suweidi explained in an injured tone. "He does not settle his debts or pay up his income tax; he simply clears out."

"Dreadful," Ronnie murmured in feigned sympathy, while I—acutely aware of my unspeakable impudence in being there at all—decided to restrict myself to a low-keyed performance and remained impassive.

Suweidi went on to explain that when he raised this issue with the heads of the Jewish community—whom he characterized as "wise and responsible men"—and asked for their help in bringing this flight to a halt, they explained that the problem lay with a few hotheaded youngsters and destitute malcontents who were determined to leave Iraq at all costs. Since they could not obtain passports and exit visas, they chose to take their chances on the wrong side of the law. But now, the Prime Minister added by way of bringing us to the matter at hand, he hoped that the law recently passed by parliament would solve that problem.

Exploiting that opening to get down to business, I proceeded to ask, "How many people do you estimate will leave?"

Suweidi looked somewhat pained, and fearing that I had touched a particularly sensitive nerve I quickly added, "We need the figure for our calculations."

"Yes, I quite understand," he said with a weak smile, as though assuring me that he had not taken offense. "Unfortunately I cannot give you an accurate answer. We thought about ten thousand would choose to leave. Now I'm told that the figure will be much higher. Just how much higher I cannot say. We are not encouraging them to go, you understand, but neither are we stopping them."

The discomfort Suweidi felt over this higher number, which tended to belie the Iraqi claim that the Jews were not being persecuted, was now quite evident. When Raouf announced—on the basis of the estimates we had given him (and in a desire to make an impression on his powerful friend)—"no less than sixty to seventy thousand will leave," the Prime Minister snapped angrily, *"I* don't know how many will go. Why should *you* make a commitment?" Suweidi soon recovered his composure, however, and went on to broach the subject for which we had been invited.

"Well now, gentlemen, I understand your company is interested in the franchise, but I must tell you that another airline has already expressed interest, and still others may yet tender bids. My friend Raouf wants the government to give him an exclusive in this matter, but I must have at least one good reason to justify giving you preference over the others."

He asked for one reason and Ronnie gave him four: first, that we were offering the lowest price, 12 dinars (about $48) per adult; second, that our four-engine aircraft were safer than the Dakotas being offered by others; third, that we had a large fleet and could regulate the flights to whatever pace the Iraqis wanted; and finally, that our company had extensive experience in moving large numbers of people from various places around the world. Manners prevented us from citing such other important reasons as the projected revenues to the Iraq Tours travel agency and a number of people associated with it, including our host. It seemed reasonable that Suweidi did not have to be reminded of that.

At that point the Prime Minister begged our indulgence while he exchanged a few words with his aides in Arabic, and I found myself in the ticklish position of being able to follow what they were saying while not letting on that I understood so much as a syllable. It was very difficult for me to maintain a blank expression, and I almost broke down and winced when I heard that they were going to invite the head of the Jewish community, Ezekiel Shemtob, to join in the meeting.

Shemtob, the scion of a family that had come to Iraq from Turkey many years back, was, as I have already noted, my mother's cousin. I had not seen him since leaving Iraq as a child, in the early 1930s, and even then we weren't in the habit of visiting his family very often, because they lived in another part of town. Nevertheless, we were relatively close kin, and I felt particularly alarmed about the prospect of his appearance (in both senses of the word), because the members of my family strongly resemble each other. The grim possibility I had feared all along—that someone would recognize me—now seemed a very concrete one, and in the very worst of places! But there wasn't a thing I could do, especially as it turned out that Shemtob lived right next door, and it was only a matter of minutes before he entered the room. We all rose in respect, Suweidi alone remaining seated and welcoming his guest informally, as befits a friend and frequenter of one's home. Then he introduced us to Shemtob and explained the purpose of our visit.

Ezekiel Shemtob seated himself opposite me, and despite myself I began to squirm in my chair, half expecting him to look me straight in the eye and say, "Excuse me, aren't you Selim, Aharon and Hanini's boy?" Or at least, "You look very familiar. Haven't we met before?" But when some time had passed and he failed to make either of these two remarks, I began to loosen up a bit. Though still convinced that he knew me, I assumed that he preferred to exercise caution until we had an opportunity to speak privately. As matters turned out, it wasn't until months later that we had that chance to talk far from curious ears—in Paris, and without the need for subterfuge—and to my surprise I learned that he hadn't recognized me at all. It simply never occurred to him that the pipe-smoking Mr. Armstrong of Near East Air Transport was in fact the youngest son of his very own cousin Hanini. "Either I'm an old man whose eyes have gone bleary or you're one big ham!" he teased. "Who ever would have thought that Hanini's son would turn out to be such a liar!"

Shemtob did not speak English but was fluent in French (from the years when he studied in Geneva), so the Prime Minister and his aides addressed him in Arabic while I conversed with him in French, adding an English translation for Ronnie's benefit. This trilingual conversation went on for quite a while until we had covered all the points that required our attention. On behalf of Near East, we promised to handle the matter of landing on Cyprus (having wisely decided not to raise the option of direct flights to Israel), while Shemtob committed the Jewish community to collect the fare from every passenger, absorb the cost of anyone who could not afford to pay, and transfer the monies to Iraq Tours.

That much settled, it appeared that the meeting was about to break up on a note of shared satisfaction when I cleared my throat and said softly, "Excuse me, Mr. Prime Minister, there is one point we haven't settled."

Ronnie shot me a puzzled look that I hoped no one else had noticed.

"Yes, Mr. Armstrong," Suweidi said with a perfunctory smile and a bemused tone suggesting his thoughts were already elsewhere.

"It has to do with the form of payment to our company," I explained. "We must have it in some form of foreign currency. As an American company, you see, we have no interest in Iraqi currency, unless there is a way it can be converted into dollars or sterling."

The smile faded from Suweidi's lips, and without even asking to be excused he plunged into a frenetic consultation with Raouf and his aides. From across the room, Ronnie was scowling at me in near fury and at one point silently mouthed the command, "Drop the subject!" But I merely glanced down and nodded, almost imperceptibly, as my way of saying, "Leave this to me." The Prime Minister seemed distraught, even angry, and I could hear from the conversation that at first he adamantly rejected my demand—making me wonder whether I should relent or at least retreat, and if so, how far. This demand for foreign currency—which had been discussed at length with the Mossad in Tel Aviv before I left for Iraq (though not with Ronnie thereafter)—had to do less with the intricacies of international finance than with a desire to reinforce our credibility as a bona fide American company.† So I knew that if I wavered now, I might actually be introducing doubts where none had existed before. Fortunately, I soon understood that Suweidi and company appreciated my argument, and I knew that if I insisted on it, they would have little choice but to concede the point. So I quietly but firmly stood by my demand until we received an explicit promise to be paid in convertible sterling.

The basic issues settled, Ronnie and I took our leave of the Prime Minister and Shemtob and returned to our hotel, accompanied by Raouf, feeling quite satisfied with ourselves. For all intents and purposes, we could consider the deal closed. At one point Raouf, who was glowing with pleasure over his own role in landing the deal and had invited himself to join us for a celebratory dinner, casually remarked that he didn't understand how the Iraqi Jews could believe they would adapt to life in Israel. They were accustomed to dealing in commerce or doing clerical work, certainly not to physical labor, so what did they think they would be able to do there? Having read about how difficult the situation was in Israel—with an austerity regime, food rationing, and all—he was sure our passengers would not hold out there for long. In fact, they would soon be begging to come back.

"You know what I think, Mr. Armstrong?" Raouf said with a sly smile. "I think we should sell them return tickets right now."

"Mr. Raouf, I'm surprised at you!" said I in mock reproof. "What kind

† Indeed, I later discovered that our British competitors were very busy casting aspersions on Near East by claiming that it was financed by the Joint Distribution Committee and was essentially a front for Israel. Such things would have been all the more convincing had I not behaved like a hard-nosed businessman and insisted on receiving "hard" currency only.

of businessman are you? If we sell them return tickets, we'll have to give them a 10 percent discount. And why should we do that? Let them pay the full price each way."

We all slept soundly that night, only to discover the next day that our celebration had been premature. The deal was emphatically not closed and not even in our pocket yet, for it was encountering fierce opposition from the Civil Aviation Authority—headed, Raouf reminded us, by Sabah Said, who was also the director of the country's national carrier. Worse yet, our meeting at the American embassy that afternoon, to deal with the matter of landing rights in Baghdad, was highly disappointing—not because of any problem with the Iraqis but because, our contact explained, it was impossible to arrange for flights via Cyprus without the consent of the authorities there, and the island's British governor was not at all disposed to agree.

"Whyever not?" Ronnie asked in a rare outburst of frustration.

And in reply our diplomat friend offered the absolutely incredible explanation that—less than two years after withdrawing from Palestine, where they had been plagued by bitter clashes with the Jews over their ban on Jewish immigration—the British were gripped by the fear that Israel would refuse to accept the refugees coming from Iraq, thereby flooding Cyprus with stateless Jews! Consequently, there was no question of routing our planes via Nicosia unless we could procure an explicit commitment from the Israeli Government to accept all the Jews sent via the island.

Ronnie rolled his eyes skyward in exasperation, but I actually had to suppress a grin of relief, for I knew that nothing could be simpler.

"Is that the whole of it?" I asked, not wanting to remove this obstacle only to run into a whole gamut of others.

"So it appears," chirped the affable American with a slight shrug.

"Well then," said Richard Armstrong, Jr., the airline executive with British repose bred into his genes and American "can-do" acquired from his training, "we had better get working on it, hadn't we?"

I began doing so the next morning by cabling Tel Aviv, with the first wireless contact, that I was flying home immediately, via Cyprus; would be arriving on a Cyprus Airways flight; and wanted to make sure that an entry visa would be awaiting Richard Armstrong at Lod Airport. My Mossad colleagues arranged far more than that, however. When my flight to Cyprus suffered a two-hour delay, simple arithmetic showed that I was going to miss the connecting flight that would get me to Israel that same day— and frankly I would be glad to spend the night in Nicosia. Though only eight days had passed since Ronnie and I had touched down in Baghdad, the rush of events and merciless tension made it seem as though we had been there for weeks, so I was pleased that I would have this opportunity to catch my breath.

What I hadn't counted on was the hyperefficiency, and the clout, of the Israeli representatives on Cyprus. Before the plane had even landed, the pilot announced over the PA system that Mr. Armstrong was requested to disembark before the other passengers because another flight was being held for him. My fellow passengers looked around them for a VIP type who would merit such treatment, and, for whatever reason, no one's gaze fell on me—which was just as well, I thought, though obviously I wouldn't remain anonymous for long. Then, as I descended the steps onto the tarmac, I saw "our man in Cyprus" waiting for me alongside a tall, red-haired Englishman who turned out to be the airport's security officer. They both trotted me over to a side runway where a Cyprus Airways plane stood, propellers turning, waiting specially for me.

"You must be a very important man if they've delayed the Lydda flight for you," the tall redhead remarked while we were jogging across the airfield.

I'm sure he had some other thoughts about Richard Armstrong too, for it wasn't every day that someone arrived from Baghdad to continue on to Israel—and on a plane delayed specially for him, at that! But I chose not to make that my concern, and soon I was far too busy to worry about a nosy airport security officer in Cyprus.

My four-day visit in Israel seemed like one long meeting, with every self-respecting official and institution in the country asking for a private briefing on our progress. I was even taken to see Ben-Gurion, who asked a few penetrating questions, seemed amused by many of the details I related, and admonished me to look after myself and not take any unnecessary risks.

Meanwhile, events kept moving along in Baghdad, and while I was away, Ronnie wrapped up the deal—for fear of losing it if he didn't act quickly. On the second day of my stay in Israel, he reported (via our clandestine wireless) that the Interior Minister had approved all the necessary forms and sent them on to the Ministry of Transport. At the same time, to make sure they wouldn't "go astray" there, he promised to make the arrangement worthwhile for Sabah Said. Two days later, Ronnie sent another wire informing us that Sabah, who was the last obstacle to the deal, "objected to granting Near East a monopoly unless it signed an agreement with Iraqi Airways. So after exhausting negotiations, I have signed a contract."

That agreement, entered into on May 9, 1950, between Iraqi Airways and Near East Air Transport, Inc., was as odd as it was historic. It spoke of Near East undertaking "the transportation by air of Jews from the Kingdom of Iraq"—never even hinting at where they were going *to,* as if all these people were flying off to infinity—and granted Iraqi Airways "exclusive ground aircraft and passenger handling of all aircraft engaged in this transportation from the Kingdom of Iraq." The cost of this service: 30 Iraqi dinars per flight. For the equivalent of $120 per planeload, Colonel Sabah Said, son of the great Nuri, the scourge of the Jews, was prepared to withdraw all his objections and append his signature to the document that would spell their salvation. Incredible!

The moment I read Ronnie's wire about the agreement, I was seized with an urgency to get back to Baghdad. What mattered more than anything now was to get those planes flying before anyone had a chance to change his mind. And that meant, most of all, handling an enormous job of coordination between the various government agencies and the Zionist underground. By the next morning, therefore, my purported boss, Jimmy Wooten, and I were on a flight for Nicosia armed with all the necessary requests and commitments, from the Israeli Government, to obtain landing rights for our planes on Cyprus. I was so driven by the need to work quickly that when we reached Nicosia and found that it would take a few days to get the clearances, I left Wooten there to deal with the formalities and grabbed the first plane to Baghdad. Within hours I was deep in the feverish preparations that would continue for over a week.

My first two stops were the Masooda Shemtob and Tweig synagogues to check the registration arrangements, and I was pleased to see that they were well under control. The men and women who came and went by the dozens had their questions answered fully and politely by the young people from the Zionist movement, whose hand was strongly felt both in the pace of the work and the creation of a soothing and cheerful atmosphere that made things easier for the prospective emigrants. Police officers were seated all around, of course, and were officially in charge of supervising the operation. But a peek into the synagogues sufficed to establish that their involvement was negligible. They busied themselves with drinking tea from the small, pot-bellied cups used for this purpose in Iraq, and with reading the papers and illustrated weeklies that our people kept in steady supply. Our hotel also became a focus of activity, with government officials, clerks from Iraq Tours, and representatives of the Jewish community coming and going in what seemed like an endless round.

For most of that week, I seemed to be going practically twenty-four hours a day. But the greatest strain for me was the physical and psychological shuttle I kept up between the two poles of the Regent Palace and the underground. Whenever I had to get through to the movement, to hold a meeting or send cables to Israel, Mordechai Ben-Porat would turn up in that jalopy of a cab and carry me off for a spin. Then back I would go to the Regent Palace to resume my life as Richard Armstrong, knowing that if ever I were to slip or a word were to pass my lips in Arabic or Hebrew, it would mean curtains for us all. Never for a second could I forget myself or be off my guard.

As a break from the constant hubbub and stress, not long after my return to Baghdad, Ronnie and I were glad to take up Raouf's invitation to go for a quiet walk along the Tigris. My strongest memories of that river were of the large boats that plied their way between the fishing skiffs and of the city's two bridges that had loomed so large to me as a child. But, most of all, I remembered the Tigris in the blazing days of summer, when the water level receded to the point where a large island covered with thick vegetation rose out of the middle of the river. It was an ideal setting for recreation spots, and our family used to visit it on outings, taking a rowboat to one of the quiet areas at the island's edge and settling in for a lazy afternoon that would culminate in a feast of *samak mazgouf,* barbecued fish prepared in a special way by the owner of the rowboat as part of his professional services.

Iraqi cuisine (and especially Iraqi Jewish cuisine) is rich in variety and palate-pleasing dishes, but its *pièce de résistance* is unquestionably *samak mazgouf.* The preparation of this one-course meal would begin before we went out rowing, with the purchase of a suitable carp, a foot and a half or longer, from one of the fishermen along the pier who kept his wares in the water, attached to a long pole, so that they remained alive until the very moment of purchase. Later, when we were ready for our feast, the owner of the rowboat would whip out a sharp knife, slit the fish down the middle, and begin preparing it with expertise. He salted it, spiced it with aromatic curry, pierced it with a wooden skewer, and laid it alongside the fire, rather than over it. A few minutes later, when it came time to turn the fish over, he would place it above the dying embers and add onions and tomatoes. Finally, when the scent of the roasted fish, curry, and onions filled the air, the picnickers were invited to sit on a mat laid out by the river and feast away on this culinary masterpiece.

Summer still lay ahead as Ronnie and I set out for our walk with Raouf, but as we strolled lazily along, taking pleasure in the sight of the crystal-clear water, I suddenly gasped and came to an abrupt halt as I caught the unmistakable aroma of *samak mazgouf.* Immediately my eye caught an open fire by the riverbank and beside it the roasting fish that filled the air with the scent of curry and onions. I stood rooted to the spot, staring at that fire as if bewitched and absolutely aching for a taste of the dish whose luscious flavor I remembered from childhood.

"Anything wrong, Dick?" I heard Ronnie ask.

I remained mute, not knowing what to say. Then I had a brainstorm.

"Look what they're doing there, Ronnie," I replied in my best approximation of fascination. "It must be some sort of sacrifice. They're burning a fish on a pyre!"

"Sacrifice? What are you talking about?" said Raouf rather testily. "They're just cooking some fish," he explained, clearly offended by my view of ordinary Iraqi customs as pagan rituals.

"Surely it's some religious rite," I insisted. "I recall reading somewhere that it's a custom to burn sacrifices. Isn't that so?"

"Mr. Armstrong," Raouf retorted in near indignation, "they're just cooking fish. It's called *samak mazgouf.*"

"That's all very well, Mr. Raouf, but then why are they burning it? Don't tell me you can actually *eat* that!"

"Of course you can! It's quite delicious," he assured me.

"Is it, now? Well then, let's taste some," I challenged, believing it couldn't hurt to try my luck.

"Oh no, Mr. Armstrong," Raouf vetoed good-naturedly. "That wouldn't be appropriate for people of our station. I'll see to it that you're invited to a fish dinner. You know, there's none like the Jews for cooking good fish, so I'll tell Shemtob to invite us. Then you'll see how tasty fish from the Tigris is!"

"That won't be necessary, Mr. Raouf," I tried to beg off. "I shouldn't want to put Mr. Shemtob to any bother. I'll order fish for dinner at the hotel."

The last thing I needed was to go to Shemtob's house and have a member of his family or social circle recognize me. But though I soon forgot the matter, Raouf would not abandon the idea—undoubtedly for motives of his own—and a few days later he informed us that we were invited to lunch at Shemtob's. My protests did no good. All I had intended was to nettle him a bit, as a way of getting a taste of some genuine *samak mazgouf.* Instead I had gotten myself into a holy mess.

I fretted all the way to Shemtob's house, but fortunately our host had invited neither relatives nor friends and had limited the guest list to government officials, who were hardly likely to recognize me as Hanini Hillel's son. It was thus with a lighter heart and a clearer conscience that I allowed myself to enjoy the spread of Iraqi specialties set out on the large table in the center of the Shemtobs' broad, tree-shaded veranda. The scene remains sharp in my mind to this day. First we helped ourselves from the bowls of steaming white and pink rice mixed with almonds and raisins, the choice cuts of chicken, meat balls in zucchini sauce, fried burghul balls formed around a variety of piquant fillings, the platters of finely diced salads, piles of flat Iraqi pitas, and pyramids of colorful and inviting fruits. Hardly had we seated ourselves around the table when a parade of servants entered with long trays, each covered with a *samak mazgouf* in all its glory, filling the air with the aroma of curry.

Ronnie and I sat flanking our host, as the guests of honor, but that was the only trace of formality—or even the standard rules of etiquette. As a matter of fact, it was as if the arrival of the fish was the signal for a free-for-all in which Ronnie and I were at a distinct disadvantage, bound as we were by *noblesse oblige* in this encounter with the "natives." While the cream of Iraq's civil service pounced on the fish, ripping off chunks with their bare hands—as *samak mazgouf* has been eaten since time immemorial —we continued to flail away at it with our knives and forks, arousing the pity and contempt of our fellow diners, who could barely keep from laughing at the ridiculous sight we made. Not only did their mocking gestures soon give way to jokes at our expense in Arabic (which they naturally assumed we did not understand), when Raouf loyally suggested offering us the best parts, he was sharply rebuked and told in no uncertain terms that it was a pity to waste such good cuts on these two persnickety Englishmen, since they would at any rate lose their savor when eaten with a knife and fork!

"What do asses know of the taste of barley?" one of the guests quoted an old Arabic proverb to the vociferous delight of the rest. I had to exercise extreme self-restraint to keep from reacting, or even showing the least sign of comprehension. And of course I had to do so while taking care not to get a bone stuck in my throat!

On another occasion, I had such an uncomfortably close call with my cover that I had to do some very fancy footwork to acquit myself. Once again, it was in a social setting. The longer we remained in Baghdad the wider our circle of acquaintances grew, until it encompassed the senior staff of Iraq Tours, members of the Civil Aviation Authority, and employees of Iraqi Airways, to say nothing of Raouf's personal friends, who regularly joined us to have a few drinks, spend the evening at a cabaret, or play cards in the hotel garden. Card playing was viewed with great disfavor on my kibbutz, but fortunately I had learned to play poker as a child, so that I not only succeeded in holding my own among the card sharks of Baghdad, occasionally I even won a fat kitty. Even so, I preferred cabarets to card games; their level of entertainment may not have been very high, but at least I was spared the tension that went along with gambling.

It was during one of these evening get-togethers on May 14—the day on which Jimmy Wooten arrived from Nicosia with all the necessary clearances—that Richard Armstrong almost met his end. A larger group than usual collected in the hotel garden that night, at Raouf's invitation, to honor the "real boss" of the airline that had appointed him its representative. We were seated in a large circle, nursing our drinks as we engaged in the usual cocktail-party conversation, when suddenly my ear picked up the exchange going on in Arabic between the two men seated to my right.

"Have you noticed the scar on his face? It looks exactly like an *ukht*," one of them remarked.

"Don't be ridiculous," the other replied impatiently. "How can he have an *ukht?* It doesn't make sense."

"I tell you it resembles an *ukht!*" the first insisted.

My stomach wrenched into a knot, for well I knew that the object of this argument was the small scar on my right cheek, the hallmark that Iraq stamps on almost all of its natives and a good many of its visitors. The so-called Rose of Baghdad is a lesion caused by a parasite carried by the sand flies and mosquitoes that thrive in areas where date palms grow. It blossoms on exposed areas of the body that are accessible to flying insects, takes an inordinately long time to heal, and leaves behind a deep scar—together with lifelong immunity to the parasite. Precisely where the "rose blooms" is a matter of luck. If it appears on the hand or the foot, the problem is not as serious, and the permanent scar may not even be noticed. But, for some reason, the face seems to be particularly vulnerable to this phenomenon, and more often than not the Rose of Baghdad will leave its lifelong mark on a child's cheek or chin—or even the tip of his nose.

While the location of the "rose" may be a matter of fate, its actual presence is practically inevitable for anyone who lives in Iraq. Folklore has it that this prevalence is the reason for its popular name, *ukht*, meaning "sister" in Arabic; for just as practically everyone has a sister, so everyone has an *ukht* in the sense of the scar left by the Rose of Baghdad.

I, too, fit this rule, with four real sisters and a fifth, metaphorical, one implanted on my cheek. It wasn't very deep, but it was (and still is) there and definitely recognizable to anyone familiar with the phenomenon. Little wonder that I had had misgivings about masquerading in Baghdad as Richard Armstrong with a typical Iraqi *ukht* engraved on my skin. So there I was, trapped at this utterly superfluous bash, desperately seeking an alternative explanation that would satisfy those two busybodies seated beside me. Instinctively I puffed away on my pipe, as though trying to create a smoke screen, and pretended to be lost in thought as my ear strained to catch the rest of the conversation.

"All right, then," said the one whose eagle eye had first discovered the mark, "I'll simply ask him. It's such a coincidence, so amazingly like an *ukht*, that I'll just come right out and ask him!"

Which is precisely what he proceeded to do.

"Mr. Armstrong," he said, addressing me in English, of course, with a strong Arabic accent, "I would like to ask you something. My friend and I were wondering how you got that scar on your face."

Here was my opportunity to deflect their attention from it and put an end to their idle speculation once and for all. Hardly had the question passed his lips when Richard Armstrong, Jr., began prattling away in reply, "I beg your pardon?" And then a second later, "Oh, you mean this small scar on my cheek! I see you have a sharp eye, sir. I should have thought it practically invisible by now. Courtesy of the Jerries, thank you. The Germans, you know. Bastards shot us down over France in '44. I was the gunner—they got one of our engines—and fortunately I didn't black out. The pilot was quite a good man, actually. Got us down in one piece. And I managed to get pretty far off before the bloody thing exploded. The plane, that is. The scar is from a burn—just a spark, really, that hit my face. Where I really got it badly was on the legs!"

And, so saying, I immodestly hiked up the pants on my left leg to reveal the large scar that remained from an injury sustained a few years back that had taken a number of operations to repair. As I had hoped, the focus of attention moved from my face to my scarred leg, and I went on to thoroughly bore them with the whole history of my ravaged limb and the doctors' efforts to rehabilitate it with steel pins, endless operations, and the like. They oozed sympathy over my tribulations, marveled over the advances of modern medicine in Europe, and never returned to the matter of my little *ukht* again. Without question, the good Lord was working overtime on my behalf during those days.

And then, just when everything seemed to be going right, on May 18, the day originally scheduled for our maiden voyage (which was postponed by a day due to a typical bureaucratic snafu), my luck seemed to change—radically. That morning, I went to the airport to check out all the arrangements for processing our passengers and then continued on to one of the centers where the emigrants were checking in and having their luggage weighed. They looked tired and anxious. Again and again they approached the young men who were in charge of these centers, asking whether this time it was certain, whether they would really be leaving the next day. Indeed, they had good reason for concern, since they had already moved out of their homes and had nowhere to return to.

After lunch at the hotel, Jimmy, Ronnie, and I went up to my room and were in the midst of finalizing some last-minute details when the door burst open and Raouf came rushing in, tie awry, panting and sweating profusely. Plopping down into a chair, he remained tantalizingly mute while trying to catch his breath, until Wooten decided to force the issue by observing in his understated, businesslike way, "You seem upset, Mr. Raouf. Is something the matter?"

"We have a problem," Raouf informed us breathlessly. "The Secret Police have received a tip that Mr. Armstrong is a Jew."

I felt a shot of pain tear through my chest and recognized it as raw fear. I knew that on the face of it, this detail should not have made any difference. Grave as the condition of Iraqi Jewry was at the time, being Jewish was still not a criminal offense. Besides, our presence in Iraq for the purpose of transporting Jews out of the country in itself implied some connection with them. Yet the fact was that during that period the Iraqi authorities had made a point of forbidding the entry of foreign Jews, of whatever nationality, and any transgression of this ban was considered an extremely grave offense. So I was truly in a pickle and sensed that I had to calculate my moves with great care. For all I knew, even Raouf might have been in the pay of the Secret Police and was testing for my reaction.

Jimmy Wooten was the first to respond to Raouf's dramatic announcement. "That's pure bunk!" he spat in annoyance.

Seeing that Raouf did not understand the idiom—though Wooten's tone had conveyed his sentiments clearly enough—I added with as much British reserve and disdain as I could muster, "That is really most amusing, Mr. Raouf."

"I know it's not true," Raouf whined defensively, "but the fact is that the Secret Police have been told otherwise."

"And what will happen now?" Wooten asked, having returned to his matter-of-fact manner.

"They'll probably want to interrogate Mr. Armstrong," Raouf predicted. "The whole thing is nonsense, but I'm afraid the consequences may be unpleasant. Rumors will begin circulating in the city, and nasty tongues will begin to wag."

If only that were the worst of it, I thought. The bolt of fear that had shot through me seconds before seemed to have settled down to a cold lump in my stomach. I glanced at the door, thinking that any minute it might burst open again and herald the beginning of the end for Richard Armstrong. I had no illusions that my cover would hold up for very long under real interrogation. How many times had I spoken about the torture cells to my colleagues, to diplomats, to journalists, depicting their horrors, trying to convey something of the anguish to which the Iraqis had subjected the Jews, and especially the members of the Zionist movement? Well, now I would have a chance to check them out for myself. Again I glanced in the direction of the door. It remained firmly closed, but I was finding the tension almost unbearable. I forced myself to concentrate on the possibility that this drama was being staged to see how I would react, and rather than stew in my fear and the suffocating feeling of being trapped, I decided to take the initiative and put on a little counterplay of my own.

"I suggest," I began jauntily, as befits a man with a clear conscience, "that we don't just sit around idly wondering what happens next. The whole matter is quite ridiculous, so perhaps I should go to the police station, introduce myself, and offer to answer any questions they may have."

Jimmy vetoed that idea on the grounds that it would further complicate matters. Raouf rejected it even more adamantly, explaining that we weren't talking about the friendly constables at the neighborhood station house, but about the Secret Police. And you couldn't just stroll into the offices of the Secret Police and say you'd heard such and such and wanted to clear up the misunderstanding!

"Then, what do you suggest, Mr. Raouf? That I sit here waiting till they come to get me?" I asked half in rebuke and half in curiosity about what he would say.

"Not at all," Raouf replied, his tone turned oddly informative. "It's afternoon already, and if they haven't come by now, they're not likely to show up today. Tomorrow is Friday, which is our day of rest, and they probably won't summon you then, either. In the meantime, perhaps we can find out who and what is behind this."

Jimmy and Ronnie found this scenario implausible. I actually thought there might be something to it, but as the man with the most to lose, I certainly wasn't banking on the possibility that the Iraqi security services worked union hours. After all, the British had been their mentors, and it was inconceivable that they had neglected to teach the Iraqis a thing or two that were not very comforting from my standpoint.

In any event, it was Jimmy Wooten who resolved the problem in his typically levelheaded way.

"Dick, I suggest that you be the one to accompany our planes to Cyprus tomorrow. You were in Nicosia with me, and you're familiar with the arrangements there. From every point of view, it's best that you take out the first flights. In the meantime, we'll try to clarify what this silliness is all about."

His logic was as faultless as his delivery, and that arrangement suited me fine. Nevertheless, to make a credible impression on Raouf, I told Wooten that I wouldn't dream of leaving Iraq under a cloud and couldn't possibly accept his suggestion.

"It's not a suggestion," he replied with just enough strain in his voice to convince the most discerning soul, "it's an order. You know what they say, Dick: the boss may not always be right, but he's always the boss."

Satisfied with that way out, I prepared to make my exit the following day—though, all the while, I was nagged by the thought that Raouf's story simply didn't wash. If he had come bearing tales that the police suspected Armstrong of being an Israeli, I could understand that someone who knew my true identity had informed on me or had simply been less than circumspect in his chatter, so that the information had reached the police through other channels. Or if someone had reported, less specifically, that I was in Iraq under an assumed identity, then I would be open to the charge of carrying a false passport—which was so serious as to make my being a Jew pale by comparison. By the same token, if the present predicament traced to my trip from Baghdad to Tel Aviv and the mad dash across Nicosia Airport (which had unquestionably caught the attention of the British there), then there was reason to wonder whether being Jewish was the worst suspicion the Iraqis had against me.

Of course, it was always possible that Major Caton or one of his cohorts was trying to torpedo our agreement by spreading malicious rumors. But that didn't seem very likely either, since Jimmy Wooten and Ronnie Barnett appeared to be far more important players than I was, and it made more sense to try to discredit them, on commercial grounds, than to float a rumor that Richard Armstrong was a Jew.

Even with the perspective of time and the advantage of access to official documents, this mystery remains unsolved—though it does appear that my trip to Cyprus had nothing to do with the "revelation" about Armstrong's ethnic background. It is reasonable to assume that if Cyprus were the source of the information, the British embassy in Baghdad would have known about it, yet there is no reference to Armstrong's background in any of the embassy's letters or documents.

All in all, I am still baffled by the episode that cut short my mission in Baghdad. But regardless of how it came about, I must say that if I was fated to have to leave Iraq quickly, the whole affair couldn't have come up at a more opportune time. The first two Near East planes were scheduled to take off the following day and, as Jimmy Wooten had pointed out, it was perfectly natural for me to be on one of them. Meanwhile, however, I still had to spend another day in Baghdad and was forced to assume that I was under surveillance. For exactly that reason, it seemed imperative to maintain a pose of business as usual. Above all, I knew that I must not appear tense or have my behavior call attention to itself as unnatural in any way: hyperactivity, inappropriately loud laughter—things like that.

Whether I actually followed all this sensible advice is not for me to judge. I can say, though, that as evening fell and the regular complement of card players and other freeloaders gathered to join us until the wee hours, I entertained them like a model host. *(At least let them remember me fondly,* I thought.) Other than glancing around from time to time to see whether anyone was following or otherwise showing any special interest in me, the only thing I did out of the ordinary was to turn in relatively early. Yet for that, at least, I had a solid explanation: I wanted to be up at dawn and get to the airport well before departure time to make sure everything was going along smoothly. On my way upstairs, I asked the desk clerk to wake me at five, though I was sure I wouldn't sleep a wink that night. And following that premise I stretched out on the bed still clothed, hoping at least to rest a bit while putting my thoughts in some semblance of order.

The next thing I knew there was loud banging on the door and I bolted off the bed in a panic, fully expecting the room to fill with policemen any second. Frantically seeking an avenue of escape, I dashed first to the window, then to the closet, only to discover—when I finally bothered to listen to the imploring tone coming from the other side of the door—that the insistent banger was the desk clerk. As I opened the door, just a crack at first to confirm that he was alone, he reminded me warily (in response, I suppose, to my ashen color and the stricken look on my face) that I had asked to be wakened at five, and it was already well past that hour. Only then did I realize that, contrary to all expectations, I had been dead to the world from the moment my head hit the pillow. Thanking the desk clerk weakly, I fumbled in my pocket for change, tipped him with whatever came to hand, and flopped back down on the bed, waiting for my heart to stop pounding. Then I methodically changed my clothes and packed my few belongings, and by the time I met Ronnie in the lobby, I had not only recovered but was feeling close to buoyant over my salvation.

My mood changed again as soon as we reached the airport—not because of any new threat, but at the sight of the dozens of emigrants crowded at the customs counters, their cartons torn open and suitcases a shambles. The customs men were turning everything inside out with pronounced malice while piling insults on the departing Jews. Seeing the bewildered old men and women being put through this final degradation and the terrified toddlers grasping at their mothers' skirts as they wailed in response to the threat they could feel but not understand, a storm of rage welled up in me. Ronnie, who was walking close beside me and evidently sensed the rush of emotion in me, or was himself moved to fury by the sight, clutched my arm and hissed through clenched teeth, "Don't you dare say a word!" He was right, of course. Since when do well-bred Englishmen, the pillars of the Empire, interfere when "natives" treat other "natives" with something less than British civility?

So we marched past the customs counters with blank expressions, but I couldn't help thinking what a pity it was that the annals of the Jewish community in Iraq were coming to a close after two and a half millennia in an atmosphere of abuse and searing insult; that a history longer and richer than the chronicles of many other peoples was ending at the customs counters of Baghdad Airport with the actors on both its sides alienated, antagonized, hardened. On one side of those counters, the faces were set in a look of tyranny, malevolence, and contempt. On the other side were the sad and frightened eyes of my people, the eyes of bruised and smarting but proud people who bit their lips rather than allow any sign of their feelings to pass them. Nevertheless, I had to remind myself, even this final, stinging humiliation was preferable to the risks involved in trying to leave the country illegally.

"Ronnie! Dick! Over here!" I heard Jimmy Wooten call, putting an end to my bitter musings. He was motioning for us to join him where he was seated together with Raouf, the pilots, and representatives of the Civil Aviation Authority. Standing stiffly beside them in a freshly ironed, button-polished uniform was a young officer introduced to us as the "inspector" who would be accompanying our flight to make sure that we were honoring the terms of our agreement and were flying to Cyprus "without any monkey business"—as one of the Aviation Authority officials put it with a smile, so as not to offend us. The officer looked unsettled and a bit dazed. When I invited him to sit down beside me, I found out why: he had never flown before and was feeling a bit queasy even before we got on the plane. I tried to win his confidence by assuring him that all would be well. I also explained that the planes would not be returning to Baghdad for two days, so that he would have to stay at a hotel in Nicosia—as our guest, of course. Naïvely he replied that he had money and even opened his wallet to show me that it was chock full of sterling. But I repeated that he was to be our guest and could save his money to buy lavish gifts for his girlfriend. When he blushed, I understood that our "inspector" was the ingenuous child of a well-to-do family who had been awarded a free plane ride by virtue of his father's connections—and had a thing or two to learn about the big wide world.

Nicosia, I decided, was as good a place as any for a beginner from Baghdad to have his first lesson. In fact, we would see to it that he was kept *very* busy there, because we had decided to improve upon the plan worked out with the Iraqis. We would fly to Nicosia, as scheduled, but, rather than transfer the passengers to other planes, as stipulated in the agreement, we intended to simplify matters and continue on to Tel Aviv in the same aircraft. My job was to ensure that, promptly upon landing in Nicosia, the interest of our Iraqi inspector was diverted from the planes and their passengers to the "vanities of this world," and fortunately this earnest, innocent young officer seemed like the perfect candidate for just the kind of sea change I had in mind.

Our immigrants boarded the planes silently, almost stonily, looking straight ahead and not permitting themselves even a parting glance at relatives, friends, or their native land. Perhaps they feared another dose of the humiliation they had suffered earlier. As the young officer and I were making ourselves comfortable in the cockpit, I opened a pack of chewing gum and held it out to him, explaining that the gum would ease the pressure on his ears. He pulled out two pieces, systematically unwrapped them, and began chewing energetically. The next time I looked his way, to my astonished delight he had removed the two still-separate wads from his mouth and was about to stuff them in his ears! By now I was finding this man-child rather endearing and softly explained how to make the gum more effective. Then I buckled him securely into his seat and readied myself for takeoff beside him.

Our plane taxied slowly to the end of the tarmac, turned around, revved its motors, swept back down the runway, and was airborne. The second plane followed immediately thereafter, initiating the great airlift that was to bring over a hundred thousand Iraqi immigrants to Israel and the oldest Jewish community in the world out of its exile. When the agreement between Near East Air Transport and Iraqi Airways was first announced, the New York *Times,* known for its restrained style, portrayed the forthcoming airlift as the "largest air migration in history." In the wireless transmission from "Berman" to "Artzi," however, the inauguration of this historic enterprise boiled down to the typically terse and pointed announcement:

Two planes took off this afternoon with Shammai. Details follow.

I must admit that my thoughts and feelings were similarly subdued during those final moments over Baghdad. As I pressed my forehead against the window and looked down on the city of my birth and the Tigris receding in the distance, while the great desert loomed before us, I remembered how we had once, not so long before, thought of that vast wilderness as a wall sealing off the Babylonian diaspora from the homeland and heartland of Jewish life. *Finally,* I recall thinking as the verse from Jeremiah came back to me, *"the wall of Babylon has fallen."*

We flew to Cyprus, as promised, and after placing the "inspector" in the capable hands of our people there, with instructions to keep him "fully entertained," we continued on to Israel in the same aircraft. As we taxied to a halt in Tel Aviv, it looked to me as if every last one of my comrades in the Mossad had come out to welcome us. I don't recall the exact roster on that occasion, but I do remember being deluged by hugs and kisses, back slaps and handshakes. Even our redheaded secretary, Zafrira, came all the way to the airport to plant a big smack of a kiss squarely on my cheek.

That unexpected reception left me aglow with feelings of triumph, sweetness, and warmth that soon dissolved into a wave of exhaustion. Suddenly all I wanted to do was sleep. Given a choice, I would have curled up into a ball and dropped off right there on the airport floor. I think I could even have slept standing up! But when the immigrants began to disembark, the sight of their first encounter with their new lives revived me. It was a very private moment for me as I watched them emerge from the aircraft hesitantly, as if reluctant to cross the line between dream and reality, and begin to walk slowly into the terminal. A few of them lingered by the plane, waiting for some token, some ceremony to mark the historic moment, until an elderly man began chanting the blessing that praises God for "giving us life, and sustaining us, and enabling us to reach this moment"—to which there was a loud chorus of "Amen."

The next day, one of the newspapers in Israel dubbed the airlift "Operation Ezra and Nehemiah," after the two biblical figures who led the Babylonian exiles back to Jerusalem to rebuild the Temple. That name stuck, winning out over a variety of other suggestions, from "Operation Ali Baba" to "Operation Babylon" (which was Moshe Sharett's proposal and my favorite). But by then, I no longer had a say in such matters. Straight from the airport I had gone home—not finally and irrevocably, as it turned out, but certainly for a long and well-deserved breather. If I had harbored any thoughts of returning to Baghdad, they were put to rest the next day, when Mordechai Ben-Porat cabled definitively: "The head of the Secret Police has informed Raouf that if you return you will be arrested." So one thing was final and irrevocable: never again did I set foot on the soil of Iraq. This time, my four-year mission—obsession, perhaps—to bring Iraqi Jews to safe harbor in their ancestral homeland was conclusively, unconditionally, and incontestably over.

TWELVE

The Curtain Falls

NO, I AM NOT GOING to reverse that ringing statement about my mission to Iraq having ended. A few months after returning home, I was drawn briefly out of "retirement" on my kibbutz to make a lightning visit to Paris for a talk with Ezekiel Shemtob, the head of the Jewish community in Iraq. But other than that, I withdrew from the Iraqi venture altogether. As a matter of fact, for much of the period covered in the narrative to come, I was working under cover for the Mossad in Egypt, completely cut off from affairs in Israel, to say nothing of Iraq. Yet my absence from the arena does not exempt me from relating the conclusion of this tale. And much as I would have liked to end it on a note of unequivocal triumph, life has a way of introducing complexities that don't allow for perfectly happy endings. In this case, our satisfaction at the Mossad's hard-won achievement in rescuing some 120,000 Jews from Iraq was considerably tempered by the ill-starred end of the Zionist underground there.

"Operation Ezra and Nehemiah" brought to Israel a total of some 104,000 people from Baghdad, the outlying cities, and the most remote villages in northern and southern Iraq in the course of a year and a half.

Such a mass population transfer would be a major challenge given even the technology of our own day, from the communications satellite to the computer. And even under the best of conditions, it was to be expected that an operation of that magnitude would be beset by hitches and delays due to technical failures—on top of grievances about everything from lost luggage to influence-peddling. But the emigration from Iraq was not carried out under ideal or even normal conditions, and the dominant mood of insecurity only aggravated the very understandable stress.

Unfortunately, the objective difficulties of running the airlift were compounded by the friction that crackled between the community's official leadership and the emissaries from the Mossad. The cause of this discord was a tangle of issues that included the priority of rank, personal prestige, and sheer differences in style. In part the problem was structural, for while the mass, legal emigration from Iraq required continuous, open contact between the community's officials and various arms of the regime, the internal organization and regulation of this exodus, as well as contact with Israel, was handled by the Mossad's chief emissary working under clandestine conditions. Yet even this division of labor was not clear-cut. By staffing the registration centers, the Zionist underground controlled the processing of the emigrants, but, nominally at least, the community leaders still had the last word on questions such as who would leave when, who was eligible for a fare exemption, and so on. On top of it all, the community board itself split into two camps, one supporting Ezekiel Shemtob, the other opposing him. In the Iraq of 1950 (and perhaps anywhere at any time), these conditions made for a veritable hotbed of tensions, misunderstandings, and clashes—all exacerbated by the stubbornly sluggish pace of transporting the stateless Jews out of Iraq.

In a matter of weeks, these strains had ballooned into a near-feud between Shemtob and Mordechai Ben-Porat, the Mossad's chief emissary in Iraq, for in addition to the struggle between the Zionist movement and the community establishment over formalities and priorities, the "chemistry" between these two men was appalling. The sixty-nine-year-old Shemtob, a man of wealth, culture, and standing in the community, with friends in high places, found his dynamic, outspoken, twenty-seven-year-old rival rather difficult to digest. Ben-Porat found Shemtob to be haughty and imperious but reported that he often swallowed his pride and yielded to the older man, to avoid a confrontation that might well end in an open breach. Even so, the friction between them could not be suppressed, and before long it had infected the community leadership as a whole.

When, at the climax of a slow boil, Shemtob threatened to resign— thereby cutting the Jewish community's direct line to Prime Minister

Suweidi—I was asked to fly to Paris to reason with him, while Moshe Carmil went to Teheran for a parallel talk with Ben-Porat. Thus in August 1950, I was on a plane again, off to Paris, where I found the venerable Shemtob ensconced in a suite in the posh Hotel Crillon, on the Place de la Concorde. (When I entered the lobby and encountered the elevator boys in caps and uniforms decorated in gold braid like admirals, I had to restrain myself from stepping aside to let them into the elevator first out of deference to their rank!) For this meeting I naturally reverted to my Richard Armstrong pose, but hardly had we finished exchanging greetings when Shemtob switched from our customary French to the Arabic dialect spoken by Iraqi Jews.

"My son, you needn't bother with all that," he said solicitously. "I know everything."

At first I stared at him in feigned bewilderment, naturally assuming that he was testing me in light of the rumor that Richard Armstrong was a Jew. But when I continued speaking in French, asking after his health and about his journey, he came right out and told me that Jimmy Wooten and Ronnie Barnett had revealed everything to him, including my real name! Unable to deny it, I settled into a deep armchair and began to answer his barrage of questions about the family and particularly about my mother, who had passed away a few years earlier and was laid to rest on Jerusalem's Mount of Olives, the most sacred burial ground for the Jews. We continued in that vein for quite a while, and although I was peeved that the Near East people had destroyed whatever remained of my Armstrong cover, I consoled myself that at least their indiscretion had boosted my rapport with Shemtob and would help me smooth his ruffled feathers.

As it happened, my optimism was short-lived. Barely had we begun to discuss the reason for my visit when his face settled into a belligerent scowl and his tone turned petulant. He had nothing but complaints about Ben-Porat and was incensed by what he felt was the ingratitude of the Zionist movement and some of his own associates on the community board. As I reported that day to Moshe Carmil:

The source of the conflict is entirely personal, and [Shemtob] makes no attempt to conceal it. He feels that essentially he did everything: he made the emigration possible, he had the Prime Minister's ear, and everyone else—Jew and non-Jew—accepted his word as law. Now this "uncouth" young man comes along and thinks that the head of the Jewish community should be taking orders from him! . . . That's essentially how he sees things, and it places [Ben-Porat] in a difficult position. . . .

Our talk wore on for over four hours, but each time I felt him begin to soften a bit, his daughter Fahima intervened in the conversation and stoked his anger all over again. I also understood that Jimmy Wooten had complicated the situation by feeding Shemtob unfounded (and unkept) promises to have Ben-Porat replaced. And my Mossad colleagues in Paris had stirred the caldron even further by getting to Shemtob before I did and making some superfluous promises of their own. At any rate, my efforts to soothe him notwithstanding, Shemtob returned to Baghdad as bitter as when he had left—so bitter, in fact, that he withdrew from all further involvement in the emigration program, and the authorities appointed a committee of Jewish notables in his stead. Ironically enough, Tawfiq Suweidi resigned soon thereafter, so that Shemtob's unique status as the one Jew with easy access to the Prime Minister no longer applied, in any case.

Moshe Carmil fared no better in his attempt to mollify his own emissary, because their rendezvous never took place. To get to Teheran, Ben-Porat had to cross the Iranian border illegally, and as luck would have it he was caught in the process. Neither, I should add, was that his first arrest. On a previous occasion, when he was likewise charged with trying to leave Iraq illegally, he spent five days in prison and was released on bail only after a tidy sum had changed hands. This second stint behind bars lasted longer (about two weeks), and as a result he never did make it to Iran to meet with Carmil. Instead, Ben-Porat stood trial in mid-October 1950 and got off with a fine of 50 dinars. There was a catch, though: by the terms of the same law that enabled the Jews to leave the country legally, any Jew convicted of trying to leave illegally automatically had his citizenship revoked and was placed on the list of prospective emigrants to Israel.* So it was that Mordechai Ben-Porat found himself about to be booted out of Iraq. Rather than yield to his fate, however, he cabled Israel with inimitable bravura: "Arrests will not stop me from carrying out my duty. We will continue with the same vigor as before." Even a third arrest did not convince him to flee, though his letters and cables began to suggest that, considering his burgeoning "criminal record," perhaps there was a point in winding up his work and returning to Israel.

All of this happened during the first few months of the airlift and certainly added to the objective difficulties of running the operation. But the worst problem during this period was unquestionably the rate of emigration from Iraq. Here the difficulties of adjustment in Israel combined with the grave shortage of tents and other supplies and the shortcomings of

* Article 2 of Law No. 1 of 1950 states: "Any Iraqi Jew who leaves Iraq or tries to leave illegally will forfeit his Iraqi nationality. . . ."

Near East Air Transport (which had difficulty supplying as many planes as necessary) to slow the pace down far below expectations. Above all, swamped as it was by its own problems, the Jewish Agency (the authority responsible for immigrant absorption) was less than acutely sensitive to the gravity of the situation in Iraq, though that was repeatedly described in the boldest terms. In a cable sent to Tel Aviv on July 17, 1950, Ben-Porat warned:

. . . The Jews are in the worst way. Citizenship has been revoked from 36,000 people. . . . Sixteen thousand people in the north and the south . . . are stateless according to law. . . . Have you taken into consideration that there will be a revolt against us . . . by the families who have left their jobs, sold their homes, and are waiting impatiently for the day when they can leave? . . . Why have you allowed us to deceive the Jews by promising them unlimited immigration? . . .

In provincial cities and remote villages, the Jews were literally thrown out of their homes by neighbors or local officials. They reached Baghdad as refugees and had to be put up in synagogues converted into emigration centers. Ronnie Barnett referred to this critical state of affairs on August 4, 1950: "In the central Tweig Synagogue, where the passengers are assembled prior to departure, there is considerable unrest. . . . The situation has become grave enough to require calling in the police. . . . Local Jews tell me that the government fears anti-Semitic riots if all this continues. . . ." And on September 22 he again described the situation in the bleakest terms:

. . . A few thousand have arrived from (been driven out of, is more accurate) the provincial cities without a penny to their names. They loiter about everywhere in a frightful state. . . . First they consume the funds they obtained to pay for the flight; then they become a burden on the community. I assume you know that there have been about fifty cases of infant deaths. . . .

Of course, the complications created by the unsatisfactory pace had not escaped the attention of the Mossad or the government in Israel. Foreign Minister Sharett himself warned on August 28 that "the existing quota [of] 2,500–3,000 a month" was highly insufficient, considering "the emergency situation that has come into being in Iraq . . . the capriciousness of the regime . . . and its ability to resort to brutal means that cause the loss of human lives." Still, the problem was an objective one—a lack of means —and it was not until months later, at the beginning of 1951, that the absorption authorities in Israel overcame these difficulties and raised the immigration quota to 13,500 a month (and thereafter to even more).

In the meantime, Sharett's forebodings took on a prophetic quality at the beginning of September 1950, when Tawfiq Suweidi's government fell and Nuri Said returned to the premiership (for the eleventh time!). Understandably, this development aroused great concern among the many people in Iraq and Israel who remembered all too clearly what Nuri had wrought in the course of 1949. Initially they feared that out of sheer spite he would rescind the March emigration law and halt the exodus completely. But Nuri had a more clever plan. He knew that it was impossible to turn the clock back, so that, rather than hold the Jews hostage, he reverted to an old idea and initially tried to step up their emigration as a way of creating a glut of immigrants in Israel and perhaps inducing its collapse.

One way of doing so was to break Near East's monopoly and bring in other airlines. According to a report by the British ambassador in Baghdad, on November 23, 1950, eighty thousand Jews were waiting for transportation out of Iraq, and Sabah Said had returned from a trip to London with the news that BOAC (British Overseas Airways Corp., now called British Airways) would be able to take fifty thousand a month—as opposed to the three thousand handled monthly by Near East. "Iraq would arrange transport and finance," the report continued, "and Israel could not plead that she could not receive them in view of Zionist insistence on unrestricted immigration during the mandate." Yet it turned out that neither BOAC nor any other airline was prepared to transport people to Israel without the prior approval of the Israeli Government, so that, willy-nilly, Jerusalem would remain in control of the rate of immigration.

Seething with frustration, Nuri began to show signs of contemplating something drastic—to the point where the British embassy reported to London that it was increasingly difficult to dissuade the Iraqis from resorting to wild measures. One possibility then being entertained was to drive the Jews over the Kuwaiti border. Sending them to Israel overland through Jordan was again mooted, more than once, though the Jordanian Government firmly quashed the idea. Nuri first raised this "solution" in October 1950 with Jordan's King Abdullah, but the king refused to cooperate, on the grounds that it would only increase the "manpower" in Israel that might someday be used against him. (It seems that like the British before him, Abdullah also feared that the Israelis would refuse to accept these Jews, leaving him stuck with them indefinitely, as well as the tens of thousands of Arab refugees in Jordan.)

Still, Nuri was so enamored of this notion that he raised it again during a state visit to Jordan at the end of January or early February 1951—as documented by Sir Alec Kirkbride, the British ambassador to Jordan.† During this visit Sir Alec was invited to attend a trilateral meeting with Jordanian Prime Minister Samir Rifai at which Nuri raised "the astounding proposition that a convoy of Iraqi Jews should be brought over in army lorries escorted by armoured cars, taken to the Jordanian-Israeli frontier and forced to cross the line." Mortified by the very thought, Kirkbride observed that "the passage of Jews through Jordan would almost certainly have touched off serious trouble amongst the very disgruntled Arab refugees who were crowded into the country. Either the Iraqi Jews would have been massacred or their Iraqi guards would have had to shoot the Arabs to protect the lives of their charges." The discussion became so heated, Sir Alec continued, that when Samir Rifai adamantly rejected the suggestion by protesting that he did "not want to be party to such a crime," Nuri responded with such a violent outburst that he feared the two prime ministers would come to blows!

Thus thwarted in his plan to "dump" the Jews on Israel, Nuri considered shipping them off to concentration camps in the wastes of the Iraqi desert, but this harrowing notion was firmly rejected by the regent, Abdul Illah (who undoubtedly recalled the international outcry against the maltreatment of the Jews in 1949). Then, just as Israel was gearing up to absorb fifteen to twenty thousand immigrants per month, thereby greatly easing the problem of the stateless Jews in Iraq, Nuri lost interest in increasing the pace of emigration and found another way to punish the departing Jews and the State of Israel alike.

March 9, 1951, was the date on which the emigration law was due to expire, and as it drew closer the tension in Iraq soared. All the Jews who intended to leave had already renounced their citizenship, but tens of thousands were still waiting for word of their departure date. With anxieties at an unprecedented height, a rumor made the rounds that the authorities were going to halt the exit of Jews after the law's expiration on March 9—causing an even greater uproar.

Then Nuri surprised everyone. Instead of blocking the departure of the remaining stateless, jobless, and in many cases homeless Jews—for after all, what would he do with all these displaced people?—on March 10 he called the Iraqi Chamber of Deputies into special session and passed a law freezing the assets of all the Jews who had renounced their citizenship (a total of 103,866 by that date) or retained Iraqi passports but were living abroad (a category that embraced some of the wealthiest of Iraq's Jewish

† From the Wings: Amman Memoirs 1947–1951.

merchants). The freeze applied to assets of every kind, including the stock in shops (which were sealed by the authorities) and holdings in banks. In a word, the law was catastrophic for the Jews.

It was hardly necessary to convince the Mossad of the grimness of the situation, for it was no secret that the government of Israel, with its own surfeit of financial distress, would hardly be cheered by the prospect of tens of thousands of additional immigrants arriving in a state of total desti-tution. One way around this problem was to establish a holding company that would take over the assets of the departing Iraqi Jews, sell them in an orderly fashion, and transfer the receipts to their owners. Even the Nazis had been amenable to an arrangement of this kind in 1933; but the Iraqis wouldn't hear of it. Thus on March 10, 1951, when more than seventy thousand stateless Jews were still waiting to leave Iraq, those who had not yet liquidated their property, or who had but were trusting enough to keep their savings and other liquid assets in the bank, became instant paupers. It was a staggering blow.

Still, the exodus continued, and as it did, the responsible bodies in Israel realized that soon the Zionist underground would have to begin dissolving itself. For the Israeli agencies with operatives in Iraq, that meant preparing to function wholly on their own; before long there would be no under-ground to fall back on in a pinch.

One of the men chosen to assume the lonely task of working in Iraq was Yudke Tajer (today Dr. Yehuda Tagar), who went to Baghdad on behalf of the Israeli Intelligence community as Isma'il Ben Mahdi Salhoun, the representative of an Iranian commercial enterprise. Yudke, who had proven his mettle as an officer during Israel's War of Independence, came from a very distinguished Sephardic family that traced its roots in Jerusa-lem back to the days of the expulsion of the Jews from Spain in 1492. As a dyed-in-the-wool "Oriental," he could presumably have resettled in Bagh-dad without attracting notice. The rub was that he spoke a distinctly Pales-tinian dialect of Arabic, so that uttering a single sentence might give him away. That's why Yudke became an Iranian—though, as covers go, this one was far from flawless, since he couldn't speak a word of Persian. Even so, he might have gotten by quite nicely had it not been for a constellation of freak circumstances that spelled his ruin.

Yudke arrived in Baghdad at a time when the tight weave of secrecy and security surrounding the Zionist movement in Iraq was in the process of coming undone. In effect, the new circumstances made it impossible to maintain the deep underground, as it had existed for close to a decade, because a clandestine movement and mass emigration were all but a contradiction in terms. Throughout Iraq, the Zionist movement was mobilized to facilitate the departure of the Jews, and more than fifty of the movement's leading activists were actually employed by the Ministry of the Interior in the registration centers, where they worked side by side with members of the police. Thus the most elementary rules of clandestine activity were being violated every day, and in time these young people were lulled into a sense of confidence and into believing that the police were as inept or indifferent as the officers working beside them day in and day out. This foray into the open also brought an almost giddy sense of relief, like the release felt by a medieval knight who spies an opportunity to remove his armor and quickly does so, not considering that the heavy, unwieldy coat that has weighed him down for so long is essentially his only protection.

As fate would have it, in Israel, too, this was a period of transition between the voluntary organs that had operated underground during the British mandate and the birth of an institutionalized apparatus befitting a sovereign state. The hallmarks of high personal motivation and nimble improvisation were giving way to a less fluid approach, and the established system that was taking its first, rather wobbly steps was periodically stricken by the usual "childhood diseases."

So it happened that Yudke Tajer found himself teamed up in Iraq with Robert Rodney, a rather peculiar young man who carried a bona fide British passport but was otherwise quite unsuited to both the mission and the locale. Fortunately, Rodney had no contact with anyone from the local underground (other than Yudke, who was his superior). Yudke, on the other hand, maintained a very close relationship with Mordechai Ben-Porat—in defiance of cold logic, to say nothing of the precautions incumbent upon professionals. Nevertheless, at that time and in that place, their closeness seemed natural, almost inevitable. Not only because Yudke, far from being the hardened spy depicted in thrillers, was a homesick young man who gravitated to Ben-Porat (an army veteran, like himself) out of plain human need, but because Ben-Porat had the advantage of wireless contact with Tel Aviv and was therefore Yudke's sole link with his headquarters in Israel. Worse yet, from a strictly professional standpoint, the lines of distinction between Ben-Porat's work and Yudke's job were not strictly drawn; it had even been suggested that Yudke might replace Ben-Porat if he was forced to leave Iraq sooner than planned.

That prospect seemed more likely with every passing day, for after three arrests—which he had weathered without arousing the least suspicion about his real role or identity—Ben-Porat's face was becoming dangerously familiar to the police. Late in April 1951, another emissary was finally sent out to replace him, but the man returned after a week, complaining of rejection by the movement people and above all by Ben-Porat himself. For his part, Ben-Porat explained that his replacement, a redhead, "stood out like a sore thumb," and argued, "We couldn't place the whole underground in peril because of him."

The muse of history must have been chuckling at the belief that it was this new man who stood to imperil the underground, for less than a month after his return from Baghdad a very different scenario began to unfold. On May 22, 1951, as Mordechai Ben-Porat and Yudke Tajer were leaving the Orozdi-Back department store after a brief shopping spree, they walked smack into a wall of three burly men whose very posture—right hands jammed into their jacket pockets as a thinly veiled threat—broadcast the fact that they were from the Secret Police. Quickly surrounding their startled prey, the three agents bundled them into a waiting car and whisked them off to Secret Police headquarters. Everything happened so quickly that there was no point in trying to resist or flee. Neither did the pedestrians on Baghdad's main street pay any attention to the drama taking place before their very eyes, so mundane was the sight of five men entering a car in the heart of the bustling city. The action was like the work of a scalpel making a cut so smooth and clean that at first there was no sensation of pain.

Ben-Porat, for whom this was the fourth arrest, was less rattled than Yudke, and for a moment he actually believed that he would get out of this spot as easily as before. But one glance at Yudke, who sat half slumped in the seat looking stunned, was enough to tell him that they were both in deep trouble. Clearly Yudke would not get very far with his Iranian cover. Worse yet, Ben-Porat had no idea why they had been arrested. In fact, we still don't know why, though there is strong support for the theory that a Palestinian Arab who knew Yudke and happened to be in Baghdad, working as a sales clerk in the department store, blew the whistle on him.

The main suspicion indeed rested on Yudke, but having been found in his company implicated Mordechai as well. His insistent claim that he was a simple clerk who worked in the center where the Jews renounced their citizenship, had met "the foreigner" by chance, and knew nothing about him failed to satisfy the interrogators. Not that they doubted he was an Iraqi Jew. He spoke the local Jewish patois flawlessly, and the address he gave checked out. But the question of his relationship with "the foreigner" (whom the police immediately suspected of being an Israeli agent) required thorough investigation. So the two men were separated and subjected to a generous dose of the Iraqis' infamous methods of torture: beatings, whippings, verbal abuse, and psychological terror.

Other people were arrested almost at once—not because either of the men broke, but apparently on the basis of the phone numbers in Yudke's address book, which was found during a search of the room he rented in one of the city's more respectable neighborhoods. Among these detainees was Robert Rodney, who decided to spare his interrogators the bother of torturing him and told them all they wanted to know—including the purpose of his mission. He confessed to being a Jew born in Germany (though he had declared himself a Christian when applying for an Iraqi visa) and related that his family had moved to the Netherlands when Hitler came to power, then on to Belgium, and finally to England at the outbreak of World War II. Ultimately he made his way to Israel and agreed to work for Israeli Intelligence in Iraq because—or so he claimed—"he believed in an understanding between Israel and the Arab countries and had come to work on its behalf." He also revealed that there was another Israeli in Baghdad, by the name of Tajer, and even identified Yudke in a lineup. He probably would have turned Ben-Porat in just as readily, but fortunately they had never met, so Rodney was unable to identify him. This failure to pick Ben-Porat out of a lineup was crucial, for it tended to shore up his claim that he had been implicated in the affair by mistake and had only an incidental connection with Tajer.

When word of the arrest got out, there was a flurry of panic in the underground. The first reaction was to ask an attorney by the name of Yosef Fatal to handle the case, because he was friendly with a number of people from the movement (though not himself a member). Fatal, who soon realized that the affair was as complex as it was sensitive, turned for help to a revered Muslim colleague by the name of Jamal Baban, a former Minister of Justice who was famed for his imposing bearing and razor-sharp tongue. (Even judges treated Baban with a healthy respect, for fear that he might return to head the Justice Ministry.) After being assured a generous fee—for which he was prepared to handle almost any matter—Baban signed on as Ben-Porat's attorney. Yudke's state was such that no sane lawyer was prepared to represent him and risk being branded the champion of a Zionist spy. Even the venerable Baban was tainted by his connection with a Jewish suspect; a booby-trapped package was sent to his home, wounding one of his servants.

Before that unfortunate incident, however, Baban combined his legal acumen with the art of bribery to get his client released on 500 dinars bail. Thus after a week of vindictive torture, Ben-Porat left prison with his eyes bleary from lack of sleep, his face swollen from the beatings, his knuckles blue and disfigured from being strung up by the hands, but his spirit unbroken. Even then he had the feeling that things weren't so bad; after all, he hadn't been charged with anything concrete. "They haven't any material evidence against me," he cabled Tel Aviv immediately after his release. "They brought me before [Rodney], and he had no idea who I was."

Almost anyone else who had undergone that kind of torture and then been set free would probably have fled the country by the fastest means possible. But Ben-Porat did more than stay at his post; incredible as it sounds, a few days after his release he actually showed up in court to stand trial on the charge of having caused a traffic accident! Though perfectly convinced of his innocence, he was to learn that in an Iraqi court, the scales of justice followed a logic of their own, especially when the accused was a Jewish driver who allegedly hit a Muslim cyclist. Worse yet, one of the witnesses to the accident was an army officer with whom Ben-Porat had come to blows and whose testimony held far more weight than the actual facts. Somewhere in the course of the trial, the issue shifted from responsibility for the accident to the nerve of the accused in sassing an Iraqi officer, and the judge sentenced the impudent upstart to two weeks' imprisonment. Just days after leaving prison, therefore, Mordechai Ben-Porat again found himself behind bars.

Ironically, that proved to be his salvation. For in the meantime, working from the list of names and phone numbers found in Yudke Tajer's room, the police had arrested a variety of other people, and soon their investigation had branched out in a number of directions. One target of their dragnet was a man called "Zakki" or "Habib"—the names by which Ben-Porat was known in the underground—whom they believed to be an important figure, since many of the detainees had mentioned him under severe torture. In this case, however, the system by which the members of the underground were known only by their *noms de guerre* proved its worth. Most of the people who spoke of "Zakki" or "Habib" had no idea that his real name was Mordechai Ben-Porat. Even fewer knew that he carried the identity card of Nissim Moshe (one of the comrades who had fled the country illegally, leaving his I.D. for the movement's use) and was known to the police by that name. For days the police inquired after the elusive "Zakki" and "Habib" in all the markets and cafés patronized by Jews but came up with nothing. After piecing together the shreds of evidence gleaned from the interrogations, they began to suspect that "Zakki," "Habib," and Nissim Moshe might be one and the same. But when they tried the house where Nissim Moshe was known to be living, they found it deserted, as everyone had left the country, and there was no trace of their quarry elsewhere. The one place they never thought to look was Baghdad Central Prison, where Mordechai Ben-Porat was serving a two-week sentence for insolence!

Through the energetic intervention of Jamal Baban, Ben-Porat was again released after a few days, whereupon the task of smuggling him out of Iraq became an urgent priority. When the usual means of escape—stealing over the Iranian border—was ruled out as being too risky, someone in Israel had the wits to remember "Operation Michaelberg" and pulled the dusty file off the Mossad's shelves to find a detailed report on the first "Michaelberg" flight. The June 12 transmission to Baghdad described the operation down to the last detail and ordered Ben-Porat to copy the timing and route to the end of the runway exactly, assuring him that "the plan has been carefully calculated and checked out." There were, however, two departures from the original "Michaelberg" conception. Rather than send a plane in specially to rescue him, he would be going on one of the Trans-Ocean flights that were leaving for Israel daily by that point. Hence the second amendment to the original plan: "If you fail to make it, the crew will claim that as they were waiting to take off, a man signaled them from the ground that he was a passenger who had been left behind. You must say the same."

Fortunately, that did not prove necessary. The plan had lost none of its virtues, and Ben-Porat's escape was a flawless "Operation Michaelberg." It also came not a minute too soon, for, as Baghdad reported just hours after he had landed in Israel: "The Iraqis are searching madly for [Ben-Porat]. Every agent in the Secret Police has a copy of his photo and is on the lookout for him."

Though Mordechai Ben-Porat was virtually snatched from the claws of doom, that was the only bright spot in an otherwise thoroughly grim episode. The torture applied to the rest of the comrades did its job all too well, and slowly the perfect discipline of the underground began to unravel. Each new strand of evidence helped the police spread their net ever farther and haul in new prey until finally, inevitably perhaps, fate smiled her crooked grin and turned a pure coincidence into tragedy.

The drama that was to play itself out over the next six months centered on two highly disparate protagonists. The first was Yosef Basri, a lawyer by profession who had once served as a senior official in the Ministry of Finance and was a respected figure in Baghdad. Basri had never been associated with the Zionist movement. He was involved in gathering intelligence data for Yudke Tajer but did not appear on any of the lists captured by the police, so that he was not being sought. One of his relatives, Yosef Khabaza, *was* on the official list of suspects but had already managed to flee the country.

Quite unaware of these last two details, Basri paid a perfectly innocent visit to Khabaza's home and had barely digested the news of his relative's abrupt departure when the police raided the house, hoping to trap its owner. Conscious of his own vulnerability, Basri panicked at their approach and made blindly for the nearest hiding place, which happened to be a wardrobe. The police failed to find their man, but on the way out they noticed the wardrobe standing at a slightly peculiar angle. One of the policemen opened the door, bent down, saw a pair of feet, whisked the clothing aside, and lo and behold, there stood Yosef Basri in a highly compromising pose that did little to support his claim to being on the premises wholly by chance, visiting relatives.

Basri was promptly taken into custody, and when all efforts to find "Habib" or "Zakki" had failed, he was elevated to the chief local figure suspected of running an Israeli spy ring. As foreigners, Yudke Tajer and Robert Rodney received very different treatment from Basri, whose background as a high-ranking official seemed to make him eminently suited to the role of spy master (or at least that's how the Iraqi Secret Police saw it).

Shalom Saleh Shalom, the other villain of the piece (as the Iraqis constructed the story), was a young carpenter, still in his teens and, as such, hardly the type to be portrayed as a leading figure in the underground. Yet his arrest proved to be fateful not only to himself but ultimately to Basri and the underground as a whole, because it introduced the element of illegal arms to the case being put together by the police.

Shalom was in charge of building weapons caches. Though he had already renounced his citizenship and could have left the country, his emigration was postponed because his skills, diligence, and eagerness to serve the cause made him absolutely invaluable at a time when moving and concealing arms was a major preoccupation of the underground. As more and more people left Iraq‡ and more and more Jewish homes were evacuated, it became increasingly urgent to consolidate the remaining stores and transfer them to safe houses. The caches contained both educational and archival material (including the names of activists, their addresses, and *noms de guerre)* and the weapons that had been accumulated over the years bit by bit, and at great risk, to be used for self-defense in an hour of need. The new caches were built mostly in synagogues—on the assumption that these buildings would serve the Jewish community till the end of the

‡ By June 1, 1951, eighty-four thousand Jews had emigrated and twenty thousand were still waiting to leave.

emigration process—and in the homes of leading movement activists, who would be among the last to go.

The educational material could always be destroyed—and rather easily, at that. But the fate of the arms was a question that had troubled the movement's leaders ever since the emigration program had begun. I myself had raised the issue of how to dissolve the Shurah in a memo written back in April 1950, before I left for Baghdad as Richard Armstrong. And Ben-Porat had repeatedly asked for instructions on what to do with the arms, but since this particular subject fell between a number of stools in Israel, he never received a reply. Consequently, the comrades in Baghdad were faced with a difficult choice: either to rid themselves of the weapons (by throwing them into the river or sealing up the caches each time a house was evacuated) or steadily to move and concentrate them until the last of the Jews had left Iraq—or at least until they received express instructions to do otherwise. Their decision was to shift the weapons from one house to another so as to keep them available as long as possible.

When Yudke Tajer and Mordechai Ben-Porat were arrested, their interrogators believed they were on to a spy ring. The search of Yudke's room yielded a haul of intelligence material but not the slightest hint of weapons, so that it is difficult to determine exactly when and why the police began searching for arms. Naturally, the most likely explanation is that one of the later detainees broke under interrogation and mentioned their existence. But whatever the case, from a certain stage onward the police began to concentrate their efforts on searching for weapons and grilled everyone in custody on the subject.

In reconstructing the investigation from oral testimony, the confessions that were wrung from the main actors, the published transcripts of the trials, the prosecutors' summaries, and the sentences passed by the judges, the following picture emerges. Shalom Saleh Shalom, the young carpenter caught in the police dragnet, was interrogated at length and, like all the others, was asked over and over, "Where are the weapons? Where have you hidden the weapons?" Each question was punctuated by an agonizing blow; each failure to reply led to new tortures. Finally Shalom concluded from the questions and the insistent beatings that the police knew about the movement's stocks of arms and his own role in keeping them hidden, but even then his conscience would not allow him to divulge any of the precious information entrusted to him. He had been educated to absolute loyalty and had been sworn to silence in the solemn ceremony inducting him into the ranks of the Shurah, so he bore up as best he could—until he thought of a way to get back at his interrogators and buy himself a respite from their torment while not doing the movement any harm.

When not engaged in building new caches, Shalom spent his time at the emigration center in the Masooda Shemtob Synagogue, and it was there, a few days earlier, that he had seen Yosef Khabaza leave for Israel. There was no mistaking that it was Khabaza; Shalom knew the man well, for he had built the large cache in his house and had seen it filled to capacity. Now that Khabaza was gone, however, he assumed that the cache had been emptied. Hence it was to Yosef Khabaza's house that he now intended to lead his tormentors and watch with sweet revenge as they discovered the cache and eagerly forced it open, only to find that it was bare. He did not know—and in his state could not have imagined—that in his haste to leave, Yosef Khabaza had not tended to emptying the cache, so that it remained as Shalom had last seen it, brimming with precisely the kind of evidence the Secret Police were hoping to find.

Having searched the Khabaza house a number of times and found nothing (other than Yosef Basri in the back of a wardrobe), the agents who now followed Shalom to this same address stood wide-eyed at the sight of the treasure trove being revealed before them: guns, ammunition, maps, account books, membership lists, texts for studying Hebrew, and other educational material ("Zionist propaganda," as the chief prosecutor and judges put it at the subsequent trials). If they were cheered by the fact that this same evidence could be connected to Yosef Basri, they absolutely exulted at the discovery of a map marked with the location of other caches in the city. All in all, twelve caches were uncovered by the police, yielding a considerable haul. The sentence passed against the twenty-one Jews eventually convicted of harboring these weapons and explosives cited 425 grenades, 33 machine guns (evidently submachine guns), 186 revolvers, 24,647 bullets, 79 cartridges for (submachine) guns, and 32 daggers.

At the same time, working from the membership lists found in the various stores, the police were able to round up precisely the people they wanted. There was no need for mass arrests this time, and, all told, fewer than one hundred people were taken into custody, of whom thirty or so were subsequently tried. However, the upshot was that the network of safeguards designed to contain any damage to the Zionist underground was unraveling at a frightening pace.

What ensued was a desperate race to destroy the contents of the remaining caches and any other incriminating evidence before the police could get to them. Whole libraries that had been created at great risk and with inordinate love and care were now put to the torch by the very people who had guarded them over the years. Simple weapons, membership lists, and whatever else had not yet fallen into unfriendly hands were hastily destroyed. But the most telling sign that the Zionist underground was bringing the curtain down on itself was the fate of the wireless set that had maintained vital contact with Israel since 1943. Every single day for eight years, the two stations, "Berman" and "Artzi," had kept up a dialogue— sometimes bristling with anger, sometimes lilting with joy—until the morning at the end of June 1951 when "Berman" failed to answer the call from Tel Aviv. The wireless operator stubbornly tapped out the familiar signal—dash dot, dot dot dash—dozens of times, his rhythm slowly shift- ing from coaxing to pleading to demanding that Berman answer him. Nothing did any good. After countless attempts to raise a response, he silently abandoned the key and placed his earphones carefully on the table. Not a word passed his lips, but the people hovering around him under- stood the message of that silence. The nerve had been cut; the pulse was stilled. The once vibrant, daring, indomitable Zionist movement in Iraq had passed into history.

A few days later, the young men who had operated the wireless in Baghdad reached Israel and filled in the story of the inglorious end they had been forced to inflict on the magical instrument that even during the days of the worst terror and despair had saved the underground from the agony of isolation and brought it renewed hope. Packing it onto a *guffa* in the dead of night, they had paddled out to the middle of the Tigris and unceremoniously chucked it overboard, consigning it to the miry clay of that mighty river's bed.

Once the wireless connection with Israel had been severed, the Mos- sad's emissaries and those movement leaders who had managed to evade arrest cleared out of Iraq with all due haste, literally one step ahead of the law. The task of seeing the emigration program through to its conclusion fell to communal leaders untainted by any association with the Zionist underground, and they performed it with great courage and skill, during some very trying days, until the last of the Jews who had chosen to leave Iraq reached Israel safely in February 1952.

So much for the bare facts of the matter. There were certainly ample grounds for the Iraqis to bring grave charges against Basri, Shalom, and the others being held in custody, based on the evidence acquired from the caches. But the indictment that followed from the evidence did not seem to satisfy the Iraqi sense of justice—or perhaps I should say the Iraqi thirst for vengeance. For instead of sticking to the facts, the police exploited the discovery of the weapons as a pretext for charging Basri and Shalom with a crime far more serious than membership in an outlawed network, illegal possession of arms, or even espionage. It was a crime of which they were totally innocent, but palming it off on them saved the police the bother of tracking down the real criminals and enabled the courts to satisfy a deep, pervasive and, to all appearances, insatiable desire to see Jews hanging from the gallows.

The crime in question comprised a series of bombings that occurred between March and June 1951. In the first, on March 19, a grenade exploded outside the information office attached to the American embassy on Al-Rashid Street, Baghdad's main thoroughfare, not far from Bab al-Agha Alley. Some two months later, on May 10, another grenade went off on Al-Rashid Street, this time in front of a building that had belonged to a Jew until the passage of the expropriation law. And about a month after that, on June 3, a third explosion occurred, alongside another building that had belonged to a Jew, not far from the offices of the local English-language newspaper, the Baghdad *Times*.

The police failed or never really tried to get to the bottom of these mysterious explosions—just as they failed to nab the perpetrators of so many explosions that had occurred before and continued to occur thereafter against a wide variety of targets. Yet the flaying they received in the press evidently left them smarting. So when the arms caches were discovered, the path of least resistance was to impute the most recent bombings to the Zionist underground—or, more specifically, to the now-absent Yosef Khabaza and anyone who could be linked with him. The fact that Khabaza was gone only made things easier, for he could be charged with anything at all, and the "proof" of his alleged crimes could be tortured out of Shalom Saleh Shalom. Then Shalom could be tried as an accomplice, and Yosef Basri would join him in the dock by virtue of having been caught in Khabaza's house. (Taken alone, that was very flimsy evidence against Basri, but it was joined by documents—found, ironically enough, in the Khabaza cache—attesting to his illegal activity and especially his association with Tajer.)

When the Basri-Shalom trial opened, in November 1951, the prosecution charged that two men, Yosef Khabaza and Yosef Basri, had perpetrated the above-mentioned bombings, with Shalom Saleh Shalom serving as an accomplice, and naturally demanded that Basri and Shalom be punished to the full extent of the law. That Basri denied any connection with the affair might have been expected under any circumstances. But what showed the state's case to be a farce was the testimony of the prosecution's own chief witness against Basri: Shalom Saleh Shalom. For the young carpenter not only repudiated his own confession, explaining that it had been extracted under torture, he also made it clear that after the discovery of the cache in Khabaza's house, the police had brutalized him relentlessly until they got him to state that Yosef Basri and Yosef Khabaza were the ones who had thrown or planted the bombs. "Each time I was brought before the judge," he related, "I asked him why they were torturing me. His reply was always that they would continue to do so until I affirmed that Yosef Khabaza was the man who had thrown the bombs. . . . My interrogators . . . pulled out my eyelashes, plucked the hairs of my mustache . . . until they got me to say that I, together with Yosef Khabaza and Yosef Basri, had thrown the bombs. . . ."

By any enlightened standard, this protest would have at least cast doubt on the admissibility of Shalom's statements to the police. But the court chose to reject Shalom's harrowing testimony, stating in its verdict that "the use of force or torture has not been proven" and accusing the defendant of claiming to have been brutalized "for the purpose of disparaging Iraqi justice and [spoiling] the name of the investigators and judges." But that was not the only lapse rendering the trial little better than a crude travesty of justice. For one thing, the court sat in a special capacity created specifically for this purpose and was presided over not by a professional judge but by one of the state prosecutors, who took his orders from above. For another, the attorneys representing the two defendants were far more involved with agonizing over their role than fulfilling it. Admittedly, Yosef Basri's first lawyer started out on the right track, challenging the composition of the court (which was in violation of the Iraqi constitution), protesting that Basri and Shalom had been forced to sign false confessions under torture, and citing precedents in which Iraqi courts had disqualified confessions so obtained. But all his objections were summarily overruled. Moreover, it wasn't long before someone took the trouble to remind him that life goes on after a trial and that he had better look to his own future. Precisely what happened is not clear, but after the second session he withdrew from the case, claiming, rather inscrutably, that while "every man has the right to a defense," the one he had conducted on Basri's behalf was being used against him for "political purposes," thus obliging him to resign.

In his place came a lawyer who went out of his way to stress that he was representing Basri against his better judgment and practically apologized to the court for assuming the task. In a similar vein, the lawyer defending Shalom told the court: "A lawyer's oath requires him to help the criminal —be he a murderer or a subversive. . . . But in this case even my family is up in arms because I have taken [his] defense upon myself. . . ." And just to be on the safe side, he concluded this abject speech with the coda: "I neglected to note that the Jews have fought against us not only with bombs but with wealth, wits, and beauty—forces that cannot be resisted.

But the question here today is one of mercy and conscience. . . . I can honestly say that my client is endowed with neither wealth nor wisdom nor beauty. . . ." Evidently he presumed that this irrelevant blather would pass for "extenuating circumstances," soften the court's heart toward his client, and thereby save his life.

As to the actual evidence presented in the trial, ironically enough Shalom's confession to the police—into which so much torture had been invested and which had served as the basis for the charges—was never introduced into the record. Instead, the prosecutor deliberately directed the case away from the bona fide evidence against the defendants and dwelled on unfounded contentions about the three above-mentioned bombings as well as two earlier incidents in which grenades had been thrown at specifically Jewish targets: the Al-Baiza café, on Abu Nuwas Street (on April 8, 1950), and the registration center in the Masooda Shemtob Synagogue (on January 14, 1951). In the first case four Jews had been injured; in the second, three Jews had been killed, including a young child, and over twenty had been injured.

The prosecution began, inexplicably, by summoning a series of witnesses—including Yosef Khabaza's mother and brothers and the landlord of the building in which the family lived—who added absolutely nothing to his case. They did, however, detail before the court the torture to which they had been subjected during their interrogations, and the picture they presented was absolutely horrific. Yet neither the defense attorneys nor the court in any way reacted to any of this testimony.

Following this strange parade of witnesses, two police officers were called to the stand. The first, Abdul Rahman Hamud Samrai, "an aide in the Special Division of the Baghdad Police," finally contributed some information that was germane to the charges by identifying the two kinds of bombs used in the assaults: No. 36 grenades and explosives known as gelignite. But then he left the realm of the concrete and went on to present "evidence" that was essentially a collection of confused and contradictory conjecture. It included such pearls as:

. . . It was clear to me that these crimes were indeed perpetrated against the Jews, but actually anyone who went into the matter in depth could see that the perpetrators did not want to cause losses to the Jews. . . . In fact there were a number of indications that these crimes were to the advantage of the Jews or to the benefit of their institutions in Palestine. . . .

As to the presumed Jewish connection of the bomb thrown at the American target, Samrai offered the explanation: "Before the explosion at the

American Information Office, an insistent rumor was afoot that the American Government had ordered its embassy in Baghdad to investigate the persecution of the Jews in Iraq. . . . This coincidence was sufficient to indicate the . . . motives of the perpetrator. . . ." And then he neatly tied the next bombing into his theory by propounding:

A few days later, while the investigation was going on, one of the
papers . . . published a report that the investigating magistrate had
released the suspects. . . . As a result of this item, an explosion
occurred at three in the morning in the building of the Lawi company
on Al-Rashid Street. The explosive used in this instance is known as
gelignite and caused slight damage to the building's façade. This
instance, too, is clear proof—if viewed in the light of the others—that
the perpetrators of these crimes were the Jews themselves, who used
them to make it appear as though they were the objects of assault. . . .

Even if the conclusion reached by this tortured logic were correct and Jews were responsible for the bombing of the Lawi building, it is still impossible to fathom why they would have thrown a grenade at the United States information office just when the American embassy was about to begin investigating charges of anti-Jewish persecution in Iraq. Surely violence of that kind would have been more likely to deter the investigators than encourage them, so that it was far more reasonable to impute an act of that sort to radical Iraqi nationalists—a few of whom were indeed apprehended after some of these bombings but were immediately released on bail. Moreover, Jews would hardly be likely to throw gelignite around the streets of Baghdad in retaliation for either the arrest or the release of Iraqi radicals hauled in after an attack on an American facility. It simply didn't make sense.

However, neither of the defense attorneys (to say nothing of the court) in any way challenged this "clear proof" presented by the prosecution's witness. Samrai was not cross-examined and not asked to clarify, let alone substantiate, his claims.

The second session of the trial opened with the testimony of another police officer, Salam Jassam al-Krayti, also a member of the special team set up to investigate the affair, who reiterated much of what his predecessor had stated but added his own emphasis. Addressing himself to the incident at the Masooda Shemtob Synagogue on January 14, 1951, Krayti noted that, according to the opinion of experts, all the grenades had been of the advanced, high-explosive No. 36 type—which was known to be *solely* in the possession of the Iraqi armed forces. No weapon of this kind, I should add, was found among the 436 grenades uncovered in the Shurah's caches, since all the arms collected by the Shurah were older, of World War II vintage. But this point was never raised by the defense.

Moreover, in his eagerness to impress the court (or perhaps his superiors) by showing the resemblance between all the actions ascribed to the defendants, Krayti volunteered the conclusion that "the crimes were carried out according to similar methods. The explosives were thrown in remote areas and were not intended to kill or wound anyone"—even though the grenade thrown at the Masooda Shemtob Synagogue was tossed into a crowd of people, and there can be no doubt that whoever threw it intended to kill and maim. Nevertheless the witness was not cross-examined on even this point.

Finally, when it came time for the defense to present its side, neither attorney called a single witness, exposed the lack of hard evidence, or made any attempt to demolish the prosecution's carelessly constructed case.

Thus all that remained was for the two sides to sum up their arguments. In his closing remarks, the prosecutor did not at first allude to the evidence presented by his witnesses and made no attempt to reconcile the contradictions in and between the testimonies of the two policemen. Instead, he launched into a soliloquy on the subject of Zionism, declaring, "The Zionist movement has strayed from the path of religion into the realm of terrorism. It cannot lay claim to being a liberation movement, because the Jews are not a people, in the legal sense of the word." When he had exhausted this line of argument, he finally turned to the case itself and proceeded to contradict his own witnesses by saying:

There is no way to explain the throwing of grenades, and especially of high-explosive grenades, into a crowd of people [at the Masooda Shemtob Synagogue] unless it was done for the purpose of killing. It was only by chance that the bombs [planted at the United States Information Office and by the Lawi building] did not cause any deaths. The crime perpetrated at the Masooda Shemtob Synagogue . . . proves that the [subsequent] throwing of a bomb at the American Information Office was also done for the purpose of political murder. . . .

It soon became clear why the prosecutor had chosen this particular formulation. Having "proved" the grave charges against Basri and Shalom, he felt constrained to draw the court's attention to Chapter 12, Clause 14, of the Iraqi Criminal Code of 1924, which states that "Any man who employs bombs or other explosives to perpetrate . . . crimes . . . or for the purpose of political murder shall be sentenced to death."

The court paid heed and did the prosecutor's bidding: on November 5,

1951, Yosef Basri and Shalom Saleh Shalom were sentenced to death by hanging on each of the three charges (the three explosions that figured in the indictment).

A few days later, they again stood trial as two of the twenty-one Jews charged with illegal possession of arms and ammunition. All of the accused were members of the Zionist movement (or their relatives), and the heaviest sentence—life imprisonment with hard labor—was passed on Yudke Tajer, because, as the court noted in its verdict, "he is not merely a clerk who came to Iraq for the purpose of spying; he came here as one of the leaders of the Zionist movement." Basri and Shalom were sentenced to fifteen years. Six of the accused (including Khabaza's mother) were acquitted; three others (all women) were sentenced to terms already covered by their period of detention and were released at the end of the proceedings. One of the Jews was sentenced to fifteen years, and all the other defendants received five years imprisonment.

This second trial lasted until December 13, and two days later a third one opened, in which Yudke Tajer, Robert Rodney, and fifteen local people—eight Jews (including Basri) and seven Arabs—were accused of espionage. At its conclusion, all were found guilty and sentenced to varying periods of imprisonment. Tajer, too, was sentenced not to death—as the prosecutor had asked—but again to life imprisonment with hard labor. Since the defense presented by his attorney in both his trials was anything but impressive, we can only conclude either that the man was working behind the scenes or that the Iraqi judges preferred not to assume responsibility for the execution of an Israeli officer. In any event, the prosecutor had difficulty accepting the court's leniency and appealed the sentence for a number of months, during which Yudke was held on death row. Robert Rodney, as a British subject, availed himself of the good offices of the British consulate in Baghdad and got off with a brief stint in prison.

Over the years, the claim that Jews were responsible for a number of bombings in Baghdad has undergone a regrettable metamorphosis. At first, few were prepared to believe that Jews had thrown grenades at Jewish or any other targets, for whatever ends. In the middle of the 1950s, however, after the famous affair known as the "Unfortunate Business,"—in which a number of Jews were arrested for executing bomb attacks on the U.S. Information Service offices in Alexandria and Cairo, among other targets, on orders from Israeli Intelligence—parallels were drawn between the Egyptian fiasco and the Baghdad bombings. In the course of time, moreover, the Arab propaganda machine began to assert that the grenades had been thrown in Baghdad to frighten the Jews into fleeing Iraq, since they had no objective reason to leave their native land and emigrate to

Israel. Over a generation after the event, this cynical claim is still being peddled by Arab parties with their own ax to grind—in the latest case even under the guise of dispassionate scholarship,* although anyone who had bothered to examine the history of the Jewish struggle to leave Iraq could not possibly take that allegation seriously. Since the propaganda persists, however, I must note in return that even a quick glance at the chronology of events shows this claim to be patently absurd.

The three bombings cited in the charges against Yosef Basri and Shalom Saleh Shalom occurred after March 9, 1951, the last date on which the law provided for renouncing one's citizenship in order to leave Iraq. Hence the insinuation that they were perpetrated to frighten the Jews into fleeing the country is sheer humbug, since it was at any rate too late for them to take advantage of the law and forfeit their citizenship as the prerequisite for emigrating. Neither did the grenade thrown at the Masooda Shemtob Synagogue on January 14, 1951, have anything to do with prompting the Jews to flee, for the fact is that by the end of 1950—two months before the final deadline for registration—fully 100,000 of the 104,000 Jews who ultimately left Iraq under the provisions of the emigration law had already relinquished their citizenship. Since it has never been denied that the people arrested and tried in 1951 were engaged in Zionist activities, which were banned by Iraqi law, it deserves to be admitted with equal candor that the charge of planting or throwing bombs, for which two young Jews paid with their lives, was completely without foundation.

As soon as the Basri-Shalom trial ended, since there was no recourse to appeal the verdict, an international effort was mounted to at least have their unconscionable sentence commuted. While their lawyers appealed the death penalty, Israeli diplomats and leading members of Jewish organizations the world over sought intervention from every possible quarter: enlightened governments, personalities known to have influence in the Arab world, and international organizations. In mid-December, after the appeals through legal channels were denied, only the regent could save them, and all the activity on their behalf was shifted in his direction. Abba Eban, Israel's ambassador to the United Nations, left a written appeal with Padilla Nervo, the president of the General Assembly. The Israeli embassy in Washington conveyed a personal message from Israel's venerated president, Dr. Chaim Weizmann, to President Truman asking him to intercede on behalf of the two doomed men. But it all proved futile. Neither pleas for mercy nor veiled threats of retaliation could move the Iraqis on this

* See Abbas Shiblak, *The Lure of Zion: The Case of the Iraqi Jews* (Worcester, 1986).

issue; even the enormous outlay of cold cash in Iraq failed to save those two lives.

Almost a decade later, upon his return to Israel,† Yudke Tajer described Yosef Basri's and Shalom Saleh Shalom's last hours, which he had spent with them in their prison cell. He described how they spoke of their love for Israel, the land they had longed for and dreamed of but would not live to see. And he told of how he sat with them in the small, dank cell singing Hebrew songs all through that night in a piteous attempt to drive the terror and darkness out of their hearts. At first light on January 21, 1952, the key turned in the lock and the cell door opened to reveal the figure of the executioner. Silently he marched Yosef Basri and Shalom Saleh Shalom out to a waiting car and drove with them to the gallows in Bab al-Muazem Square, in the heart of Baghdad, where they were hanged by the neck until dead to the cheers of the thousands of citizens who had come to feast their eyes on the grisly sight.

Returning to the prison, the hangman paid a call on Yudke Tajer and somberly reported that his two comrades had gone to their deaths with dignity. When the noose was placed around their necks, their last words were the cry "Long live the State of Israel!" And with that proud prayer, they surrendered their martyred souls to their creator.

A few weeks after the executions, in February 1952, the final flights of "Operation Ezra and Nehemiah" took off from Baghdad carrying the last of the Jews back to Zion from their seat by the rivers of Babylon. Neither Moshe Carmil, Mordechai Ben-Porat, nor I—nor any other of the twenty-five emissaries who had worked in Iraq and Iran since 1942 nurturing the Zionist movement, laying the groundwork for escape, doing all that had to be done to make that moment possible—could find it in his heart to celebrate the successful conclusion of the undertaking that had rescued over one hundred thousand of our people from a land where the death of a Jew was cause for exultation. The loss of Yosef Basri and Shalom Saleh Shalom had brought this ancient dispersion to a painful close. "There we sat down, yea we wept," the Psalmist wrote of our ancestors' exile in Babylon—and so were we fated to weep in our hour of redemption as well.

† Tajer was released in January 1960, after serving nine years of his life sentence.

THIRTEEN

The Aftermath

TO BE PERFECTLY HONEST, there were times when many of the people we brought out of Iraq wondered whether they hadn't just traded one grief for another. Leaving persecution and fear behind them, they headed hopefully for what was in essence an abstraction, a collection of broad and comforting expectations like safety and freedom—all of which were indeed the point of having created a sovereign state. But there were also everyday realities to be faced, and on that score it appeared during the early 1950s that the grim vision aired to me by Levi Eshkol was, if anything, an understatement.

The people who came from Iraq in the framework of "Operation Ezra and Nehemiah" were only one part of a massive influx of immigrants to Israel. Together with those who had fled via Iran, the total number of Iraqi Jews who immigrated to Israel from May 1948 through the beginning of 1952 was 121,512. They joined another 565,225 immigrants coming from literally the farthest corners of the earth to more than double Israel's Jewish population in the course of three and a half years. If you stop to think about it, these are astounding statistics. They also go a long way toward explaining why, from an economic standpoint, the early 1950s were critically difficult years for the country. The same papers that trumpeted the arrival of the first planeloads of immigrants from Iraq were filled with items about the shortage of food, the black market in sugar and oil, and the prospect of "new cuts in imports." Unemployment, still rampant, was now leading to violent clashes between veteran, unionized workers and new immigrants who were willing to work outside the union framework for lower pay.

But most difficult of all were the conditions in the transit camps. Fresh off the boat or plane, the immigrants were taken by truck (buses being considered a luxury) to one of the camps dotting the countryside, where whole families, from infants to the elderly, were crowded into asbestos huts or tattered tents from British Army surplus. The furnishings they received for their temporary home consisted of narrow iron cots and straw mattresses. The water faucets and sanitary facilities (field latrines designed for outlying army units) were located at the far edges of these sprawling camps, and reaching them required waiting on long lines in all kinds of weather. Speaking of the weather, it seemed to be particularly ungracious to us in those years: the winter rains turned the camps into seas of mud, and the cold was nothing short of numbing. In a way, the immigrants from Iraq were even worse hit than the others, because their short and relatively comfortable journey made the shock of these conditions all the more stunning. Some of them had left large and well-appointed homes in Baghdad in the morning and within hours found themselves installed in a tent or hut somewhere in a remote and seemingly forsaken transit camp.

Add to these trying physical conditions the natural anxieties about the future; the culture shock of being lumped together with countless people from different backgrounds and outlooks, speaking a cacophony of languages; and the short shrift or condescending treatment they felt they were getting from the camp staff, government officials, representatives of the national labor union (the Histadrut), and the like, and it is easy to see why a generous store of bitterness built up in no time. Contrary to Eshkol's forecast, the immigrants did not hold many demonstrations. But their distress and disappointment were not easily assuaged—as I had ample opportunity to learn in my new role as a member of the Knesset, Israel's parliament.

That radical change in my status, from an underground agent to the most public of public servants, traced to June 1951, when I was working as a Mossad emissary in Egypt and found myself forced to leave the country on very short notice. At Orly Airport, in Paris, still shaken by my narrow escape, I was glad to see that friends were waiting for me. Little did I suspect that they had come with the unenviable task of breaking the news about the fall of our network in Iraq and the arrest of Mordechai, Yudke, and the other comrades taken in the initial sweep. And while reeling from this second blow, suddenly I was accosted by a complete stranger who introduced himself as a representative of Mapai, the centrist Labor Party in Israel, and urged me to sign a preworded cable committing myself to stand as one of the party's candidates for the Knesset.

All I could do at first was glare at him in disbelief. Then I concluded that this must be someone's idea of a joke—someone who couldn't have known how singularly inappropriate the timing would be. It had to be a hoax; why anyone would have the impression that I was cut out for (or the least interested in) politics was beyond me. Still, there was no glint of mischief in the man's eye, and from what he and the others were saying, I began to understand that Mapai's kingmakers believed that gracing the election list with a name known (at least by reputation) to the tens of thousands of Iraqi newcomers who had already acquired the vote would certainly do the party no harm. That may not have been very flattering, but it was certainly sensible.

The fortunes of the Mapai Party, however, were not my concern just then, and I refused to sign anything. Not only did I consider myself to be the antithesis of a political animal, the Israeli legislature struck me as being the province of the country's elder statesmen and dignitaries, and at the tender age of twenty-seven I had bolder plans than to languish in their shadow. Nevertheless, under the pressure of the messenger from Mapai, plus the gentle prodding of my friends, I finally capitulated and signed— though not before they explained that there was a great difference between standing for election and actually winning a seat. According to the system of proportional representation practiced in Israel, the voters cast their ballots for parties, and on election day each party is represented by a numbered list of 120 candidates. Thus the chances of winning a seat in the Knesset depend on where one's name is slotted on this list, and I was told that I could probably depend on mine being in a safely unrealistic spot.

Indeed, I turned out to be number fifty, and since the party won only forty-five seats, I did not enter the Knesset—not immediately, that is. My life did undergo a few fundamental changes, however. Either because of my candidacy (which had placed me in the public domain, as it were) or because my Mossad colleagues feared that my luck had lost its elasticity, they came to the conclusion that it was neither responsible nor fair to send me on another covert mission. Instead of putting me out to pasture, though, they kept me busy in the office until the middle of 1952 and then made me an offer so tempting and revolutionary that I could not refuse: to work in an overt, official capacity in our Paris embassy.

That certainly helped me persuade Temima that I had slaked my thirst for adventure and was resolved to become a sober, upstanding citizen. Well, perhaps she wasn't entirely convinced, but she did agree to marry me. So, together with my bride, I set off for Paris, this time on an Israeli diplomatic passport made out in my real name. It was an odd but wonderful feeling to be traveling as my very own self, without the fear of making a misstep and blowing my cover. To celebrate this unaccustomed freedom (and our honeymoon), we traveled via Vienna so that Temima could take me along on a sentimental journey to the house where she had been born and raised, teasing that when we got to Baghdad she would reciprocate by accompanying me to the old Hillel family abode—for we both knew that there was little chance of that happening in our lifetimes. By the time we had settled into our small flat near the Bois de Boulogne, all memory of the Knesset episode had faded into oblivion, and we geared up to enjoy the magic of the City of Light—when we weren't simply enjoying the charm of our home and being with each other.

If this sounds too good to be true, all I say is that it didn't last very long. At the end of 1952, after four Mapai deputies had withdrawn from the Knesset or passed on and a fifth was elected president of the state, my turn came to enter the house. I suppose I could have waived that right to eminence without much of an uproar. Certainly others were more eager for and perhaps more suited to the role. But reality barged in on me in the form of friends who argued that the critical situation in the transit camps obliged me to make my presence felt and give the immigrants a voice, lest I add the element of bad faith to their long list of grievances. So early in the spring of 1953, we found ourselves sailing across the Mediterranean on our way home to Israel. If the truth be told, we both felt a bit disappointed. "Then again, perhaps it's for the best," Temima observed one morning in an attempt to cheer me up. "After all," she reasoned while absently patting her rounded middle, "we always wanted the baby to be born on the kibbutz."

I was sworn in as a member of the Knesset on May 4 and overnight was up to my neck in public affairs: visiting the transit camps, talking to the immigrants still housed there, listening as they poured their hearts out about bleak conditions and cavalier treatment. But the most painful part was the oft-heard question (or perhaps it was an accusation) about whether, in our arrogance, we hadn't miscalculated; whether we hadn't in fact misled these understandably worn and frazzled people, first making them wait for months on end in Iraq, sick with anxiety; then bringing them to the very gates of salvation only to dump them in these unspeakably wretched camps and leave them to rot there, again for months on end. I could only wince whenever I heard someone, in a state of exasperation or despair, repeat the obscene Iraqi lie that it was the Zionists who had thrown the grenades at the café and the synagogue to scare the Jews into leaving the country in droves.

Time and again, the conversation turned to the fate of the five thousand Jews who had spurned the Zionist idea and, against all odds and all reason, had chosen to remain in Iraq. We knew from letters that came through various circuitous routes and from rumors that filtered through the Sand Curtain sealing Israel off to the east that the condition of these Jews was satisfactory, some might even say enviable. Their sources of livelihood were ample—certainly by the standards of the unemployed immigrants living in the tent camps—and their spiritual and ritual needs continued to be met by the small community organization. Of course, the process of cultural assimilation was in high gear, but Jewish schools did continue to function (admittedly minus the study of Hebrew, the Bible, and Jewish history), and their graduates were accepted in Iraq's universities. Even if some fields were "off limits" to these high school graduates, rather than become dispirited they simply concentrated on other professions—and flourished in them.

That situation remained fairly stable throughout the decade. Even during the military coup of July 14, 1958—in which such prominent figures as Abdul Illah and Nuri Said met horribly violent ends—the expression of anti-Jewish sentiment was limited to placards carried at prerevolutionary demonstrations or occasional taunts against Zionism and Israel. Long familiar with such behavior, the remaining Jews of Iraq reverted to their traditional stance—lying low until the fury had spent itself—and were soon able to congratulate themselves on being no worse off than before. In some spheres, such as the ability to obtain a higher education or travel abroad, the revolution even brought an easing of restrictions. Another promising sign was that after the coup a number of Jews were released from prison. Even Yudke Tajer was set free and allowed to return home. One of the officers who got to know him in prison and was highly impressed by Yudke arranged for him to meet with General Abdul Karim Kassem, the leader of the revolution and head of Iraq's new government, as a result of which he was given his freedom.

By the early 1960s, however, the picture in both countries—along with the above comparison—was looking very different. In Israel, virtually all of the immigrants had been installed in permanent housing, were working or studying, and in general had found their place in the country's economic and social life, so that the wounds of the previous decade were on the mend. (I cannot resist adding that many of the people who spent a chunk of their childhood in those camps are today leading figures in the government, army, academy, and especially the business world in Israel.) In Iraq, meanwhile, the domestic situation deteriorated rapidly after another coup brought the Ba'ath Party to power, in 1963. One of the casualties of that takeover was the stability which had enabled the Jews to prosper. Coups and countercoups, purges and counterpurges now rocked the country, and it was almost axiomatic in such circumstances that the small Jewish community was subjected to threats and restrictions. Traveling abroad, even for medical treatment, was nigh onto impossible; the universities were almost totally closed to Jews; Jewish property (individual and communal) was confiscated; and the ancient Jewish cemetery of Baghdad was totally destroyed. But the final insult was that these Jews, who, rather than leave with the rest of their people, had chosen to regard themselves as Iraqis in every way, were now forced to carry special yellow identity cards so that no one would mistake them for true sons and daughters of Iraq.

With the fall of the Ba'ath regime and the installation of a more moderate government, at the end of 1963, the small Jewish community began to look forward to better days—and they did follow, for a while. But less than four years later, in June 1967, the Six-Day War broke out, and what ensued seemed like a tasteless replay of the events of 1948. Once again, Iraqi troops moved westward through Jordan to join in the assault on Israel (and although their participation in the fighting was almost nil, Iraq still bore responsibility for all the consequences). On the first day of the fighting, the country was awash with celebration as the martial music blaring out of radios alternated with ecstatic (and wholly fictional) bulletins about crushing Egyptian victories. The next day, the situation reversed itself when Israeli planes attacked H-3, the forward base of the Iraqi Air Force—and the cheering crowds turned ugly. Before the week was out, Iraq's state radio had exchanged the marching songs for broadcasts inciting against the "fifth column" and the "Zionist agents." As though out of sheer habit, the Jews were cast in the role of scapegoat.

Then came a wave of arrests, abuse, torture, extortion—ominous signs that the Iraqis were warming up to some inexorable climax, and it didn't take much imagination to guess what that would be. In July 1968 the Ba'ath Party returned to power under the leadership of General Ahmed Hassan al-Bakr, and in October the dread announcement came: the official spokesman of the party's Revolutionary Council gravely reported the capture of a spy network that had been operating on behalf of "Zionism and

Imperialism." (Now that the Iraqi Government had snuggled up to the Kremlin, the old cry against "Zionism and Communism" was no longer appropriate.) When reports reached Israel of the disproportionately high number of Jews among the suspects arrested on espionage charges, our sense of *déjà vu* grew stronger, and we began to fear the worst.

Needless to say, these trumped-up charges were so implausible as to be preposterous. Of the 150,000 Jews who had thrived in Iraq on the eve of the country's independence in 1932, a mere five thousand remained and were totally divorced from the Zionist movement and the State of Israel. They had not joined the mass exodus to Israel, because they did not hold with the Zionist approach to the age-old "Jewish question," on either the ideological or the pragmatic level. They did not even exploit the opportunity to leave Iraq under the relatively comfortable terms of the 1950 law to build new lives in Europe or America. We must therefore assume that their preference for remaining in their native land was based on the belief that they would enjoy peaceful and comfortable lives as citizens whose loyalty had been proven by their very decision to stay when 95 percent of their fellow Jews had chosen otherwise.

The Iraqi authorities knew, of course, that the remaining Jews had no contact with Israel. More likely than not, it was this very isolation that made them such an attractive choice as scapegoats, especially since fulminating against the Jews was then in vogue in the Arab world. The Amman summit conference of September 1967, for example, had pronounced sanctimoniously (and very ominously) that "the Jews in the Arab countries have not behaved honorably, considering the protection Islam has accorded them for generations, [for] they have encouraged world Zionism and Israel." It also prescribed that "the Muslim governments [should] treat [the Jews who are proven to have ties with Zionism and Israel] as belligerents and aggressors, just as it is incumbent upon the Muslim peoples . . . to treat them as sworn enemies." Thus the problem was not restricted to Iraq alone.

But Iraq was more defiant and callous than the other Arab states—as I knew all too well, because since the Six-Day War I had been directly involved in efforts to ease the plight of the Jews in the Arab lands in my capacity as deputy director-general of Israel's Foreign Ministry in charge of Middle Eastern affairs. We chose the route of quiet diplomacy and were rewarded by help from sympathetic governments—particularly France—and a number of internationally known figures who quietly interceded on behalf of these Jews. Their efforts bore fruit in Egypt, which was generally sensitive to world opinion and was persuaded to release the Jews being held in custody. But the same could not be said of Iraq. The "suspects" arrested there in October 1968 remained in detention, and we could only assume they were being interrogated by the methods at which the Iraqis were so adept. After months of fruitless efforts to ascertain their fate, at the beginning of January 1969 we learned that a military court, holding its proceedings behind closed doors, had condemned a number of Jews to death.

Seventeen years had passed since that frightful January day when Yosef Basri and Shalom Saleh Shalom had swung lifeless from the gallows in the heart of Baghdad, but the memory of that day sent a shudder of dismay through me as I envisioned this gruesome ritual again being enacted. My instinct was to sound a shrill alarm that would shame the Iraqis, once and for all, into halting this senseless killing of defenseless people. But we were caught in the bind of wanting to speak out while fearing that any protest coming from Israel would do the Jews in Iraq more harm than good. Once the Iraqis discovered that they were touching a particularly sensitive nerve, they might massacre even more people.

So we swallowed our pride and anger and opted again for lobbying behind the scenes. The parties to whom we appealed for help, from the pope and the secretary-general of the United Nations to various sovereign governments, all promised to make their feelings known to the Iraqis. But it did no good.

Just after midnight on January 26, 1969, Radio Baghdad began to broadcast selections from the trials, and our people immediately grasped what was about to happen. Alerted by Army Intelligence (which monitors the broadcasts from the Arab countries), the duty officer at the Foreign Ministry called me for instructions. I told him to assemble a skeleton staff while I rushed to the office, desperately hoping to exploit the time difference between the Middle East and the United States to mobilize some kind of force to stop the words that, once pronounced, would never be retracted. We were too late. As if jeering at our impotence, at seven o'clock the next morning the voice of the chief justice of the special military court boomed out of our radio sets, announcing that the fourteen traitors, caught red-handed, had been condemned to death and had already been executed. The bodies of the eleven men executed in Baghdad had been transported to the city's main plaza, Liberation Square, for the public to view; the other three had been executed in Basra. The names read over the airwaves seemed to mock us with every syllable: nine of the fourteen men hanged from the gallows that day were Jews.

Le Monde gave the following all too familiar description of the "occasion": "More than a million demonstrators are estimated to have taken to the streets of Baghdad in answer to the calls broadcast over the radio to treat this day, Monday, January 27, as a national holiday."

In Jerusalem, January 27 was a particularly cold winter's day. The city was covered by stark white snow, but our mood was as black as the hearts of the benighted men in Baghdad who took such pride and pleasure in institutionalized murder. I doubt whether in all the two thousand five hundred years of Jewish history in Iraq, there had been anything to match the sheer malevolence of executing nine Jews on the same day. I felt overcome by helpless rage, for there was nothing we could do to ensure that the killing would not go on. But I was convinced that, at the very least, we had to speak out. If quiet diplomacy was not working, we had nothing to lose by telling the Iraqis, and the world at large, that the State of Israel considered itself the guardian of the Jews living in Iraq. We owed it to them, and we owed it to ourselves. When I called a press conference to proclaim this position on behalf of the Israeli Government, I was surprised and gratified to see that, despite the inclement weather, the press had come out in full force and immediately began spreading our message far and wide.

The results more than justified my decision to bring the issue directly before the public, for the reaction around the world was outrage at Iraq's cynical display of brutality. Even the Egyptian Government condemned the hangings as "doing harm to the Arab cause," and the semiofficial newspaper *Al Ahram* described the affair as "a tactical error." For public consumption, the Iraqi Government dismissed the outcry as "world propaganda." Nevertheless, when a second closed espionage trial ended on March 19, 1969, although the list of the accused included thirteen Jews, we noted with enormous relief that none of them was sent to the gallows. Three Jews were executed later on—two following trials that ended on August 18, 1969, and the third on January 21, 1970—but that brought the tragic chapter of the Baghdad trials and execution of Jews to an end.

Unfortunately the persecution went on—in a less spectacular but more insidious form. Jews were not only arrested but were now kidnapped in unprecedented numbers. Dozens met their deaths under torture in the infamous "Summer Palace" (which had housed the regent until the July 1958 coup); many others were dragged out of their homes or simply snatched off the streets, never to be seen again, and we can only assume that they met a violent end.

Once again we appealed, cajoled, and above all simply kept the world informed of this intolerable situation until critical editorials, questions raised in parliaments, and the demonstrations and vigils held outside Iraqi embassies in a number of cities made it clear to the Iraqis that it was pointless to contend that the fate of its citizens was Iraq's business alone and that no outside party had the right to interfere in its internal affairs. On the initiative of our Foreign Ministry, and as a result of vigorous action by Israel's ambassadors, the International Conference for the Rescue of Jews in the Middle East was established, under the chairmanship of Alain Poher, the president of the French Senate. Its first convention, held in Paris on January 27, 1970—a year after the hangings in Baghdad—was attended by representatives of all faiths from no fewer than thirty countries.

While this international pressure ultimately moved the Iraqis to demonstrate a bit of humanity by occasionally allowing some Jews to leave the country, most of the others were forced to take illegal routes of escape. Thus in one sense this story ends as it began, with Iraqi Jews stealing over borders to freedom. The northern route, which had been opened by the bold young men and women of the Zionist underground some twenty years earlier, became particularly popular, because the fugitives knew they could count on support from the Kurds living in the area. One way or another, most of the Jews who had remained in Iraq after "Operation Ezra and Nehemiah" now left the country and made their way to Israel to embark on new lives.

And so the circle closed. The last page in the annals of the Babylonian diaspora had been turned, the story ended. If the mass emigration from Iraq in 1950–51 was testimony to the power of the Zionist idea, surely its coda—the lot of those few thousand Jews who elected to sever themselves from their people and perpetuate an age-old exile—is signal proof of its validity. Indeed, it is one of the ironies of the Jewish experience that even those who would divorce themselves from their people's fate find that it has a way of overtaking them—in this case, even as they sat in the shade of the palm trees by the distant rivers of Babylon.

One last personal account was closed for me when these refugees trickled out of Iraq. In the early 1970s my cousin Fahima, the daughter of Ezekiel Shemtob, passed through Israel on her way to Canada and came to see me. We had last met in Paris in 1951, when Fahima was simmering with resentment over what she saw as incursions on her father's prerogatives during the difficult early months of the airlift. I knew that Ezekiel Shemtob had died in 1954 at the age of seventy-three, but now Fahima told me of the sad circumstances of his passing; he had died in Beirut on his way home from England after being treated for a malignant growth. Finally I had an opportunity to tell her how much I had admired and respected him as an extraordinary and courageous man whose influence had been so instrumental in making the legal exit of the Jews possible.

From this talk of her father, we soon found ourselves reminiscing about our childhood in Baghdad. I waxed nostalgic about the family, the food, the romps by the river, but most of all about our innocence. How far we had come since the days when we believed that closing the shutters and barring the door was enough to keep evil at bay. Fahima's eyes reflected a deep sadness as she related what had befallen her and the other Jews of Iraq since the Six-Day War. When she spoke of her own shattering despair, I asked whether she and the others believed we had forgotten them.

"There were many moments when I was sure you had," she said without bitterness, "but when I listened to the BBC on the day of the terrible hangings in January 1969 and heard your voice at that press conference, for the first time ever I felt a sense of closeness, a feeling of belonging, and I knew that you hadn't and wouldn't ever abandon us."

She lowered her eyes and fell silent, embarrassed perhaps by her candor and emotion. But I sensed that there was more to come, and I was rewarded.

"You know, Selim," she said, using my childhood name, "for the longest time I nursed a grudge. I felt that all the horrible things that were happening to us were because of Israel, because of your dream and your wars. You celebrated the victories, and we paid the price of those wars."

She paused, steeped in some private thought, then raised her gaze to me. "Now I can see that we were saved because of the existence and the efforts of Israel. So you see, we've settled our debts to each other. We're quits now!" she concluded with a soft laugh as tears of repentance or relief, I cannot say which, streamed down her flushed cheeks.

AUTHOR'S NOTE

This is a true story. It is a tale told from a personal perspective, but it is not a personal story. Rather, it is the drama of the modern exodus of the Jews of Iraq, the oldest Jewish community in the Diaspora, dating back to the destruction of the First Temple, more than twenty-five hundred years ago.

The Psalms relate that when the Jews were exiled to Babylonia (modern-day Iraq) after the Temple was laid waste, they hung their harps upon the willows, sat down by the rivers, wept, and vowed, "If I forget you, O Jerusalem, let my right hand wither." From then onward, notwithstanding periods of persecution and danger, they never lost their faith, never became severed from their Jewish roots, never abandoned their oath of setting Jerusalem above their highest joy or their hope of returning to the Promised Land.

Finally they began to act upon their dream. When a few young men from the Haganah underground in Palestine arrived in Iraq with the naïve audacity to help smuggle Jews out of the country and into Palestine (and later on bring them openly into the sovereign State of Israel), the circle had come full. Now, almost forty years after the events, the story can finally be told.

Descriptions of the illegal immigration of Jews from Europe to Palestine, of the heroic struggle by the survivors of the Nazi extermination camps to make their way to Palestine at all costs, are well known. Sagas of overcrowded immigrant boats such as the *Exodus 1947* have sparked the imagination of novelists and screenwriters alike. But the story of the immigration of Jews from the Arab lands, the dangers they faced, and the resourcefulness they displayed in breaking through the wall of enmity and crossing the desert separating their native countries from the Promised Land has remained unknown.

The cloak of secrecy shrouding this subject was for the most part justified as long as there was concern over the fate of the Jews still living in the

Arab countries and a chance of rescuing them. Those of us touched by this
ongoing concern and involved in the rescue attempts imposed the silence
upon ourselves. But as a result, an injustice was done to them, for their
struggle and sacrifice for the sake of redemption became obscured.

Now, when no less than 95 percent of the million or so Jews who lived
in the Arab countries have left them, and most of them are living in Israel,
there is no longer any reason not to relate the drama without which it is
difficult to imagine the character of the State of Israel today.

I feel it is my duty to tell this story, warts and all, for I was fortunate to
have taken an active part in some of its most crucial episodes. I have
written this book in the first person singular and focused primarily on the
years 1946–50, the period in which I worked undercover in Iraq, Syria,
Lebanon, and Iran. The experiences, feelings, and thoughts that fill these
pages are personal, but the events are based on historical fact, as well as on
sources from the archives of the Haganah, the Israeli Foreign Ministry,
and the British Foreign Office (which are made available to researchers
after thirty years, and most of which are published here for the first time).

It is also pertinent to keep in mind that the book tells mainly of events
that occurred at the end of the 1940s and beginning of the 1950s. Many
things have changed since then. Iran, which during those years displayed
great magnanimity toward Jewish refugees who had fled from Iraq, has
changed its colors radically with the rise of the Ayatollah Khomeini and is
today one of Israel's most fervent enemies. On the other hand, Great
Britain, which, during the period prior to the establishment of Israel,
found itself literally in combat with refugees from Nazi Europe and the
Arab lands, has today become one of Israel's good friends. So to anyone
who may be concerned or puzzled about some of the heroes and villains of
this piece, I can at best quote the terse wisdom of an old Arab proverb:
"The world changes."

I owe a number of debts of gratitude. The first is to the many people
who helped me take part in the drama described in this book, though I
could not possibly list them all by name. Therefore let me express my
thanks to all the members of the Mossad for Illegal Immigration; to the
commanders who sent me on my missions and guided me in my work; to
the members of my kibbutz, Ma'agan Michael, who gave me the feeling
that I had a warm home during the many years I spent far away, absorbed
in rescue work; to my fellow emissaries; to the leaders and members of the
Zionist movement in Iraq; and to the entire Jewish community of Iraq,
who are the real heroes of this tale and without whose perseverance and
daring there would have been no story to tell.

Many people helped me contend with the challenge of writing this book, encouraging me during moments of crisis and urging me on for over four long years of searching out documents, sifting through old files, and committing this story to paper. I will not mention them here by name; they know who they are, and I want them to know that their help will always be remembered with gratitude and affection.

I owe special thanks and an apology to the members of my family for bouts of short temper and impatience as I was immersed in writing the book—especially to my son, Ari, who devoted many hours of the precious free time he had as a soldier on active duty to reading the manuscript and suggesting corrections and improvements, and to my daughter, Hagar, whose incisive comments and knowledge of history made a great contribution to avoiding errors and oversights.

But most of all I owe special thanks to my wife, Temima, who spent countless days engaged in the search for source materials in archives and libraries, sorting and deciphering letters and documents, and separating the historical wheat from the mounds of chaff. She read every chapter, more than once, and was liberal in her criticism, forcing me to weed out much of the wild grass that has a way of growing rampant in the field of my writing.

For the publication of the English edition, I owe special thanks to Asher Weill, managing director of the Edanim Publishing House in Israel, who followed and encouraged the writing of this book in Hebrew and its translation into English; to my friend Chaim Potok, who simply ordered me to sit down and write; to Avi Primor, his late wife, Michal, and Beverly Gordey, who, ever since hearing the outline of this story years ago, warmly encouraged me to commit it to paper; to Nita Shechet, who read the manuscript and contributed a number of important comments; and above all to Ina Friedman, who translated the book from the Hebrew. The translation was not a strictly technical affair, for it was necessary to tailor this edition to a readership not familiar with much of the background. Thus the translation required both additions and excisions, and it is due to Ms. Friedman's talent, experience, and great patience that we were able to arrive at a rendition faithful to the spirit (if not always the letter) of the original book in an atmosphere of friendship and appreciation.

Jerusalem   Shlomo Hillel

GLOSSARY

Amo Yusuf   Shlomo Hillel's *nom de guerre* in the Iraqi Zionist underground from July 1946 to August 1947

Artzi   The code name for Palestine, and thereafter Israel, in the Mossad's secret wireless communications

Berichah   From 1945 to mid-1948, the secret migration across Europe of Jewish survivors of the Holocaust in an effort to reach Palestine

Berman   The code name for Baghdad, and Iraq in general, in the Mossad's secret wireless communications

farhoud   The two-day pogrom that took place in Baghdad on June 1–2, 1941

Goldman   The code name for Teheran, and Iran in general, in the Mossad's secret wireless communications

Habib   One of Mordechai Ben-Porat's *noms de guerre* as a Mossad emissary in Iraq

Haganah   Jewish underground in Palestine during the period of the British mandate

jihad   Muslim holy war

mandate   The British mandate for Palestine, granted by the League of Nations in 1920

Mossad   The Mossad for Illegal Immigration, an arm of the Haganah that dealt with bringing Jews to Palestine in defiance of the British ban on Jewish immigration; not to be confused with the arm of Israeli Intelligence now widely referred to as the Mossad

moshav   Small-holders' collective settlement in Israel

Mujaheddin   Arab volunteers from neighboring countries sent to fight in Palestine and encourage the local Arab population to acts of terrorism prior to the establishment of Israel

Palmach   The Haganah's permanently mobilized "shock troops"

Palmachnik   Member of the Palmach

regent   Abdul Illah, uncle of King Feisal II, who effectively ruled Iraq until the young king reached majority

Ruthie   Code name for Beirut

Sammi   Shmuel Moriah, one of author's closest associates in Baghdad and subsequently in Teheran

Shammai	Shlomo Hillel's *nom de guerre* in the Mossad
Shurah	Armed self-defense organization of the Iraqi Zionist underground
Zakki	One of Mordechai Ben-Porat's *noms de guerre* as a Mossad emissary in Iraq

325. 2567
H557
1987

325.
2567
H557
1987

124071